Lecture Notes in Computer Science   10329

Commenced Publication in 1973
Founding and Former Series Editors:
Gerhard Goos, Juris Hartmanis, and Jan van Leeuwen

More information about this series at http://www.springer.com/series/7407

Arnaud Carayol · Cyril Nicaud (Eds.)

Implementation and Application of Automata

22nd International Conference, CIAA 2017
Marne-la-Vallée, France, June 27–30, 2017
Proceedings

 Springer

Editors
Arnaud Carayol
LIGM (UMR 8049), CNRS
Université Paris-Est
Marne-la-Vallée Cedex 2
France

Cyril Nicaud
LIGM (UMR 8049)
Université Paris-Est
Marne-la-Vallée Cedex 2
France

ISSN 0302-9743   ISSN 1611-3349   (electronic)
Lecture Notes in Computer Science
ISBN 978-3-319-60133-5   ISBN 978-3-319-60134-2   (eBook)
DOI 10.1007/978-3-319-60134-2

Library of Congress Control Number: 2017942998

LNCS Sublibrary: SL1 – Theoretical Computer Science and General Issues

Printed on acid-free paper

This Springer imprint is published by Springer Nature
The registered company is Springer International Publishing AG
The registered company address is: Gewerbestrasse 11, 6330 Cham, Switzerland

Preface

This volume contains the papers presented at the 22nd International Conference on Implementation and Application of Automata (CIAA 2017) organized by the Laboratoire d'Informatique Gaspard-Monge (CNRS UMR 8049), Université Paris-Est, during June 27–30, 2017, in Paris, France.

The CIAA conference series is a major international venue for the dissemination of new results in the implementation, application, and theory of automata. The previous 21 conferences were held in various locations all around the globe: Seoul (2016), Umeå (2015), Giessen (2014), Halifax (2013), Porto (2012), Blois (2011), Winnipeg (2010), Sydney (2009), San Francisco (2008), Prague (2007), Taipei (2006), Nice (2005), Kingston (2004), Santa Barbara (2003), Tours (2002), Pretoria (2001), London Ontario (2000), Potsdam (WIA 1999), Rouen (WIA 1998), and London Ontario (WIA 1997 and WIA 1996). Like its predecessors, the theme of CIAA 2017 was the implementation of automata and applications in related fields. The topics of the presented papers include state complexity of automata, implementations of automata and experiments, enhanced regular expressions, and complexity analysis.

There were 31 submissions from 20 different counties: Algeria, Brazil, Bulgaria, Canada, Chile, China, Czech Republic, France, Germany, Iceland, India, Italy, Malta, Poland, UK, Russia, Slovakia, South Africa, South Korea, and Sweden. Each submission was reviewed by at least three reviewers and thoroughly discussed by the Program Committee (PC). The committee decided to accept 17 papers for oral presentation. The program also includes three invited talks by Véronique Cortier, Kim G. Larsen, and Damien Pous.

We would like to thank the members of the PC and the external reviewers for their work and for the thorough discussions that took place. We also thank all the authors of submitted papers who made CIAA 2017 possible. The work of the PC and the collating of the proceedings were greatly simplified by the EasyChair conference system.

We would furthermore like to thank the editorial staff at Springer, and in particular Alfred Hofmann and Anna Kramer, for their guidance and help during the process of publishing this volume. We are also grateful to the IUT de Marne-la-Vallée for providing the rooms for the conference. Finally, we are grateful to the conference sponsors for their generous financial support: Labex Bézout, Laboratoire d'Informatique Gaspard-Monge (UMR 8049) and Université Paris-Est Marne-la-Vallée.

We all look forward to CIAA 2018 in Charlottetown, Canada.

June 2017

Arnaud Carayol
Cyril Nicaud

Organization

CIAA 2017 was organized by the Laboratoire d'Informatique Gaspard-Monge at Université Paris-Est Marne-la-Vallée, France.

Invited Speakers

Véronique Cortier	CNRS, LORIA, France
Kim G. Larsen	Aalborg University, Denmark
Damien Pous	CNRS, ENS Lyon, France

Program Committee

Cezar Câmpeanu	University of Prince Edward Island, Canada
Arnaud Carayol (Co-chair)	CNRS, Université Paris-Est, France
Jean-Marc Champarnaud	Université de Rouen, France
Julien Clément	Université de Caen, France
Jan Daciuk	Gdańsk University of Technology, Poland
Frank Drewes	Umeå University, Sweden
Manfred Droste	University of Leipzig, Germany
Matthew Hague	Royal Holloway, University of London, UK
Yo-Sub Han	Yonsei University, South Korea
Markus Holzer	Justus-Liebig-Universität Giessen, Germany
Oscar Ibarra	University of California, Santa Barbara, USA
Galina Jirásková	Slovak Academy of Sciences, Slovak Republic
Juhani Karhumäki	University of Turku, Finland
Christof Löding	RWTH Aachen University, Germany
Markus Lohrey	University of Siegen, Germany
Sylvain Lombardy	Bordeaux Institute of Technology, France
Andreas Maletti	University of Leipzig, Germany
Sebastian Maneth	University of Edinburgh, UK
Denis Maurel	Université François Rabelais de Tours, France
Nelma Moreira	Universidade do Porto, Portugal
Cyril Nicaud (Chair)	Université Paris-Est, France
Kemal Oflazer	Carnegie Mellon University, Qatar
Bala Ravikumar	Sonoma State University, USA
Daniel Reidenbach	Loughborough University, UK
Kai T. Salomaa	Queen's University, Kingston, Canada
Marinella Sciortino	Università degli studi di Palermo, Italy
Shinnosuke Seki	University of Electro-Communications, Japan
Brink van der Merwe	University of Stellenbosch, South Africa

Mikhail Volkov   Ural Federal University, Ekaterinburg, Russia
Hsu-Chun Yen   National Taiwan University, Taipei, Taiwan

Steering Committee

Jean-Marc Champarnaud   Université de Rouen, France
Markus Holzer   Justus-Liebig-Universität Giessen, Germany
Oscar Ibarra   University of California, Santa Barbara, USA
Denis Maurel   Université François Rabelais Tours, France
Kai T. Salomaa   Queen's University, Kingston, Canada
Hsu-Chun Yen   National Taiwan University, Taipei, Taiwan

Additional Reviewers

Alhazov, Artiom	Guillon, Bruno	Ng, Timothy
Berglund, Martin	Guingne, Franck	Okhotin, Alexander
Cho, Da-Jung	Ivan, Szabolcs	Pradella, Matteo
Dück, Stefan	Jeandel, Emmanuel	Rampersad, Narad
Freydenberger,	Ko, Sang-Ki	Restivo, Antonio
Dominik D.	Mamouras, Konstantinos	Richomme, Gwenaël
Ganardi, Moses	Masopust, Tomas	Terrier, Véronique
Garavel, Hubert	McQuillan, Ian	Trakhtman, Avraham
Grädel, Erich	Mio, Matteo	Zetzsche, Georg

Organizing Committee

Chloé Athénosy
Arnaud Carayol
Claire David
Julien David
Pavel Heller
Revekka Kyriakoglou
Cyril Nicaud
Carine Pivoteau
Nathalie Rousseau

Sponsoring Institutions

Labex Bézout, Université Paris-Est
Laboratoire d'Informatique Gaspard-Monge (UMR 8049)
Université Paris-Est Marne-la-Vallée

Abstract of Invited Papers

Electronic Voting: How Logic Can Help

Véronique Cortier

LORIA - CNRS, Nancy, France

Electronic voting should offer at least the same guarantees than traditional paper-based voting systems. In particular, voting systems should ensure ballot privacy (no one knows how I voted) and verifiability (voters can check the whole voting process). In order to achieve this, electronic voting protocols make use of cryptographic primitives, as in the more traditional case of authentication or key exchange protocols. All these protocols are notoriously difficult to design and flaws may be found years after their first release. Formal models, such as process algebra, Horn clauses, or constraint systems, have been successfully applied to automatically analyze traditional protocols and discover flaws. Electronic voting protocols however significantly increase the difficulty of the analysis task. Indeed, they involve for example new and sophisticated cryptographic primitives such as mixnets (e.g. in Civitas [4]) or homomorphic encryption (e.g. in [1, 5]), new dedicated security properties, and new execution structures.

Standard protocols like authentication or key-exchange protocols typically involve trace based properties, for which many procedures and tools have been developed in the context of security protocols. Tools include for example, ProVerif [3], Avispa [2], Scyther [6], or Tamarin [8]. However, ballot privacy is modeled as an equivalence property [7], for which fewer techniques exist.

After an introduction to electronic voting, we will describe the current techniques for e-voting protocols analysis and review the key challenges towards a fully automated verification.

References

1. Adida, B., de Marneffe, O., Pereira, O., Quisquater, J.-J.: Electing a university president using open-audit voting: analysis of real-world use of Helios. In: Proceedings of the 2009 Conference on Electronic Voting Technology/Workshop on Trustworthy Elections (2009)
2. Armando, A., Basin, D., Boichut, Y., Chevalier, Y., Compagna, L., Cuellar, J., Hankes Drielsma, P., Héam, P.-C., Kouchnarenko, O., Mantovani, J., Mödersheim, S., von Oheimb, D., Rusinowitch, M., Santiago, J., Turuani, M., Viganò, L., Vigneron, L.: The AVISPA Tool for the automated validation of internet security protocols and applications. In: Etessami, K., Rajamani, S.K. (eds.) CAV 2005. LNCS, vol. 3576, pp. 281–285. Springer, Berlin (2005)
3. Blanchet, B.: An automatic security protocol verifier based on resolution theorem proving (invited tutorial). In: 20th International Conference on Automated Deduction (CADE-20) (2005)

4. Clarkson, M.R., Chong, S., Myers, A.C.: Civitas: toward a secure voting system. In: Proceeding of IEEE Symposium on Security and Privacy, pp. 354–368 (2008)
5. Cortier, V., Galindo, D., Glondu, S., Izabachene, M.: Election verifiability for Helios under weaker trust assumptions. In: Kutyłowski, M., Vaidya, J. (eds.) ESORICS 2014. LNCS, vol. 8713, pp. 327–344. Springer, Switzerland (2014)
6. Cremers, C.: The Scyther tool: verification, falsification, and analysis of security protocols. In: Gupta, A., Malik, S. (eds.) CAV 2008. LNCS, vol. 5123, pp. 414–418. Springer, Berlin (2008)
7. Kremer, S., Ryan, M.: Analysis of an electronic voting protocol in the applied Pi calculus. In: Sagiv, M. (eds.) ESOP 2005. LNCS, vol. 3444, pp. 186–200. Springer, Berlin (2005)
8. Schmidt, B., Meier, S., Cremers, C., Basin, D.: Automated analysis of Diffie-Hellman protocols and advanced security properties. In: Chong, S. (ed.) 25th IEEE Computer Security Foundations Symposium, CSF 2012, Cambridge, MA, USA, June 25–27, 2012, pp. 78–94. IEEE (2012)

Timed and Untimed Energy Games

Kim Guldstrand Larsen

Department of Computer Science, Aalborg University,
Selma Lagerlöfs Vej 300, 9220 Aalborg, Denmark
kgl@cs.aau.dk

Abstract. Energy games have recently attracted a lot of attention. These are games played on finite weighted (timed) automata and concern the existence of infinite runs subject to boundary constraints on the accumulated weight, allowing e.g. only for behaviours where a resource is always available (non-negative accumulated weight), yet does not exceed a given maximum capacity. In this extended abstract we give an overview of the various results that have been obtained on this topic.

Untimed Energy Games

In [9] we have extend energy games to a multiweighted and parameterized setting, allowing us to model systems with multiple quantitative aspects. We present reductions between Petri nets and multiweighted automata and among different types of multi-weighted automata and identify new complexity and (un)decidability results for both one- and two-player games. We also investigate the tractability of an extension of multiweighted energy games in the setting of timed automata.

In [11] we reconsider the multiweighted energy problem assuming an unknown upper bound and calculate the set of vectors of upper bounds that allow an infinite run to exist. For both a strict and a weak upper bound we show how to construct this set by employing results from previous works, including an algorithm given by Valk and Jantzen for finding the set of minimal elements of an upward closed set.

In [8] we introduce and study average-energy games, where the goal is to optimize the long-run average of the accumulated energy. We show that this objective arises naturally in several applications, and that it yields interesting connections with previous concepts in the literature. We prove that deciding the winner in such games is in NP inter coNP and at least as hard as solving mean-payoff games, and we establish that memoryless strategies suffice to win. We also consider the case where the system has to minimize the average-energy while maintaining the accumulated energy within pre-defined bounds at all times: this corresponds to operating with a finite-capacity storage for energy. We give results for one-player and two-player games, and establish complexity bounds and memory requirements.

In [12] we reconsider average-energy games focusing on the problem of deter-mining upper bounds on the average accumulated energy or on the capacity while satisfying a given lower bound, i.e., we do not determine whether a given bound is sufficient to meet the specification, but if there exists a sufficient bound to meet it. In the classical setting with positive and negative weights, we show that the problem of determining the existence of a sufficient bound on the long-run average accumulated energy can be solved in doubly-exponential time. We consider recharge game, where all weights are negative, but there are recharge edges that recharge the energy to some fixed capacity. We show that bounding the long-run average energy in such games is complete for exponential time.

Weighted Timed Automata and Games

The model of weighted timed automata was introduced in [1] as an extension of timed automata, with prices on both transitions and locations. For this model we considered the minimum-cost reachability problem: i.e. given a weighted timed automaton and a target state, determine the minimum cost of executions from the initial state to the target state. This problem generalizes the minimum-time reachability problem for ordinary timed automata. We prove decidability of this problem by offering an algorithmic solution, which is based on a combination of branch-and-bound techniques and a new notion of priced regions. The latter allows symbolic representation and manipulation of reachable states together with the cost of reaching them. Later the associated decision problem has been shown to be PSPACE-complete.

Now considering weighted timed *games* the cost-optimal reachability problem is shown to be undecidable in [2] already in the setting of three clocks. For the case of weighted timed games with a single clock decidability of cost-optimal reachability was shown decidable in [7] in triple-exponential time. This result is improved in [10] which provides a single-exponential algorithm. For this improvement a new algorithm for solving one-clock weighted timed games, based on the sweep-line technique from computational geometry and the strategy iteration paradigm from the algorithmic theory of Markov decision processes has been introduced.

Timed Energy Games

The paper [4] introduces the problem of existence and construction of infinite schedules for finite weighted automata and one-clock weighted timed automata, subject to boundary constraints on the accumulated weight. More specifically, the paper considers automata equipped with positive and negative weights on transitions and locations, corresponding to the production and consumption of some resource (e.g. energy). We ask the question whether there exists an infinite path for which the accumulated weight for any finite prefix satisfies certain constraints (e.g. remains between 0 and some given upper-bound). We also consider a game version of the above, where certain transitions may be uncontrollable. In the setting of one-player, one-clock weighted timed automata we show that the problem of deciding the existence of an infinite admissible run is decidable.

In [3] we study one-clock priced timed automata in which prices can grow linearly (dp/dt = k) or exponentially (dp/dt = kp), with discontinuous updates on edges. We propose EXPTIME algorithms to decide the existence of controllers that ensure existence of infinite runs or reachability of some goal location with non-negative observer value all along the run. These algorithms consist in computing the optimal delays that should be elapsed in each location along a run, so that the final observer value is maximized (and never goes below zero).

In [5, 6] we show that the existence of an infinite lower-bound-constrained run is in general undecidable for weighted timed automata with four or more clocks.

Also in [13] and [9] it is shown that the lower- and upper-bound-constrained run problem is undecidable in case of 2 costs or 2 clocks.

References

1. Behrmann, G., Fehnker, A., Hune, T., Larsen, K.G., Pettersson, P., Romijn, J., Vaandrager, F.W.: Minimum-cost reachability for priced timed automata. In: Di Benedetto, M.D., Sangiovanni-Vincentelli, A. (eds.) HSCC 2001. LNCS, vol. 2034, pp. 147–161. Springer, Berlin (2001)

2. Bouyer, P., Brihaye, T., Markey, N.: Improved undecidability results on weighted timed automata. Inf. Process. Lett. **98**(5), 188–194 (2006)

3. Bouyer, P., Fahrenberg, U., Larsen, K.G., Markey, N.: Timed automata with observers under energy constraints. In: Johansson, K.H., Yi, W. (eds.) Proceedings of the 13th ACM International Conference on Hybrid Systems: Computation and Control. HSCC 2010, Stockholm, Sweden, April 12–15, 2010, pp. 61–70. ACM (2010)

4. Bouyer, P., Fahrenberg, U., Larsen, K.G., Markey, N., Srba, J.: Infinite runs in weighted timed automata with energy constraints. In: Cassez, F., Jard, C. (eds.) FORMATS 2008. LNCS, vol. 5215, pp. 33–47. Springer, Berlin (2008)

5. Bouyer, P., Larsen, K.G., Markey, N.: Lower-bound-constrained runs in weighted timed automata. Perform. Eval. **73**, 91–109 (2014)

6. Bouyer, P., Larsen, K.G., Markey, N.: Lower-bound constrained runs in weighted timed automata. In: Ninth International Conference on Quantitative Evaluation of Systems. QEST 2012, London, UK, September 17–20, 2012, pp. 128–137. IEEE Computer Society (2012)

7. Bouyer, P., Larsen, K.G., Markey, N., Rasmussen, J.I.: Almost optimal strategies in one clock priced timed games. In: Arun-Kumar, S., Garg, N. (eds.) FSTTCS 2006. LNCS, vol. 4337, pp. 345–356. Springer, Berlin (2006)

8. Bouyer, P., Markey, N., Randour, M., Larsen, K.G., Laursen, S.: Average-energy games. In: Esparza, J., Tronci, E. (eds.) Proceedings Sixth International Symposium on Games, Automata, Logics and Formal Verification. GandALF 2015, Genoa, Italy, September 21–22, 2015. EPTCS, vol. 193, pp. 1–15 (2015)

9. Fahrenberg, U., Juhl, L., Larsen, K.G., Srba, J.: Energy games in multiweighted automata. In: Cerone, A., Pihlajasaari, P. (eds.) ICTAC 2011. LNCS, vol. 6916, pp. 95–115. Springer, Berlin (2011)

10. Hansen, T.D., Ibsen-Jensen, R., Miltersen, P.B.: A faster algorithm for solving one-clock priced timed games. In: D'Argenio, P.R., Melgratti, H. (eds.) CONCUR 2013. LNCS, vol. 8052, pp. 531–545. Springer, Berlin (2013)

11. Juhl, L., Larsen, K.G., Raskin, J.-F.: Optimal bounds for multiweighted and parametrised energy games. In: Liu, Z., Woodcock, J., Zhu, H. (eds.) Theories of Programming and Formal Methods - Essays Dedicated to Jifeng He on the Occasion of His 70th Birthday. LNCS, vol. 8051, pp. 244–255. Springer, Berlin (2013)
12. Larsen, K.G., Laursen, S., Zimmermann, M.: Limit your consumption! finding bounds in average-energy games. In: Tribastone, M., Wiklicky, H. (eds.) Proceedings 14th International Workshop Quantitative Aspects of Programming Languages and Systems. QAPL 2016, Eindhoven, The Netherlands, April 2–3, 2016. EPTCS, vol. 227, pp. 1–14 (2016)
13. Quaas, K.: On the interval-bound problem for weighted timed automata. In: Dediu, A.-H., Inenaga, S., Martín-Vide, C. (eds.) LATA 2011. LNCS, vol. 6638, pp. 452–464. Springer, Berlin (2011)

CoInductive Automata Algorithms

Damien Pous

University of Lyon, CNRS, ENS de Lyon, UCB Lyon 1, LIP
Lyon, France
damien.pous@ens-lyon.fr

We consider the problem of checking equivalence or inclusion of finite automata. Algorithms for such a task are used in model-checking for instance, where one can build an automaton for a formula and an automaton for a model, and then check that the latter is included in the former. More advanced constructions need to build a sequence of automata by applying a transducer, and to stop whenever two subsequent automata recognise the same language [4]. Another field of application is that of various extensions of Kleene algebra [7], whose equational theories are reducible to language equivalence of various kinds of automata: regular expressions and finite automata for plain Kleene algebra [12], "closed" automata for Kleene algebra with converse [2, 9], or guarded string automata for Kleene algebra with tests (KAT) [14].

Equivalence of deterministic finite automata (DFA) can be checked either via minimisation [10] or, more directly, through Hopcroft and Karp's algorithm [11]. The complexity of the latter algorithm has been studied by Tarjan [18]: checking language equivalence of two states in a DFA with n states over an alphabet of size k requires $O(nk\alpha(k,n))$ operations, where $\alpha(k,n)$ is a *very* slow-growing inverse of Ackermann's function. This might look rather satisfactory, except that: (1) in most applications one starts with non-deterministic automata (NFA), and (2) sometimes the alphabet is too large to be iterated naively.

For the first point, it is well-known that NFA can be determinised using the powerset construction, and that there can be exponentially many reachable sets. In fact, language equivalence becomes PSPACE-complete for NFA over an alphabet with at least two letters [15]—and coNP-complete with one letter. De Wulf, Doyen, Henzinger and Raskin have proposed algorithms based on *antichains* [19], that exploit the specific structure of determinised automata to avoid systematically exploring all reachable states. Together with Filippo Bonchi, we have discovered that both Hopcroft and Karp's algorithm and the antichain algorithms actually make use of a reasoning principle which is well-known in concurrency theory: *coinduction* [16]. This lead us to a new algorithm [3], which can improve exponentially over both Hopcroft and Karp's algorithm and more recent antichain-based algorithms [1, 8, 19].

This author is funded by the European Research Council (ERC) under the European Unions Horizon 2020 programme (CoVeCe, grant agreement No 678157). This work was supported by the LABEX MILYON (ANR-10-LABX-0070) of Université de Lyon, within the program "Investissements d'Avenir" (ANR-11-IDEX-0007) operated by the French National Research Agency (ANR).

The second point is raised for instance with the automata required for deciding Kleene algebra with tests [13]. We propose to use symbolic automata [17], where the transition function is represented in a compact way using binary decision diagrams (BDD) [5, 6]. Coinductive algorithms such as above then make it possible to explore reachable pairs symbolically, and to avoid redundancies. We show in particular a nice integration with the disjoint sets forest data-structure from Hopcroft and Karp's algorithm.

References

1. Abdulla, P.A., Chen, Y.-F., Holík, L., Mayr, R., Vojnar, T.: When simulation meets antichains. In: Esparza, J., Majumdar, R. (eds.) TACAS. LNCS, vol. 6015, pp. 158–174. Springer, Berlin (2010)
2. Bloom, S.L., Ésik, Z., Stefanescu, G.: Notes on equational theories of relations. Algebra Universalis **33**(1), 98–126 (1995)
3. Bonchi, F., Pous, D.: Checking NFA equivalence with bisimulations up to congruence. In: Proceedings of POPL, pp. 457–468. ACM (2013)
4. Bouajjani, A., Habermehl, P., Vojnar, T.: Abstract regular model checking. In: Alur, R., Peled, D.A. (eds.) CAV 2004. LNCS, vol. 3114, pp. 372–386. Springer, Heidelberg (2004)
5. Bryant, R.E.: Graph-based algorithms for Boolean function manipulation. IEEE Trans. Comput. **35**(8), 677–691 (1986)
6. Bryant, R.E.: Symbolic Boolean manipulation with ordered binary-decision diagrams. ACM Comput. Surveys **24**(3), 293–318 (1992)
7. Conway, J.H.: Regular Algebra and Finite Machines. Chapman and Hall (1971)
8. Doyen, L., Raskin, J.-F.: Antichain algorithms for finite automata. In: Esparzam, J., Majumdar, R. (eds.) TACAS 2010. LNCS, vol. 6015, pp. 2–22. Springer, Berlin (2010)
9. Ésik, Z., Bernátsky, L.: Equational properties of Kleene algebras of relations with conversion. Theoret. Comput. Sci. **137**(2), 237–251 (1995)
10. Hopcroft, J.E.: An n log n algorithm for minimizing in a finite automaton. In: Proceedings of International Symposium of Theory of Machines and Computations, pp. 189–196. Academic Press (1971)
11. Hopcroft, J.E., Karp, R.M.: A linear algorithm for testing equivalence of finite automata. Technical report 114, Cornell University (1971)
12. Kozen, D.: A completeness theorem for Kleene algebras and the algebra of regular events. Inf. Comput. **110**(2), 366–390 (1994)
13. Kozen, D.: Kleene algebra with tests. Trans. Program. Lang. Syst. **19**(3), 427–443 (1997)
14. Kozen, D.: On the coalgebraic theory of Kleene algebra with tests. Technical report, CIS, Cornell University (2008)
15. Meyer, A., Stockmeyer, L.J.: Word problems requiring exponential time. In: Proceedings of STOC, pp. 1–9. ACM (1973)
16. Milner, R.: Communication and Concurrency. Prentice Hall (1989)
17. Pous, D.: Symbolic algorithms for language equivalence and Kleene algebra with tests. In: Proceedings of POPL 2015, pp. 357–368. ACM (2015)
18. Tarjan, R.E.: Efficiency of a good but not linear set union algorithm. J. ACM **22**(2), 215–225 (1975)
19. Wulf, M.D., Doyen, L., Henzinger, T.A., Raskin, J.-F.: Antichains: a new algorithm for checking universality of finite automata. In: Ball, T., Jones, R.B. (eds.) CAV 2006. LNCS, vol. 4144, pp. 17–30. Springer, Berlin (2006)

Contents

On the Complexity of Determinizing Monitors

Luca Aceto[1], Antonis Achilleos[1], Adrian Francalanza[2(✉)], Anna Ingólfsdóttir[1], and Sævar Örn Kjartansson[1]

[1] School of Computer Science, Reykjavik University, Reykjavik, Iceland
{luca,antonios,annai}@ru.is
[2] Department of Computer Science, ICT, University of Malta, Msida, Malta
adrian.francalanza@um.edu.mt

Abstract. We examine the determinization of monitors. We demonstrate that every monitor is equivalent to a deterministic one, which is at most doubly exponential in size with respect to the original monitor. When monitors are described as CCS-like processes, this doubly-exponential bound is optimal. When (deterministic) monitors are described as finite automata (as their LTS), then they can be exponentially more succinct than their CCS process form.

1 Introduction

Monitors [10,23] are computational entities that execute alongside a system so as to *observe* its runtime behavior and possibly determine whether a property is satisfied or violated from the exhibited (system) execution. They are used extensively in runtime verification [17] and are central to software engineering techniques such as monitor-oriented programming [6]. Monitors are often considered to be part of the trusted computing base and, as a result, are expected to behave correctly. A prevailing correctness criterion requires monitors to exhibit *deterministic behavior*. Determinism is also important for lowering the runtime overheads of monitoring a system: in order not to miss possible detections of a non-deterministic monitor, one would need to keep track of all the monitor states that are reachable for the currently observed execution trace.

Non-determinism is inherent to various computational models used to express monitors, such as Büchi automata [8,26] or process calculi [5,10,27]. As a matter of fact, non-deterministic monitor descriptions are often more succinct than deterministic ones, and thus easier to formulate and comprehend. Non-deterministic computation is also intrinsic to concurrent and distributed programming — used increasingly for runtime monitoring [3,5,9,18,24] —, where the absence of global clocks makes it hard to rule it out, and interleaving underspecification can be used to improve execution efficiency.

In [11], Francalanza *et al.* identified a maximally-expressive monitorable fragment for the branching-time logic μHML [15,16] and their results relied on a

This research was supported by the project "TheoFoMon: Theoretical Foundations for Monitorability" (grant number: 163406-051) of the Icelandic Research Fund.

A. Carayol and C. Nicaud (Eds.): CIAA 2017, LNCS 10329, pp. 1–13, 2017.
DOI: 10.1007/978-3-319-60134-2_1

monitor-synthesis procedure for every monitorable μHML-formula. In order to achieve a simple compositional definition, this synthesis procedure may yield non-deterministic monitors. In this paper we tackle the problem of determinizing monitors in the framework of [11], which are described using syntax close to the regular fragment of CCS processes [20]. We demonstrate that every monitor can be transformed into an equivalent deterministic one, which strengthens the results in [11]. However, we also show that the price of determinization can be a hefty one: there are monitors which require a doubly exponential blow-up in size to determinize. Note that, although our results employ the monitor framework of [11], our methods and findings can be extended to other forms of automata-like monitor descriptions such as those in [2,5,10,27].

Overview: Section 2 provides the preliminaries. In Sect. 3, we prove that all monitors can be determinized and give methods to transform monitors to automata and back. Section 4 provides lower bounds to complement the constructions of Sect. 3. Section 5 discusses the main technical results in this paper. Omitted proofs and an extensive treatment of the determinization of monitors can be found in an extended version [1].

2   Background

We overview the main definitions for the monitoring set-up of [11] that we used in our study.

2.1   Basic Definitions: Monitoring Processes

Systems are denoted as processes whose semantics is given in terms of a labeled transition system (LTS). An LTS is a triple $\langle \text{PROC}, (\text{ACT} \cup \{\tau\}), \rightarrow \rangle$ where PROC is a set of process states ($p \in \text{PROC}$), ACT is a finite set of observable actions ($\alpha \in \text{ACT}$), $\tau \notin \text{ACT}$ is the distinguished silent action, and $\rightarrow \subseteq (\text{PROC} \times (\text{ACT} \cup \{\tau\}) \times \text{PROC})$ is a transition relation. Monitors are described via the specific syntax given below, but their semantics is also given as an LTS.

Table 1. Monitor and Instrumentation Semantics ($\alpha \in \text{ACT}$ and $\mu \in \text{ACT} \cup \{\tau\}$)

Monitor semantics			
ACT$\dfrac{}{\alpha.m \xrightarrow{\alpha} m}$	SEL$\dfrac{m_i \xrightarrow{\mu} m' \quad i \in I}{\sum_{i \in I} m_i \xrightarrow{\mu} m'}$	REC$\dfrac{}{rec x.m \xrightarrow{\tau} m[rec x.m/x]}$	VER$\dfrac{}{v \xrightarrow{\alpha} v}$
Instrumentation semantics			
MON$\dfrac{p \xrightarrow{\alpha} p' \quad m \xrightarrow{\alpha} m'}{m \lhd p \xrightarrow{\alpha} m' \lhd p'}$	TER$\dfrac{p \xrightarrow{\alpha} p' \quad m \xrightarrow{\alpha} \!\!\!\!\!/ \quad m \xrightarrow{\tau} \!\!\!\!\!/}{m \lhd p \xrightarrow{\alpha} \mathbf{end} \lhd p'}$	AsP$\dfrac{p \xrightarrow{\tau} p'}{m \lhd p \xrightarrow{\tau} m \lhd p'}$	AsM$\dfrac{m \xrightarrow{\tau} m'}{m \lhd p \xrightarrow{\tau} m' \lhd p}$

Definition 1. *A monitor is described by the following grammar:*

$$m \in \text{Mon} :: = \textbf{\textit{yes}} \quad | \quad \textbf{\textit{no}} \quad | \quad \textbf{\textit{end}} \quad | \quad \alpha.m \quad | \quad \sum_{i \in I} m_i \quad | \quad \textbf{\textit{rec}} \, x.m \quad | \quad x$$

where x comes from a countably infinite set of variables and $I \neq \emptyset$ is a finite index set. We write $m + n$ in lieu of $\sum_{i \in I} m_i$ when $|I| = 2$. Constants **yes**, **no**, *and* **end** *are called verdicts (denoted by v) and represent acceptance, rejection and inconclusive termination respectively. The behavior of a monitor is defined by the rules of Table 1.* ∎

A *monitored system* is a monitor m and a system p instrumented to execute side-by-side, denoted as $m \lhd p$; its behavior is defined by the instrumentation rules in Table 1. Intuitively, a monitor m mirrors visible actions performed by p (rule MON). Whenever m cannot match an action from p and cannot internally transition to a state that might enable it to do so, $m \not\xrightarrow{\tau}$, then m aborts to the inconclusive **end** verdict (rule TER). Finally instrumentation monitors only for visible actions, and thus we allow m and p to perform internal τ actions independently of each other (rules AsP and AsM). Given an LTS with a set of states P (of processes, monitors, or monitored systems) with $r, r' \in P$ and a set of actions ($\text{ACT} \cup \{\tau\}$), we write $r \xRightarrow{\alpha} r'$ to mean that r can weakly transition to r' using a single α action and any number of τ actions, $r(\xrightarrow{\tau})^* \cdot \xrightarrow{\alpha} \cdot (\xrightarrow{\tau})^* r'$. For each $r, r' \in P$ and trace $t = \alpha_1.\alpha_2.\ldots.\alpha_k \subset \text{ACT}^*$, we use $r \xRightarrow{t} r'$ to mean $r \xRightarrow{\alpha_1} \cdot \xRightarrow{\alpha_2} \ldots \xRightarrow{\alpha_k} r'$ if t is non-empty and $r(\xrightarrow{\tau})^* r'$ if t is the empty trace.

In the monitorability results of [11] the verdicts **yes** and **no** (referred to hereafter as *conclusive* verdicts) are linked to satisfaction and violation of μHML formulas, respectively. We say that a monitor m accepts (resp. rejects) process p when there are a trace $t \in \text{Act}^*$ and process p' such that $m \lhd p \xRightarrow{t} \textbf{yes} \lhd p'$ (resp. $m \lhd p \xRightarrow{t} \textbf{no} \lhd p'$). In this setting, acceptance is equivalent to saying that p can produce a trace t along which the monitor can derive the **yes** verdict, and similarly for rejection and verdict **no**. Thus, we say that a monitor m accepts (resp. rejects) a trace $t \in \text{Act}^*$ when $m \xRightarrow{t} \textbf{yes}$ (resp. when $m \xRightarrow{t} \textbf{no}$). We say that two monitors, m and n are (verdict) equivalent, denoted as $m \sim n$, if for every trace t and verdict $v \in \{\textbf{yes}, \textbf{no}\}$, $m \xRightarrow{t} v$ iff $n \xRightarrow{t} v$. The utility of this monitor equivalence relation stems from the following fact: whenever $m \sim n$, then for *every* process state p, if monitor m accepts (resp. rejects) process p, then monitor n must accept (resp. reject) process p as well.

Multiple Verdicts. In [11] the authors show that monitors with a *single conclusive verdict* suffice to adequately monitor for μHML formulae; these monitors can use either **yes** or **no**, but not both. We therefore confine our study to determinizing single-verdict monitors (particularly monitors that use the **yes** verdict), but note that there is a straightforward approach for dealing with multi-verdict monitors, which are used in other settings such as in [10]. For details on determinizing multi-verdict monitors consult [1]. Given a single-verdict monitor m that uses the **yes** verdict, $L(m)$ is the set of traces that m accepts.

Finite Automata. We overview briefly Finite Automata Theory, used in Sect. 3; the interested reader should consult [25] for further details. A nondeterministic finite automaton (NFA) is a quintuple $A = (Q, \Sigma, \delta, q_0, F)$, where Q is a finite set of states, Σ is a finite set of symbols, called the alphabet (in our context, $\Sigma = \text{ACT}$), $\delta \subseteq Q \times \Sigma \times Q$ is a transition relation, $q_0 \in Q$ is the initial state, and $F \subseteq Q$ is the set of final or accepting states. Given a word $t \in \Sigma^*$, a run r of A on $t = t_1 \cdots t_k$ ($t_i \in \Sigma$, $1 \le i \le k$) is a sequence $q_0 q_1 \cdots q_k$, such that $(q_{i-1}, t_i, q_i) \in \delta$ for $1 \le i \le k$; r is an accepting run if $q_k \in F$. We say that A accepts t when A has an accepting run on t, and A accepts/recognizes a language $L \subseteq \Sigma^*$ whenever A accepts exactly all $t \in L$. In such cases L is unique and we call it $L(A)$. If δ is a function $\delta : Q \times \Sigma \to Q$ then A is a deterministic finite automaton (DFA). A classical result is that for every NFA A with n states, there is an equivalent DFA (i.e. a DFA that recognizes the language $L(A)$) with at most 2^n states [21]; this upper bound is optimal [19].

2.2 Determinism and Other Choices

The purpose of this paper is to examine the determinization of monitors, which is the process of constructing a deterministic monitor from an equivalent nondeterministic one. We must therefore establish what we understand by a deterministic monitor. For the purposes of [11], deterministic monitor behavior need only concern itself with the definite verdicts that can be reached after observing a particular trace t. Stated otherwise, we can say that a monitor m behaves deterministically whenever it transitions to verdict-equivalent monitors for every trace t. The work in [11] contains several examples of monitors that break this behavioral condition: an easy one is $m_c = \alpha.\alpha.\mathsf{yes} + \alpha.\beta.\mathsf{yes}$, because when this monitor reads an α, it has to make a choice and transition to either $\alpha.\mathsf{yes}$ or $\beta.\mathsf{yes}$ which are *not* equivalent, $\alpha.\mathsf{yes} \not\sim \beta.\mathsf{yes}$. A deterministic monitor that is equivalent to m_c is $\alpha.(\alpha.\mathsf{yes} + \beta.\mathsf{yes})$.

For Turing machines, algorithms, and finite automata, determinism is typically more restrictive, requiring that from every state (in our case, monitor) and input symbol (in our case, action), there is a *unique* transition to follow. In the case of monitors, we can transition either by means of an observable action, α, but also via a τ-action, which can occur without reading from a trace. In finite automata, these τ actions could perhaps correspond to ϵ-transitions, which are eliminated from deterministic automata. However, we cannot readily eliminate τ-transitions from deterministic monitors. For instance, we need to be able to activate the recursive operators. Instead we require that monitor transitions denote functions that take us to a unique next state, and moreover that whenever a monitor can transition with an observable action α, it cannot perform silent actions. A closer inspection of the derivation rules of Table 1 immediately reveals that such choices can only be introduced by sums — that is, monitors of the form $\sum_{i \in I} m_i$ with $|I| \ge 2$; we can therefore attain the required behavior via syntactic constraints.

Definition 2. *A monitor m is syntactically deterministic (s-deterministic) iff every sum of at least two summands that appears in m is of the form $\sum_{\alpha \in A} \alpha.m_\alpha$, where $A \subseteq$ ACT.* ∎

As we will see below, this set of monitors is in fact maximally expressive. Lemma 1 demonstrates that the syntactic determinism of Definition 2 ensures that such monitors will always arrive at the same verdict for a given trace. Following Lemma 1, we simply refer to s-deterministic monitors as deterministic monitors.

Lemma 1. *If m is s-deterministic, $m \overset{t}{\Rightarrow} n$, and $m \overset{t}{\Rightarrow} n'$, then $n \sim n'$.* □

The first main result of the paper is that given a nondeterministic monitor, we can always find an equivalent deterministic monitor.

Theorem 1. *For each monitor $m \in$ MON there exists a deterministic monitor, $m' \in$ MON, such that $m \sim m'$.* □

Besides the constructions we present in this paper, in [1] we present two more methods to determinize monitors. The first is by reducing monitor determinization to the determinization of CCS processes modulo trace equivalence, which has been accomplished by Rabinovich in [22]. The second method is specific to the synthesis procedure of [11] via the determinization of μHML formulas. In either case, it is not easy to extract complexity bounds from these methods. See [1] for more details.

Size Conventions. When we extract complexity bounds for our constructions, we assume that the set of actions, ACT, is of constant size. The size $|m|$ of a monitor m is the size of its syntactic description as given in Sect. 2.1, defined recursively thus: $|x| = |\mathbf{yes}| = 1$; $|a.m| = |m|+1$; $|\sum_{i \in I} m_i| = \sum_{i \in I} |m_i| + |I| - 1$; and $|\mathbf{rec}\ x.m| = |m| + 1$. Notice that $|m|$ coincides with the total number of submonitor occurrences — namely, symbols in m.

Example 1. Consider the monitor $m = \mathbf{rec}\ x.(0.x + 1.x + 1.2.\mathbf{yes})$. It accepts process states that can produce traces from the language $(0+1)^*12(0+1+2)^*$, that is, traces (words) in which the action 2 appears at least once and the action preceding this 2 action is a 1. An equivalent deterministic monitor is

$$m' = \mathbf{rec}\ y.(0.y + 1.\mathbf{rec}\ x.(0.y + 1.x + 2.\mathbf{yes}))$$

Notice that the size of the deterministic monitor m' is greater than that of its original non-deterministic counterpart m. In fact, $|m| = 10$ and $|m'| = 14$. ∎

2.3 Semantic Transformations

For convenience, we slightly alter the behavior of monitors from [11] to simplify our constructions and arguments. Specifically, we provide another set of transition rules and show that the new and old rules are equivalent with respect to the

Table 2. System N is the result of replacing rule REC by rules RECF and RECB.

$$\text{RecF}\,\frac{}{rec x.m_x \xrightarrow{\tau} m_x} \qquad\qquad \text{RecB}\,\frac{}{x \xrightarrow{\tau} p_x}$$

traces that can reach a **yes** verdict (the same applies for **no** verdicts). Consider a single monitor, m_0, which appears at the beginning of the derivation under consideration — that is, all other monitors are submonitors of m_0. We assume, without loss of generality, that each variable x appears in the scope of a unique monitor of the form **rec** $x.m$, which we call p_x; namely, m_x is the monitor such that $p_x = \textbf{rec } x.m_x$. The monitors may behave according to one of two systems of rules. System O is the old system of rules, as given in Table 1. System N is given by replacing rule REC by the rules given in Table 2. The transition relations $\xrightarrow{\mu}$ and $\xRightarrow{t}$ are defined as before, but they are called $\xrightarrow{\mu}_O$ and $\xRightarrow{t}_O$ when they result from System O and $\xrightarrow{\mu}_N$ and $\xRightarrow{t}_N$ when they result from System N. We can show that the two LTSs are equivalent with respect to verdicts.

Lemma 2. *For a monitor m and trace t, $m \xRightarrow{t}_N$ yes iff $m \xRightarrow{t}_O$ yes.*   □

There are three reasons for changing the operational semantics rules of monitors. One is that, for the bounds we prove, we need to track when recursion is used in a derivation. Another is that in System N (unlike in System O) it is clear which monitors may appear in a derivation starting from monitor m (namely, at most all submonitors of m), which in turn makes it easier to construct an LTS — and also to transform a monitor into an automaton. For instance, consider $m = \textbf{rec } x.(\alpha.x + \beta.\textbf{yes})$. In System O, $m \xrightarrow{\tau} \alpha.(\textbf{rec } x.(\alpha.x + \beta.\textbf{yes})) + \beta.\textbf{yes}$, which is *not* a subterm of m. On the other hand, in System N, $m \xrightarrow{\tau} \alpha.x + \beta.\textbf{yes}$, which is a subterm of m. Finally, and partly due to the previous observation, we can see that a monitor, viewed as an LTS, has a specific form: it is a rooted tree with labeled edges provided by $\xrightarrow{\mu}$, with some back edges, which result from recursion (namely, from the rule RECB in Table 2). For the remainder, we use system N and drop subscripts from $\xrightarrow{\mu}_N$ and $\xRightarrow{t}_N$.

When using System N, we need to be more careful with the definition of determinism. Notice that it is possible to have a nondeterministic monitor, which has a deterministic submonitor. For instance, $p_x = \textbf{rec } x.(\alpha.x + \alpha.\textbf{yes})$ is nondeterministic, while according to our definition of determinism, $\alpha.x$ is deterministic (specifically, all variables are deterministic). The issue here is that although $\alpha.x$ is deterministic in form, it can transition to (x and then to) p_x, which is not. This is not a situation we encountered in System O, because there variables do not derive anything on their own and all monitors we consider are closed. In System N, though, a variable x can appear in a derivation and it can derive p_x, so it is not prudent to judge that any variable is deterministic — and thus judge the determinism of a monitor only from its structure. In other words, our definition of a deterministic monitor additionally demands that said monitor is closed; alternatively, for a monitor which appears in a derivation to be deterministic, we demand that the initial monitor p_0 be deterministic (by Definition 2).

3 Monitor Determinization

We provide methods to transform monitors to automata and back, allowing us to use the classic subset construction for the determinization of NFAs and thus determinize monitors. This approach yields upper bounds on the size of the constructed monitors. Furthermore, when transforming a monitor into an equivalent automaton, the constructed NFA may be smaller than the original monitor, thus resulting in a smaller deterministic monitor.

3.1 From Monitors to Finite Automata

A monitor can be seen as a finite automaton with its submonitors as states and the composition $\stackrel{\epsilon}{\Rightarrow} \cdot \stackrel{\alpha}{\rightarrow}$ as its transition relation. Here we make this observation explicit. For a monitor m, we define the automaton $A(m)$ to be $(Q, \text{ACT}, \delta, q_0, F)$, where

- Q, the set of states, is the set of submonitors of m;
- ACT, the set of actions, is also the alphabet of the automaton;
- $q' \in \delta(q, \alpha)$ iff $q \stackrel{\epsilon}{\Rightarrow} \cdot \stackrel{\alpha}{\rightarrow} q'$;
- q_0, the initial state, is m;
- $F = \{\text{yes}\} \cap Q$, that is, yes is the only accepting state (if it exists).

Proposition 1. *For every monitor m, $A(m)$ accepts $L(m)$.*   □

Thus, all languages recognized by monitors are regular. Notice that $A(m)$ has at most $|m|$ states (because Q only includes submonitors of m), but possibly fewer, since two occurrences of the same monitor as submonitors of m give the same state; we can cut the state size down further by removing submonitors which can only be reached through τ-transitions. Furthermore, if m is deterministic, then $A(m)$ is deterministic.

Corollary 1. *For every monitor m, there is an automaton of at most $|m|$ states that accepts $L(m)$. The automaton is deterministic if so is m.*   □

3.2 From Automata to Monitors

We would also like to be able to transform a finite automaton to a monitor and thus recognize regular languages by monitors. However, this is not always possible because there are simple regular languages that are not recognized by any monitor. Consider, for example, the language $(11)^*$, which includes all strings of ones of even length. Since ϵ is in that language, a monitor m for $(11)^*$ is such that $m \stackrel{\epsilon}{\Rightarrow} \text{yes}$ and thus accepts everything (so, this conclusion is also true for any regular language of the form $\epsilon + L \neq \text{ACT}^*$).

One of the properties differentiating monitors from automata is that verdicts are irrevocable for monitors. Therefore, if for a monitor m and finite trace t, $m \stackrel{t}{\Rightarrow} \text{yes}$, then for every trace t', it is also the case that $m \stackrel{tt'}{\Rightarrow} \text{yes}$ (this is due to rule VER which ensures that **yes** $\xRightarrow{t'}$ **yes**, for every t'). Stated otherwise, if L is a regular language on ACT that is recognized by a monitor, then L must be *suffix-closed*. Since this property stems from the fact that monitor verdicts are irrevocable, in the rest of this paper we instead call such languages *irrevocable*.

Now, consider an automaton that recognizes an irrevocable language L. Then, if q is any (reachable) accepting state of the automaton, and q can be reached through a word t, then t is clearly in L but so is every word $t\alpha$. Thus, we can safely add an α-transition from q to an accepting state (for example, itself) if no such transition exists. We call an automaton that can *always* transition from an accepting state to an accepting state for each $\alpha \in$ ACT irrevocable. Note that, in the case of an irrevocable DFA, all transitions from accepting states *must* go to accepting states.

Corollary 2. *A language is regular and irrevocable if and only if it is recognized by an irrevocable NFA (or DFA).* □

Given an irrevocable NFA, we can construct an equivalent monitor through a procedure that can be described informally as follows (see Fig. 1 for an example). We first unravel the NFA into a tree: for every transition sequence that starts from the initial state and that does not repeat any states, we keep a copy of its ending state. For example, for the automaton of Fig. 1, we can reach q_2 through $q_0 \xrightarrow{0} q_1 \xrightarrow{1} q_2$ and $q_0 \xrightarrow{1} q_1 \xrightarrow{1} q_2$, which gives us two copies of q_2. Then, we map each node of this tree to a monitor, so that, at the end, the root is mapped to the resulting equivalent monitor. The leaves that correspond to an accepting state are mapped to **yes**. We use action transitions to describe forward tree edges and recursion for back edges — there is no need for cross edges. If the automaton is deterministic, so is the resulting monitor.

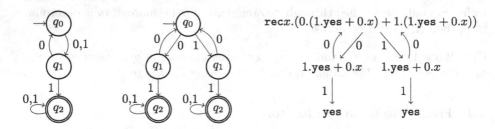

Fig. 1. Transforming an automaton into a monitor: DFA to tree unraveling to monitor.

Theorem 2. *Given an irrevocable NFA (resp. DFA) A of n states, there is a monitor (resp. deterministic monitor) of size $2^{O(n \log n)}$ (resp. $2^{O(n)}$) that accepts $L(A)$.* □

We use the transformations from a monitor into an NFA, into a DFA, and into a deterministic monitor to obtain the following space complexity upper bound.

Corollary 3. *For every monitor m, there exists an equivalent deterministic monitor of size $2^{O(2^{|m|})}$.* □

4   Lower Bounds

We demonstrate that we cannot significantly improve the bounds of Sect. 3.

4.1   Lower Bound for (Nondeterministic) Monitor Size

It is easier to understand the intuition behind the lower bounds for constructing monitors after realizing that the LTS of a monitor is a rooted tree with additional back edges (when we consider each submonitor occurrence to be distinct). The tree is the monitor's syntactic tree; a transition generated by rules ACT and RECF (and then, possibly, SEL) is a transition from a parent to a child and a transition generated by rule RECB (and then, possibly, SEL) is a transition to an ancestor (rule VER gives self-loops for the leaves). Furthermore, from every node, distinct actions transition to distinct nodes. This is the form generated from the construction of Theorem 2.

We initially consider the family of regular languages $(L_n)_n$, where L_n, for $n \geq 1$, is described by $(0+1)^*1(0+1)^{n-1}$. This is a well-known example of a regular language recognizable by an NFA of $n+1$ states, by a DFA of 2^n states, but by no DFA of fewer than 2^n states. As we have previously remarked, monitors do not behave exactly the same way automata do and can only recognize irrevocable languages. Therefore, we modify L_n to mark the ending of a word with a special character, e, and make it irrevocable. Let $M_n = \{\alpha e \beta \in \{0, 1, e\}^* \mid \alpha \in L_n\}$.

Note that an automaton (deterministic or not) accepting L_n can easily be transformed into one (of the same kind) accepting M_n by introducing two new states, Y and N, where Y is accepting and N is not, so that all transitions from Y go to Y and from N go to N (N is a junk state, thus unnecessary for NFAs); then we add an e-transition from all accepting states to Y and from all other states to N. The reverse transformation is also possible: From an automaton accepting M_n, we can have a new one accepting L_n by removing all e-transitions and turning all states that can e-transition to an accepting state of the old automaton to accepting states. The details are left to the reader.

So, there is an NFA for M_n with $n + 2$ states and a DFA for M_n with $2^n + 2$ states, but no fewer. Let $m = \mathbf{rec}\ x.(0.x + 1.x + 1.\sum_{t \in \{0,1\}^{n-1}} t.e.\mathbf{yes})$. Then, m mimics the behavior of the NFA for M_n and $|m| = O(2^n)$.

The idea behind showing that there is no monitor for M_n of size less than 2^n is that, for every $w \in \{0, 1\}^{n-1}$, the trace $1we$ constitutes an accepted trace. Furthermore, after reading the first letter, the monitor tree is not allowed to use a back edge (i.e. recursion), or else it could accept a shorter trace. By the above observation regarding the tree-form of monitors, the monitor is (at least) a complete binary tree of height $n - 1$.

Proposition 2. *Let m be a monitor for M_n. Then, $|m| \geq 3 \cdot 2^{n-1}$.*   □

The above result means that monitors of size exponential with respect to n are required to recognize languages M_n, and thus we have a lower bound on the construction of a monitor from an NFA, which is close to the respective upper bound of Theorem 2.

4.2   Lower Bounds for the Size of Deterministic Monitors

Theorem 3. *Let m be a deterministic monitor for M_n. Then, $|m| = 2^{2^{\Omega(n)}}$.* $\square$

Therefore, a construction of a deterministic monitor from an equivalent NFA can result in a doubly-exponential blow-up in the size of the monitor, and building a deterministic monitor from an equivalent nondeterministic one can result in an exponential blow-up in the size of the monitor. Hence, the upper bounds provided by Theorem 2 cannot be improved significantly. As Theorem 4 demonstrates, the situation is actually even worse for the determinization of monitors.

Theorem 4. *For every $n \in \mathbb{N}$, there is an irrevocable regular language on two symbols[1] that is recognized by a nondeterministic monitor of size $O(n)$, but which cannot be recognized by any deterministic monitor of size $2^{2^{o(\sqrt{n \log n})}}$.* $\square$

The proof of Theorem 4 relies on a result by Chrobak [7] for unary languages (languages on only one symbol), who showed that, for every n, there is a unary language Ch_n that is recognized by an NFA with n states, but by no DFA with $e^{o(\sqrt{n \log n})}$ states. U_n is then the set of words $w \in \{0,1\}$, such that the 0's or the 1's in w are a word from Ch_n. Then, from a deterministic monitor for U_n we can extract a unary DFA for Ch_n by following the 0*1- or 1*0-transitions of the monitor, until the first time recursion was used (i.e. a back edge was followed). Therefore, the first time the deterministic monitor has a back edge is at distance at least $e^{\Omega(\sqrt{n \log n})}$ from the root; so, the deterministic monitor contains at least a complete binary tree of height $e^{\Omega(\sqrt{n \log n})}$.

Table 3. Bounds on the cost of construction (X signifies that the conversion is trivial)

from/to	DFA	monitor	det. monitor
NFA	tight: $O(2^n)$	upper: $2^{O(n \log n)}$ lower: $2^{2^{\Omega(\sqrt{n \log n})}}$	tight: $2^{O(2^n)}$
DFA	X	upper: $2^{O(n)}$	tight: $2^{O(n)}$
nondet.monitor	upper: $2^{O(2^n)}$ lower: $2^{2^{\Omega(\sqrt{n \log n})}}$	X	upper: $2^{O(2^n)}$ lower: $2^{2^{\Omega(\sqrt{n \log n})}}$

5   Conclusions

We provided a method for determinizing monitors. We have focused on monitors for the co-safety fragment of μHML, as constructed in [11]. We showed that we can add a runtime monitor to a system without having a significant effect on the execution time of the system. Specifically, evaluating a nondeterministic monitor for a runtime trace may amount to keeping track of all possible monitor

---

[1] For unary languages, determinizing monitors is significantly easier; see [1].

states reachable along that trace. By using a deterministic monitor, each trace event leads to a unique monitor state from the current state, which is easier to compute. However, this speed-up can come at a severe cost, since we may have to use up to doubly-exponential more space to store the monitor; even if this is stored in a more efficient form such as its LTS, the deterministic monitor may require an exponential additional space.

From the established bounds, NFAs can be exponentially more succinct than monitors as a specification language, and doubly exponentially more succinct than deterministic monitors; DFAs can be exponentially more succinct than deterministic monitors. Therefore, it is much more efficient to use monitors not in their syntactic forms, but as automata — or to use a monitor's syntax DAG instead of its syntax tree.

Summary of Bounds: We proved upper and lower bounds for several constructions related to monitor determinization. Table 3 summarizes the bounds we have proven, those which were known, and the ones we can further infer from these results. We discuss these below:

- Corollary 3 informs us that from a nondeterministic monitor of size n, we can construct a deterministic one of size $2^{O(2^n)}$.
- Theorem 4 explains that we cannot do much better, because there is an infinite family of monitors such that, for each monitor of size n in the family, there is no equivalent deterministic monitor of size $2^{2^{o(\sqrt{n \log n})}}$.
- Theorem 2 tells us that an irrevocable NFA of n states can be converted to an equivalent monitor of size $2^{O(n \log n)}$.
- Proposition 2 reveals that there is an infinite family of NFAs, for which every n-state NFA of the family is not equivalent to any monitor of size $2^{o(n)}$.
- Corollary 3 yields that an irrevocable NFA of n states can be converted to an equivalent deterministic monitor of size $2^{O(2^n)}$; Theorem 3 makes this bound tight.
- Theorem 2 also allows us to convert a DFA of n states to a deterministic monitor of $2^{O(n)}$ states; Theorem 3 makes this bound tight.
- We can convert a (single-verdict) monitor of size n to an equivalent DFA of $O(2^n)$ states, by first converting the monitor to an NFA of n states (Proposition 1) and then using the classical subset construction.
- If we could convert any monitor of size n to a DFA of $2^{o(\sqrt{n \log n})}$ states, then we could use the construction in the proof of Theorem 2 to construct a deterministic monitor of $2^{2^{o(\sqrt{n \log n})}}$ states, which contradicts the lower bound of Theorem 4; therefore, $2^{\Omega(\sqrt{n \log n})}$ is a lower bound for converting monitors to equivalent DFAs.

Optimizations: Monitors to be used in runtime verification are expected not to affect the systems they monitor as much as possible. Therefore, the efficiency of monitoring must be taken into account to reduce overhead. To use a deterministic monitor, we would naturally want to keep its size as small as possible. It would help to preserve space (and time for each transition) to store the monitor in its LTS form — as a DFA. We should also aim to use the smallest possible monitor we can. There are efficient methods for minimizing a DFA, so one can use these to find a minimal DFA and then turn it into monitor form using the construction from Theorem 2, if such a form is required. The resulting monitor will be (asymptotically) minimal.

On the other hand, it would be good to keep things small from an earlier point of the construction, before the exponential explosion of states of the subset construction takes place. In other words, it would be good to minimize the NFA we construct from the monitor, which can already be smaller than the original monitor. Unfortunately, NFA minimization is a hard problem — specifically PSPACE- complete [14] — and it remains NP-hard even for classes of NFAs that are very close to DFAs [4]. NFA minimization is even hard to approximate or parameterize [12,13]. Still, it would be better to use an efficient approximation algorithm from [13] to process the NFA and save on the number of states before we determinize. This raises the question of whether (nondeterministic) monitors are easier to minimize than NFAs, although a positive answer seems unlikely in the light of the hardness results for NFA minimization.

References

1. Aceto, L., Achilleos, A., Francalanza, A., Ingólfsdóttir, A., Kjartansson, S.Ö.: Determinizing monitors for HML with recursion. arXiv preprint arXiv:1611.10212 (2016)
2. Barringer, H., Falcone, Y., Havelund, K., Reger, G., Rydeheard, D.: Quantified event automata: towards expressive and efficient runtime monitors. In: Giannakopoulou, D., Méry, D. (eds.) FM 2012. LNCS, vol. 7436, pp. 68–84. Springer, Heidelberg (2012). doi:10.1007/978-3-642-32759-9_9
3. Berkovich, S., Bonakdarpour, B., Fischmeister, S.: Runtime verification with minimal intrusion through parallelism. Formal Methods Syst. Des. **46**(3), 317–348 (2015)
4. Björklund, H., Martens, W.: The tractability frontier for NFA minimization. J. Comput. Syst. Sci. **78**(1), 198–210 (2012)
5. Bocchi, L., Chen, T.-C., Demangeon, R., Honda, K., Yoshida, N.: Monitoring networks through multiparty session types. In: Beyer, D., Boreale, M. (eds.) FMOODS/FORTE -2013. LNCS, vol. 7892, pp. 50–65. Springer, Heidelberg (2013). doi:10.1007/978-3-642-38592-6_5
6. Cassar, I., Francalanza, A.: On implementing a monitor-oriented programming framework for actor systems. In: Ábrahám, E., Huisman, M. (eds.) IFM 2016. LNCS, vol. 9681, pp. 176–192. Springer, Cham (2016). doi:10.1007/978-3-319-33693-0_12
7. Chrobak, M.: Finite automata and unary languages. Theor. Comput. Sci. **47**, 149–158 (1986)
8. dAmorim, M., Roşu, G.: Efficient monitoring of ω-languages. In: Etessami, K., Rajamani, S.K. (eds.) CAV 2005. LNCS, vol. 3576, pp. 364–378. Springer, Heidelberg (2005). doi:10.1007/11513988_36
9. Fraigniaud, P., Rajsbaum, S., Travers, C.: On the number of opinions needed for fault-tolerant run-time monitoring in distributed systems. In: Bonakdarpour, B., Smolka, S.A. (eds.) RV 2014. LNCS, vol. 8734, pp. 92–107. Springer, Cham (2014). doi:10.1007/978-3-319-11164-3_9

10. Francalanza, A.: A theory of monitors. In: Jacobs, B., Löding, C. (eds.) FoSSaCS 2016. LNCS, vol. 9634, pp. 145–161. Springer, Heidelberg (2016). doi:10.1007/978-3-662-49630-5_9

11. Francalanza, A., Aceto, L., Ingolfsdottir, A.: On verifying hennessy-milner logic with recursion at runtime. In: Bartocci, E., Majumdar, R. (eds.) RV 2015. LNCS, vol. 9333, pp. 71–86. Springer, Cham (2015). doi:10.1007/978-3-319-23820-3_5

12. Gramlich, G., Schnitger, G.: Minimizing NFA's and regular expressions. J. Comput. Syst. Sci. **73**(6), 908–923 (2007)

13. Gruber, H., Holzer, M.: Inapproximability of nondeterministic state and transition complexity assuming **P** $\neq$ **NP**. In: Harju, T., Karhumäki, J., Lepistö, A. (eds.) DLT 2007. LNCS, vol. 4588, pp. 205–216. Springer, Heidelberg (2007). doi:10.1007/978-3-540-73208-2_21

14. Jiang, T., Ravikumar, B.: Minimal NFA problems are hard. SIAM J. Comput. **22**(6), 1117–1141 (1993)

15. Kozen, D.: Results on the propositional μ-calculus. Theor. Comput. Sci. **27**(3), 333–354 (1983)

16. Larsen, K.G.: Proof systems for satisfiability in Hennessy-Milner logic with recursion. Theor. Comput. Sci. **72**(2&3), 265–288 (1990)

17. Leucker, M., Schallhart, C.: A brief account of runtime verification. J. Logic Algebraic Program. **78**(5), 293–303 (2009)

18. Luo, Q., Roşu, G.: EnforceMOP: a runtime property enforcement system for multi-threaded programs. In: International Symposium on Software Testing and Analysis, New York, USA, pp. 156–166 (2013)

19. Meyer, A.R., Fischer, M.J.: Economy of description by automata, grammars, and formal systems. In: 12th Annual Symposium on Switching and Automata Theory (1971)

20. Milner, R. (ed.): A Calculus of Communicating Systems. Springer, Heidelberg (1980)

21. Rabin, M.O., Scott, D.: Finite automata and their decision problems. IBM J. Res. Dev. **3**(2), 114–125 (1959)

22. Rabinovich, A.: A complete axiomatisation for trace congruence of finite state behaviors. In: Brookes, S., Main, M., Melton, A., Mislove, M., Schmidt, D. (eds.) MFPS 1993. LNCS, vol. 802, pp. 530–543. Springer, Heidelberg (1994). doi:10.1007/3-540-58027-1_25

23. Schneider, F.B.: Enforceable security policies. ACM Trans. Inf. Syst. Secur. (TISSEC) **3**(1), 30–50 (2000)

24. Sen, K., Vardhan, A., Agha, G., Roşu, G.: Efficient decentralized monitoring of safety in distributed systems. In: International Conference on Software Engineering, pp. 418–427 (2004)

25. Sipser, M.: Introduction to the Theory of Computation, Computer Science. PWS Publishing Company (1997)

26. Vardi, M.Y., Wolper, P.: Reasoning about infinite computations. Inf. Comput. **115**(1), 1–37 (1994)

27. Yamagata, Y., Artho, C., Hagiya, M., Inoue, J., Ma, L., Tanabe, Y., Yamamoto, M.: Runtime monitoring for concurrent systems. In: Falcone, Y., Sánchez, C. (eds.) RV 2016. LNCS, vol. 10012, pp. 386–403. Springer, Cham (2016). doi:10.1007/978-3-319-46982-9_24

On the Semantics of Atomic Subgroups
in Practical Regular Expressions

Martin Berglund[1,3], Brink van der Merwe[2(✉)], Bruce Watson[1,3],
and Nicolaas Weideman[2,3]

[1] Department of Information Science,
Stellenbosch University, Stellenbosch, South Africa
[2] Department of Computer Science,
Stellenbosch University, Stellenbosch, South Africa
abvdm@cs.sun.ac.za
[3] Center for AI Research, CSIR, Stellenbosch University, Stellenbosch, South Africa

Abstract. Most regular expression matching engines have operators and features to enhance the succinctness of classical regular expressions, such as interval quantifiers and regular lookahead. In addition, matching engines in for example Perl, Java, Ruby and .NET, also provide operators, such as atomic operators, that constrain the backtracking behavior of the engine. The most common use is to prevent needless backtracking, but the operators will often also change the language accepted. As such it is essential to develop a theoretical sound basis for the matching semantics of regular expressions with atomic operators. We here establish that atomic operators preserve regularity, but are exponentially more succinct for some languages. Further we investigate the state complexity of deterministic and non-deterministic finite automata accepting the language corresponding to a regular expression with atomic operators, and show that emptiness testing is PSPACE-complete.

1 Introduction

In this paper we study atomic subgroups, a generalization of the feature described by Jeffrey Friedl, in the first edition of his book on regular expressions, as follows [Fri97]:

> "A feature I think would be useful, but that no regex flavor that I know of has, is what I would call possessive quantifiers. They would act like normal quantifiers except that once they made a decision that met with local success, they would never backtrack to try the other option. The text they match could be unmatched if their enclosing subexpression was unmatched, but they would never give up matched text of their own volition, even in deference to an overall match."

In the five and a half years between the first and second edition of Friedl's book, possessive quantifiers were introduced, and in the process gave way to

© Springer International Publishing AG 2017
A. Carayol and C. Nicaud (Eds.): CIAA 2017, LNCS 10329, pp. 14–26, 2017.
DOI: 10.1007/978-3-319-60134-2_2

atomic subgroups, making the prior a syntactic sugar for the latter. For example, E*+ denotes a regular expression E with a possessive Kleene star applied, which may also be written as (?>E*), where ?> makes the surrounding parenthesis an "atomic subgroup". Atomic subgroups "lock up" the part of the pattern it contains once it has matched, a failure further on in the pattern is not allowed to backtrack into the atomic group, but backtracking past it to previous subexpressions works as usual. A common use of atomic subgroups is to prevent needless backtracking and thus speedup matching time. For example, while the matcher in Java will take exponential time in the length of the input string to establish that input strings of the form $a \ldots ab$ can not be matched by (a|a)*, by essentially trying each possible way of matching an a in the input string with respectively the first or the second a in (a|a), matching happens in linear time when using (?>a|a)*, since the matcher "forgets" each time after using the first a in (?>a|a) to match an a, that it was also possible to use the second. Atomic subgroups are implemented in, among others, the Java, .NET, Python, Perl, PHP, and Ruby standard libraries, and in libraries such as Boost and PCRE.

Paper outline. In the next section we introduce the required notation followed by a section on the matching semantics of a-regexes (regular expressions with atomic subgroups). Then a section on the descriptional complexity of a-regexes and the complexity of deciding emptiness follows. After this, we briefly discuss how we arrived at our matching semantics definition, followed by our conclusions.

2   Definitions and Notation

An alphabet is a finite set of symbols. When not otherwise specified, Σ denotes an arbitrary alphabet. A regular expression over Σ is, as usual, an element of $\Sigma \cup \{\varepsilon, \emptyset\}$ (ε denotes the empty string), or an expression of one of the forms $(E_1 | E_2)$, $(E_1 \cdot E_2)$, or (E_1^*), where E_1 and E_2 are regular expressions. Some parenthesis may be elided using the rule that the Kleene closure '*' takes precedence over concatenation '·', which takes precedence over union '|'. In addition, outermost parenthesis may be dropped and $E_1 \cdot E_2$ abbreviated as $E_1 E_2$. The language matched by an expression is defined in the usual way. Furthermore, an alphabet $S = \{s_1, \ldots, s_n\}$ used as an expression S is an abbreviation for $s_1 | \cdots | s_n$, and for any expression E we may write E^k as an abbreviation for $E \cdots E$, i.e. k copies of E (so $|E^k| = k|E|$, where $|E|$ denotes the number of symbols in $|E|$, i.e. the *size* of E). Regular expressions set in typewriter font are examples of the Java syntax (same as most other libraries), which is not fully described here.

For a set S let 2^S denote the powerset of S. For a string w and a set of strings S, let $w \diagdown S = \{v \mid wv \in S\}$. A singleton set S and the single string may be used interchangeably. The union, concatenation and Kleene star of languages (over an alphabet Σ) is defined as usual. For a possibly infinite sequence $v_1, v_2, \ldots$ let $\text{dedup}(v_1, v_2, \ldots)$ denote the list (always finite in the uses in this paper) resulting when only the first instance of each value in the sequence is retained (e.g. $\text{dedup}(1, 2, 2, 1, 4, 3, 4) = 1, 2, 4, 3$). The concatenation of two sequences

$\sigma = v_1, \ldots, v_m$ and $\sigma' = v'_1, \ldots, v'_n$ is denoted by σ, σ' and defined to be the sequence $v_1, \ldots, v_m, v'_1, \ldots, v'_n$. For a string $w \in \Sigma^*$ and sequence $\sigma = v_1, \ldots, v_m$ with $v_i \in \Sigma^*$, we denote by $w\sigma$ the sequence $wv_1, \ldots, wv_m$.

Remark 1. In many real-world systems the primary primitive for regular expression matching is a *substring finding* one, where an input string w is searched for the left-most longest substring which matches the expression. Here we take (mostly) the more classical view, concerning ourselves with the strings matched entirely by the expression (with the exception of Definition 4). When we write e.g. a^*b the corresponding Java regular expression is `^a*b$`, the caret and dollar sign being special operators which "anchor" the match to the ends of the string.

As usual we will need to consider finite automata in some of the following.

Definition 1. *A non-deterministic finite automaton (NFA) is a tuple $A = (Q, \Sigma, q_0, \delta, F)$ where: (i) Q is the finite set of states; (ii) Σ is the input alphabet; (iii) $q_0 \in Q$ is the initial state; (iv) $\delta \subseteq Q \times (\Sigma \cup \{\varepsilon\}) \times Q$ is the transition relation; and (v) $F \subseteq Q$ is the set of final states.*

The language $\mathcal{L}(A)$ accepted by A is precisely the strings $w = \alpha_1 \cdots \alpha_n$ where $\alpha_i \in \Sigma \cup \{\varepsilon\}$ for all i, such that there exists states $q_0, \ldots, q_n \in Q$, where q_0 is the initial state, $(q_i, \alpha_{i+1}, q_{i+1}) \in \delta$ for each i, and $q_n \in F$.

For brevity we may write e.q. A_Q to denote the states of A, A_δ for the transition function, and so on. Also, $|A|$ denotes the number of states in A.

Definition 2. *An NFA with negative regular lookaheads (NFA with lookaheads for short) is an NFA $A = (Q, \Sigma, q_0, \delta, F)$, where δ may contain transitions of the form $(q, \alpha, \neg E, q') \in \delta$, where E is a regular expression over Σ.*

The language is as in Definition 1 except a transition $(q, \alpha, \neg E, q') \in \delta$ may only be used when the remainder of the input string is not in $\mathcal{L}(E)$.

We use lookaheads to demonstrate the regularity of atomic subgroups in an intuitive way. For this purpose, note that NFA with lookahead can only represent regular languages, as the lookaheads may be implemented by complementation and intersection of regular languages (that is, a product automaton tracking all lookaheads in parallel with the main expression).

3   Regular Expression Semantics and Atomic Subgroups

Informally, atomic subgroups are defined in terms of the depth-first search nature of matchers (such as in e.g. Java), in that the implementation will discard the portion of the stack (recording decisions made) corresponding to the atomic subgroup upon exiting the group. That is, the matcher will not reconsider choices made within the atomic subgroup once it has started to match the expression immediately following the group, though it may reconsider the choices made before entering the atomic subgroup, in which case the atomic subgroup matching will also be reconsidered.

Definition 3. *An* a-regex *over* Σ *is an element of* $\Sigma \cup \{\varepsilon, \emptyset\}$, *or an expression of the form* $(E_1 | E_2)$, $(E_1 \cdot E_2)$, (E_1^*), *or* $(\triangleright E_1)$, *where* E_1 *and* E_2 *are* a-regexes. *A subexpression of the form* $(\triangleright E)$, *for an expression* E, *is referred to as an* atomic subgroup *(that is, where it is styled as* (?>E) *in e.g. Java we write* $(\triangleright E)$*).*

Before going into the definition proper let us first give some informal examples of the semantics of atomic subgroups (agreeing with those in practical software).

Example 1. The expression $(\triangleright b^*)b$ matches nothing, as the atomic subgroup will consume all bs available and refuse to give one up for the final b subexpression. Meanwhile, the expression $a^*(\triangleright ab | b^*)b$ will match $\{a^n b^2 \mid n \geq 1\}$. For example, on $a^2 b^2$ the matcher will first have the $a*$ subexpression consume all as, then the $b*$ in the atomic subgroup "steals" all bs, making the match fail. However, as the atomic subgroup will not relinquish a b the matcher will backtrack past it into a^*, having it match one less a, after which reconsidering the atomic subgroup instead matches its preferred ab, leaving the final b to be matched by the end of the expression. Note that there exist E such that $\mathcal{L}(\triangleright E) \neq \mathcal{L}(E)$, and more precisely, $\mathcal{L}(\triangleright E) \subseteq \mathcal{L}(E)$ in general. For example $(\triangleright a | aa)$ does not match aa as it will always prefer to just match the first a without possibility of backtracking.

Example 2. A key use of atomic subgroups in practical matching is to limit ambiguity for performance reasons (e.g. avoiding pitfalls such as those formalized in [WvdMBW16]). Consider the following expression for matching email addresses, extracted from the RegExLib repository [Reg] (here slightly simplified):

```
[0-9a-z]([-.\w]*[0-9a-z])*@(([0-9a-z])+([-\w]*[0-9a-z])*\.)+[a-z]{2,9}
```

We do not give a complete explanation of the syntax and matching behavior of this expression, but there are two dangerous subexpressions here. Firstly, $([-.\backslash w]*[0-9a-z])*$ is (exponentially) ambiguous on the string $a \cdots a$ since both $[-.\backslash w]$ and $[0-9a-z]$ represents subalphabets containing a, and thus aa can be matched in more than one way by $([-.\backslash w]*[0-9a-z])*$. Using this regular expression, in e.g. a Java system, to validate that a user has provided a valid email address, would leave the system open to a regular expression denial of service attack. To make it safe one would replace this subexpression by $(?>([-.\backslash w]*[0-9a-z])*)$. The refusal to backtrack, introduced by using ?>, will have no effect on the language accepted, as the next symbol in the input sting must be an @, and the subgroup cannot read @. A similar problem, and solution, exist for the subexpression $([-\backslash w]*[0-9a-z])*$. This kind of performance concern apply especially in expressions using back references, which are necessarily very expensive to match in the face of ambiguity (unless P equals NP [Aho90]).

Example 3. The example eliciting the quote from [Fri97] on the introductory page concerned writing a regular expression for rounding decimal numbers. The expression should match a decimal number if it; either has more than two digits on the right of the decimal point; and; if the third is non-zero, it has more than three. It would match 12.750001 with the intent of rounding to 12.75, and match 2.1250 to round to 2.125, but not match 2.125 (in almost all practical regular expression matchers the substring matched by a certain subexpression can be extracted after matching, which is used in this example). Friedl suggests the expression `([1-9][0-9]*\.([0-9][0-9]([1-9]|ε)))[0-9][0-9]*`, where `[x-z]` is shorthand for $x \mid \cdots \mid z$, with the intent of using the first parenthesized subexpression (i.e. `([1-9][0-9]*\.([0-9][0-9]([1-9]|ε)))`) to "capture" the rounded number. This is incorrect however, as the number 2.125 would get 2.12 captured with the 5 being used to satisfy the final `[0-9]`. It is non-trivial to rewrite without interfering with having the rounded substring be the one matched by the first subexpression. This suggested the invention of atomic subgroups, i.e. the ability to force the first subexpression to not not give up the trailing 5 once it has matched it in for example 2.125, even though this makes the overall match fail, realizing the intended language.

For classical regular expressions the language being accepted can be defined inductively in terms of operations on the languages accepted by the subexpressions, e.g. $\mathcal{L}(E_1 \cdot E_2) = \{wv \mid w \in \mathcal{L}(E_1), v \in \mathcal{L}(E_2)\}$, but this is not the case for a-regexes. Instead we have to opt for a left-to-right approach on a specified input string w, where a subexpression acts upon some prefix of the suffix of w left to be matched. This definition was arrived at by careful analysis of the Java implementation – see Sect. 5 for a discussion on this process.

Definition 4. *For any a-regex E and string w let $m(E, w)$ denote the sequence of (not necessarily strict) prefixes of w which E matches, in order of priority. Then for all w:*

- *$m(\varepsilon, w) = \varepsilon$, the list consisting of a single element, the empty string,*
- *$m(\alpha, w) = \alpha$ if $\alpha \in \Sigma$ and w starts with α, otherwise $m(\alpha, w)$ is empty,*
- *$m(E \mid E', w) = dedup(m(E, w), m(E', w))$ (the concatenation deduplicated),*
- *$m(E^*, w) = dedup(v_1 \sigma_1, v_2 \sigma_2, \ldots, v_n \sigma_n, \varepsilon)$ where $m(E, w) = v_1, \ldots, v_n$ and for each i, $\sigma_i = m(E^*, v_i \smallsetminus w)$ if $v_i \neq \varepsilon$, and $\sigma_i = \varepsilon$ otherwise,*
- *$m(E \cdot E', w) = dedup(v_1 m(E', v_1 \smallsetminus w), \ldots, v_n m(E', v_n \smallsetminus w))$ where $m(E, w) = v_1, \ldots, v_n$,*
- *$m((\triangleright E), w) = v_1$ if $m(E, w)$ is non-empty and equal to $v_1, \ldots, v_n$, otherwise $m((\triangleright E), w)$ is empty.*

The language matched by E is denoted $\mathcal{L}_a(E)$ and defined as

$$\{w \mid w \in \Sigma^* \text{ occurs in } m(E, w)\}.$$

Remark 2. Note that setting $\sigma_i = \varepsilon$ when $v_i = \varepsilon$ in the definition of $m(E^*, w)$ above, is required in order to avoid infinite recursion in the definition. Regular expressions with subexpressions of the form E^*, such that $\varepsilon \in \mathcal{L}(E)$, are so-called *problematic regular expressions*. These are special enough that they are a source for differences in matching behavior in some implementations, and are considered in for example [SMV12, BvdM16].

Remark 3. We can define $m(E^{*?}, w)$, where $E^{*?}$ denotes the lazy Kleene star of E by moving the ε to the front in a definition otherwise similar to $m(E^*, w)$: $m(E^{*?}, w) = \text{dedup}(\varepsilon, v_1\sigma_1, v_2\sigma_2, \ldots, v_n\sigma_n)$. Intuitively, $E^{*?}$ repeats matching with E as few times as possible, whereas E^* does the opposite. Thus $m(E^{*?}, a^n) = \{\varepsilon, a, \ldots, a^n\}$ whereas $m(E^*, a^n) = \{a^n, a^{n-1}, \ldots, \varepsilon\}$.

Remark 4. Atomic subgroups may be compared to *cuts* [BBD+13], a proposed alternative to concatenation, denoted $R_1 ! R_2$ for expressions R_1 and R_2. The expression $R_1 ! R_2$ forces a "greedy" (i.e. longest possible prefix) match with R_1, whereas $(\triangleright R_1)R_2$ forces R_1 to pick the "first" match according to a priority implied by the syntactic details of the expression R_1. So, for example, whereas $\mathcal{L}((\triangleright\varepsilon|a)ab^*)$ equals ab^*, the cut expression $(\varepsilon|a)!ab^*$ would match aab^*. As such the cut is a normal operator on languages with two arguments, whereas atomic subgroups depend on the structure of the expressions.

Lemma 1. *For a regular expression E the sequence $m(E, w)$ contains each prefix w' of w with $w' \in \mathcal{L}(E)$ precisely once, and $m(E, w)$ contains no other strings. As a direct effect it holds that $\mathcal{L}(E) = \mathcal{L}_a(E)$.*

Proof. Follows by induction on the number of operators appearing in E. $\square$

In the remainder of the paper we simply use the notation $\mathcal{L}(E)$, instead of $\mathcal{L}_a(E)$, for an a-regex E. Let us consider some of the properties of a-regexes.

Lemma 2. *For a-regexes E and F we have the following properties.*

(i) $\mathcal{L}(EF) \subseteq \mathcal{L}(E)\mathcal{L}(F)$ (ii) $\mathcal{L}(E|F) = \mathcal{L}(E) \cup \mathcal{L}(F) = \mathcal{L}(F|E)$
(iii) $\mathcal{L}(E^*) \subseteq \mathcal{L}(E)^*$ (iv) $\mathcal{L}(\triangleright E) \subseteq \mathcal{L}(E)$

Also (i) is an equality if E is a regular expression. In addition, there exists E and F such that $\mathcal{L}(EF) \subsetneq \mathcal{L}(E) \cdot \mathcal{L}(F)$, $\mathcal{L}(E^*) \subsetneq \mathcal{L}(E)^*$ and $\mathcal{L}(\triangleright E) \subsetneq \mathcal{L}(E)$.

Proof. Follows from Definition 4, e.g. $abab \notin \mathcal{L}((\triangleright aba^*)^*) \subsetneq \mathcal{L}((\triangleright aba^*))^* \ni abab$ exemplifies property (iii). $\square$

In addition to the language captured, let us make the ordered nature of the semantics which Definition 4 gives to each expression an explicit property.

Definition 5. *For a-regexes F and G, we define F and G to be* language equivalent, *denoted by $F \equiv_{\mathcal{L}} G$, if $\mathcal{L}(F) = \mathcal{L}(G)$, whereas F and G are* order equivalent, *denoted by $F \equiv_{\mathcal{O}} G$, if $m(F, w) = m(G, w)$ for all $w \in \Sigma^*$.*

Lemma 3. *The following language and order equivalences hold.*

(i) $(FG)H \equiv_{\mathcal{O}} F(GH)$ (ii) $(F|G)|H \equiv_{\mathcal{O}} F|(G|H)$
(iii) $(F^*)^* \equiv_{\mathcal{O}} F^*$ (iv) $F \equiv_{\mathcal{O}} G$ implies $F \equiv_{\mathcal{L}} G$

However, there exists some F and G fulfilling each of the following inequalities.

(v) $F|G \not\equiv_{\mathcal{O}} G|F$ (vi) $(\triangleright FG) \not\equiv_{\mathcal{L}} (\triangleright F)(\triangleright G)$ (vii) $F \equiv_{\mathcal{L}} G$ but $F \not\equiv_{\mathcal{O}} G$

Proof. Follows directly from Definition 4. For $(\triangleright FG) \not\equiv_\mathcal{O} (\triangleright F)(\triangleright G)$ take e.g. $F = \Sigma^*$ and $G = a$, which makes $\mathcal{L}((\triangleright F)(\triangleright G))$ empty.   □

Order equivalence captures the semantics precisely: if two expressions are *not* order-equivalent contexts exist where replacing one with the other (as subexpressions of some expression) will result in different languages being accepted.

Lemma 4. *Let F and G be two a-regexes over Σ. Let E and E' be a-regexes over $\Sigma \cup \{\#\}$ (we assume $\# \notin \Sigma$) such that E' is obtained from E by replacing the subexpression F by the subexpression G. Then: (i) $F \equiv_\mathcal{O} G$ implies $E \equiv_\mathcal{O} E'$ for all E; and; (ii) $F \not\equiv_\mathcal{O} G$ implies $E \not\equiv_\mathcal{L} E'$ for some E.*

Proof. Statement (i) follows from Definitions 4 and 5, since having order equivalence means that $m(F, w) = m(G, w)$ for all w, and the sequences $m(F, w)$ and $m(G, w)$ entirely determine the influence of the subexpressions F and G on $m(E, w)$ and $m(E', w)$, respectively.

For statement (ii), take w such that $m(F, w) \neq m(G, w)$ and let $m(F, w) = v_1 \cdots v_n$ and $m(G, w) = v_1' \cdots v_{n'}'$. If $\{v_1, \ldots, v_n\} \neq \{v_1', \ldots, v_{n'}'\}$ the languages $\mathcal{L}(F)$ and $\mathcal{L}(G)$ already differ when restricted to prefixes of w, so just take $E = F$, $E' = G$ and we are done. Otherwise, let i be the smallest index with $v_i \neq v_i'$. As v_i and v_i' are both prefixes of w, we may assume without loss of generality that $w = v_i w_2 = v_i' w_1 w_2$, with $w_1 \neq \varepsilon$. Now construct $E = (\triangleright F(w_2 \#\# \mid w_1 w_2 \#))\#$, which makes $E' = (\triangleright G(w_2 \#\# \mid w_1 w_2 \#))\#$. Then $w\#\# \notin \mathcal{L}(E)$, while $w\#\# \in \mathcal{L}(E')$. To see, for example, why $w\#\# \notin \mathcal{L}(E)$, note that as a subexpression, F has to match either v_i or v_i' in order to make it through the atomic subgroups in E, when attempting to match $w\#\#$ with E. However, during this matching process, the a-regex F will in fact use v_i and not v_i', since v_i appears before v_i' in $m(E, w)$. Since using v_i will cause both $\#$ end-markers to be used in the atomic subgroup, we have that $w\#\#$ is not matched by E.   □

4   Automata Construction and Complexity Results

Despite the rather special semantics, adding atomic subgroups to regular expressions *does* in fact preserve regularity, though with a high state complexity.

Lemma 5. *For every a-regex E there exists a finite automaton A with $\mathcal{L}(E) = \mathcal{L}(A)$.*

Proof. We first consider the case where E contains no subexpression of the form F^*, with $\varepsilon \in \mathcal{L}(F)$. This restriction ensures that the constructed NFA contain no ε-loops, and thus each input string has only finitely many acceptance paths.

We inductively construct an NFA for each a-regex E, denoted by $M(E)$, with lookaheads and prioritized ε-transitions (a concept to be defined below), such that not only $\mathcal{L}(M(E)) = \mathcal{L}(E)$, but also such that $M(E)$ encodes (to be made precise below) for each string w the order in which prefixes w' of w with $w' \in \mathcal{L}(E)$, appear in $m(E, w)$. $M(E)$ has a single accept state with no outgoing transitions. With the exception of the final state, each state p in $M(E)$ has outgoing transitions of one of the following forms: (i) p has a single transition to a state q on a symbol from $\Sigma \cup \{\varepsilon\}$; (ii) p has transitions on ε to states q_1 and q_2, but $p \to q_1$ has higher priority (a concept used and defined next to ensure that each $w \in \mathcal{L}(E)$ has a unique accepting path in $M(E)$) than $p \to q_2$. Also, prioritized ε-transitions may have regular lookahead.

Given a string $w \in \mathcal{L}(G)$, we define an accepting path for w as usual, but whenever we encounter a state with transitions of type (ii), we always pick the higher priority transition if taking this transition will still make acceptance of w possible. By doing this, each $w \in \mathcal{L}(E)$ will have a unique accepting path in $M(E)$. Note that in terms of language accepted, the priorities on transitions play no role. Also, note that if w' and w'' are both prefixes of a string w, with $w', w'' \in \mathcal{L}(E)$, then the accepting paths $ap(w')$ and $ap(w'')$ of w' and w'' respectively, will be such that at some state p with prioritized outgoing ε-transitions, the one acceptance path will take the higher priority transition and the other the lower priority transition. The priorities on transitions at states with two outgoing ε-transitions can thus be used to define an ordering on all prefixes of w in $\mathcal{L}(E)$, denoted by the sequence $M(E, w)$. By constructing $M(E)$ inductively over the operators in E, we show that $M(E, w) = m(E, w)$ for all $w \in \Sigma^*$, which will also imply that we have $\mathcal{L}(M(E)) = \mathcal{L}(E)$. See Fig. 1 for examples.

The construction of $M(E)$, when $E = \emptyset$, ε or a, for $a \in \Sigma$, is as usual. Now suppose $M(E_i)$, for $i = 1, 2$, is already constructed, and $M(E_i, w) = m(E_i, w)$ for all $w \in \Sigma^*$. Also, assume p_i and q_i are the initial and final states in E_i. Next we describe the construction of (i) $M(E_1|E_2)$, (ii) $M(E_1 E_2)$, (iii) $M(E_1^*)$ and (iv) $M((\triangleright E_1))$, and leave it to the reader to verify from Definition 4 that $M(E, w) = m(E, w)$, for all $w \in \Sigma^*$, in each of these four cases.

(i) Create a new initial state p and final state q. In addition to these two states, we use the states and transitions as in E_1 and E_2. We add prioritized ε-transitions from p to p_1 and p_2, with $p \to p_1$ having higher priority. We also add ε transitions from q_1 and q_2 to q.

(ii) We use the states and transitions as in E_1 and E_2 and merge states q_1 and p_2. We use p_1 as initial and q_2 as final state.

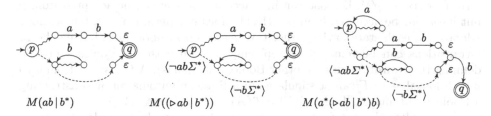

$$M(ab\,|\,b^*) \qquad M((\triangleright ab\,|\,b^*)) \qquad M(a^*(\triangleright ab\,|\,b^*)b)$$

Fig. 1. NFA with lookahead constructed as defined in Lemma 5. Wavy and dashed lines represent high and low priority transitions respectively. Negative lookaheads are shown in angle brackets. On the left the expression $ab\,|\,b^*$, in the middle the same expression inside an atomic subgroup, getting the prioritized edges augmented by lookaheads on the low-priority case. Right is the full result for an expression discussed in Example 1.

(iii) Create a new final state q and relabel the old final state q_1 in E_1 as the new initial state. In addition to the state q, we use the states and transitions as in E_1. We add prioritized ε-transitions from q_1 to p_1 and q, with $q_1 \to p_1$ having higher priority.

(iv) We keep the states and transitions as in E_1, but for all states p' having prioritized ε-transitions to q_1' and q_2' (with $p' \to q_1'$ having highest priority), we add regular lookahead $\neg(E_1)_{p',q_2'}$ to $p' \to q_2'$, where $(E_1)_{p',q_2'}$ is obtained as follows. Let $(E_1)_{q_1'}$ be a regular expression for the language accepted by $M(E_1)$ when q_1' is initial, then $(E_1)_{p',q_2'} = (E_1)_{q_1'} \Sigma^*$.

Next we discuss the modifications required for subexpression of the form E_1^*, with $\varepsilon \in \mathcal{L}(E_1)$. In the construction of E_1^* given in (iii) above we end up with potentially infinitely many acceptance paths for some strings when $\varepsilon \in \mathcal{L}(E_1)$. This problem can be addressed by a procedure called *flattening*, described in the proof of Theorem 3 in [BvdM16]. According to Definition 4, in cases where ε is the next prefix that should be matched (by the subexpression E_1) based on priority of prefix matching, the process of matching with E_1 (again) is disallowed. Flattening ensures this behavior by replacing consecutive ε-transitions (on a path in the NFA) with a single ε-transition, while taking all lookaheads on a given path of ε-transitions and replacing them with a regular expression equivalent to the intersection of encountered lookaheads. Once we apply this procedure, ε-selfloops may be obtained, which are simply not used in the flattened version of $M(E_1^*)$. It should be noted that applying the flattening procedure may produce states with more than two outgoing prioritized transitions.   □

Remark 5. The proof above can allow for lazy Kleene closures by switching the priorities of the outgoing ε-transitions from state q_1 in $M(E_1^*)$.

Lemma 6. *For every a-regex E there exists an NFA A such that $\mathcal{L}(E) = \mathcal{L}(A)$ and $|A| \in 2^{\mathcal{O}((k+1)|E|)}$ where k is the number of atomic subgroups in E.*

Proof (sketch). A Boolean automaton with n states can be simulated by an NFA with $2^n + 1$ states [HK11], and can be used to implement lookaheads. Without a complete definition, note that Boolean automata may have transitions of the form $(q, \alpha, (p \wedge \neg p'))$, i.e., one can in q accept αw if w can be accepted from p but it *cannot* be accepted from p' ([HK11] does not permit $\alpha = \varepsilon$, but without ε-loops and each state having either transitions on symbols or ε, but not both, ε-transitions can be removed by replacing a state with the Boolean formula defining the transition on ε, in other Boolean formulas). A transition from q to p with lookahead $\neg F$ can be simulated in a Boolean automaton by constructing a Boolean automaton A with $\mathcal{L}(F) = \mathcal{L}(A)$ and $(q, \varepsilon, (p \wedge \neg A_{q_0})) \in A_\delta$.

To complete the proof we argue that the NFA with lookaheads $M(E)$ constructed in the proof of Lemma 5 can be converted into a Boolean automaton with $\mathcal{O}((k + 1)|M(E)|)$ states, where k is the number of atomic subgroups in E. Notice that $M(E)$ has $\mathcal{O}(|E|)$ states as constructed. As only the language matters, prioritized transitions are treated as ε-transitions.

Consider a lookahead $\neg G\Sigma^*$ added to a transition when constructing $M(\triangleright F)$ in Lemma 5. Notice that there will exist some $q \in M(F\Sigma^*)_Q$ such that $\mathcal{L}(G\Sigma^*)$ is accepted by $M(F\Sigma^*)$ when starting in q (choosing the q which corresponds to the higher-priority choice). As such, let $\{E_1, \ldots, E_k\}$ be all the subexpressions such that each $(\triangleright E_i)$ occurs in E. Then construct the disjoint union of all these automata $A = M(E) \cup M(E_1\Sigma^*) \cup \cdots \cup M(E_k\Sigma^*)$ taking $A_{q_0} = M(E)_{q_0}$. Then, for each transition $(q, \alpha, \neg G\Sigma^*, p)$ in A find the state r such that A accepts $\mathcal{L}(G\Sigma^*)$ when started in r (as noted above r was originally in $M(E_i\Sigma^*)_Q$ for the E_i most closely enclosing this transition), and replace the transition by $(q, \alpha, (p \wedge \neg r))$. The intersected lookaheads created by the flattening at the end of Lemma 5 can be handled by a conjunction of lookaheads in the formula. $\square$

Theorem 1. *The class of languages matched by a-regexes is precisely the class of regular languages.*

Proof. This follows from the combination of Lemma 1, as a regular expression is an a-regex representing the same language, and Lemma 5, demonstrating that a finite automaton can describe the language of an a-regex. $\square$

We now demonstrate that a-regexes are exponentially more succinct than regular expressions for some languages. We start with two utility lemmas, which demonstrate that we can perform a limited set subtraction and intersection of languages using atomic subgroups.

Lemma 7. *For a-regexes F and G over the alphabet Σ with $\varepsilon \notin \mathcal{L}(G)$ we have that $\mathcal{L}((\triangleright(F\Sigma^* \mid \varepsilon))G) = \mathcal{L}(G) \setminus \mathcal{L}(F\Sigma^*)$.*

Proof. From $\mathcal{L}(\triangleright F\Sigma^*) = \mathcal{L}(F\Sigma^*)$ (both consist of all strings which have a prefix in $\mathcal{L}(F)$) and $\varepsilon \notin \mathcal{L}(G)$ it follows that $\mathcal{L}((\triangleright(F\Sigma^* \mid \varepsilon))G) \cap \mathcal{L}(F\Sigma^*) = \emptyset$. To complete the proof we need to show that if $w \in \mathcal{L}(G)$ but $w \notin \mathcal{L}(F\Sigma^*)$, then $w \in \mathcal{L}((\triangleright(F\Sigma^* \mid \varepsilon))G)$. This is indeed the case since $w \notin \mathcal{L}(F\Sigma^*)$ implies that ε, and not $F\Sigma^*$, is used when matching a string w with $(\triangleright(F\Sigma^* \mid \varepsilon))G$. $\square$

Lemma 8. *Let $E_1, \ldots, E_n$ be a-regexes over the alphabet Σ and $\# \notin \Sigma$. Then there is an a-regex E over the alphabet $\Sigma \cup \{\#\}$ such that $|E| \leq cn|\Sigma| + \sum_{i=1}^n |E_i|$, for some constant c, and $\mathcal{L}(E) = (\mathcal{L}(E_1) \cap \ldots \cap \mathcal{L}(E_n))\#$.*

Proof. Let $\Gamma = \Sigma \cup \{\#\}$. The language equality when replacing Σ by Γ in Lemma 7 becomes:

$$\mathcal{L}((\triangleright(F\Gamma^* \mid \varepsilon))G) = \mathcal{L}(G) \setminus \mathcal{L}(F\Gamma^*) \tag{1}$$

Let $E_1' = (\triangleright(E_1 \# \Gamma^* \mid \varepsilon))\Sigma^* \#$ be the lhs of (1) when setting $F = E_1\#$ and $G = \Sigma^*\#$. Then from (1) we have $\mathcal{L}(E_1') = \mathcal{L}(\Sigma^*\#) \setminus \mathcal{L}(E_1\#\Gamma^*) = (\mathcal{L}(\Sigma^*) \setminus \mathcal{L}(E_1))\#$.

Next, let $E_{1,2} = (\triangleright(E_1'\Gamma^* \mid \varepsilon))E_2\#$, again forming the lhs of (1) when taking $F = E_1'$ and $G = E_2\#$. Again from (1) we have $\mathcal{L}(E_{1,2}) = \mathcal{L}(E_2\#) \setminus \mathcal{L}(E_1') = (\mathcal{L}(E_1) \cap \mathcal{L}(E_2))\#$. The result now follows by repeating this construction. $\square$

Using the above lemmas we can now demonstrate a lower bound on the worst-case state complexity of an a-regex.

Theorem 2. *There exists a sequence $F_1, F_2, \ldots$ of a-regexes of increasing size such that the number of states in a minimal DFA for $\mathcal{L}(F_n)$ is in $2^{2^{\Omega(\sqrt{|F_n|})}}$.*

Proof. By using Lemma 8 we obtain a sequence of a-regexes F_n with $\mathcal{L}(F_n) = \Sigma^* a((\Sigma^{p_1})^+ \cap \ldots \cap (\Sigma^{p_1})^+)\#$ and $|F_n| \in \Theta(p_1 + \ldots + p_n)$, where $a \in \Sigma$, $|\Sigma| \geq 2$ and $p_1, \ldots, p_n$ the first n prime numbers. Note that $\mathcal{L}(F_n) = \Sigma^* a(\Sigma^{r_n})^+\#$, where $r_n = p_1 \cdot p_2 \cdot \ldots \cdot p_n$. Let $D(L_n)$ be the complete minimal DFA for $\mathcal{L}(F_n)$ and $s(n)$ the number of states in $D(F_n)$. Thus $s(n) = 2^{r_n+1} + 2$ (which can for example be verified by using derivatives). By showing that $r_n \in 2^{\Omega(\sqrt{p_1 + \ldots + p_n})}$ we thus have that $s(n) \in 2^{2^{\Omega(\sqrt{|F_n|})}}$. To obtain that $r_n \in 2^{\Omega(\sqrt{p_1 + \ldots + p_n})}$, make use of the results stating that; the sum of the first n prime numbers is asymptotically equal to $(n^2 \ln n)/2$; and; the product of the first n prime numbers (the so called primorial function), is equal to $e^{(1+o(1))n \ln n}$. □

For NFA the lower bound on worst-case state complexity indirectly established in Theorem 2 ($2^{\Omega(\sqrt{n})}$ for NFA) can be improved upon.

Theorem 3. *For every integer $k \geq 1$ there exists an a-regex E_k of size $\mathcal{O}(k)$ such that a state minimal NFA (and thus also every regular expression) for $\mathcal{L}(E_k)$ contains $2^{\Omega(k)}$ states. Furthermore, E_k contains only one atomic subgroup.*

Proof. Let $\Sigma = \{0, 1\}$ and for $k \geq 1$ let $F = \Sigma^*(0\Sigma^{k-1}1 | 1\Sigma^{k-1}0)$ and $G = \Sigma^{2k}$ in Lemma 7. Then if $E_k = (\triangleright(F\Sigma^* | \varepsilon))G$, we have, via Lemma 7, that

$$\mathcal{L}(E_k) = \mathcal{L}(G) \setminus \mathcal{L}(F\Sigma^*) = \Sigma^{2k} \setminus \mathcal{L}(\Sigma^*(0\Sigma^{k-1}1 | 1\Sigma^{k-1}0)\Sigma^*) = \{ww \,|\, w \in \Sigma^k\}.$$

To complete the proof, note that from the pigeon-hole principle it follows that no NFA with fever than 2^k states can accept the language $\mathcal{L}(E_k)$ (for a detailed argument see the proof of Theorem 6 in [BBD+13] where a language very similar to $\mathcal{L}(E_k)$ is considered). □

Finally we show that deciding emptiness of a-regexes is PSPACE-complete.

Theorem 4. *The problem of deciding whether $\mathcal{L}(E) = \emptyset$, for an a-regex E, is PSPACE-complete.*

Proof. First we show that deciding emptiness is PSPACE-hard. With $\Gamma = \Sigma \cup \{\#\}$, where $\# \notin \Sigma$, and $E_1' = (\triangleright(E_1\#\Gamma^* | \varepsilon))\Sigma^*\#$, we have from the proof of Lemma 8 that $\mathcal{L}(E_1') = (\mathcal{L}(\Sigma^*) \setminus \mathcal{L}(E_1))\#$. Thus $\mathcal{L}(E_1') = \emptyset$ precisely when $\mathcal{L}(E_1) = \Sigma^*$. Since deciding if $\mathcal{L}(E_1) = \Sigma^*$ for a regular expression E_1 is PSPACE-hard, we have that deciding emptiness for a-regexes is PSPACE-hard.

It can be decided whether $\mathcal{L}(E) = \emptyset$ in PSPACE by constructing the Boolean automaton described in the proof of Lemma 6 (polynomial in the size of E), this automaton can then be converted into an alternating finite automaton and emptiness-checked in PSPACE using results from [HK11]. □

5 On Arriving at the Semantics

The atomic subgroups semantics defined in this paper should agree with most common regular expression libraries, but the reference point primarily used has been the Java implementation (where they are called "independent subgroups"). The priorities of Definition 4 follow from the depth-first search implementation which Java and many others use (or at least simulate the effects of), semantics which are treated at length in [BvdM16], where the specifics of the Java implementation are also described. For atomic subgroups specifically a further analysis of the Java source code (version 8u40-25) was performed. In so doing we informally deduced the stack-discarding behavior which causes the atomic subgroup semantics in Java. However, the source code for the matcher itself is close to 6000 lines, supported by several other classes, and has little documentation, making a truly formal proof of equivalence fall outside the scope of this paper.

To corroborate the semantics of Definition 4 without a formal proof an implementation computing $m(E, w)$ for any expression E and string w was created. This was compared to Java using both a full match (i.e. verifying that $w \in m(E, w)$ if and only if E matches w in Java), and by comparing the preferred prefixes (where the prefix of a string w matched by an expression E in Java is compared with the first element in $m(E, w)$). All strings $w \in \{a, b, c\}^*$ with $|w| \leq 5$ were tested against all expressions with up to three operations, with no discrepancies found between Java and the definition.

6 Conclusions and Future Work

While this paper gives formal definitions and some key results on the previously only informally documented atomic subgroups, numerous open questions remain. Specifically, the complexity of the uniform membership problem (it is linear in the non-uniform case due to the regularity of a-regexes) remains open ($\mathcal{O}(n^3)$ appears likely). Also, the worst-case bounds on the minimum number of states required to accept the language matched by an a-regex are not tight, with DFA having the span between $2^{2^{\Omega(\sqrt{|E|})}}$ and $2^{2^{\mathcal{O}((k+1)|E|)}}$ (where k is the number of atomic subgroups in E), and NFA between $2^{\Omega(|E|)}$ and $2^{\mathcal{O}((k+1)|E|)}$.

References

[Aho90] Aho, A.: Algorithms for finding patterns in strings. In: van Leeuwen, J. (ed.) Handbook of Theoretical Computer Science, vol. A, pp. 255–300. MIT Press (1990)

[BBD+13] Berglund, M., Björklund, H., Drewes, F., van der Merwe, B., Watson, B.: Cuts in regular expressions. In: Béal, M.-P., Carton, O. (eds.) DLT 2013. LNCS, vol. 7907, pp. 70–81. Springer, Heidelberg (2013). doi:10. 1007/978-3-642-38771-5_8

[BvdM16] Berglund, M., van der Merwe, B.: On the semantics of regular expression parsing in the wild. Theor. Comput. Sci. (2016). doi:10.1016/j.tcs. 2016.09.006

[Fri97] Friedl, J.: Mastering regular expressions, 1st edn. O'Reilly & Associates Inc. (1997)

[HK11] Holzer, M., Kutrib, M.: Descriptional and computational complexity of finite automata—a survey. Inf. Comput. **209**(3), 456–470 (2011)

[Reg] RegexAdvice.com. Regular expression library. http://regexlib.com. Accessed 9 Jan 2017

[SMV12] Sakuma, Y., Minamide, Y., Voronkov, A.: Translating regular expression matching into transducers. J. Appl. Logic **10**(1), 32–51 (2012)

[WvdMBW16] Weideman, N., van der Merwe, B., Berglund, M., Watson, B.: Analyzing matching time behavior of backtracking regular expression matchers by using ambiguity of NFA. In: Han, Y.-S., Salomaa, K. (eds.) CIAA 2016. LNCS, vol. 9705, pp. 322–334. Springer, Cham (2016). doi:10.1007/978-3-319-40946-7_27

On the Regularity and Learnability of Ordered DAG Languages

Henrik Björklund$^{(\boxtimes)}$, Johanna Björklund, and Petter Ericson

Department of Computing Science, Umeå University, Umeå, Sweden
henrikb@cs.umu.se

Abstract. Order-Preserving DAG Grammars (OPDGs) is a subclass of
Hyper-Edge Replacement Grammars that can be parsed in polynomial
time. Their associated class of languages is known as Ordered DAG Languages, and the graphs they generate are characterised by being acyclic,
rooted, and having a natural order on their nodes. OPDGs are useful
in natural-language processing to model abstract meaning representations. We state and prove a Myhill-Nerode theorem for ordered DAG
languages, and translate it into a MAT-learning algorithm for the same
class. The algorithm infers a minimal OPDG G for the target language
in time polynomial in G and the samples provided by the MAT oracle.

1 Introduction

Graphs are one of the fundamental data structures of computer science, and
appear in every conceivable application field. We see them as atomic structures in physics, as migration patterns in biology, and as interaction networks
in sociology. For computers to process potentially infinite sets of graphs, i.e.,
graph languages, these must be represented in a finite form akin to grammars
or automata. However, the very expressiveness of graph languages often causes
problems, and many of the early formalisms have NP-hard membership problems; see, for example, [16] and [9, Theorem 2.7.1].

Motivated by applications in natural language processing (NLP) that require
more light-weight forms of representation, there is an on-going search for grammars that allow polynomial-time parsing. A recent addition to this effort was
the introduction of order-preserving DAG grammars (OPDGs) [4]. This is a
restricted type of hyper-edge replacement grammars [9] that generate languages
of directed acyclic graphs in which the nodes are inherently ordered. The authors
provide a parsing algorithm that exploits this order, thereby limiting nondeterminism and placing the membership problem for OPDGs in $O(n^2 + nm)$, where
m and n are the sizes of the grammar and the input graph, respectively. This is
to be compared with the unrestricted case, in which parsing is NP-complete.

The introduction of OPDGs is a response to the recent application [6] of
Hyperedge Replacement Grammars (HRGs) to abstract meaning representations
(AMRs) [2]. An AMR is a directed acyclic graph that describes the semantics

---

J. Björklund—Supported by the Swedish Research Council, Grant No. 621-2012-4555.

A. Carayol and C. Nicaud (Eds.): CIAA 2017, LNCS 10329, pp. 27–39, 2017.
DOI: 10.1007/978-3-319-60134-2_3

of a natural language sentence, and a corpus with approx. 8 000 AMRs has been compiled by the Information Sciences Institute (ISI) at USC.[1] The formalisation of AMRs is still under discussion, but although restricted, OPDGs retain sufficient expressive power to capture the AMRs in the ISI corpus.

In this paper, we continue to explore the OPDGs mathematical properties. We provide an algebraic representation of their domain, and a Myhill-Nerode theorem for the ordered DAG languages. We show that every ordered DAG language L is generated by a minimal unambiguous OPDG G_L, and that this grammar is unique up to renaming of nonterminals. In this context, 'unambiguous' means that every graph is generated by at most one nonterminal. This is similar the behaviour of deterministic automata, in particular that of bottom-up deterministic tree automata which take each input tree to at most one state.

One way of understanding the complexity of the class of ordered DAG languages, is to ask what kind of information is needed to infer its members. MAT learning [1], where MAT is short for minimal adequate teacher, is one of the most popular and well-studied learning paradigms. In this setting, we have access to an oracle (often called the teacher) that can answer *membership queries* and *equivalence queries*. In a membership query, we present the teacher with a graph g and are told whether g is in the target language L. In an *equivalence* query, we give the teacher an OPDG H and receive in return an element in the symmetric difference of $L(H)$ and L. This element is called a *counterexample*. If L has been successfully inferred and no counterexample exists, then the teacher instead returns the special token $\perp$.

MAT learning algorithms have been presented for a range of language classes and representational devices [1,5,10,12,14,17,18]. There have also been some results on MAT learning for graph languages. Okada et al. present an algorithm for learning unions of linear graph patterns from queries [15]. These patterns are designed to model structured data (HTML/XML). The linearity of the patterns means that no variable can appear more than once. Hara and Shoudai consider MAT learning for context-deterministic regular formal graph systems [11]. Intuitively, the context determinism means that a context uniquely determines a nonterminal, and only graphs derived from this nonterminal may be inserted into the context. Both restrictions are interesting, but neither is compatible with our intended applications.

Due to space limitations, most proofs have been omitted, but are available in a technical report [3].

2   Preliminaries

Sets, sequences, and numbers. The set of non-negative integers is denoted by $\mathbb{N}$. For $n \in \mathbb{N}$, $[n]$ abbreviates $\{1, \ldots, n\}$, and $\langle n \rangle$ the sequence $1 \cdots n$. In particular, $[0] = \emptyset$ and $\langle 0 \rangle = \lambda$. We also allow the use of sets as predicates: Given a set S and an element s, $S(s)$ is *true* if $s \in S$, and *false* otherwise. When $\equiv$ is an

---

[1] The ISI corpus is available at http://amr.isi.edu.

equivalence relation on S, $(S/\equiv)$ denotes the partitioning of S into equivalence classes induced by $\equiv$. The *index* of $\equiv$ is $|(S/\equiv)|$.

Let S° be the set of non-repeating sequences of elements of S. We refer to the ith member of a sequence s as s_i. When there is no risk for confusion, we use sequences directly in set operations, as the set of their members. Given a partial order $\preceq$ on S, the sequence $s_1 \cdots s_k \in S^\circ$ respects $\preceq$ if $s_i \preceq s_j$ implies $i \le j$.

A *ranked alphabet* is a pair $(\Sigma, rank)$ consisting of a finite set Σ of symbols and a *ranking function* $rank : \Sigma \mapsto \mathbb{N}$ which assigns a rank $rank(a)$ to every symbol $a \in \Sigma$. The pair $(\Sigma, rank)$ is typically identified with Σ, and the second component is kept implicit.

Graphs. Let Σ be a ranked alphabet. A (directed edge-labelled) *hypergraph* over Σ is a tuple $g = (V, E, src, tar, lab)$ consisting of

- finite sets V and E of *nodes* and *edges*, respectively,
- *source* and *target mappings* $src \colon E \mapsto V$ and $tar \colon E \mapsto V^\circ$ assigning to each edge e its source $src(e)$ and its sequence $tar(e)$ of targets, and
- a *labelling* $lab \colon E \mapsto \Sigma$ such that $rank(lab(e)) = |tar(e)|$ for every $e \in E$.

Since we are only concerned with hypergraphs, we simply call them graphs.

A *path* in g is a finite and possibly empty sequence $p = e_1, e_2, \ldots, e_k$ of edges such that for each $i \in [k-1]$ the source of e_{i+1} is a target of e_i. The *length* of p is k, and p is a *cycle* if $src(e_1)$ appears in $tar(e_k)$. If g does not contain any cycle then it is a *directed acyclic graph* (DAG). The *height* of a DAG G is the maximum length of any path in g. A node v is a *descendant* of a node u if $u = v$ or there is a nonempty path $e_1, \ldots, e_k$ in g such that $u = src(e_1)$ and $v \in tar(e_k)$. An edge e' is a *descendant edge* of an edge e if there is a path $e_1, \ldots, e_k$ in g such that $e_1 = e$ and $e_k = e'$.

The *in-degree* and *out-degree* of a node $u \in V$ is $|\{e \in E \mid u \in tar(e)\}|$ and $|\{e \in E \mid u = src(e)\}|$, respectively. A node with in-degree 0 is a *root* and a node with out-degree 0 is a *leaf*. For a single-rooted graph g, we write $root(g)$ for the unique root node.

For a node u of a DAG $g = (V, E, src, tar, lab)$, the *sub-DAG rooted at* u is the DAG $g{\downarrow}u$ induced by the descendants of u. Thus $g{\downarrow}u = (U, E', src', tar', lab')$ where U is the set of all descendants of u, $E' = \{e \in E \mid src(e) \in U\}$, and src', tar', and lab' are the restrictions of src, tar and lab to E'. A leaf v of $g{\downarrow}u$ is *reentrant* if there exists an edge $e \in E \setminus E'$ such that v occurs in $tar(e)$. Similarly, for an edge e we write $g{\downarrow}e$ for the subgraph induced by $src(e)$, $tar(e)$, and all descendants of nodes in $tar(e)$. This is distinct from $g{\downarrow}src(e)$ iff $src(e)$ has out-degree greater than 1.

Marked graphs. Although graphs, as defined above, are the objects we are ultimately interested in, we will mostly discuss marked graphs. When combining smaller graphs into larger ones, whether with a grammar or algebraic operations, the markings are used to know which nodes to merge with which.

A *marked DAG* is a tuple $g = (V, E, src, tar, lab, X)$ where (V, E, src, tar, lab) is a DAG and $X \in V^\circ$ is nonempty. The sequence X is called the *marking* of g,

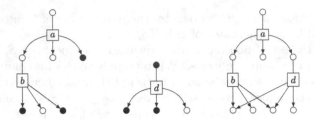

Fig. 1. A 2-context c, a 2-graph g, and the substitution $c[\![g]\!]$. Filled nodes convey the marking of c and g, respectively. Both targets of edges and external nodes of marked graphs are drawn in order from left to right.

and the nodes in X are referred to as *external nodes*. For $X = v_0v_1 \cdots v_k$, we write $head(g) = v_0$ and $ext(g) = v_1 \cdots v_k$. We say that two marked graphs are isomorphic modulo markings if their underlying unmarked graphs are isomorphic. The *rank* of a marked graph g is $|ext(g)|$.

Graph operations. Let g be a single-rooted marked DAG with external nodes X and $|ext(g)| = k$. Then g is called a *k-graph* if $head(g)$ is the unique root of g, and all nodes in $ext(g)$ are leaves.

If $head(g)$ has out-degree at most 1 (but is not necessarily the root of g), and either $head(g)$ has out-degree 0 or $ext(g)$ is exactly the reentrant nodes of $g \downarrow head(g)$, then g is a *k-context*. We denote the set of all *k*-graphs over Σ by $\mathbb{G}_\Sigma^k$, and the set of all *k*-contexts over Σ by $\mathbb{C}_\Sigma^k$. Furthermore, $\mathbb{G}_\Sigma = \cup_{k\in\mathbb{N}}\mathbb{G}_\Sigma^k$ and $\mathbb{C}_\Sigma = \cup_{k\in\mathbb{N}}\mathbb{C}_\Sigma^k$. Note that the intersection $\mathbb{G}_\Sigma\cap\mathbb{C}_\Sigma$ is typically not empty. Finally, the *empty context* consisting of a single node, which is external, is denoted by ϵ.

Given $g \in \mathbb{G}_\Sigma^k$ and $c \in \mathbb{C}_\Sigma^k$, the *substitution* $c[\![g]\!]$ of g into c is obtained by first taking the disjoint union of g and c, and then merging $head(g)$ and $head(c)$, as well as the sequences $ext(g)$ and $ext(c)$ element-wise. The results is a single-rooted, unmarked DAG. For an example, see Fig. 1.

Let g be a graph in $\mathbb{G}_\Sigma^0$, e an edge and let h be the marked graph given by taking $g \downarrow e$ and marking the (single) root, and all reentrant nodes. Then the *quotient* of $g \in \mathbb{G}_\Sigma^0$ with respect to h, denoted g/h is the unique context $c \in \mathbb{C}_\Sigma^k$ such that $c[\![h]\!] = g$. The *quotient* of a graph language $L \subseteq \mathbb{G}_\Sigma$ with respect to $g \in \mathbb{G}_\Sigma$ is the set of contexts $L/g = \{c \mid c[\![g]\!] \in L\}$.

Let A be a symbol of rank k. Then $A^\bullet$ is the graph $(V, \{e\}, src, tar, lab, X)$, where $V = \{v_0, v_1, \ldots, v_k\}$, $src(e) = v_0$, $tar(e) = v_1 \ldots v_k$, $lab(e) = A$, and $X = v_0 \ldots v_k$. Similarly, $A^\odot$ is the very same graph, but with only the root marked, in other words, $X = v_0$.

3   Well-Ordered DAGs

In this section, we present two formalisms for generating languages of DAGs, one grammatical and one algebraic. Both generate graphs that are *well-ordered* in the sense defined below. We show that the two formalisms define the same families of languages. This allows us to use the algebraic formulation as a basis for the upcoming Myhill-Nerode theorem and MAT learning algorithm.

An edge e with $tar(e) = w$ is a *common ancestor edge* of nodes u and u' if there are t and t' in w such that u is a descendant of t and u' is a descendant of t'. If, in addition, there is no edge with its source in w that is a common ancestor edge of u and u', we say that e is a *closest common ancestor edge* of u and u'. If e is a common ancestor edge of u and v we say that e *orders* u and v, with u before v, if $tar(e)$ can be written as wtw', where t is an ancestor of u and every ancestor of v in $tar(e)$ can be found in w'.

The relation $\preceq_g$ is defined as follows: $u \preceq_g v$ if every closest common ancestor edge e of u and v orders them with u before v. It is a partial order on the leaves of g [4]. Let g be a graph. We call g *well-ordered*, if we can define a total order $\trianglelefteq$ on the leaves of g such that $\preceq_g \subseteq \trianglelefteq$, and for every $v \in V$ and every pair u, u' of leaves of $g \downarrow v$, $u \preceq_{g \downarrow v} u'$ implies $u \trianglelefteq u'$.

3.1   Order-Preserving DAG Grammars

Order-preserving DAG grammars (OPDGs) are essentially hyper-edge replacement grammars with added structural constraints to allow efficient parsing.[2] The idea is to enforce an easily recognisable order on the nodes of the generated graphs, that provides evidence of how they were derived. The constraints are rather strict, but even small relaxations make parsing NP-hard; for details, see [4]. Intuitively, the following holds for any graph g generated by an OPDG:

- g is a connected, single-rooted DAG,
- only leaves of g have in-degree greater than 1, and
- g is well-ordered.

Definition 1 (Order-preserving DAG grammar [4]). *An* order-preserving DAG grammar *is a system* $H = (\Sigma, N, I, P)$ *where* Σ *and* N *are disjoint ranked alphabets of terminals and nonterminals, respectively,* I *is the set of starting nonterminals, and* P *is a set of productions. Each production is of the form* $A \to f$ *where* $A \in N$ *and* $f \in \mathbb{G}_{\Sigma \cup N}^{rank(A)}$ *satisfies one of the following two cases:*

1. *f consists of exactly two nonterminal edges e_1 and e_2, both labelled by A, such that $src(e_1) = src(e_2) = head(f)$ and $tar(e_1) = tar(e_2) = ext(f)$. In this case, we call $A \to f$ a* clone rule.
2. *f meets the following restrictions:*
    - *no node has out-degree larger than 1*
    - *if a node has in-degree larger than one, then it is a leaf;*
    - *if a leaf has in-degree exactly one, then it is an external node or its unique incoming edge is terminal*

---

[2] In [4], the grammars are called Restricted DAG Grammars, but we prefer to use a name that is more descriptive.

- *for every nonterminal edge e in f, all nodes in $tar(e)$ are leaves, and $src(e) \neq head(f)$*
- *the leaves of f are totally ordered by $\preceq_f$ and $ext(f)$ respects $\preceq_f$.*

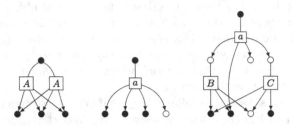

Fig. 2. Examples right-hand sides f of normal form rules of types (a), (b), and (c) for a nonterminal of rank 3.

A derivation step of H is defined as follows. Let $\rho = A \to f$ be a production, g a graph, and g_A a subgraph of g isomorphic modulo markings to $A^\odot$. The result of applying ρ to g at g_A is the graph $g' = (g/g_A)[\![f]\!]$, and we write $g \Rightarrow_\rho g'$. Similarly, we write $g \Rightarrow_H^* g'$ if g' can be derived from g in zero or more derivation steps. The language $\mathcal{L}(H)$ of H are all graphs g over the terminal alphabet Σ such that $S^\bullet \Rightarrow_H^* g$, for some $S \in I$. Notice that since a derivation step never removes nodes and never introduces new markings, if we start with a graph g with $|ext(g)| = k$, all derived graphs g' will have $|ext(g')| = k$. In particular, if we start from $S^\bullet$, all derived graphs will have $|ext(g')| = rank(S)$.

Definition 2 (Normal form [4]). *An OPDG H is on normal form if every production $A \to f$ is in one of the following forms:*

(a) The rule is a clone rule.
(b) f has a single edge e, which is terminal.
(c) f has height 2, the unique edge e with $src(e) = head(f)$ is terminal, and all other edges are nonterminal.

We say that a pair of grammars H and H' are *language-equivalent* if $\mathcal{L}(H) = \mathcal{L}(H')$. As shown in [4], every OPDG H can be rewritten to a language-equivalent OPDG H' in normal form in polynomial time. For an example of normal form rules, see Fig. 2.

For a given alphabet Σ, we denote the class of graphs $\cup_{H \text{ is an OPDG}} \mathcal{L}(H)$ that can be generated by some OPDG by $\mathcal{H}_\Sigma$, and by $\mathcal{H}_\Sigma^k$ the class of rank k marked graphs that can be generated from a rank k nonterminal.

3.2 DAG Concatenation

In Sects. 4 and 5, we need algebraic operations to assemble and decompose graphs. For this purpose, we define graph concatenation operations that mimic the behaviour of our grammars and show that the class of graphs that can be constructed in this way is equal to $\mathcal{H}_\Sigma$.

In particular, we construct our graphs in two separate ways, mirroring the cloning and non-cloning rules of the grammars:

- 2-concatenation, which takes 2 rank-m graphs and merges their external nodes, preserving their order, corresponding to the clone rules in Definition 2.
- a-concatenation, for $a \in \Sigma$, takes an a-labelled $rank(a)$ terminal edge and a number (less than or equal to $rank(a)$) of marked graphs, puts the graphs under targets of the terminal edge, and merges some of the leaves. This corresponds to rules of type (b) or (c) in Definition 2.

The second operation is more complex, since we must make sure that order is preserved. Given a terminal a of rank k and a sequence $g_1, \ldots, g_n$, with $n \leq k$, of marked graphs, new graphs are created in the following way. We start with $a^{\odot}$ and, for each $i \in [n]$ identify $head(g_i)$ with a unique leaf of $a^{\odot}$, intuitively "hanging" $g_1, \ldots, g_n$ under an edge labelled a. We then identify some of the leaves of the resulting graph. To specify the result of such a concatenation, and to ensure that it preserves order, we equip it with the following parameters.

(1) A number m. This is the number of nodes we will merge the external nodes of the graphs $g_1, \ldots, g_n$ and the remaining leaves of the a-labelled edge into.
(2) A subsequence $s = s_1 \ldots s_n$ of $\langle k \rangle$ of length n. This sequence defines under which leaves of $a^{\odot}$ we are going to hang which graph.
(3) A subsequence x of $\langle m \rangle$. This sequence defines which of the leaves of the resulting graph will be external.
(4) An order-preserving function φ that defines which leaves to merge. Its domain consists of the external leaves of the graphs $g_1, \ldots, g_n$ as well as the leaves of $a^{\odot}$ to which no graph from $g_1, \ldots, g_n$ is assigned. Its range is $[m]$.

Before we describe the details of the concatenation operation, we must go into the rather technical definition of what it means for φ to be order-preserving. It has to fulfil the following conditions:

(i) If both u and v are marked leaves of g_i, for some $i \in [n]$, and u comes before v in $ext(g_i)$, then $\varphi(u) < \varphi(v)$.
(ii) If $|\varphi^{-1}(i)| = 1$, then either $i \in x$ or the unique node v with $\varphi(v) = i$ belongs to $a^{\odot}$.
(iii) If there are i and j in $[m]$, with $i < j$ such that no graph g_ℓ for $\ell \in [n]$ contains both a member of $\varphi^{-1}(i)$ and a member of $\varphi^{-1}(j)$, then there exists a $p \in [k]$ such that either
    - p is the qth member of s, and g_q contains a member of $\varphi^{-1}(i)$, or
    - the pth member of $tar(a)$ is in $\varphi^{-1}(i)$
    and furthermore there is no $r < p$ such that either
    - r is the tth member of s and g_t contains a member of $\varphi^{-1}(j)$, or
    - the rth member of $tar(a)$ is itself in $\varphi^{-1}(j)$

Definition 3 (*a-concatenation*). *Given a terminal a, the a-concatenation of $g_1, \ldots, g_n$, parameterized by m, s, x, ϕ is the graph g obtained by doing the following. For each $i \in [n]$, identify head(g_i) with the leaf of $a^\odot$ indicated by s_i. For each $j \in [m]$, identify all nodes in $\varphi^{-1}(j)$. Finally, ext(g) is the subsequence of the m nodes from the previous step indicated by x.*

We denote by $\mathcal{A}_\Sigma$ the class of marked graphs that can be assembled from Σ through a- and 2-concatenation, and by $\mathcal{A}_\Sigma^k \subseteq \mathcal{A}_\Sigma$ the graphs of rank k. Each concatenation operation can be defined as an algebraic operation that is defined for a sequence of graphs if they have the appropriate ranks. Let ψ be a concatenation operator and $g_1, \ldots, g_n$ a sequence of graphs for which it is defined. Let $g = \psi(g_1, \ldots, g_n)$. For some $i \in n$, let g' be a graph of the same rank as g_i. Then $\psi(g_1, \ldots, g_{i-1}, g', g_{i+1}, \ldots, g_n) = (g/g_i)[\![g']\!]$.

The following is the main result of this section.

Theorem 4. $\mathcal{A}_\Sigma = \mathcal{H}_\Sigma$, and $\mathcal{A}_\Sigma^k = \mathcal{H}_\Sigma^k$ for all k.

4   A Myhill-Nerode Theorem

This section defines the Nerode congruence $\equiv_L$ for an ordered DAG language L. A pair of graphs are congruent with respect to L, if they can be replaced by one another in any context in $\mathbb{C}_\Sigma$, without disturbing the encompassing graph's membership in L. The learning algorithm in Sect. 5 produces increasingly more refined approximations of $\equiv_L$ until it reaches $\equiv_L$ itself. This treats $\equiv_L$ as a corner case in a family of relations, each induced by a subset of $\mathbb{C}_\Sigma$.

Definition 5. *Let $C \subseteq \mathbb{C}_\Sigma$. The equivalence relation $\equiv_{L,C}$ on $\mathcal{A}_\Sigma$ is given by: $g \equiv_{L,C} g'$ if and only if $(L/g \cap C) = (L/g' \cap C)$. The relation $\equiv_{L,\mathbb{C}_\Sigma}$ is known as the* Nerode congruence *with respect to L and written $\equiv_L$.*

It is easy to see that for two graphs to be equivalent, they must have equally many external nodes. The graph g is *dead* (with respect to L) if $L/g = \emptyset$, and graphs that are not dead are *live*. Thus, if $\equiv_L$ has finite index, there must be a $k \in \mathbb{N}$ such that every $g \in \mathcal{A}_\Sigma$ with more than k external nodes is dead.

In the following, we use $\Psi(\Sigma)$ to denote the set of all concatenation operators applicable to graphs over Σ.

Definition 6 (*Σ-expansion*). *Given $N \subseteq \mathcal{A}_\Sigma$, we write $\Sigma(N)$ for the set:*

$$\{\psi(g_1, \ldots, g_m) \mid \psi \in \Psi(\Sigma), g_1, \ldots, g_m \in N \text{ and } \psi(g_1, \ldots, g_m) \text{ is defined}\}.$$

In the upcoming Sect. 5, Theorem 9 will form the basis for a MAT learning algorithm. As is common, this algorithm maintains an *observation table* T that collects the information needed to build a finite-state device for the target language L. The construction of an OPDG G^T from T is similar to that from the Nerode congruence, so introducing it here avoids repetition. Intuitively, the observation table is made up of two sets of graphs N and P, representing nonterminals and production rules, respectively, and a set of contexts C used to explore the congruence classes of $N \cup P$ with respect to L.

To facilitate the design of new MAT learning algorithms, the authors of [7] introduce the notion of an *abstract observation table* (AOT); an abstract data type guaranteed to uphold certain helpful invariants.

Definition 7 (Abstract observation table, see [7]). *Let $N \subseteq P \subseteq \Sigma(N) \subseteq A_\Sigma$, with N finite. Let $C \subseteq \mathbb{C}_\Sigma$, and let $\rho : P \mapsto N$. The tuple (N, P, C, ρ) is an abstract observation table with respect to L if for every $g \in P$,*

1. *$L/g \neq \emptyset$, and*
2. *$\forall g' \in N \setminus \{\rho(g)\} : g \not\equiv_{L,C} g'$.*

The AOT in [7] accommodates production weights taken from general semirings. The version recalled here has a number of modifications: First, we dispense with the sign-of-life function that maps every graph $g \in N$ to an element in L/g. Its usages in [7] are to avoid dead graphs, and to compute the weights of productions involving g. From the way new productions and nonterminals are discovered, we already know that they are live, and as we are working in the Boolean setting, there are no transition weights to worry about. Second, we explicitly represent the set of contexts C to prove that the nonterminals in N are distinct. Both realisations of the AOT discussed in [7] collect such contexts, though it is not enforced by the AOT. Third, we do not require that $L(y) = L(\rho(y))$, as this condition is not necessary for correctness, though it may reduce the number of counterexamples needed. The data fields and procedures have also been renamed to reflect the shift from automata to grammars. This change is only superficial, as there is a direct correspondence between states and nonterminals, transitions and productions, and accepting states and initial nonterminals. From here on, a bold font is used to refer to graphs as nonterminals.

Definition 8. *Let $T = (N, P, C, \rho)$ be an AOT with respect to L. Then G^T is the OPDG (Σ, N^T, I^T, P^T) where $N^T = N$, $I^T = N \cap L$, and*

$$P^T = \{\rho(g) \to \psi(\rho(g_1), \dots, \rho(g_m)) \mid g = \psi(g_1, \dots, g_m) \in P\} \ .$$

Given an ODPG $G = (\Sigma, N, I, P)$ and a nonterminal $f \in N$, we let $G_f = (\Sigma, N, \{f\}, P)$. The grammar G is *unambiguous* if for every $g, h \in N$, $\mathcal{L}(G_g) \cap \mathcal{L}(G_h) \neq \emptyset$ implies that $g = h$.

Theorem 9 (Myhill-Nerode theorem). *The language $L \subseteq A_\Sigma$ can be generated by an OPDG if and only if $\equiv_L$ has finite index. Furthermore, there is a minimal unambiguous OPDG G_L with $\mathcal{L}(G_L) = L$ that has one nonterminal for every live equivalence class of $\equiv_L$, and this is unique up to nonterminal names.*

In the following proof sketch, $D = \{g \in A_\Sigma \mid g \text{ is dead}\}$. In the "if" direction, we consider an AOT (N, P, C, ρ) where N contains representative elements of $(A_\Sigma/ \equiv_L) \setminus \{D\}$, $P = \Sigma(N) \setminus D$, $C = \mathbb{C}_\Sigma$, and, for every $g \in P$, $\rho(g)$ is the representative of g's equivalence class in N. From the fact that $g \in \mathcal{L}(G^T_{\rho(g)})$, for every $g \in \mathcal{A}_\Sigma$, the first result follows. In the "only if" direction, we note that if G is an OPDG with nonterminals N, and $\mathcal{L}(G_A)(g) = \mathcal{L}(G_A)(h)$ for $g, h \in \mathcal{A}_\Sigma$ and all $A \in N$, then $g \equiv_{\mathcal{L}(G)} h$. As N is finite, so is the index of $\equiv_{\mathcal{L}(G)}$.

Notice that when L only contains ordered ranked trees (i.e., when the root has out-degree one and no node has in-degree greater than one), Theorem 9 turns into the Myhill-Nerode theorem for regular tree languages [13], and the constructed device is essentially the minimal bottom-up tree automaton for L.

5   MAT Learnability

In Sect. 4, the data fields of the AOT were populated with a so-called characteristic set for L, and this yielded the minimal unambiguous OPDG G_L for L. In this section, we describe how the necessary information can be incrementally built up by querying a MAT oracle. Due to space restrictions, background results are covered in brief and we refer to [3] for a detailed exposition.

The learning algorithm (henceforth; the learner) interacts with the oracle (the teacher) through the following procedures:

- EQUALS?(H) returns a graph in $\mathcal{L}(H) \ominus L$, or $\bot$ if no such exists.
- MEMBER?(g) returns the Boolean value $L(g)$.

The information gathered from the teacher is written and read from the AOT through the procedures listed below. In the declaration of these, (N, P, C, ρ) and (N', P, C', ρ') are the data values before and after application, respectively.

- INITIALISE sets $N' = P' = C' = \emptyset$.
- ADDPRODUCTION(g) with $g \in \Sigma(N) \setminus P$. Requires that $L/g \neq \emptyset$, and guarantees that $N \subseteq N'$ and $P \cup \{g\} \subseteq P'$.
- ADDNONTERMINAL(c, g) with $g \in P \setminus N$ and $c \in \mathbb{C}_\Sigma$. Requires that $\forall g' \in N : g \not\equiv_{L, C \cup \{c\}} g'$, and guarantees that $N \cup \{g\} \subseteq N'$, $P \subseteq P'$, and $C \subseteq C' \subseteq C \cup \{c\}$.
- GRAMMAR returns G^T without modifying the data fields.

The learner and the procedure EXTEND are as they stand in [7]. The learner maintains an AOT T, from which it induces an OPDG G^T. This OPDG is given to the teacher in the form of an equivalence query. If the teacher responds with the token $\bot$, then the language has been successfully acquired. Otherwise, the learner receives a counterexample $g \in \mathcal{L}(G^T) \ominus L$, from which it extracts new facts about L through the procedure EXTEND and includes these in T.

The procedure EXTEND uses contradiction backtracking to gain new knowledge from the counterexample g [8]. This consists in simulating the parsing of g with respect to the OPDG G^T. The simulation is done incrementally, and in each step a subgraph $h \in \Sigma(N) \setminus N$ of g is nondeterministically selected. If h is not in P, this indicates that a production is missing from G^T and the problem is solved by a call to ADDPRODUCTION. If h is in P, then the learner replaces it by $\rho(h)$ and checks whether the resulting graph g' is in L. If $L(g) \neq L(g')$,

---

Algorithm 1. The procedure ADDPRODUCTION

Data: $p \in \Sigma(N) \setminus P$

$P \leftarrow P \cup \{g\}$;

if $\exists g' \in N : g \equiv_{L,C} g'$ **then**

$\quad | \quad \rho(g) \leftarrow g'$;

else

$\quad$ **if** $\exists g' \in N$ **then**

$\quad\quad | \quad \rho(g) \leftarrow g'$;

$\quad$ **else**

$\quad\quad | \quad$ ADDNONTERMINAL(ϵ, g);

Algorithm 2. The procedure ADDNONTERMINAL

Data: $g \in P \setminus N$, $c \in \mathbb{C}_\Sigma$, and $\forall g' \in N : g \not\equiv_{L,C\cup\{c\}} g'$

$N \leftarrow N \cup \{g\}$;

if $g \equiv_{L,C} \rho(g)$ **then**

$\quad | \quad C \leftarrow C \cup \{c\}$;

$g' \leftarrow \rho(g)$;

for $h \in \rho^{-1}(g')$ **do**

$\quad$ **if** $h \equiv_{L,C} g$ **then**

$\quad\quad | \quad \rho(h) \leftarrow g$;

---

then evidence has been found that h and $\rho(h)$ do not represent the same congruence class and the learner calls ADDNONTERMINAL. If the membership has not changed, then the procedure calls itself recursively with the graph g' as argument, which has strictly fewer subgraphs not in P. Since g is a counterexample, so is g'. If this parsing process succeeds in replacing all of g with a graph $g' \in N$, then $L(g) = L(g')$ and $g \in \mathcal{L}(G_{g'}^{\mathrm{T}})$. Since $g' \in N$, $\mathcal{L}(G^{\mathrm{T}})(g') = L(g')$. It follows that $\mathcal{L}(G^{\mathrm{T}})(g) = L(g)$ which contradicts g being a counterexample.

From [7], we know that if EXTEND adheres to the pre- and postconditions of the AOT procedures, and the target language L can be computed by an OPDG, then the learner terminates and returns a minimal OPDG generating L. It thus remains to discuss the procedures ADDPRODUCTION and ADDNONTERMINAL (Algorithms 1 and 2, respectively), and show that these behave as desired. The procedure ADDPRODUCTION simply adds its argument g to the set P of graphs representing productions. It then looks for a representative g' for g in N, such that $g' \equiv_{L,C} g$. If no such graph exists, it chooses any $g' \in N$, or if N is empty, adds g itself to N with a call to ADDNONTERMINAL. Similarly, ADDNONTERMINAL adds g to the set N of graphs representing nonterminals. If g cannot be distinguished from $\rho(g)$, which is the only element in N that could possibly be indistinguishable from g, then c is added to C to tell g and $\rho(g)$ apart. Finally, the representative function ρ is updated to satisfy Definition 7.

It is easy to verify that (i) the proposed procedures deliver on their guarantees if their requirements are fulfilled, (ii) that where they are invoked, the requirements are indeed fulfilled, and (iii) the conditions on the observation table given in Definition 7 are always met. By [7, Corollary 8], we arrive at Theorem 10.

Theorem 10. *The learner terminates and returns G_L.*

We close this section with a discussion of the learner's complexity. To infer the canonical ODGP $G_L = (\Sigma, N, I, P)$ for L, the learner must gather as many graphs as there are nonterminals and transitions in G_L. In each iteration of the main loop, it parses a counterexample g in polynomial time in the size of g and T (the latter is limited by the size of G_L), and is rewarded with at least one production or nonterminal. The learner is thus polynomial in $|G_L| = |N| + |P|$ and the combined size of the counterexamples provided by the teacher.

Acknowledgments. We thank the anonymous reviewers for their careful reading of our manuscript and their helpful comments.

References

1. Angluin, D.: Learning regular sets from queries and counterexamples. Inf. Comput. **75**, 87–106 (1987)
2. Banarescu, L., Bonial, C., Cai, S., Georgescu, M., Griffitt, K., Hermjakob, U., Knight, K., Koehn, P., Palmer, M., Schneider, N.: Abstract meaning representation for sembanking. In: 7th Linguistic Annotation Workshop & Interoperability with Discourse, Sofia, Bulgaria (2013)
3. Björklund, H., Björklund, J., Ericson, P.: On the regularity and learnability of ordered DAG languages. Technical report UMINF 17.12, Umeå University (2017)
4. Björklund, H., Drewes, F., Ericson, P.: Between a rock and a hard place - uniform parsing for hyperedge replacement DAG grammars. In: 10th International Conference on Language and Automata Theory and Applications, Prague, Czech Republic, pp. 521–532 (2016)
5. Björklund, J., Fernau, H., Kasprzik, A.: Polynomial inference of universal automata from membership and equivalence queries. Inf. Comput. **246**, 3–19 (2016)
6. Chiang, D., Andreas, J., Bauer, D., Hermann, K.M., Jones, B., Knight, K.: Parsing graphs with hyperedge replacement grammars. In: 51st Annual Meeting of the Association for Computational Linguistics (ACL 2013), Sofia, Bulgaria, pp. 924–932 (2013)
7. Drewes, F., Björklund, J., Maletti, A.: MAT learners for tree series: an abstract data type and two realizations. Acta Informatica **48**(3), 165 (2011)
8. Drewes, F., Högberg, J.: Query learning of regular tree languages: how to avoid dead states. Theory Comput. Syst. **40**(2), 163–185 (2007)
9. Drewes, F., Kreowski, H.-J., Habel, A.: Hyperedge replacement graph grammars. In: Rozenberg, G. (ed.), Handbook of Graph Grammars, vol. 1, pp. 95–162. World Scientific (1997)
10. Drewes, F., Vogler, H.: Learning deterministically recognizable tree series. J. Automata, Lang. Comb **12**(3), 332–354 (2007)
11. Hara, S., Shoudai, T.: Polynomial time MAT learning of c-deterministic regular formal graph systems. In: International Conference on Advanced Applied Informatics (IIAI AAI 2014), Kitakyushu, Japan, pp. 204–211 (2014)

12. Högberg, J.: A randomised inference algorithm for regular tree languages. Nat. Lang. Eng. **17**(02), 203–219 (2011)

13. Kozen, D.: On the Myhill-Nerode theorem for trees. Bull. EATCS **47**, 170–173 (1992)

14. Maletti, A.: Learning deterministically recognizable tree series — revisited. In: Bozapalidis, S., Rahonis, G. (eds.) CAI 2007. LNCS, vol. 4728, pp. 218–235. Springer, Heidelberg (2007). doi:10.1007/978-3-540-75414-5_14

15. Okada, R., Matsumoto, S., Uchida, T., Suzuki, Y., Shoudai, T.: Exact learning of finite unions of graph patterns from queries. In: Hutter, M., Servedio, R.A., Takimoto, E. (eds.) ALT 2007. LNCS (LNAI), vol. 4754, pp. 298–312. Springer, Heidelberg (2007). doi:10.1007/978-3-540-75225-7_25

16. Rozenberg, G., Welzl, E.: Boundary NLC graph grammars-basic definitions, normal forms, and complexity. Inf. Control **69**(1–3), 136–167 (1986)

17. Sakakibara, Y.: Learning context-free grammars from structural data in polynomial time. Theor. Comput. Sci. **76**(2–3), 223–242 (1990)

18. Shirakawa, H., Yokomori, T.: Polynomial-time MAT learning of c-deterministic context-free grammars. Trans. Inf. Process. Soc. Jpn. **34**, 380–390 (1993)

On the Number of Active States in Deterministic and Nondeterministic Finite Automata

Henning Bordihn[1] and Markus Holzer[2(✉)]

[1] Institut für Informatik, Universität Potsdam,
August-Bebel-Straße 89, 14482 Potsdam, Germany
henning@cs.uni-potsdam.de
[2] Institut Für Informatik, Universität Giessen,
Arndtstraße 2, 35392 Giessen, Germany
holzer@informatik.uni-giessen.de

Abstract. We introduce a new measure of descriptional complexity on finite automata, called the number of active states. Roughly speaking, the number of active states of an automaton A on input w counts the number of different states visited during the most economic computation of the automaton A for the word w. This concept generalizes to finite automata and regular languages in a straightforward way. We show that the number of active states of both finite automata and regular languages is computable, even with respect to nondeterministic finite automata. We further compare the number of active states to related measures for regular languages. In particular, we show incomparability to the radius of regular languages and that the difference between the number of active states and the total number of states needed in finite automata for a regular language can be of exponential order.

1 Introduction

The concept of finite (state) automata is fundamental for nearly all areas of computer science. The class of finite automata possesses many nice features, for instance, decidability properties and algebraic characterizations. This led to several efficient algorithms available for finite automata, making them accessible for a bench of different applications. However, the finite automata used in applications typically have a fairly large number of states, in the sense that minimal finite automata need hundreds of thousands or even millions of states in order to express all relevant properties of the systems to be modeled. For example, in the field of reactive or embedded systems, where concurrent processes cause an "explosion" of the state space, Mealy automata or Kripke structures used for modeling controllers may be of enormous size, e.g., see [3] and [7, Table 5.1].

M. Holzer—Part of the work was done while the author was at Institut für Informatik, Technische Universität München, Arcisstraße 21, 80290 München, Germany and at Institut für Informatik, Technische Universität München, Boltzmannstraße 3, 85748 Garching bei München, Germany.

A. Carayol and C. Nicaud (Eds.): CIAA 2017, LNCS 10329, pp. 40–51, 2017.
DOI: 10.1007/978-3-319-60134-2_4

Consequently, the efficiency of algorithms such as those for model checking may become less feasible or can be applied only to relatively small subsystems.

In this paper, a new measure of descriptional complexity for finite automata, namely the number of active states, is introduced, which may contribute to better cope with huge finite automata. In contrast to other, well-known measures for finite automata such as the state complexity or the radius, the number of active states is a dynamic measure: for any computation, the number of different states is counted that are visited during the computation. This notion generalizes to words by taking the computation with the smallest number of active states into account, and it is defined for automata as the number of active states of the "most expensive" word. Finally, the number of active states of a regular language with respect to deterministic (nondeterministic) finite automata is the measure of the best deterministic (nondeterministic, respectively) automaton accepting the language. The notion of active states is defined in a similar way as the number of active symbols for Lindenmayer and cooperating distributed grammar systems, where a symbol is referred to as active if it can be non-identically rewritten, that is, if there is a production of the form $a \rightarrow x$ with $a \neq x$ [2,6,9]. Then, an active symbol can contribute to the generation (evolution) of sentential forms in a similar way as active states are used during the analysis of strings. Clearly, the measure of active symbols also allows for a dynamic interpretation [2], which parallels the dynamic definition of the number of active states.

We investigate basic properties of the newly defined measure. It is shown that the measure is algorithmically computable, even in the nondeterministic case. While in the deterministic case the number of active states can be read off from the minimal deterministic finite automaton of the language in question, the number of active states in the nondeterministic case can be determined by a brute force search on an exponentially large search space. Moreover, the number of active states is compared to related measures, the state complexity and the radius. One of the results shows that there is an infinite sequence of regular languages for which the number of active states is bounded by some constant while the (total) number of states in their minimal automata cannot be bounded. Here, the alphabet grows with the state complexity. If the languages are restricted to binary alphabets, then the (total) number of states of the minimal automata can be exponential in the number of active states. That is, in such cases, the amount of random access memory needed during the computations can be logarithmic in the size of the automata. In general, the size of the random access memory needed for the computations of finite automata can be calculated in advance due to the computability of the measure of active states. In this paper, most of the proofs are omitted due to space constraints.

2   Definitions

We assume the reader to be familiar with some basic notation of automata and formal language theory as contained in the book of Wood [8]. In particular, let Σ be a finite alphabet. Then the cardinality of Σ (or any other set) is denoted by $|\Sigma|$ and the set of finite words over Σ including the empty word λ is referred to as Σ^*, which is the *free monoid* over Σ. Let $\Sigma^+ = \Sigma^* \setminus \{\lambda\}$. The length of a word w is denoted by $|w|$, where $|\lambda| = 0$. By convention, a singleton set will usually be identified with its element.

A *(nondeterministic) finite automaton* (NFA) is a 5-tuple $A = (Q, \Sigma, \delta, q_0, F)$, where Q is the finite set of *states*, Σ is the finite set of *input symbols*, $q_0 \in Q$ is the *initial state*, $F \subseteq Q$ is the set of *accepting states*, and $\delta : Q \times \Sigma \to 2^Q$ is the *transition function*—here 2^Q denotes the power-set of Q. Observe that by our definition the transition function δ is a *total* mapping. The set of rejecting states is $Q \setminus F$. Moreover, a finite automaton is *deterministic* (DFA) if and only if for all $q \in Q$ and $a \in \Sigma$ the set $\delta(q, a)$ is a singleton, i.e., $|\delta(q, a)| = 1$. In this case we simply write $\delta(q, a) = p$ instead of $\delta(q, a) = \{p\}$.

Let $A = (Q, \Sigma, \delta, q_0, F)$ be a finite automaton. A *configuration* of a finite automaton is a tuple (q, w), where $q \in Q$ and w is a string. If a is in Σ and w in Σ^*, then we write $(q, aw) \vdash_A (p, w)$ if p is in $\delta(q, a)$. As usual, the reflexive transitive closure of $\vdash_A$ is denoted by $\vdash_A^*$. The subscript A will be dropped from $\vdash_A$ and $\vdash_A^*$ if the meaning is clear. Then the *language accepted* by A is defined as

$$L(A) = \{\, w \in \Sigma^* \mid (q_0, w) \vdash_A^* (p, \lambda) \text{ for some } p \in F \,\}.$$

Let $X \in \{D, N\}$. Then $\mathscr{L}(XFA)$ refers to the family of languages accepted by finite automata of type X. Note that $\mathscr{L}(DFA) = \mathscr{L}(NFA)$ and that this language class is equal to the family of regular languages REG.

Although DFAs and NFAs are equally powerful their descriptional complexity may vary significantly. We define the *state complexity of a finite automaton* $A = (Q, \Sigma, \delta, q_0, F)$, denoted by $\mathsf{sc}(A)$, by $\mathsf{sc}(A) = |Q|$. Then the *state complexity of a regular language with respect to automata of type* X is

$$\mathsf{sc}_{XFA}(L) = \min\{\, \mathsf{sc}(A) \mid A \text{ is an } XFA \text{ with } L = L(A) \,\}.$$

It is well known that $\mathsf{sc}_{NFA}(L) \leq \mathsf{sc}_{DFA}(L) \leq 2^{\mathsf{sc}_{NFA}(L)}$ for all regular languages L.

Now we are ready to introduce the notion of active states in DFAs and NFAs.

Definition 1. *Let* $X \in \{D, N\}$ *and* $A = (Q, \Sigma, \delta, q_0, F)$ *be an XFA. The number of active states in a computation*

$$C = (q_0, w) \vdash_A (q_1, a_2 \cdots a_n) \vdash_A \cdots \vdash_A (q_n, \lambda)$$

of A *on word* $w = a_1 a_2 \ldots a_n$ *in* Σ^* *is* $\mathsf{as}(C) = |\{\, q \in Q \mid q \text{ occurs in } C \,\}|$; *the computation* C *is accepting, if* q_n *is in* F. *For a word* $w \in \Sigma^*$, *this measure is defined by*

$$\mathsf{as}(w, A) = \min\{\, \mathsf{as}(C) \mid C \text{ is an accepting computation on } w \text{ according to } A \,\},$$

if word w *is in* $L(A)$, *and*

$$\mathsf{as}(w, A) = \min\{\, \mathsf{as}(C) \mid C \text{ is a computation on } w \text{ according to } A \,\},$$

otherwise, and for the automaton A*, we set* $\mathsf{as}(A) = \max\{\,\mathsf{as}(w, A) \mid w \in \Sigma^*\,\}$.
Finally, we define $\mathsf{as}_{XFA}(L) = \min\{\,\mathsf{as}(A) \mid L = L(A) \quad and \quad A \quad is \ an \quad XFA\,\}$,
for any regular language L.

Observe that in the definition of $\mathsf{as}(w, A)$, for w in Σ^*, one has to distinguish the cases when w is in $L(A)$ and w is *not* in $L(A)$. This is necessary because of the following observation: if, for all words w one had the unified definition

$$\mathsf{as}(w, A) = \min\{\,\mathsf{as}(C) \mid C \text{ is a computation of } w \text{ according to } A\,\},$$

then the counter intuitive fact that $\mathsf{as}_{NFA}(L) \leq 2$ would be obtained, because for every NFA one can construct an equivalent finite automaton whose states are connected to a new sink state. Furthermore, one might wonder whether one should use the maximum or even the sum norm instead of the minimum in the definition of $\mathsf{as}(w, A)$ since it cannot be determined which computation will be used on input w. The minimum norm is preferred because of the following arguments. If A is a DFA and w in Σ^*, the definition of $\mathsf{as}(w, A)$ can be simplified to $\mathsf{as}(w, A) = \mathsf{as}(C)$, where C is the unique computation for w according to A. In the nondeterministic case, where one can only speculate about the computation performed on input w, we are interested in the state space that is indispensable in order to deal with arbitrary input. This intuition is best captured by the minimum norm in the definition of $\mathsf{as}(w, A)$.

In order to clarify our notation we give an example.

Example 2. Consider the unary regular language

$$L = \{\,a^{2n} \mid n \geq 1\,\} \cup \{\,a^{3n} \mid n \geq 1\,\}$$

accepted by the DFA $A = (Q_A, \{a\}, \delta_A, q_0, F_A)$, where $Q_A = \{q_0, q_1, \ldots, q_6\}$, $F_A = \{q_2, q_3, q_4, q_6\}$, and $\delta_A(q_i, a) = q_{i+1}$, if $0 \leq i < 6$, and $\delta_A(q_6, a) = q_1$. The automaton is depicted on the left of Fig. 1. Then it is easy to see that $\mathsf{as}(\lambda, A) = 1$, $\mathsf{as}(a, A) = 2$, ..., $\mathsf{as}(a^5, A) = 6$, and $\mathsf{as}(w, A) = 7$, if $|w| \geq 6$. Thus, $\mathsf{as}(A) = 7$. In fact, in this example it is easily seen that $\mathsf{as}_{DFA}(L) = 7$, since

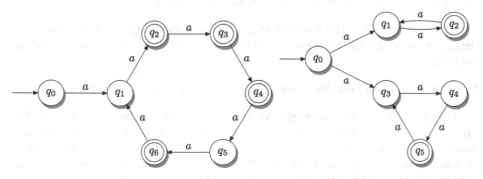

Fig. 1. DFA A (left) and NFA B (right) accepting $L = \{\,a^{2n} \mid n \geq 1\,\} \cup \{\,a^{3n} \mid n \geq 1\,\}$.

otherwise words of not appropriate length can be accepted. Later we will see, that in general $\mathsf{as}_{\mathrm{DFA}}(L)$ can be computed from the minimal DFA accepting L.

Finally we consider an NFA accepting L. Let $B = (Q_B, \{a\}, \delta_B, q_0, F_B)$, where $Q_B = \{q_0, q_1, \ldots, q_5\}$, $F_B = \{q_2, q_5\}$, and $\delta_B(q_0, a) = \{q_1, q_3\}$, $\delta_B(q_i, a) = \{q_{i+1}\}$, if $i = 1$ or $i \in \{3, 4\}$, $\delta_B(q_2, a) = \{q_1\}$, and $\delta_B(q_5, a) = \{q_3\}$. The automaton B is depicted on the right of Fig. 1. Clearly, $\mathsf{as}(\lambda, B) = 1$, $\mathsf{as}(a, B) = 2$, $\mathsf{as}(a^2, B) = 3$, and $\mathsf{as}(w, B) \in \{3, 4\}$, if $|w| \geq 3$. Hence, $\mathsf{as}(B) = 4$. As in the previous example one can verify that $\mathsf{as}_{\mathrm{NFA}}(L) = 4$. We have already mentioned that $\mathsf{as}_{\mathrm{DFA}}(L)$ is computable. This is also true for $\mathsf{as}_{\mathrm{NFA}}(L)$, but as we will see the situation is much more involved compared to the deterministic case.

By definition, the ordinary state measure for a regular language is an upper bound for the number of active states, i.e., if L is accepted by an XFA, for $X \in \{\mathrm{D}, \mathrm{N}\}$, with most n states, then $\mathsf{as}_{x\mathrm{FA}}(L) \leq n$. A lower bound statement on the number of active states reads as follows:

Lemma 3. *Let $L \subseteq \Sigma^*$ be a non-empty regular language and w be a shortest word in L. Then $\mathsf{as}_{X\mathrm{FA}}(L) \geq |w| + 1$, for $X \in \{\mathrm{D}, \mathrm{N}\}$.*

3   On the Number of Active States

In this section we show how to compute the measure of active states both for a given finite automaton and even for a regular language. First we show that given some finite automaton A, deterministic or not, the measure $\mathsf{as}(A)$ can be computed.

Theorem 4. *Let $X \in \{\mathrm{D}, \mathrm{N}\}$ and $A = (Q, \Sigma, \delta, q_0, F)$ be an n-state XFA. Then there is an integer m with $0 \leq m \leq \frac{n(n+1)}{2} - 1$ and a word w of length at most m, such that $\mathsf{as}(A) = \mathsf{as}(w, A)$.*

In conclusion measure $\mathsf{as}_{\mathrm{DFA}}(L)$ is computable *via* the minimal DFA.

Theorem 5. *Let $L \subseteq \Sigma^*$ be a regular language. Then $\mathsf{as}_{\mathrm{DFA}}(L) = \mathsf{as}(A)$, where A is the minimal state DFA accepting the language L.*

Before we consider the measure $\mathsf{as}_{\mathrm{NFA}}(L)$, for a given regular language L, in detail, we state the following easy observation. Since the proof is straightforward we omit it.

Lemma 6. *For any regular language $L \subseteq \Sigma^*$ we have $\mathsf{as}_{\mathrm{NFA}}(L) \leq \mathsf{as}_{\mathrm{DFA}}(L)$.* $\square$

It is well known that minimal NFAs with respect to the number of states are *not* unique in general. The situation is even more involved, since distinct minimal NFAs A and B can have different measures with respect to the number of active states, i.e., the inequality $\mathsf{as}(A) \neq \mathsf{as}(B)$ may hold. This shows that one cannot rely the computation of the measure $\mathsf{as}_{\mathrm{NFA}}(L)$, for a regular language L, on some minimal NFA L. Nevertheless, the following theorem shows that for a regular language the measure is computable, although the search space is quite large. In the proof of the next theorem we need the notion of multiple entry finite automata—see, e.g., [5]. This is a finite-state device with several initial states. Formally, a *multiple entry* finite automaton is a quintuple $A = (Q, \Sigma, \delta, Q_0, F)$, where Q, Σ, δ, and F are as for ordinary (nondeterministic) finite automata and $Q_0 \subseteq Q$ is the non-empty set of initial states. Then $L(A) = \bigcup_{q_0 \in Q_0} L(A_{q_0})$, where $A_q = (Q, \Sigma, \delta, q, F)$, for $q \in Q$. In order to simplify the presentation in the proof of the next theorem we also need an operation that takes two finite automata and returns an equivalent multiple entry automaton. Let $A = (Q_A, \Sigma, \delta_A, q_{0,A}, F_A)$ and $B = (Q_B, \Sigma, \delta_B, q_{0,B}, F_B)$ with $Q_A \cap Q_B = \emptyset$. Then $A \oplus B = (Q_A \cup Q_B, \Sigma, \delta, \{q_{0,A}, q_{0,B}\}, F_A \cup F_B)$, where

$$\delta(q, a) = \begin{cases} \delta_A(q, a) & \text{if } q \in Q_A \text{ and } a \in \Sigma \\ \delta_B(q, a) & \text{if } q \in Q_B \text{ and } a \in \Sigma. \end{cases}$$

Obviously, $L(A \oplus B) = L(A) \cup L(B)$ and both automata A and B are sub-automata of $A \oplus B$ that are *not* connected with each other by any transition. Moreover, the operation $\oplus$ generalizes to more than two automata and to multiple entry finite automata as well. Now we are ready to state the next theorem, which states an upper bound on the number of states of an NFA, if the nondeterministic active state complexity is known.

Theorem 7. *Let $L \subseteq \Sigma^*$ be a regular language with $\mathsf{as}_{\mathrm{NFA}}(L) = n$. Then there is an NFA A with at most $n \cdot 2^{|\Sigma| \cdot n^2 + n}$ states that accepts the language L and satisfies $\mathsf{as}(A) = n$.*

Proof. By definition there is an NFA B such that $\mathsf{as}(B) = \mathsf{as}_{\mathrm{NFA}}(L)$. Note that we do not know how many states B has. Nevertheless, every computation of B on a word needs at most n states, i.e., every computation induces an n-state subautomaton of B. Let $\mathcal{B} = \{B_1, B_2, \ldots, B_m\}$ be the set of all n-state subautomata of B that contain the initial state of B. Clearly, $\mathcal{B}$ is finite. Without loss of generality we may assume that the states of all these automata are disjoint (by appropriately renaming them) and that all automata are non-isomorphic. But then the multiple entry finite automaton $C := B_1 \oplus B_2 \oplus \cdots \oplus B_m$ is language equivalent to B, i.e., $L(C) = L(B)$. The number of states of C is $n \cdot m$. It remains to estimate m. An n-state automaton has at most n^2 transitions that can be labeled with letters from a subset of Σ. Thus, there are at most $2^{|\Sigma| \cdot n^2}$ possible combinations for transitions. Moreover, there are at most 2^n possible combinations for n states to be either accepting or non-accepting. Thus, $2^{|\Sigma| \cdot n^2 + n}$ is an upper bound on the number of automata with n states. Therefore the multiple entry NFA C has at most $n \cdot 2^{|\Sigma| \cdot n^2 + n}$ states. See Fig. 2 (left and middle) for a schematic drawing of this construction.

Then we construct the NFA A from the multiple entry NFA C by identifying all initial states—in A we can still name the subautomata $B_1, B_2, \ldots, B_m$ from C. We show $L(A) = L(C)$. Obviously, $L(C) \subseteq L(A)$. Conversely, we argue as follows: consider any computation (not necessarily an accepting one) of a

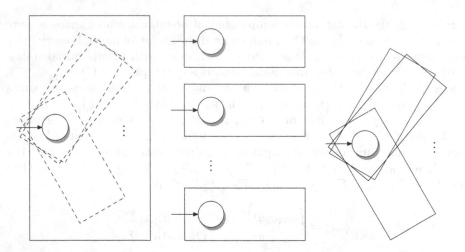

Fig. 2. Schematic drawings of the automata from the proof of Theorem 7. (Left): the NFA B satisfying $\mathsf{as}(B) = \mathsf{as}_{\mathrm{NFA}}(L) = n$ and its n-state subautomata depicted by rectangles with dashed lines. (Middle): the multiple entry NFA C build from the n-state subautomata of B. (Right): the NFA A satisfying $\mathsf{as}(A) = \mathsf{as}_{\mathrm{NFA}}(L)$ obtained from the multiple entry NFA C by identifying all initial states.

word w on A. If the computation only runs through a single subautomaton B_i, for $1 \le i \le m$, then this computation can also be found in C. On the other hand, if the computation under consideration runs through at least two different sub-automata, then the initial state must be part of this computation at least twice. In fact, whenever the computation changes from one to another subautomaton, it must pass the initial state. Since C is built from B, we find a corresponding computation in the original NFA B. Because $\mathsf{as}(B) = \mathsf{as}_{\mathrm{NFA}}(L)$, every word has a computation that contains at most n states. Thus, for the word w there is a computation in B that is completely within one n-state subautomaton, say B_i. Thus, by construction of C and A we can find a corresponding computation in the subautomaton B_i of C and A. Therefore we conclude $L(A) \subseteq L(C)$. Again see Fig. 2 (middle and right) for a schematic drawing of this part of the construc-tion. In fact, the previous argument shows a little bit more than $L(A) = L(C)$, namely that $\mathsf{as}(A) = \mathsf{as}_{\mathrm{NFA}}(L)$. As the number of states of A is bounded by the number of states of C, that is, by $n \cdot 2^{|\Sigma| \cdot n^2 + n}$, the proof of the stated claim is complete.   □

We summarize the results of the previous theorems:

Corollary 8. *Let $X \in \{\mathrm{D}, \mathrm{N}\}$ and A be a finite automaton. Then the measures $\mathsf{as}_{X\mathrm{FA}}(L(A))$ are algorithmically computable.*

The exact complexity of determining the active state complexity in the deter-ministic and nondeterministic case is left open.

4   Comparing Number of Active States, Radius, and Number of States

We examine how the measure of active states for regular languages is related to other measures of descriptional complexity. These other measures are the radius of a regular language and more importantly the ordinary state complexity of a regular language. In particular, the comparison with the latter measure is of interest, since it tells us how effective the dynamic state savings modelled by the number of active states can be. We start our investigation with the comparison to the ordinary state complexity of a regular language.

We have seen that the number of active states is a lower bound on the state complexity of a regular language. While there are obviously regular languages, where both measures meet, such as, e.g., the finite language $L_n = \{a^{n-1}\}$, there are other languages, where arbitrarily large savings in the number of active states are possible. This situation is described in the following theorem.

Theorem 9. *Let $X \in \{D, N\}$. There is a sequence of languages $(L_n)_{n \geq 1}$ over a linearly growing size alphabet such that $\text{sc}_{X\text{FA}}(L_n) \geq n + 2$ but $\text{as}_{X\text{FA}}(L_n) = c$, for some constant c.*

Proof. Let $\Sigma_n = \{a_1, a_2, \ldots, a_n\}$. Define the language $L_n = \{a_i a_i \mid 1 \leq i \leq n\}$. In order to determine the nondeterministic state complexity of L_n we use the extended fooling set technique.[1] Now consider the following set

$$S = \{(\lambda, a_1 a_1), (a_1 a_1, \lambda)\} \cup \{(a_i, a_i) \mid 1 \leq i \leq n\},$$

which is easily seen to be a fooling set for the language L_n. Thus, the minimal NFA accepting L_n has at least $n + 2$ states, i.e., $\text{sc}_{\text{NFA}}(L_n) \geq n + 2$.

It remains to determine and upper bound on $\text{as}_{\text{DFA}}(L_n)$. Define the DFA $A_n = (Q_n, \Sigma_n, \delta_n, q_0, F_n)$, where $Q_n = \{q_0, q_1, \ldots, q_{n+2}\}$, $F_n = \{q_{n+1}\}$, and the transition function δ_n is given by

$$\delta_n(q_i, a_j) = \begin{cases} q_j & \text{if } i = 0 \text{ and } 1 \leq j \leq n \\ q_{n+1} & \text{if } 1 \leq i, j \leq n \text{ and } i = j \\ q_{n+2} & \text{if } 1 \leq i, j \leq n \text{ and } i \neq j \\ q_{n+2} & \text{if } (i = n+1 \text{ or } i = n+2) \text{ and } 1 \leq j \leq n. \end{cases}$$

The automaton A_n is depicted in Fig. 3. As *any* computation done in A_n needs at most four states, we have $\text{as}_{\text{DFA}}(L_n) \leq 4$. This proves the stated claim.   □

For languages over a fixed alphabet we still can observe an exponential increase when going from the active state complexity to the state complexity when considering regular languages.

---

[1] A set $S = \{(x_i, y_i) \mid 1 \leq i \leq n\}$ is an *extended fooling set* of size n for the regular language $L \subseteq \Sigma^*$, if (i) $x_i y_i \in L$ for $1 \leq i \leq n$, and (ii) $i \neq j$ implies $x_i y_j \notin L$ or $x_j y_i \notin L$, for $1 \leq i, j \leq n$. Then any NFA accepting language L has at least n states [1].

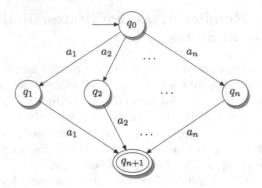

Fig. 3. The $n + 3$-state minimal DFA A_n, which proves $\mathsf{as}_{\mathrm{DFA}}(L_n) \leq 4$. The sink state q_{n+2} is not shown.

Theorem 10. *Let $X \in \{\mathrm{D}, \mathrm{N}\}$. There is a sequence of languages $(L_n)_{n \geq 1}$ over a binary alphabet such that $\mathsf{sc}_{\mathrm{DFA}}(L_n) \geq 2^n$ but $\mathsf{as}_{\mathrm{DFA}}(L_n) = 2n + c$, for some constant c.*

It is easy to see that the statement of the previous theorem generalizes to sequences of languages over a k-letter alphabet, for some constant k. On the other hand, the stated exponential state savings between the state complexity and the number of active states is best possible for constant size alphabets. The statement is proven for the deterministic case; whether a similar statement holds in the nondeterministic case is left open.

Theorem 11. *There is no sequence of languages $(L_n)_{n \geq 1}$ over a fixed size alphabet of at least two letters, such that $\mathsf{sc}_{\mathrm{DFA}}(L_n) \geq 2^n$ and $\mathsf{as}_{\mathrm{DFA}}(L_n) = o(n)$.*

In the remainder of this section we investigate the relationship between the active state complexity and the radius of a regular language. The radius of a regular language was introduced in [4] and is defined as follows: let $A = (Q, \Sigma, \delta, q_0, F)$ be a finite automaton. For every state $q \in Q$, the *depth* of q, denoted by $\mathsf{depth}_A(q)$ is defined to be the minimal distance from the initial state to q. Formally, let

$$\mathsf{depth}_A(q) = \min_{w \in \Sigma^*} \{\, |w| \mid (q_0, w) \vdash_A^* (q, \lambda) \,\}.$$

If q is not reachable from q_0 then $\mathsf{depth}_A(q)$ is defined to be infinite. Next, the *radius of a finite automaton* $A = (Q, \Sigma, \delta, q_0, F)$ is defined to be

$$\mathsf{rad}(A) = \max\{\, \mathsf{depth}_A(q) \mid q \in Q \,\}.$$

This is extended to define the *radius of a regular language with respect to finite automata of type X*, which is the minimum radius of all XFAs that accept the language L. Formally, if L is a regular language, then

$$\mathsf{rad}_{X\mathrm{FA}}(L) = \min\{\, \mathsf{rad}(A) \mid A \text{ is an } X\mathrm{FA} \text{ with } L = L(A) \,\}.$$

The following relation between the radius of a regular language and the number of active states is obvious and therefore stated without proof.

Lemma 12. *Let $X \in \{D, N\}$. Then* $\mathrm{rad}_{X\mathrm{FA}}(L) \leq \mathrm{as}_{X\mathrm{FA}}(L)$, *if L is a regular language.* $\square$

In other words, the radius of a regular language is a lower bound for the number of active states. When comparing the exact values of these measures we find the following situation in the nondeterministic case.

Theorem 13. *There is a sequence of languages $(L_n)_{n \geq 2}$ over a one letter alphabet such that* $\mathrm{as}_{\mathrm{NFA}}(L_n) = n$ *but* $\mathrm{rad}_{\mathrm{NFA}}(L_n) = 1$.

Proof. Consider the languages $L_n = \{a^k \mid 0 \leq k \leq n-1\}$. In [4] it was shown that $\mathrm{rad}_{\mathrm{NFA}}(L_n) = 1$. An NFA that proves this fact is depicted in Fig. 4. By this NFA we already know that $\mathrm{as}_{\mathrm{NFA}}(L_n) \leq n$. It remains to show that $\mathrm{as}_{\mathrm{NFA}}(L_n) = n$. To this end assume to the contrary that $\mathrm{as}_{\mathrm{NFA}}(L_n) < n$. By definition there is an NFA A_n such that $\mathrm{as}(A_n) = \mathrm{as}_{\mathrm{NFA}}(L_n)$. Now consider an accepting computation of A_n on the word a^{n-1}. Then by our assumption $\mathrm{as}(w, A) = k$, for some k with $1 \leq k \leq \mathrm{as}(A_n)$. Note that $k < n$. Thus, for this particular accepting computation the NFA A_n is only allowed to use k different states, which means that there exists a state q that appears at least twice in the accepting computation of A_n on a^{n-1}. Then by a simple pumping argument similar as that used in the proof of Lemma 3 the automaton A_n is forced to accept a word that is too long. This is a contradiction, and thus it follows that $\mathrm{as}_{\mathrm{NFA}}(L_n) = n$ as stated. $\square$

The idea used in the previous proof to keep the radius small can also be adopted to DFAs, if the underlying input alphabet is growing.

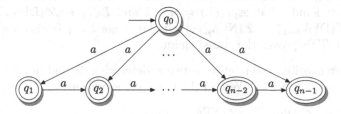

Fig. 4. NFA with n states that accepts $L_n = \{a^k \mid 0 \leq k \leq n-1\}$ and shows that $\mathrm{rad}_{\mathrm{NFA}}(L_n) = 1$.

Theorem 14. *There is a sequence of languages $(L_n)_{n \geq 1}$ on a linearly growing size alphabet such that* $\mathrm{as}_{\mathrm{DFA}}(L_n) = n+1$ *but* $\mathrm{rad}_{\mathrm{DFA}}(L_n) = 1$.

Finally, let us consider the case where the alphabet is of constant size.

Theorem 15. *There is a sequence of languages $(L_n)_{n \geq 1}$ over a fixed size alphabet of at least two letters, such that* $\mathrm{as}_{\mathrm{DFA}}(L_n) = 2^n$ *but* $\mathrm{rad}_{\mathrm{DFA}}(L) = n$.

5 Hierarchies Induced by the Number of Active States

In this section it is shown that, both for DFA and NFA, the number of active states induces infinite hierarchies that are strict. To this end, for $X \in \{D, N\}$, we define the class of automata

$$X\mathrm{FA}_n = \{\, A \mid A \text{ is an } X\mathrm{FA} \text{ with } \mathsf{as}(A) \leq n \,\},$$

for $n \geq 1$. Correspondingly, the set of all languages L with $\mathsf{as}_{X\mathrm{FA}}(L) \leq n$ is referred to as $\mathscr{L}(X\mathrm{FA}_n)$, $n \geq 1$. By definition

$$\mathscr{L}(\mathrm{DFA}_n) \subseteq \mathscr{L}(\mathrm{DFA}_{n+1}) \quad \text{and} \quad \mathscr{L}(\mathrm{NFA}_n) \subseteq \mathscr{L}(\mathrm{NFA}_{n+1}),$$

for $n \geq 1$, and by Lemma 6 we have $\mathscr{L}(\mathrm{DFA}_n) \subseteq \mathscr{L}(\mathrm{NFA}_n)$, for every $n \geq 1$. In the forthcoming we show that all these inclusions are strict. We start with the bottom level of both hierarchies

Theorem 16. $\{\emptyset, \Sigma^*\} = \mathscr{L}(\mathrm{DFA}_1) \subset \mathscr{L}(\mathrm{NFA}_1) = \{\emptyset\} \cup \{\, (\Sigma')^* \mid \Sigma' \subseteq \Sigma \,\}.$

Next we show that the hierarchies on the number of active states for both types of finite automata are strict.

Theorem 17. *Let $X \in \{D, N\}$. Then $\mathscr{L}(XFA_n) \subset \mathscr{L}(XFA_{n+1})$, for $n \geq 1$.*

Proof. Both inclusions hold by definition. For their strictness consider the unary language $L_{n+1} = a^n a^*$, for $n \geq 1$. The shortest word in L_{n+1} is a^n and therefore we conclude $\mathsf{as}_{X\mathrm{FA}}(L) \geq n+1$, for $X \in \{D, N\}$, by Lemma 3. Thus language L_{n+1} cannot be a member of $\mathscr{L}(\mathrm{DFA}_n)$ or $\mathscr{L}(\mathrm{NFA}_n)$. On the other hand a DFA accepting L_{n+1} consists of a chain of $n + 1$ states connected by a-transitions, where the first state in the chain is the initial one and the last state has an a-loop and is accepting. For this automaton the number of active states is exactly $n + 1$. Thus we conclude that $\mathsf{as}_{\mathrm{DFA}}(L) = n + 1$ and $L_{n+1} \in \mathscr{L}(\mathrm{DFA}_{n+1})$. Since obviously $\mathscr{L}(\mathrm{DFA}_{n+1}) \subseteq \mathscr{L}(\mathrm{NFA}_{n+1})$, the language L_{n+1} is also a member of $\mathscr{L}(\mathrm{NFA}_{n+1})$. This proves the stated claim. $\square$

Finally we consider the relation between deterministic and nondeterministic language families in detail. We find the following situation.

Theorem 18. $\mathscr{L}(\mathrm{DFA}_n) \subset \mathscr{L}(\mathrm{NFA}_n)$, *for $n \geq 1$.*

Proof. By Theorem 16 we have $\mathscr{L}(\mathrm{DFA}_1) \subset \mathscr{L}(\mathrm{NFA}_1)$. For the other inclusions $\mathscr{L}(\mathrm{DFA}_n) \subset \mathscr{L}(\mathrm{NFA}_n)$ with $n \geq 2$ we argue as follows: consider the NFA $A_n = (Q_n, \{a\}, \delta_n, q_0, F_n)$ where $Q_n = \{q_0, q_1, \ldots, q_{n-1}\}$, $F = \{q_0\}$, and the transition function is defined by

$$\delta(q_i, a) = \begin{cases} \{q_{i+1}\} & \text{if } 0 \leq i < n - 1 \\ \{q_0, q_1, \ldots, q_{n-1}\} & \text{if } i = n - 1. \end{cases}$$

The NFA A_n is depicted in Fig. 5. By construction we have $\mathsf{as}_{\mathrm{NFA}}(L(A_n)) \leq n$ and thus $L(A_n) = \{\lambda\} \cup \{\, a^{n+k} \mid k \geq 0 \,\} \in \mathscr{L}(\mathrm{NFA}_n)$. Since the minimal DFA for

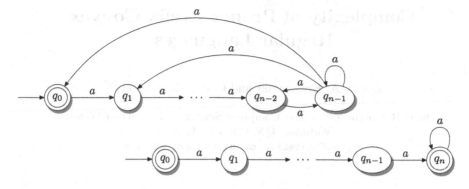

Fig. 5. The NFA A_n accepting a language $L(A_n)$ with $\mathsf{as}_{\mathrm{NFA}}(L(A_n)) \leq n$. The equivalent minimal DFA proves that $\mathsf{as}_{\mathrm{DFA}}(L(A_n)) = n + 1$.

the language $L(A_n)$ consists of $n+1$ states in a chain connected by a-transitions, where the initial state and the last state in the chain is accepting and the latter one has an a-loop. The minimal DFA for $L(A_n)$ is shown on the bottom of Fig. 5. Thus by Theorem 5 we conclude that $\mathsf{as}_{\mathrm{DFA}}(L(A_n)) = n + 1$ and therefore $L(A_n) \notin \mathscr{L}(\mathrm{DFA}_n)$. This proves the stated claim. □

Hence both hierarchies on the families $\mathscr{L}(\mathrm{DFA}_n)$ and $\mathscr{L}(\mathrm{NFA}_n)$ are strict and exhaust the family of regular languages REG.

References

1. Birget, J.-C.: Intersection and union of regular languages and state complexity. Inform. Process. Lett. **43**, 185–190 (1992)
2. Bordihn, H., Holzer, M.: On the number of active symbols in L and CD grammar systems. J. Autom. Lang. Comb. **6**(4), 411–426 (2001)
3. Burch, J.R., Clarke, E.M., McMillan, K.L.: Symbolic model checking: 10^{20} states and beyond. Inform. Comput. **98**(2), 142–170 (1992)
4. Ellul, K.: Descriptional complexity measures of regular languages. Master thesis, Computer Science, University of Waterloo, Ontario, Canada (2002)
5. Gill, A., Kou, L.T.: Multiple-entry finite automata. J. Comput. System Sci. **9**, 1–19 (1974)
6. Kleijn, H.C.M., Rozenberg, G.: A study in parallel rewriting systems. Inform. Control **44**, 134–163 (1980)
7. Lockefeer, L.: Formal specification and verification of TCP extended with the Window Scale Option. Master thesis, Vrije Universiteit Amsterdam, The Netherlands (2013)
8. Wood, D.: Theory of Computation. Wiley (1987)
9. Yokomori, T., Wood, D., Lange, K.-J.: A three-restricted normal form theorem for ET0L languages. Inform. Process. Lett. **14**(3), 97–100 (1982) and **21**(1), 53 (1985)

Complexity of Proper Prefix-Convex
Regular Languages

Janusz A. Brzozowski and Corwin Sinnamon[(✉)]

David R. Cheriton School of Computer Science, University of Waterloo,
Waterloo, ON N2L 3G1, Canada
brzozo@uwaterloo.ca, sinncore@gmail.com

Abstract. A language L over an alphabet Σ is prefix-convex if, for
any words $x, y, z \in \Sigma^*$, whenever x and xyz are in L, then so is xy.
Prefix-convex languages include right-ideal, prefix-closed, and prefix-free
languages, which were studied elsewhere. Here we concentrate on prefix-
convex languages that do not belong to any one of these classes; we call
such languages *proper*. We exhibit most complex proper prefix-convex
languages, which meet the bounds for the size of the syntactic semigroup,
reversal, complexity of atoms, star, product, and Boolean operations.

Keywords: Atom · Most complex · Prefix-convex · Proper · Quotient
complexity · Regular language · State complexity · Syntactic semigroup

1 Introduction

Prefix-Convex Languages. We examine the complexity properties of a class
of regular languages that has never been studied before: the class of proper
prefix-convex languages [7]. Let Σ be a finite alphabet; if $w = xy$, for $x, y \in \Sigma^*$,
then x is a prefix of w. A language $L \subseteq \Sigma^*$ is *prefix-convex* [1,16] if whenever
x and xyz are in L, then so is xy. Prefix-convex languages include three special
cases:

1. A language $L \subseteq \Sigma$ is a *right ideal* if it is non-empty and satisfies $L = L\Sigma^*$.
   Right ideals appear in pattern matching [11]: $L\Sigma^*$ is the set of all words in
   some text (word in Σ^*) beginning with words in L.
2. A language is *prefix-closed* [6] if whenever w is in L, then so is every prefix
   of w. The set of allowed sequences to any system is prefix-closed. Every prefix-
   closed language other than Σ^* is the complement of a right ideal [1].
3. A language is *prefix-free* if $w \in L$ implies that no prefix of w other than w
   is in L. Prefix-free languages other than $\{\varepsilon\}$, where ε is the empty word, are
   prefix codes and are of considerable importance in coding theory [2].

This work was supported by the Natural Sciences and Engineering Research Council
of Canada grant no. OGP0000871.

© Springer International Publishing AG 2017
A. Carayol and C. Nicaud (Eds.): CIAA 2017, LNCS 10329, pp. 52–63, 2017.
DOI: 10.1007/978-3-319-60134-2_5

The complexities of these three special prefix-convex languages were studied in [8]. We now turn to the "real" prefix-convex languages that do not belong to any of the three special classes.

Omitted proofs can be found in [7].

Complexities of Operations. If $L \subseteq \Sigma^*$ is a language, the *(left) quotient* of L by a word $w \in \Sigma^*$ is $w^{-1}L = \{x \mid wx \in L\}$. A language is regular if and only if it has a finite number of distinct quotients. So the number of quotients of L, the *quotient complexity* [3] $\kappa(L)$ of L, is a natural measure of complexity for L. An equivalent concept is the *state complexity* [15,17,18] of L, which is the number of states in a complete minimal deterministic finite automaton (DFA) over Σ recognizing L. We refer to quotient/state complexity simply as *complexity*.

If L_n is a regular language of complexity n, and $\circ$ is a unary operation, the *complexity of* $\circ$ is the maximal value of $\kappa(L_n^\circ)$, expressed as a function of n, as L_n ranges over all languages of complexity n. If L'_m and L_n are regular languages of complexities m and n respectively, and $\circ$ is a binary operation, the *complexity of* $\circ$ is the maximal value of $\kappa(L'_m \circ L_n)$, expressed as a function of m and n, as L'_m and L_n range over all languages of complexities m and n. The complexity of an operation is a lower bound on its time and space complexities. The operations reversal, (Kleene) star, product (concatenation), and binary boolean operations are considered "common", and their complexities are known; see [4,17,18].

Witnesses. To find the complexity of a unary operation we find an upper bound on this complexity, and languages that meet this bound. We require a language L_n for each n, that is, a sequence, $(L_k, L_{k+1}, \dots)$, called a *stream* of languages, where k is a small integer, because the bound may not hold for small values of n. For a binary operation we need two streams. The same stream cannot always be used for both operands, but for all common binary operations the second stream can be a "dialect" of the first, that is it can "differ only slightly" from the first [4]. Let $\Sigma = \{a_1, \dots, a_k\}$ be an alphabet ordered as shown; if $L \subseteq \Sigma^*$, we denote it by $L(a_1, \dots, a_k)$. A *dialect* of L is obtained by deleting letters of Σ in the words of L, or replacing them by letters of another alphabet Σ'. More precisely, for an injective partial map $\pi \colon \Sigma \mapsto \Sigma'$, we get a dialect of L by replacing each letter $a \in \Sigma$ by $\pi(a)$ in every word of L, or deleting the word if $\pi(a)$ is undefined. We write $L(\pi(a_1), \dots, \pi(a_k))$ to denote the dialect of $L(a_1, \dots, a_k)$ given by π, and we denote undefined values of π by "$-$". Undefined values for letters at the end of the alphabet are omitted; for example, $L(a, c, -, -)$ is written as $L(a, c)$. Our definition of dialect is more general than that of [5], where only the case $\Sigma' = \Sigma$ was allowed.

Finite Automata. A *deterministic finite automaton (DFA)* is a quintuple $\mathcal{D} = (Q, \Sigma, \delta, q_0, F)$, where Q is a finite non-empty set of *states*, Σ is a finite non-empty *alphabet*, $\delta \colon Q \times \Sigma \to Q$ is the *transition function*, $q_0 \in Q$ is the *initial state*, and $F \subseteq Q$ is the set of *final states*. We extend δ to a function $\delta \colon Q \times \Sigma^* \to Q$ as usual. A DFA $\mathcal{D}$ *accepts* a word $w \in \Sigma^*$ if $\delta(q_0, w) \in F$. The set of all words accepted by $\mathcal{D}$ is the *language of* $\mathcal{D}$. If $q \in Q$, then the *language L_q of* q is the language accepted by the DFA $(Q, \Sigma, \delta, q, F)$. A state is *empty or dead or a sink* if its language is empty. Two states p and q of $\mathcal{D}$ are *equivalent* if $L_p = L_q$. A state q is *reachable* if there exists $w \in \Sigma^*$ such that $\delta(q_0, w) = q$. A DFA is *minimal* if all of its states are reachable and no two states are equivalent. A *nondeterministic finite automaton (NFA)* is a quintuple $\mathcal{D} = (Q, \Sigma, \delta, I, F)$, where Q, Σ and F are defined as in a DFA, $\delta \colon Q \times \Sigma \to 2^Q$ is the *transition function*, and $I \subseteq Q$ is the *set of initial states*. An ε-*NFA* is an NFA in which transitions under the empty word ε are also permitted.

Transformations. We use $Q_n = \{0, \ldots, n-1\}$ as the set of states of every DFA with n states. A *transformation* of Q_n is a mapping $t \colon Q_n \to Q_n$. The *image* of $q \in Q_n$ under t is qt. In any DFA, each letter $a \in \Sigma$ induces a transformation δ_a of the set Q_n defined by $q\delta_a = \delta(q, a)$; we denote this by $a \colon \delta_a$. Often we use the letter a to denote the transformation it induces; thus we write qa instead of $q\delta_a$. We extend the notation to sets: if $P \subseteq Q_n$, then $Pa = \{pa \mid p \in P\}$. We also write $P \xrightarrow{a} Pa$ to indicate that the image of P under a is Pa. If s, t are transformations of Q_n, their composition is $(qs)t$.

For $k \geqslant 2$, a transformation (permutation) t of a set $P = \{q_0, q_1, \ldots, q_{k-1}\} \subseteq Q_n$ is a k-*cycle* if $q_0 t = q_1, q_1 t = q_2, \ldots, q_{k-2} t = q_{k-1}, q_{k-1} t = q_0$. This k-cycle is denoted by $(q_0, q_1, \ldots, q_{k-1})$. A 2-cycle (q_0, q_1) is called a *transposition*. A transformation that sends all the states of P to q and acts as the identity on the other states is denoted by $(P \to q)$, and $(Q_n \to p)$ is called a *constant* transformation. If $P = \{p\}$ we write $(p \to q)$ for $(\{p\} \to q)$. The identity transformation is denoted by $\mathbb{1}$. Also, $\binom{j}{i}\, q \to q + 1)$ is a transformation that sends q to $q + 1$ for $i \leqslant q \leqslant j$ and is the identity for the remaining states; $\binom{j}{i}\, q \to q - 1)$ is defined similarly.

Semigroups. The *syntactic congruence* of $L \subseteq \Sigma^*$ is defined on Σ^+: For $x, y \in \Sigma^+$, $x \approx_L y$ if and only if $wxz \in L \Leftrightarrow wyz \in L$ for all $w, z \in \Sigma^*$. The quotient set $\Sigma^+/\approx_L$ of equivalence classes of $\approx_L$ is the *syntactic semigroup* of L. Let $\mathcal{D}_n = (Q_n, \Sigma, \delta, q_0, F)$ be a DFA, and let $L_n = L(\mathcal{D}_n)$. For each word $w \in \Sigma^*$, the transition function induces a transformation δ_w of Q_n by w: for all $q \in Q_n$, $q\delta_w = \delta(q, w)$. The set $T_{\mathcal{D}_n}$ of all such transformations by non-empty words is a semigroup under composition called the *transition semigroup* of $\mathcal{D}_n$. If $\mathcal{D}_n$ is a minimal DFA of L_n, then $T_{\mathcal{D}_n}$ is isomorphic to the syntactic semigroup T_{L_n} of L_n, and we represent elements of T_{L_n} by transformations in $T_{\mathcal{D}_n}$. The size of the syntactic semigroup has been used as a measure of complexity for regular languages [4, 10, 12, 14].

Atoms. are defined by a left congruence, where two words x and y are equivalent if $ux \in L$ if and only if $uy \in L$ for all $u \in \Sigma^*$. Thus x and y are equivalent if $x \in u^{-1}L$ if and only if $y \in u^{-1}L$. An equivalence class of this relation is an *atom* of L [9, 13].

One can conclude that an atom is a non-empty intersection of complemented and uncomplemented quotients of L. That is, every atom of a language with quotients $K_0, K_1, \ldots, K_{n-1}$ can be written as $A_S = \bigcap_{i \in S} K_i \cap \bigcap_{i \in \overline{S}} \overline{K_i}$ for some set $S \subseteq Q_n$. The number of atoms and their complexities were suggested as possible measures of complexity [4], because all the quotients of a language and the quotients of its atoms are unions of atoms [9].

Most Complex Regular Stream. The stream $(\mathcal{D}_n(a,b,c) \mid n \geqslant 3)$ of Definition 1 and Fig. 1 will be used as a component in the class of proper prefix-convex languages. This stream together with some dialects meets the complexity bounds for reversal, star, product, and all binary boolean operations [7,8]. Moreover, it has the maximal syntactic semigroup and most complex atoms, making it a most complex regular stream.

Definition 1. *For* $n \geqslant 3$, *let* $\mathcal{D}_n = \mathcal{D}_n(a,b,c) = (Q_n, \Sigma, \delta_n, 0, \{n-1\})$, *where* $\Sigma = \{a,b,c\}$, *and* δ_n *is defined by* $a \colon (0, \ldots, n-1)$, $b \colon (0,1)$, $c \colon (1 \to 0)$.

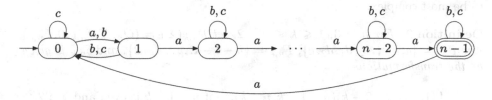

Fig. 1. Minimal DFA of a most complex regular language.

Most complex streams are useful in systems dealing with regular languages and finite automata. To know the maximal sizes of automata that can be handled by a system it suffices to use the most complex stream to test all the operations.

2 Proper Prefix-Convex Languages

We begin with some properties of prefix-convex languages that will be used frequently in this section. The following lemma and propositions characterize the classes of prefix-convex languages in terms of their minimal DFAs.

Lemma 1. *Let* L *be a prefix-convex language over* Σ. *Either* L *is a right ideal or* L *has an empty quotient.*

Proposition 1. *Let* L_n *be a regular language of complexity* n, *and let* $\mathcal{D}_n = (Q_n, \Sigma, \delta, 0, F)$ *be a minimal DFA recognizing* L_n. *The following are equivalent:*

1. L_n *is prefix-convex.*
2. *For all* $p, q, r \in Q_n$, *if* p *and* r *are final,* q *is reachable from* p, *and* r *is reachable from* q, *then* q *is final.*
3. *Every state reachable in* $\mathcal{D}_n$ *from any final state is either final or empty.*

Proposition 2. *Let* L_n *be a non-empty prefix-convex language of complexity* n, *and let* $\mathcal{D}_n = (Q_n, \Sigma, \delta, 0, F)$ *be a minimal DFA recognizing* L_n.

1. L_n is prefix-closed if and only if $0 \in F$.
2. L_n is prefix-free if and only if $\mathcal{D}_n$ has a unique final state p and an empty state p' such that $\delta(p, a) = p'$ for all $a \in \Sigma$.
3. L_n is a right ideal if and only if $\mathcal{D}_n$ has a unique final state p and $\delta(p, a) = p$ for all $a \in \Sigma$.

A prefix-convex language L is *proper* if it is not a right ideal and it is neither prefix-closed nor prefix-free. We say it is *k-proper* if it has k final states, $1 \leqslant k \leqslant n - 2$. Every minimal DFA for a k-proper language with complexity n has the same general structure: there are $n - 1 - k$ non-final, non-empty states, k final states, and one empty state. Every letter fixes the empty state and, by Proposition 1, no letter sends a final state to a non-final, non-empty state.

Next we define a stream of k-proper DFAs and languages, which we will show to be most complex.

Definition 2. *For $n \geqslant 3$, $1 \leqslant k \leqslant n - 2$, let $\mathcal{D}_{n,k}(\Sigma) = (Q_n, \Sigma, \delta_{n,k}, 0, F_{n,k})$ where $\Sigma = \{a, b, c_1, c_2, d_1, d_2, e\}$, $F_{n,k} = \{n - 1 - k, \ldots, n - 2\}$, and $\delta_{n,k}$ is given by the transformations*

$$
a: \begin{cases}
(1, \ldots, n - 2 - k)(n - 1 - k, n - k), & \text{if } n - 1 - k \text{ is even and } k \geqslant 2; \\
(0, \ldots, n - 2 - k)(n - 1 - k, n - k), & \text{if } n - 1 - k \text{ is odd and } k \geqslant 2; \\
(1, \ldots, n - 2 - k), & \text{if } n - 1 - k \text{ is even and } k = 1; \\
(0, \ldots, n - 2 - k), & \text{if } n - 1 - k \text{ is odd and } k = 1.
\end{cases}
$$

$$
b: \begin{cases}
(n - k, \ldots, n - 2)(0, 1), & \text{if } k \text{ is even and } n - 1 - k \geqslant 2; \\
(n - 1 - k, \ldots, n - 2)(0, 1), & \text{if } k \text{ is odd and } n - 1 - k \geqslant 2; \\
(n - k, \ldots, n - 2), & \text{if } k \text{ is even and } n - 1 - k = 1; \\
(n - 1 - k, \ldots, n - 2), & \text{if } k \text{ is odd and } n - 1 - k = 1.
\end{cases}
$$

$$
c_1: \begin{cases}
(1 \to 0), & \text{if } n - 1 - k \geqslant 2; \\
\mathbb{1}, & \text{if } n - 1 - k = 1.
\end{cases}
$$

$$
c_2: \begin{cases}
(n - k \to n - 1 - k), & \text{if } k \geqslant 2; \\
\mathbb{1}, & \text{if } k = 1.
\end{cases}
$$

$d_1: (n - 2 - k \to n - 1)\binom{n-3-k}{0} q \to q + 1)$.

$d_2: \binom{n-2}{n-1-k} q \to q + 1)$.

$e: (0 \to n - 1 - k)$.

Also, let $E_{n,k} = \{0, \ldots, n - 2 - k\}$; it is useful to partition Q_n into $E_{n,k}$, $F_{n,k}$, and $\{n - 1\}$. Letters a and b have complementary behaviours on $E_{n,k}$ and $F_{n,k}$, depending on the parities of n and k. Letters c_1 and d_1 act on $E_{n,k}$ in exactly the same way as c_2 and d_2 act on $F_{n,k}$. In addition, d_1 and d_2 send states $n - 2 - k$ and $n - 2$, respectively, to state $n - 1$, and letter e connects the two parts of the DFA. The structure of $\mathcal{D}_n(\Sigma)$ is shown in Figs. 2 and 3 for certain parities of $n - 1 - k$ and k. Let $L_{n,k}(\Sigma)$ be the language recognized by $\mathcal{D}_{n,k}(\Sigma)$.

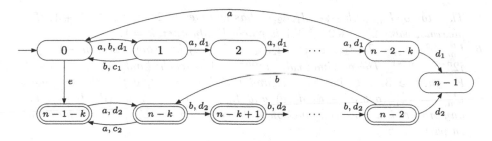

Fig. 2. DFA $\mathcal{D}_{n,k}(a, b, c_1, c_2, d_1, d_2, e)$ of Definition 2 when $n - 1 - k$ is odd, k is even, and both are at least 2; missing transitions are self-loops.

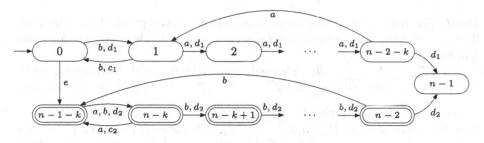

Fig. 3. DFA $\mathcal{D}_{n,k}(a, b, c_1, c_2, d_1, d_2, e)$ of Definition 2 when $n - 1 - k$ is even, k is odd, and both are at least 2; missing transitions are self-loops.

Theorem 1 (Proper Prefix-Convex Languages). *For $n \geqslant 3$ and $1 \leqslant k \leqslant n - 2$, the DFA $\mathcal{D}_{n,k}(\Sigma)$ of Definition 2 is minimal and $L_{n,k}(\Sigma)$ is a k-proper language of complexity n. The bounds below are maximal for k-proper prefix-convex languages. At least seven letters are required to meet these bounds.*

1. *The syntactic semigroup of $L_{n,k}(\Sigma)$ has cardinality $n^{n-1-k}(k+1)^k$; the maximal value $n(n - 1)^{n-2}$ is reached only when $k = n - 2$.*
2. *The non-empty, non-final quotients of $L_{n,k}(a, b, -, -, -, d_2, e)$ have complexity n, the final quotients have complexity $k + 1$, and $\emptyset$ has complexity 1.*
3. *The reverse of $L_{n,k}(a, b, -, -, -, d_2, e)$ has complexity 2^{n-1}; moreover, the language $L_{n,k}(a, b, -, -, -, d_2, e)$ has 2^{n-1} atoms for all k.*
4. *For each atom A_S of $L_{n,k}(\Sigma)$, write $S = X_1 \cup X_2$, where $X_1 \subseteq E_{n,k}$ and $X_2 \subseteq F_{n,k}$. Let $\overline{X_1} = E_{n,k} \setminus X_1$ and $\overline{X_2} = F_{n,k} \setminus X_2$. If $X_2 \neq \emptyset$, then $\kappa(A_S) =$*

$$1 + \sum_{x_1=0}^{|X_1|} \sum_{x_2=1}^{|X_1|+|X_2|-x_1} \sum_{y_1=0}^{|\overline{X_1}|} \sum_{y_2=0}^{|\overline{X_1}|+|\overline{X_2}|-y_1} \binom{n-1-k}{x_1}\binom{k}{x_2}\binom{n-1-k-x_1}{y_1}\binom{k-x_2}{y_2}.$$

If $X_1 \neq \emptyset$ and $X_2 = \emptyset$, then $\kappa(A_S) =$

$$1 + \sum_{x_1=0}^{|X_1|} \sum_{x_2=0}^{|X_1|-x_1} \sum_{y_1=0}^{|\overline{X_1}|} \sum_{y_2=0}^{k} \binom{n-1-k}{x_1}\binom{k}{x_2}\binom{n-1-k-x_1}{y_1}\binom{k-x_2}{y_2} - 2^k \sum_{y=0}^{|\overline{X_1}|} \binom{n-1-k}{y}.$$

Otherwise, $S = \emptyset$ and $\kappa(A_S) = 2^{n-1}$.

5. *The star of $L_{n,k}(a, b, -, -, d_1, d_2, e)$ has complexity $2^{n-2} + 2^{n-2-k} + 1$. The maximal value $2^{n-2} + 2^{n-3} + 1$ is reached only when $k = 1$.*

6. *$L'_{m,j}(a, b, c_1, -, d_1, d_2, e)L_{n,k}(a, d_2, c_1, -, d_1, b, e)$ has complexity $m - 1 - j + j2^{n-2} + 2^{n-1}$. The maximal value $m2^{n-2} + 1$ is reached only when $j = m - 2$.*

7. *For $m, n \geqslant 3$, $1 \leqslant j \leqslant m - 2$, and $1 \leqslant k \leqslant n - 2$, define the languages $L'_{m,j} = L'_{m,j}(a, b, c_1, -, d_1, d_2, e)$ and $L_{n,k} = L_{n,k}(a, b, e, -, d_2, d_1, c_1)$. For any proper binary boolean function $\circ$, the complexity of $L'_{m,j} \circ L_{n,k}$ is maximal. In particular,*

   (a) $L'_{m,j} \cup L_{n,k}$ and $L'_{m,j} \oplus L_{n,k}$ have complexity mn.
   (b) $L'_{m,j} \setminus L_{n,k}$ has complexity $mn - (n - 1)$.
   (c) $L'_{m,j} \cap L_{n,k}$ has complexity $mn - (m + n - 2)$.

Proof. The remainder of this paper is an outline of the proof of this theorem. The longer parts of the proof are separated into individual propositions and lemmas.

DFA $\mathcal{D}_{n,k}(a, b, -, -, -, d_2, e)$ is easily seen to be minimal. Language $L_{n,k}(\Sigma)$ is k-proper by Propositions 1 and 2.

1. See Lemma 2 and Proposition 3.
2. If the initial state of $\mathcal{D}_{n,k}(a, b, -, -, -, d_2, e)$ is changed to $q \in E_{n,k}$, the new DFA accepts a quotient of $L_{n,k}$ and is still minimal; hence the complexity of that quotient is n. If the initial state is changed to $q \in F_{n,k}$ then states in $E_{n,k}$ are unreachable, but the DFA on $\{n - 1 - k, \ldots, n - 1\}$ is minimal; hence the complexity of that quotient is $k + 1$. The remaining quotient is empty, and hence has complexity 1. By Proposition 1, these are maximal.
3. See Proposition 4 for the reverse. It was shown in [9] that the number of atoms is equal to the complexity of the reverse.
4. See [7].
5. See Proposition 5.
6. See [7].
7. By [3, Theorem 2], all boolean operations on regular languages have the upper bound mn, which gives the bound for (a). The bounds for (b) and (c) follow from [3, Theorem 5]. The proof that all these bounds are tight for $L'_{m,j} \circ L_{n,k}$ can be found in [7]. □

Lemma 2. *Let $n \geqslant 1$ and $1 \leqslant k \leqslant n - 2$. For any permutation t of Q_n such that $E_{n,k}t = E_{n,k}$, $F_{n,k}t = F_{n,k}$, and $(n - 1)t = n - 1$, there is a word $w \in \{a, b\}^*$ that induces t on $\mathcal{D}_{n,k}$.*

Proof. Only a and b induce permutations of Q_n; every other letter induces a properly injective map. Furthermore, a and b permute $E_{n,k}$ and $F_{n,k}$ separately, and both fix $n - 1$. Hence every $w \in \{a, b\}^*$ induces a permutation on Q_n such that $E_{n,k}w = E_{n,k}$, $F_{n,k}w = F_{n,k}$, and $(n - 1)w = n - 1$. Each such permutation naturally corresponds to an element of $S_{n-1-k} \times S_k$, where S_m denotes the symmetric group on m elements. To be consistent with the DFA, assume S_{n-1-k} contains permutations of $\{0, \ldots, n - 2 - k\}$ and S_k contains permutations of $\{n - 1 - k, \ldots, n - 2\}$. Let s_a and s_b denote the group elements corresponding to the transformations induced by a and b respectively. We show that s_a and s_b generate $S_{n-1-k} \times S_k$.

It is well known that $(0, \ldots, m-1)$, and $(0, 1)$ generate the symmetric group on $\{0, \ldots, m-1\}$ for any $m \geq 2$. Note that $(1, \ldots, m-1)$ and $(0, 1)$ are also generators, since $(0, 1)(1, \ldots, m-1) = (0, \ldots, m-1)$.

If $n-1-k = 1$ and $k = 1$, then $S_{n-1-k} \times S_k$ is the trivial group. If $n-1-k = 1$ and $k \geqslant 2$, then $s_a = (1, (n-1-k, n-k))$ and s_b is either $(1, (n-1-k, \ldots, n-2))$ or $(1, (n-k, \ldots, n-2))$, and either pair generates the group. There is a similar argument when $k = 1$.

Assume now $n-1-k \geqslant 2$ and $k \geqslant 2$. If $n-1-k$ is odd then $s_a = ((0, \ldots, n-2-k), (n-1-k, n-k))$, and hence $s_a^{n-1-k} = ((0, \ldots, n-2-k)^{n-1-k}, (n-1-k, n-k)^{n-1-k}) = (1, (n-1-k, n-k))$. Similarly if $n-1-k$ is even then $s_a = ((1, \ldots, n-2-k), (n-1-k, n-k))$, and hence $s_a^{n-2-k} = (1, (n-1-k, n-k))$. Therefore $(1, (n-1-k, n-k))$ is always generated by s_a. By symmetry, $((0, 1), 1)$ is always generated by s_b regardless of the parity of k.

Since we can isolate the transposition component of s_a, we can isolate the other component as well: $(1, (n-1-k, n-k))s_a$ is either $((0, \ldots, n-2-k), 1)$ or $((1, \ldots, n-2-k), 1)$. Paired with $((0, 1), 1)$, either element is sufficient to generate $S_{n-1-k} \times \{1\}$. Similarly, s_a and s_b generate $\{1\} \times S_k$. Therefore s_a and s_b generate $S_{n-1-k} \times S_k$. It follows that a and b generate all permutations t of Q_n such that $E_{n,k}t = E_{n,k}$, $F_{n,k}t = F_{n,k}$, and $(n-1)t = n-1$. $\square$

Proposition 3 (Syntactic Semigroup). *The syntactic semigroup of $L_{n,k}(\Sigma)$ has cardinality $n^{n-1-k}(k+1)^k$, which is maximal for a k-proper language. Furthermore, seven letters are required to meet this bound. The maximum value $n(n-1)^{n-2}$ is reached only when $k = n-2$.*

Proof. Let L be a k-proper language of complexity n and let $\mathcal{D}$ be a minimal DFA recognizing L. By Lemma 1, $\mathcal{D}$ has an empty state. By Proposition 1, the only states that can be reached from one of the k final states are either final or empty. Thus, a transformation in the transition semigroup of $\mathcal{D}$ may map each final state to one of $k+1$ possible states, while each non-final, non-empty state may be mapped to any of the n states. Since the empty state can only be mapped to itself, we are left with $n^{n-1-k}(k+1)^k$ possible transformations in the transition semigroup. Therefore the syntactic semigroup of any k-proper language has size at most $n^{n-1-k}(k+1)^k$.

Now consider the transition semigroup of $\mathcal{D}_{n,k}(\Sigma)$. Every transformation t in the semigroup must satisfy $F_{n,k}t \subseteq F_{n,k} \cup \{n-1\}$ and $(n-1)t = n-1$, since any other transformation would violate prefix-convexity. We show that the semigroup contains every such transformation, and hence the syntactic semigroup of $L_{n,k}(\Sigma)$ is maximal.

First, consider the transformations t such that $E_{n,k}t \subseteq E_{n,k} \cup \{n-1\}$ and $qt = q$ for all $q \in F_{n,k} \cup \{n-1\}$. By Lemma 2, a and b generate every permutation of $E_{n,k}$. When t is not a permutation, we can use c_1 to combine any states p and q: apply a permutation on $E_{n,k}$ so that $p \to 0$ and $q \to 1$, and then apply c_1 so that $1 \to 0$. Repeat this method to combine any set of states, and further apply permutations to induce the desired transformation while leaving the states of $F_{n,k} \cup \{n-1\}$ in place. The same idea applies with d_1; apply permutations and d_1 to send any states of $E_{n,k}$ to $n-1$. Hence a, b, c_1, and d_1 generate every transformation t such that $E_{n,k}t \subseteq E_{n,k} \cup \{n-1\}$ and $qt = q$ for all $q \in F_{n,k} \cup \{n-1\}$.

We can make the same argument for transformations that act only on $F_{n,k}$ and fix every other state. Since c_2 and d_2 act on $F_{n,k}$ exactly as c_1 and d_1 act on $E_{n,k}$, the letters a, b, c_2, and d_2 generate every transformation t such that $F_{n,k}t \subseteq F_{n,k} \cup \{n-1\}$ and $qt = q$ for all $q \in E_{n,k} \cup \{n-1\}$. It follows that a, b, c_1, c_2, d_1, and d_2 generate every transformation t such that $E_{n,k}t \subseteq E_{n,k} \cup \{n-1\}$, $F_{n,k}t \subseteq F_{n,k} \cup \{n-1\}$, and $(n-1)t = n-1$.

Note the similarity between this DFA restricted to the states $E_{n,k} \cup \{n-1\}$ (or $F_{n,k} \cup \{n-1\}$) and the witness for right ideals introduced in [7]. The argument for the size of the syntactic semigroup of right ideals is similar to this; see [10].

Finally, consider an arbitrary transformation t such that $F_{n,k}t \subseteq F_{n,k} \cup \{n-1\}$ and $(n-1)t = n-1$. Let j_t be the number of states $p \in E_{n,k}$ such that $pt \in F_{n,k}$. We show by induction on j_t that t is in the transition semigroup of $\mathcal{D}$. If $j_t = 0$, then t is generated by $\Sigma \setminus \{e\}$. If $j_t \geqslant 1$, there exist $p, q \in E_{n,k}$ such that $pt \in F_{n,k}$ and q is not in the image of t. Consider the transformations s_1 and s_2 defined by $qs_1 = pt$ and $rs_1 = r$ for $r \neq q$, and $ps_2 = q$ and $rs_2 = rt$ for $r \neq p$. Then $(rs_2)s_1 = rt$ for all $r \in Q_n$. Notice that $j_{s_2} = j_t - 1$, and hence Σ generates s_2 by inductive assumption. One can verify that $s_1 = (n - 1 - k, pt)(0, q)(0 \to n - 1 - k)(0, q)(n - 1 - k, pt)$. From this expression, we see that s_1 is the composition of transpositions induced by words in $\{a, b\}^*$ and the transformation $(0 \to n - 1 - k)$ induced by e, and hence s_1 is generated by Σ. Thus, t is in the transition semigroup. By induction on j_t, it follows that the syntactic semigroup of $L_{n,k}$ is maximal.

Now we show that seven letters are required to meet this bound. Two letters (like a and b) are required to generate the permutations, since clearly one letter is not sufficient. Every other letter will induce a properly injective map. A letter (like c_1) that induces a properly injective map on $E_{n,k}$ and permutes $F_{n,k}$ is required. Similarly, a letter (like c_2) that permutes $E_{n,k}$ and induces a properly injective map on $F_{n,k}$ is required. A letter (like d_1) that sends a state in $E_{n,k}$ to $n-1$ and permutes $F_{n,k}$ is required. Similarly, a letter (like d_2) that sends a state in $F_{n,k}$ to $n-1$ and permutes $E_{n,k}$ is required. Finally, a letter (like e) that connects $E_{n,k}$ and $F_{n,k}$ is required.

For a fixed n, we may want to know which $k \in \{1, \ldots, n-2\}$ maximizes $s_n(k) = n^{n-1-k}(k+1)^k$; this corresponds to the largest syntactic semigroup of a proper prefix-convex language with n quotients. We show that $s_n(k)$ is largest at $k = n - 2$. Consider the ratio $\frac{s_n(k+1)}{s_n(k)} = \frac{(k+2)^{k+1}}{n(k+1)^k}$. Notice this ratio is increasing with k, and hence s_n is a convex function on $\{1, \ldots, n-2\}$. It follows that the maximum value of s_n must occur at one the endpoints, 1 and $n-2$.

Now we show that $s_n(n-2) \geqslant s_n(1)$ for all $n \geqslant 3$. We can check this explicitly for $n = 3, 4, 5$. When $n \geqslant 6$, $s_n(n-2)/s_n(1) = \frac{n}{2} \left(\frac{n-1}{n}\right)^{n-2} \geqslant 3(1/e) > 1$; so the largest syntactic semigroup of $L_{n,k}(\Sigma)$ occurs only at $k = n - 2$ for all $n \geqslant 3$. $\square$

Proposition 4 (Reverse). *For any regular language L of complexity n with an empty quotient, the reversal has complexity at most 2^{n-1}. Moreover, the reverse of $L_{n,k}(a, b, -, -, -, d_2, e)$ has complexity 2^{n-1} for $n \geqslant 3$ and $1 \leqslant k \leqslant n - 2$.*

Proof. The first claim is left for the reader to verify. For the second claim, let $\mathcal{D}_{n,k} = (Q_n, \{a, b, d_2, e\}, \delta_{n,k}, 0, F_{n,k})$ denote the DFA $\mathcal{D}_{n,k}(a, b, -, -, -, d_2, e)$ in Definition 2 and let $L_{n,k} = L(\mathcal{D}_{n,k})$. Construct an NFA $\mathcal{N}$ recognizing the reverse of $L_{n,k}$ by reversing each transition, letting the initial state 0 be the unique final state, and letting the final states in $F_{n,k}$ be the initial states. Applying the subset construction to $\mathcal{N}$ yields a DFA $\mathcal{D}^R$ whose states are subsets of Q_{n-1}, with initial state $F_{n,k}$ and final states $\{U \subseteq Q_{n-1} \mid 0 \in U\}$. We show that $\mathcal{D}^R$ is minimal, and hence the reverse of $L_{n,k}$ has complexity 2^{n-1}.

Recall from Lemma 2 that a and b generate all permutations of $E_{n,k}$ and $F_{n,k}$ in $\mathcal{D}_{n,k}$ and, although the transitions are reversed in $\mathcal{D}^R$, they still generate all such permutations. Let $u_1, u_2 \in \{a, b\}^*$ be such that u_1 induces $(0, \ldots, n-2-k)$ and u_2 induces $(n - 1 - k, \ldots, n - 2)$ in $\mathcal{D}^R$.

Consider a state $U = \{q_1, \ldots, q_h, n - 1 - k, \ldots, n - 2\}$ where $0 \leqslant q_1 < q_2 < \cdots < q_h \leqslant n - 2 - k$. If $h = 0$, then U is the initial state. When $h \geqslant 1$, $\{q_2 - q_1, q_3 - q_1, \ldots, q_h - q_1, n - 1 - k, \ldots, n - 2\}eu_1^{q_1} = U$. By induction, all such states are reachable.

Now we show that any state $U = \{q_1, \ldots, q_h, p_1, \ldots, p_i\}$ where $0 \leqslant q_1 < q_2 < \cdots < q_h \leqslant n - 2 - k$ and $n - 1 - k \leqslant p_1 < p_2 < \cdots < p_i \leqslant n - 2$ is reachable. If $i = k$, then $U = \{q_1, \ldots, q_h, n - 1 - k, \ldots, n - 2\}$ is reachable by the argument above. When $0 \leqslant i < k$, choose $p \in F_{n,k} \setminus U$ and see that U is reached from $U \cup \{p\}$ by $u_2^{n-1-p} d_2 u_2^{p-(n-2-k)}$. By induction, every state is reachable.

To prove distinguishability, consider distinct states U and V. Choose $q \in U \oplus V$. If $q \in E_{n,k}$, then U and V are distinguished by $u_1^{n-1-k-q}$. When $q \in F_{n,k}$, they are distinguished by $u_2^{n-1-q}e$. So $\mathcal{D}^R$ is minimal. $\square$

Proposition 5 (Star). *Let L be a regular language with $n \geqslant 2$ quotients, including $k \geqslant 1$ final quotients and one empty quotient. Then $\kappa(L^*) \leqslant 2^{n-2} + 2^{n-2-k} + 1$. This bound is tight for prefix-convex languages; in particular, the language $(L_{n,k}(a, b, -, -, d_1, d_2, e))^*$ meets this bound for $n \geqslant 3$ and $1 \leqslant k \leqslant n - 2$.*

Proof. Since L has an empty quotient, let $n - 1$ be the empty state of its minimal DFA $\mathcal{D}$. To obtain an ε-NFA for L^*, we add a new initial state $0'$ which is final and has the same transitions as 0. We then add an ε-transition from every state in F to 0. Applying the subset construction to this ε-NFA yields a DFA $\mathcal{D}' = (Q', \Sigma, \delta', \{0'\}, F')$ recognizing L^*, in which Q' contains non-empty subsets of $Q_n \cup \{0'\}$.

Many of the states of Q' are unreachable or indistinguishable from other states. Since there is no transition in the ε-NFA to $0'$, the only reachable state in Q' containing $0'$ is $\{0'\}$. As well, any reachable final state $U \neq \{0'\}$ must contain 0 because of the ε-transitions. Finally, for any $U \in Q'$, we have $U \in F'$ if and only if $U \cup \{n - 1\} \in F'$, and since $\delta'(U \cup \{n - 1\}, w) = \delta'(U, w) \cup \{n - 1\}$ for all $w \in \Sigma^*$, the states U and $U \cup \{n - 1\}$ are equivalent in $\mathcal{D}'$.

Hence $\mathcal{D}'$ is equivalent to a DFA with the states $\{\{0'\}\}\cup\{U\subseteq Q_{n-1}\mid U\cap F = \emptyset\}\cup\{U\subseteq Q_{n-1}\mid 0\in U \text{ and } U\cap F\neq\emptyset\}$. This DFA has $1+2^{n-1-k}+(2^{n-2}-2^{n-2-k})=2^{n-2}+2^{n-2-k}+1$ states. Thus, $\kappa(L^*)\leqslant 2^{n-2}+2^{n-2-k}+1$.

This bound applies when L is a prefix-convex language and $n\geqslant 3$. By Lemma 1, L is either a right ideal or has an empty state. If L is a right ideal, then $\kappa(L^*)\leqslant n+1$, which is at most $2^{n-2}+2^{n-2-k}+1$ for $n\geqslant 3$.

For the last claim, let $\mathcal{D}_{n,k}(a,b,-,-,d_1,d_2,e)$ of Definition 2 be denoted by $\mathcal{D}_{n,k}=(Q_n,\{a,b,d_1,d_2,e\},\delta_{n,k},0,F_{n,k})$ and let $L_{n,k}=L(\mathcal{D}_{n,k})$. We apply the same construction and reduction as before to obtain a DFA $\mathcal{D}'_{n,k}$ recognizing $L^*_{n,k}$ with states $Q'=\{\{0'\}\}\cup\{U\subseteq E_{n,k}\}\cup\{U\subseteq Q_{n-1}\mid 0\in U \text{ and } U\cap F_{n,k}\neq\emptyset\}$. We show that the states of Q' are reachable and pairwise distinguishable.

By Lemma 2, a and b generate all permutations of $E_{n,k}$ and $F_{n,k}$ in $\mathcal{D}_{n,k}$. Choose $u_1,u_2\in\{a,b\}^*$ such that u_1 induces $(0,\ldots,n-2-k)$ and u_2 induces $(n-1-k,\ldots,n-2)$ in $\mathcal{D}_{n,k}$.

For reachability, we consider three cases. (1) State $\{0'\}$ is reachable by ε. (2) Let $U\subseteq E_{n,k}$. For any $q\in E_{n,k}$, we can reach $U\setminus\{q\}$ by $u_1^{n-2-k-q}d_1u_1^q$; hence if U is reachable, then every subset of U is reachable. Observe that state $E_{n,k}$ is reachable by $eu_1^{n-2-k}d_2^k$, and we can reach any subset of this state. Therefore, all non-final states are reachable. (3) If $U\cap F_{n,k}\neq\emptyset$, then $U=\{0,q_1,q_2,\ldots,q_h,r_1,\ldots,r_i\}$ where $0<q_1<\cdots<q_h\leqslant n-2-k$ and $n-1-k\leqslant r_1<\cdots<r_i<n-1$ and $i\geqslant 1$. We prove that U is reachable by induction on i. If $i=0$, then U is reachable by (2). For any $i\geqslant 1$, we can reach U from $\{0,q_1,\ldots,q_h,r_2-(r_1-(n-1-k)),\ldots,r_i-(r_1-(n-1-k))\}$ by $eu_2^{r_1-(n-1-k)}$. Therefore, all states of this form are reachable.

Now we show that the states are pairwise distinguishable. (1) The initial state $\{0'\}$ is distinguishable from any other final state U since $\{0'\}u_1$ is non-final and Uu_1 is final. (2) If U and V are distinct subsets of $E_{n,k}$, then there is some $q\in U\oplus V$. We distinguish U and V by $u_1^{n-1-k-q}e$. (3) If U and V are distinct and final and neither one is $\{0'\}$, then there is some $q\in U\oplus V$. If $q\in E_{n,k}$, then $Ud_2^k=U\setminus F_{n,k}$ and $Vd_2^k=V\setminus F_{n,k}$ are distinct, non-final states as in (2). Otherwise, $q\in F_{n,k}$ and we distinguish U and V by $u_2^{n-1-q}d_2^{k-1}$. $\square$

Table 1. Complexities of prefix-convex languages

	Right-ideal	Prefix-closed	Prefix-free	Proper
SeGr	n^{n-1}	n^{n-1}	n^{n-2}	$n^{n-1-k}(k+1)^k$
Rev	2^{n-1}	2^{n-1}	$2^{n-2}+1$	2^{n-1}
Star	$n+1$	$2^{n-2}+1$	n	$2^{n-2}+2^{n-2-k}+1$
Prod	$m+2^{n-2}$	$(m+1)2^{n-2}$	$m+n-2$	$m-1-j+j2^{n-2}+2^{n-1}$
$\cup$	$mn-(m+n-2)$	mn	$mn-2$	mn
$\oplus$	mn	mn	$mn-2$	mn
$\setminus$	$mn-(m-1)$	$mn-(n-1)$	$mn-(m+2n-4)$	$mn-(n-1)$
$\cap$	mn	$mn-(m+n-2)$	$mn-2(m+n-3)$	$mn-(m+n-2)$

3   Conclusions

The bounds for prefix-convex languages (see also [8]) are summarized in Table 1. The largest bounds are shown in boldface type, and they are reached either in the class of right-ideal languages or the class of proper languages. Recall that for regular languages we have the following results: semigroup n^n, reverse 2^n, star $2^{n-1} + 2^{n-2}$, product $m2^n - 2^{n-1}$, boolean operations mn.

References

1. Ang, T., Brzozowski, J.A.: Languages convex with respect to binary relations, and their closure properties. Acta Cybernet. **19**(2), 445–464 (2009)
2. Berstel, J., Perrin, D., Reutenauer, C.: Codes and Automata (Encyclopedia of Mathematics and its Applications). Cambridge University Press, New York (2010)
3. Brzozowski, J.A.: Quotient complexity of regular languages. J. Autom. Lang. Comb. **15**(1/2), 71–89 (2010)
4. Brzozowski, J.A.: In search of the most complex regular languages. Int. J. Found. Comput. Sci **24**(6), 691–708 (2013)
5. Brzozowski, J.A., Davies, S., Liu, B.Y.V.: Most complex regular ideal languages. Discrete Math. Theoret. Comput. Sci. **18**(3), 1–25 (2016). Paper #15
6. Brzozowski, J.A., Jirásková, G., Zou, C.: Quotient complexity of closed languages. Theory Comput. Syst. **54**, 277–292 (2014)
7. Brzozowski, J.A., Sinnamon, C.: Complexity of prefix-convex regular languages (2016). http://arxiv.org/abs/1605.06697
8. Brzozowski, J.A., Sinnamon, C.: Complexity of right ideal, prefix-closed, and prefix-free regular languages. Acta Cybernet. (2017, to appear)
9. Brzozowski, J.A., Tamm, H.: Theory of átomata. Theoret. Comput. Sci. **539**, 13–27 (2014)
10. Brzozowski, J., Ye, Y.: Syntactic complexity of ideal and closed languages. In: Mauri, G., Leporati, A. (eds.) DLT 2011. LNCS, vol. 6795, pp. 117–128. Springer, Heidelberg (2011). doi:10.1007/978-3-642-22321-1_11
11. Crochemore, M., Hancart, C.: Automata for pattern matching. In: Rozenberg, G., Salomaa, A. (eds.) Handbook of Formal Languages, vol. 2, pp. 399–462. Springer, Heidelberg (1997)
12. Holzer, M., König, B.: On deterministic finite automata and syntactic monoid size. Theoret. Comput. Sci. **327**(3), 319–347 (2004)
13. Iván, S.: Complexity of atoms, combinatorially. Inform. Process. Lett. **116**(5), 356–360 (2016)
14. Krawetz, B., Lawrence, J., Shallit, J.: State complexity and the monoid of transformations of a finite set. In: Domaratzki, M., Okhotin, A., Salomaa, K., Yu, S. (eds.) CIAA 2004. LNCS, vol. 3317, pp. 213–224. Springer, Heidelberg (2005). doi:10.1007/978-3-540-30500-2_20
15. Maslov, A.N.: Estimates of the number of states of finite automata. Dokl. Akad. Nauk SSSR **194**, 1266–1268 (1970). (Russian). English translation: Soviet Math. Dokl. **11**, 1373–1375 (1970)
16. Thierrin, G.: Convex languages. In: Nivat, M. (ed.) Automata, Languages and Programming, pp. 481–492. North-Holland (1973)
17. Yu, S.: State complexity of regular languages. J. Autom. Lang. Comb. **6**, 221–234 (2001)
18. Yu, S., Zhuang, Q., Salomaa, K.: The state complexities of some basic operations on regular languages. Theoret. Comput. Sci. **125**(2), 315–328 (1994)

Equivalence of Probabilistic μ-Calculus and p-Automata

Claudia Cauli$^{(\boxtimes)}$ and Nir Piterman

University of Leicester, Leicester, UK
cc488@leicester.ac.uk

Abstract. An important characteristic of Kozen's μ-calculus is its strong connection with parity alternating tree automata. Here, we show that the probabilistic μ-calculus μ^p-calculus and p-automata (parity alternating Markov chain automata) have an equally strong connection. Namely, for every μ^p-calculus formula we can construct a p-automaton that accepts exactly those Markov chains that satisfy the formula. For every p-automaton we can construct a μ^p-calculus formula satisfied in exactly those Markov chains that are accepted by the automaton. The translation in one direction relies on a normal form of the calculus and in the other direction on the usage of vectorial μ^p-calculus. The proofs use the game semantics of μ^p-calculus and automata to show that our translations are correct.

1 Introduction

The verification of probabilistic systems is an increasingly important area that has led to the development of new formalisms and tools for the evaluation of quantitative properties over stochastic models. These tools range from temporal logics and quantitative variants of Kozen's modal μ-calculus [15] to probabilistic automata and games [2,13,17–19].

This work focuses on two such formalisms, μ^p-calculus and p-automata. The μ^p-calculus has been introduced in [8] as a probabilistic extension of Kozen's modal μ-calculus. The so-called p-automata [9] are probabilistic alternating parity automata that read Markov chains as input. Acceptance of a Markov chain by a p-automaton is decided by an obligation game, that is, a turn-based stochastic parity game with obligations.

The key contribution given by this paper is the proof of the equivalence between μ^p-calculus and p-automata. We provide a framework to translate μ^p-formulas into p-automata and, using the vectorial syntax, define the inverse conversion from p-automata into μ^p-calculus. Thus, we show that the two formalisms have the same expressive power and that they enjoy a close relationship similar to those of Kozen's μ-calculus and alternating tree automata (see below).

Related Work. This study belongs to a general field of research that aims to define a connection between logics and automata theory. An interesting survey conducted by Kupferman et al. in [16] provides insights into this relationship by presenting translations from a number of temporal logics – linear-time,

© Springer International Publishing AG 2017
A. Carayol and C. Nicaud (Eds.): CIAA 2017, LNCS 10329, pp. 64–75, 2017.
DOI: 10.1007/978-3-319-60134-2_6

branching-time, μ-calculus, and its alternation-free fragment – into different classes of alternating tree automata.

Over the last three decades, several studies have focused on the definition of an automata-theoretic approach to Kozen's μ-calculus. In [10], Emerson and Jutla proposed a framework to convert μ-calculus formulas into alternating tree automata, then reduced to their non-deterministic counterpart. Their result complements previous studies by Niwiński [20] that defined the inverse translation from non-deterministic tree automata to μ-calculus, thus showing that Kozen's μ-calculus is equivalent to tree automata in expressive power. In [14], Janin and Walukiewicz introduced μ-automata, alternating automata with a parity acceptance condition that easily translate to and from μ-calculus formulas in disjunctive normal form. In a subsequent work, [21], Niwiński extends his previous result to a broader scope establishing the equivalence between alternating automata over arbitrary algebraic structures – thus including trees – and fixed point terms, a general fixpoint formalism that finds a natural interpretation as a system of equations. Wilke, in [23], addresses the interplay among μ-calculus, alternating tree automata, and games. In particular, he gives a translation from logic to automata and then defines the acceptance problem for automata by reduction to the winner problem in parity games. A comprehensive outline of the relationship among logics, automata, and parity games is given in [12]. Overviews of μ-calculus, including its mathematical foundation, axiomatic system, properties, guarded form, vectorial syntax, game semantics, and equivalence with automata, can be found in [1, 3, 5].

Huth and Kwiatkowska suggested a quantitative μ-calculus to reason about Markov chains [13]. This calculus was extended in [7] by adding a bounded number of probabilistic quantifications and allowing to define PCTL*. The μ^p-calculus allows to nest probabilistic quantifications inside fixpoint operators and, thus, allows for unbounded probabilistic quantifications. It is a subset of the calculus defined in [17, 19]. The μ^p-calculus expressive enough to include PCTL and PCTL*, the complexity of its decision procedures is reduced, and the algorithms involved wrap up standard algorithms for solution of (quantitative) two-player stochastic parity games in extra layer rather than bespoke algorithms.

2   Background

2.1   Markov Chains

A Markov chain M over a set AP of atomic propositions is a probabilistic labelled transition system defined by the tuple $M = (S, s^{in}, L, P)$, where S is the set of locations; $s^{in} \in S$ is the initial location; L is a labelling function, overloaded to both denote $L : S \to 2^{AP}$ and $L : AP \to 2^S$; and P is the probability transition function $P : S \times S \to [0, 1]$. For every location s we define the set $succ(s)$ of its successors as the set of locations s' such that $P(s, s') > 0$. Clearly, the sum of the probabilities of moving from a location to all its successors must be equal to 1, that is $\sum_{s' \in succ(s)} P(s, s') = 1$, and every location has at least one successor.

2.2   Obligation Games

Obligation games [9] are two-player stochastic parity games with obligations that are played on a graph amongst a probabilistic system and two players, called Player 0 and Player 1.

Definition 1 (Obligation Game). *An obligation game G is the tuple*

$$G = ((V, E), (V_0, V_1, V_p), \mathcal{K}, \langle \alpha, O \rangle),$$

where V is the set of configurations, partitioned in Player 0 (V_0), Player 1 (V_1), and probabilistic configurations (V_p); $E \subseteq V \times V$ is the set of edges; $\mathcal{K} : V_p \times V \to [0, 1]$ is the probability function such that $(v, v') \notin E$ implies $\mathcal{K}(v, v') = 0$ and for every $v \in V_p$ we have $\sum_{v' \in V} \mathcal{K}(v, v') = 1$; and the pair $\langle \alpha, O \rangle$ defines the goal: $\alpha : V \to [0..k]$ is the parity condition, and $O : V \to (\{>, \geq\} \times [0, 1]) \cup \{\bot\}$ marks the obligations, with the symbol $\bot$ denoting no obligation.

Obligations are statements applied to some configurations that impose constraints on the winning paths that depart from them. An obligation has the form $>x$ or $\geq x$, where $x \in [0, 1]$, so as to indicate that the measure of the paths starting from that configuration must be greater than, or greater than or equal to, a given value x. Fixing a pair of strategies – σ for Player 0 and π for Player 1 – and a prefix of configurations $w \in V^+$, the game is reduced to only probabilistic vertices and, hence, can be seen as a Markov chain enriched with a *goal* $\langle \alpha, O \rangle$, that is, a winning condition and a set of obligations. We denote such structure as $G^{w(\sigma, \pi)}$. Value and winner of G are decided by analysing $G^{w(\sigma, \pi)}$ using the notion of *choice set*.

A choice set is the set of finite paths that extend the prefix w and end in a configuration with an obligation that can be met. It must be extended through infinite paths that either reach another obligation or never reach another obligation and are winning. The measure of the choice set is the measure of these infinite paths and determines the value of the game on every configuration for each player, denoted as $val_i(v)$ for $i \in \{0, 1\}$. We refer the reader to [9] for further details concerning the measure of choice sets and the value of obligation parity Markov chains. We write the value of game G on configuration v as $val_G(v)$ and we define it as the value for Player 0 on v.

Player 0 wins the game G from prefix w with a value of 1 if for every value $r < 1$ there exists a strategy σ such that for all Player 1's strategies π in the corresponding Markov chain $G^{w(\sigma, \pi)}$ it is possible to determine a choice set whose measure is at least r.

2.3   The μ^p-Calculus

The μ^p-calculus [8] is an extension of Kozen's μ-calculus [15] that allows one to specify properties that are bounded by a specific probability. This is done through the distinction between qualitative (Φ) and quantitative (Ψ) formulas that are evaluated to values in the sets $\{0, 1\}$ and $[0, 1]$, respectively.

A μ^p-calculus sentence is qualitative and might contain one or more quantitative sub-formulas within a probabilistic quantification operator $[\cdot]_J$. The operator $[\cdot]_J$ checks whether the value of the enclosed formula satisfies the bound J and gets the value 1 or 0 accordingly. The syntax of the μ^p-calculus is given by the following BNF grammar.

$$J ::= \{\geq, >\} \times [0,1]$$
$$\Phi ::= p \mid \neg p \mid \varphi_1 \wedge \varphi_2 \mid \varphi_1 \vee \varphi_2 \mid [\Psi]_J \mid \mu X_i.\varphi \mid \nu X_i.\varphi$$
$$\Psi ::= \Phi \mid X_i \mid \psi_1 \wedge \psi_2 \mid \psi_1 \vee \psi_2 \mid \bigcirc\psi \mid \mu X_i.\psi \mid \nu X_i.\psi$$

Fixed point formulas are of the form $\sigma X_i.\varphi$, where $\sigma \in \{\mu, \nu\}$ and X_i is a variable in the set $\mathcal{V} = \{X_0, X_1, ...\}$. Variable X_i is bound by the fixed point operator to the formula φ, which we also denote by $\varphi(X_i)$ or φ_{X_i}.

Semantics. The semantics of a μ^p-calculus formula φ is given with respect to a Markov chain M and an interpretation $\rho : \mathcal{V} \to (S \to [0,1])$. That is, ρ associates a function from locations to values in the domain $[0,1]$ with each variable X_i appearing in φ. Therefore, the semantics is a mapping of type $S \to [0,1]$ denoted by $[\![\varphi]\!]_M^\rho$ and defined as follows:

$$[\![p]\!]_M^\rho = \chi_{L(p)} \qquad\qquad [\![\neg p]\!]_M^\rho = 1 - \chi_{L(p)}$$
$$[\![\varphi_1 \wedge \varphi_2]\!]_M^\rho = \min\{[\![\varphi_1]\!]_M^\rho, [\![\varphi_2]\!]_M^\rho\} \qquad [\![\varphi_1 \vee \varphi_2]\!]_M^\rho = \max\{[\![\varphi_1]\!]_M^\rho, [\![\varphi_2]\!]_M^\rho\}$$
$$[\![X]\!]_M^\rho = \rho(X)$$
$$[\![\varphi]_J]\!]_M^\rho = \begin{cases} 1 \text{ If } [\![\varphi]\!]_M^\rho(s)\, J \\ 0 \text{ Otherwise} \end{cases}$$
$$[\![\bigcirc\varphi]\!]_M^\rho = \lambda s. \sum_{s'} P(s,s')[\![\varphi]\!]_M^\rho(s')$$
$$[\![\mu X.\varphi]\!]_M^\rho = \mathrm{lfp}(\lambda f.[\![\varphi]\!]_M^{\rho[f/X]}) \qquad [\![\nu X.\varphi]\!]_M^\rho = \mathrm{gfp}(\lambda f.[\![\varphi]\!]_M^{\rho[f/X]})$$

where $\chi_{L(p)}$ is the function that associates to a location s the value 0 if $s \notin L(p)$, or the value 1 if $s \in L(p)$. The only elements of the calculus that are evaluated exclusively to values in the set $\{0,1\}$ are p, $\neg p$, and $[\cdot]_J$. All the other operators get real values in $[0,1]$, thus, can specify both quantitative and qualitative properties depending on their nested sub-formulas.

Alternation Depth. The alternation depth of a formula φ, denoted by $ad(\varphi)$, is the maximum number of fixed point operators that occur nested and alternated [8,11]. A formula, or sub-formula, with no fixpoints has an alternation depth of 0. A formula with a single fixed point operator has alternation depth 1. In addition to the alternation depth, with every μ^p-calculus sub-formula ψ of φ is associated a colour $c(\psi)$. If ψ is a greatest fixed point then $c(\psi) = 2\big(ad(\varphi) - ad(\psi)\big)$; if ψ is a least fixed point then $c(\psi) = 2\big(ad(\varphi) - ad(\psi)\big) + 1$; and in every other case $c(\psi) = 2ad(\varphi) - 1$.

Game Semantics. Given a μ^p-calculus formula φ and a Markov chain M, we construct an obligation game $G_{M,\varphi}$ and we refer to such game as *semantics game*. Game $G_{M,\varphi}$ is the tuple $\big((V,E), (V_0, V_1, V_p), \mathcal{K}, \langle\alpha, O\rangle\big)$, where:

- $V = S \times sub(\varphi)$
- $V_0 = \{(s, \varphi_1 \vee \varphi_2) \mid \varphi_1 \vee \varphi_2 \in sub(\varphi)\}$
- $V_1 = \{(s, \varphi_1 \wedge \varphi_2) \mid \varphi_1 \wedge \varphi_2 \in sub(\varphi)\}$
- $V_p = V \setminus (V_0 \cup V_1)$
- $E = \{((s,p),(s,p)),((s,\neg p),(s,\neg p))\} \cup \{((s,X),(s,\sigma X.\varphi(X)))\} \cup$
  $\{((s,\varphi_1 \vee \varphi_2),(s,\varphi_i)) \mid i \in \{1,2\}\} \cup \{((s,\varphi_1 \wedge \varphi_2),(s,\varphi_i)) \mid i \in \{1,2\}\} \cup$
  $\{((s,\bigcirc\varphi),(s',\varphi)) \mid s' \in succ(s)\} \cup \{((s,[\varphi]_J),(s,\varphi))\} \cup$
  $\{((s,\sigma X.\varphi(X)),(s,\varphi(X))) \mid \sigma \in \{\mu,\nu\}\}$
- $\mathcal{K}((s,\bigcirc\psi),(s',\psi)) = P(s,s')$
- $\alpha(s,\psi) = \begin{cases} 0 & \text{if } \psi = p, p \in L(s) \text{ or } \psi = \neg p, p \notin L(s) \\ 1 & \text{if } \psi = p, p \notin L(s) \text{ or } \psi = \neg p, p \in L(s) \\ c(\psi) & \text{otherwise} \end{cases}$
- $O(s,[\psi]_J) = J, \quad O(v) = \bot$ for all other $v \in V$

Lemma 1 [8]. *For every Markov chain M, every location s, and every formula φ we have $\llbracket \varphi \rrbracket_M^\rho(s) = val_0(s,\varphi)$, where $val_0(s,\varphi)$ is the value of configuration (s,φ) in game $G_{M,\varphi}$.*

For a qualitative μ^p-calculus formula φ we say that M satisfies φ, denoted $M, s^{in} \models \varphi$ or $M \models \varphi$, iff $\llbracket \varphi \rrbracket_M^\rho(s^{in}) = 1$. That is, $M \models \varphi$ iff $val_{G_{M,\varphi}}(s^{in},\varphi) = 1$.

2.4 p-Automata

A p-automaton A is an alternating parity automaton that reads Markov chains as input [9]. From a state q, the p-automaton reads a location s of a Markov chain M and, according to the labelling $L(s)$, performs a transition. Since Markov chains have probabilities and the paths starting from a location s are characterised by a measure, the p-automaton A might need to mark the states by a bound J. The bound J is an element of the set $(\{\geq,>\} \times [0,1])$ and, analogously to the obligations over configurations of games, imposes a constraint over the measure of the accepted paths starting in s.

For the set of states Q, we denote by $\llbracket Q \rrbracket_>$ the set of states $q \in Q$ that are marked by a bound J defined as $\{\llbracket q \rrbracket_J \mid q \in Q, J \in (\{\geq,>\} \times [0,1])\}$. Moreover, we denote by $B^+(X)$ the set of *positive boolean formulas* over elements x in the set X, given by the following grammar:

$$\theta ::= x \mid true \mid false \mid \theta_1 \wedge \theta_2 \mid \theta_1 \vee \theta_2$$

Given a formula $\theta \in B^+(X)$ its *closure* $\mathsf{cl}(\theta)$ is the set of all sub-formulas of θ defined according to the grammar above. For a set Θ of formulas, the closure is computed as $\mathsf{cl}(\Theta) = \bigcup_{\theta \in \Theta} \mathsf{cl}(\theta)$.

Definition 2 (p-Automata). *A p-automaton A over the set AP of atomic propositions is defined by the tuple:*

$$A = (\Sigma, Q, \varphi^{in}, \delta, \Omega)$$

where $\Sigma = 2^{AP}$ is a finite input alphabet, Q is a possibly infinite set of states, $\varphi^{in} \in B^+(\llbracket Q \rrbracket_>)$ is the initial condition, $\delta : Q \times \Sigma \to B^+(Q \cup \llbracket Q \rrbracket_>)$ is the transition function, and $\Omega : Q \to [0 \ldots k]$ is the parity acceptance condition.

Acceptance Game. The set of Markov chains accepted by a p-automaton A is the language of A, denoted by $\mathcal{L}(A)$. Acceptance of a Markov chain M by A is decided through the obligation game $G_{M,A} = (V, E, (V_0, V_1, V_p), \mathcal{K}, \mathcal{G})$, where:

- $V = S \times \mathsf{cl}(\delta(Q, \Sigma))$
- $V_0 = \{(s, \theta_1 \vee \theta_2) \mid s \in S \text{ and } \theta_1 \vee \theta_2 \in \mathsf{cl}(\delta(Q, \Sigma))\}$
- $V_1 = \{(s, \theta_1 \wedge \theta_2) \mid s \in S \text{ and } \theta_1 \wedge \theta_2 \in \mathsf{cl}(\delta(Q, \Sigma))\}$
- $V_p = V \setminus (V_0 \cup V_1)$
- $E = \{((s, \theta_1 \wedge \theta_2), (s, \theta_i)) \mid i \in \{1, 2\}\} \cup$
  $\quad \{((s, \theta_1 \vee \theta_2), (s, \theta_i)) \mid i \in \{1, 2\}\} \cup$
  $\quad \{((s, q), (s', \delta(q, L(s)))) \mid s' \in succ(s)\} \cup$
  $\quad \{((s, \llbracket q \rrbracket_J), (s', \delta(q, L(s)))) \mid s' \in succ(s)\}$
- $\mathcal{K}((s, q), (s', \delta(q, L(s)))) = \mathcal{K}((s, \llbracket q \rrbracket_J), (s', \delta(q, L(s)))) = P(s, s')$
- $\mathcal{G} = \langle \alpha, O \rangle$, where $\alpha(s, q) = \alpha(s, \llbracket q \rrbracket_J) = \Omega(q)$, and $O(s, \llbracket q \rrbracket_J) = J$.

The Markov chain M is accepted if the configuration (s^{in}, φ^{in}) has value 1 in $G_{M,A}$. That is, $M \in \mathcal{L}(A)$ iff $val_{G_{M,A}}(s^{in}, \varphi^{in}) = 1$.

3 Vectorial μ^p-Calculus

We introduce the vectorial form as an alternative syntax for formulas in μ^p-calculus. This form exposes the distinction between the fixpoint operators, which appear as a prefix of the formula, and the modal formulas that they bind, allowing one to focus on the modal properties rather than on an intricate nesting of fixed-point terms. Through this syntax, the alternation depth of a sentence is easier to identify, as the number of pairwise distinct fixpoint operators within the prefix of the formula, and the most complex properties can be expressed in a succinct way.

Let F_i be the set of functions $(S \rightarrow [0,1])_i$ from locations to values in the unit interval, and φ_i be a modal μ^p-formula over the product lattice $(F_1 \times \ldots \times F_n)^m$ with range F_i, i.e. φ_i takes m vectors of n variables $\langle X_1^1, \ldots, X_n^1, \ldots, X_1^m, \ldots, X_n^m \rangle$ and evaluates to a single function in F_i. If we consider the vector φ of all modal terms $\langle \varphi_1, \ldots, \varphi_n \rangle$, each of which has range F_i, then, φ can be seen as a mapping of type $\varphi : (F_1 \times \ldots \times F_n)^m \rightarrow F_1 \times \ldots \times F_n$, whose monotonicity derives from the monotonicity of each single component and for which, by the Knaster-Tarski theorem, least and greatest fixpoints are always defined. For $m = 1$, we denote as $\mu X.\varphi$, resp. $\nu X.\varphi$, the least, resp. greatest, fixpoint of the mapping φ, as a compact notation for:

$$\sigma \begin{pmatrix} X_1 \\ \vdots \\ X_n \end{pmatrix} . \begin{pmatrix} \varphi_1(X_1, \ldots, X_n) \\ \vdots \\ \varphi_n(X_1, \ldots, X_n) \end{pmatrix} = \begin{pmatrix} f_1 \\ \vdots \\ f_n \end{pmatrix}.$$

Vectorial μ^p-calculus has the same expressive power as scalar μ^p-calculus. By the application of the Bekič principle [1], whose effect is to push the fixpoint operators inwards, every vectorial formula $\sigma X.\varphi$ can be reduced to a vector f of scalar formulas $\langle f_1, \ldots, f_n \rangle$.

Semantics. Given a Markov chain M and a valuation $\rho : (\mathcal{V}_1 \times \ldots \times \mathcal{V}_n)^m \to$
$(F_1 \times \ldots \times F_n)^m$ that associates a vector of functions with a vector of variables, the
semantics of φ is defined as $[\![\varphi]\!]^\rho_M = [\![\varphi_1]\!]^\rho_M \times \ldots \times [\![\varphi_n]\!]^\rho_M$; that is, the semantics
of a vector of μ^p-formulas is the vector of the semantics of each component.
Accordingly, the semantics of $\sigma \boldsymbol{X}.\varphi$ is the vector of semantics:

$$[\![\sigma \boldsymbol{X}.\varphi]\!]^\rho_M = [\![\sigma X_1.\varphi]\!]^\rho_M \times \ldots \times [\![\sigma X_n.\varphi]\!]^\rho_M.$$

We use the projection operator on vectors $\downarrow_i$ to select the i-th component:
$[\![\sigma \boldsymbol{X}.\varphi \downarrow_i]\!]^\rho_M = [\![\sigma X_i.\varphi]\!]^\rho_M = f_i$. The meaning of choosing a component is to
define an *entry point* to the computation performed by the vectorial formula [6].

Game Semantics. The semantics of a vectorial μ^p-calculus sentence $\sigma_1 \boldsymbol{X}_1 \ldots$
$\sigma_m \boldsymbol{X}_m.\varphi$ of depth m and height n for a Markov chain M is given by the obligation game $G_{M,\varphi}$ defined by the tuple $(V, E, (V_0, V_1, V_p), \mathcal{K}, \langle \alpha, O \rangle)$. The set of
configurations of the game is the set of pairs of a location from the Markov chain
and a subformula in $\bigcup_{i \leq n} sub(\varphi_i)$ and, since φ is a vector of modal formulas, do
not contain pairs whose second element is a fixpoint term. As a consequence of
the absence of such configurations, vertices of the form (s, X_i^j) link directly to
(s, φ_i) and carry the relevant priority j, which is the depth of the fixpoint that
the variable X_i^j binds in the vectorial formula. The remaining components are
defined exactly as in the semantics game for the scalar μ^p-calculus.

The value of the game $G_{M,\varphi}$ on the initial location s^{in} of a Markov chain
M is the vector of values: $val_{G_{M,\varphi}} = val_{G_{M,\varphi}}(s^{in}, \varphi_1) \times \ldots \times val_{G_{M,\varphi}}(s^{in}, \varphi_n)$,
where the value of the i-th component is $val_{G_{M,\varphi}}(s^{in}, \varphi_i)$.

Lemma 2. *For every Markov chain M, every location s, every μ^p-calculus vec-
torial sentence $\sigma_1 \boldsymbol{X}_1 \ldots \sigma_m \boldsymbol{X}_m.\varphi$ of height n, and index $i \leq n$ we have*

$$[\![\sigma_1 \boldsymbol{X}_1 \ldots \sigma_m \boldsymbol{X}_m.\varphi \downarrow_i]\!]^\rho_M(s) = val_{G_{M,\varphi}}(s, \varphi_i).$$

Proof. The proof is conducted as that of Theorem 6 in [8] with the exception
that configurations $(s, \sigma X.\varphi(X))$ do not appear in the game and those of the
form (s, X_i) link directly to (s, φ_i).   □

4   From μ^p-Calculus to p-Automata

We show that every qualitative μ^p-calculus formula can be translated into an
equivalent p-automaton. The translation relies on the formulas satisfying some
syntactic requirements.

Well-Formedness. The set of well-formed μ^p-calculus formulas is semantically
equivalent to the standard form of the calculus; however, it poses some constraints on the syntax allowing for the conversion into p-automata. We require
that the variables be bound exactly once and that well-formed formulas be
guarded; that is, all the occurrences of a variable must be in the scope of a

next modality, which is itself in the scope of a fixpoint operator. To this end, formulas can be re-written in guarded form, as explained in [5,16], by the iterated replacement of every open occurrence of a variable X by *false* in least fixed point formulas and by *true* in greatest fixed point formulas. Also, we consider the probabilistic quantification operator over a bound J that is restricted to the set $(\{\geq, >\} \times [0,1]) \setminus \{\geq 0, >1\}$; this restriction does not affect the expressive power of the language since properties of the form $[\cdot]_{\geq 0}$ and $[\cdot]_{>1}$ correspond to *true* and *false* statements. Moreover, we are interested in formulas where all the instances of the probabilistic quantification operator $[\cdot]_J$ are directly applied to a next $\bigcirc$. This requirement is necessary because the statements enclosed in a probabilistic operator will translate into states of the corresponding automaton that performs a transition moving to read the next locations of the model. One can achieve this form by transforming the formulas according to the equivalences stated in the lemma below.

Lemma 3. *The following μ^p-calculus formulas are semantically equivalent.*

$$[p]_J \equiv p$$
$$[\neg p]_J \equiv \neg p$$
$$[\varphi_1 \wedge \varphi_2]_J \equiv [\varphi_1]_J \wedge [\varphi_2]_J$$
$$[\varphi_1 \vee \varphi_2]_J \equiv [\varphi_1]_J \vee [\varphi_2]_J$$
$$[\sigma X.\varphi(X)]_J \equiv [\varphi(\sigma X.\varphi(X))]_J$$

Proof. The proof arises from the semantics of the μ^p-calculus and the fixed point axioms. $\qquad\square$

Translation. Let φ be a qualitative well-formed μ^p-calculus formula over the set AP of atomic propositions. The p-automaton A_φ is the tuple $(2^{AP}, Q, \delta, \varphi^{in}, \Omega)$, where 2^{AP} is the alphabet, Q is the set of states $\{\bot, \top\} \cup \{p, \neg p, (\bigcirc \psi, c) \mid$ for all $p, \neg p, \bigcirc \psi \in sub(\varphi)$ and $c \in [0 \ldots 2ad(\varphi) - 1]\}$, the transition function δ (and the auxiliary function δ_ϵ) is defined by the rules in Fig. 1.

$$\delta(p, a) = \begin{cases} \top & \text{if } p \in a \\ \bot & \text{if } p \notin a \end{cases} \qquad\qquad \delta_\epsilon(p, c) = p$$

$$\delta_\epsilon(\neg p, c) = \neg p$$

$$\delta(\neg p, a) = \begin{cases} \top & \text{if } p \notin a \\ \bot & \text{if } p \in a \end{cases} \qquad \delta_\epsilon(\psi_1 \vee \psi_2, c) = \delta_\epsilon(\psi_1, c) \vee \delta_\epsilon(\psi_2, c)$$

$$\delta_\epsilon(\psi_1 \wedge \psi_2, c) = \delta_\epsilon(\psi_1, c) \wedge \delta_\epsilon(\psi_2, c)$$

$$\delta(\top, a) = \top \qquad\qquad \delta_\epsilon(\sigma X.\varphi(X), c) = \delta_\epsilon(\varphi(X), c)$$

$$\delta(\bot, a) = \bot \qquad\qquad \delta_\epsilon(X, c) = \delta_\epsilon(\varphi(X), c(X))$$

$$\delta((\bigcirc \psi, c), a) = \delta_\epsilon(\psi, c) \qquad\qquad \delta_\epsilon(\bigcirc \psi, c) = (\bigcirc \psi, c)$$

$$\delta_\epsilon([\bigcirc \psi]_J, c) = [(\bigcirc \psi, c)]_J$$

Fig. 1. Transition of A_φ.

The initial condition φ^{in} is the expression $\delta_\epsilon(\varphi, c(\varphi))$; the priority Ω is $\Omega(\bot) = 1$, $\Omega(\top) = 0$, $\Omega(\bigcirc\psi, c) = c$, and maximum colour otherwise.

Transitions of A_φ always consume the input label a of a location in a Markov chain and move forward to its successors. The computation starts from the states within the initial condition φ^{in}. From a state p or $\neg p$, the p-automaton reads the current label a and moves to one of the special states $\top$ or $\bot$ defining an infinite computation that is accepting or rejecting, respectively. When in a state $(\bigcirc\psi, c)$ reading a label a, the p-automaton moves to a new set of states determined by unfolding the formula ψ through the epsilon transition function δ_ϵ. The outcome of δ_ϵ, as well as of δ, is a positive boolean formula over states q and bounded states $[\![q]\!]_J$ that represents the requirement from the system. States within such formula are evaluated over the successor locations in M. Acceptance of a Markov chain M by the p-automaton A_φ is decided by the *acceptance game* G_{M,A_φ}: if the value in such game of the initial configuration is 1 M is accepted, otherwise, it is rejected.

The following theorem states the correctness of the translation from μ^p-calculus into p-automata.

Theorem 1. *Let φ be a well-formed μ^p-calculus formula and A_φ the automaton resulting from its translation. Then, φ and A_φ are equivalent: the set of Markov chains that satisfy the formula φ corresponds to the language $\mathcal{L}(A_\varphi)$ recognised by the p-automaton A_φ. That is, $M \models \varphi$ iff $M \in \mathcal{L}(A_\varphi)$.*

The proof is conducted by showing that for all Markov chains M the *acceptance game* G_{M,A_φ} simulates the *semantics game* $G_{M,\varphi}$. In particular, there is a mapping between prefixes of paths in the two games, within which probabilities, obligations, and infinite winning sets are preserved. Therefore, the acceptance game has the same value as that of the semantics game, leading the p-automaton A_φ to accept all the Markov chains that satisfy the formula φ.

5   From p-Automata to μ^p-Calculus

We show that every p-automaton can be translated into an equivalent μ^p-calculus formula. Transitions of p-automata define an infinite computation tree whose nodes are states marked by priorities. The sequence of such priorities within the paths of the tree determines whether the computation is accepted or not: infinitely many visits to a minimal even priority mean acceptance, whereas passing infinitely often through a minimal odd priority causes rejection. All these elements have their analogue in μ^p-calculus: transitions and modal formulas, applying a transition from a state and passing through variables, odd/even priorities and least/greatest fixpoints, and levels of priorities and nesting of fixpoint formulas. We exploit this analogy in the conversion from p-automata to μ^p-calculus, using the syntax that most emphasises the role of each component, the vectorial form.

Translation. Let A be a p-automaton over the set AP of atomic propositions defined by the tuple $(2^{AP}, Q, \delta, \varphi^{in}, \Omega)$, with n the number of states of the automaton. Let $i_1, \ldots, i_m$ be the ordered chain of increasing priorities in the set $\bigcup_{q \in Q} \Omega(q)$. For each index $j \leq m$ we introduce a vector $\boldsymbol{X}_{i_j}$ of $n+1$ fresh variables. The first variable of each j-th vector is a dummy variable that refers to the initial condition of the automaton, and we indicate it as $X_{i_j}^{in}$. The remaining n variables of each j-th vector bind the n formulas corresponding to the transitions that the p-automaton A performs from each of its n states; we write such variables as $X_{i_j}^1, \ldots, X_{i_j}^n$. Accounting for the initial condition of the automaton as the first component of these vectors allows one to retrieve the semantics of the resulting formula as the semantics of its first element. As a consequence, the ordering of the other n components is not relevant.

In order to turn states into variables we use a function t that takes a formula in $B^+(Q \cup [\![Q]\!]_>)$ and returns a formula over variables and bounded variables:

$$t(\theta_1 \vee \theta_2) = t(\theta_1) \vee t(\theta_2)$$
$$t(\theta_1 \wedge \theta_2) = t(\theta_1) \wedge t(\theta_2)$$
$$t([\![q]\!]_J) = [X_{\Omega(q)}^q]_J$$
$$t(q) = X_{\Omega(q)}^q$$

We employ this function in the definition of the vector $\boldsymbol{\varphi}$ of modal μ^p-formulas. The first component of $\boldsymbol{\varphi}$ is $t(\varphi^{in})$, the other n components are denoted by φ^k for $k \leq n$ and are specified by the following modal formula

$$\varphi^k = \bigvee_{a \in 2^{AP}} \left(\bigcirc t\left(\delta\left(q^k, a\right)\right) \wedge \bigwedge_{p \in a} p \wedge \bigwedge_{p \notin a} \neg p \right).$$

Finally, the vectorial μ^p-calculus formula $\boldsymbol{\varphi}_A$ is defined as the prefix chain of ordered fixpoints and vectors enclosing $\boldsymbol{\varphi}$, where $\sigma_{i_j} = \mu$ if i_j is odd or $\sigma_{i_j} = \nu$ if i_j is even:

$$\boldsymbol{\varphi}_A = \sigma_{i_1} \begin{pmatrix} X_{i_1}^{in} \\ X_{i_1}^1 \\ \vdots \\ X_{i_1}^n \end{pmatrix} \ldots \sigma_{i_m} \begin{pmatrix} X_{i_m}^{in} \\ X_{i_m}^1 \\ \vdots \\ X_{i_m}^n \end{pmatrix} \cdot \begin{pmatrix} t\left(\varphi^{in}\right) \\ \varphi^1 \\ \vdots \\ \varphi^n \end{pmatrix}.$$

The semantics of the vectorial formula $\boldsymbol{\varphi}_A$ for a Markov chain M and a valuation ρ is the semantics of its first component over the initial location s^{in} of M and it is equivalent to the value of the configuration $(s^{in}, t(\varphi^{in}))$ in the semantics game G_{M, φ_A}. That is, $[\![\boldsymbol{\varphi}_A \downarrow_1]\!]_M^\rho (s^{in}) = val_{G_{M, \varphi_A}} (s^{in}, t(\varphi^{in}))$.

It is worth noticing that only a maximum of n out of $m \times (n+1)$ variables are bound within the formula $\boldsymbol{\varphi}_A$. Therefore, $\boldsymbol{\varphi}_A$ can be seen as a system of $n+1$ equations in n variables that can be reduced by substitution and Gauss elimination techniques to a single scalar μ^p-calculus sentence (see [22]). In particular, it is sufficient to derive a solution, or expression, for each of the n variables and by syntactical substitution embed such expressions in $t(\varphi^{in})$. However, we are interested in giving a characterization in terms of semantics game G_{M,φ_A}, in which the effect of the syntactical substitution of variables is handled by the edges connecting configurations (s, X^k) to (s, φ^k).

Theorem 2. *Let A be a p-automaton over the set AP of atomic propositions and φ_A the vectorial μ^p-calculus formula resulting from its conversion. Then, A and φ_A are equivalent: the set of Markov chains that constitute the language $\mathcal{L}(A)$ recognised by the p-automaton A coincides with the set of Markov chains that satisfy the vectorial formula φ_A. That is, $M \in \mathcal{L}(A)$ iff $M \models \varphi_A$.*

Similarly to the case of the inverse translation, the proof shows that the semantics game G_{M,φ_A} for the vectorial formula φ_A simulates the acceptance game $G_{M,A}$ for the original p-automaton A. As a result, the two games have the same value and, therefore, the Markov chains that satisfy the formula φ_A are exactly those that are accepted by A.

6   Conclusion

The aim of this paper was to investigate the connection between μ^p-calculus and p-automata and to assess their equivalence in expressive power. We introduced the vectorial syntax and focused on its semantics in terms of obligation games. We presented the notion of well-formed formulas as a necessary preliminary step for their translation into p-automata. We showed that for every well-formed μ^p-calculus sentence there exists an equivalent p-automaton that recognises exactly all the Markov chains that model the formula. Conversely, we proved that for every p-automaton there is an equivalent μ^p-formula that is satisfied by the same Markov chains that form the language of the p-automaton.

Throughout this work, obligation games have played a key linking role in defining the semantics of the structures resulting from the conversions and, therefore, proving the correctness of our claims.

References

1. Arnold, A., Niwiński, D.: Rudiments of μ-calculus. Studies in Logic and the Foundations of Mathematics, vol. 146. Elsevier, New York (2001)
2. Baier, C., Katoen, J.P.: Principles of Model Checking. The MIT Press, Cambridge (2008)
3. Blackburn, P., Benthem, J., Wolter, F.: Handbook of Modal Logic. Studies in Logic and Practical Reasoning. Elsevier, New York (2007)
4. Bradfield, J., Stirling, C.: Modal μ-calculi. In: Handbook of Modal Logic, pp. 721–756. Elsevier (2007)
5. Bradfield, J., Walukiewicz, I.: The μ-calculus and model-checking. In: Handbook of Model Checking. Springer (2015)
6. Bruse, F., Friedmann, O., Lange, M.: On guarded transformation in the modal μ-calculus. Logic J. IGPL **23**(2), 194–216 (2015)

7. Cleaveland, R., Purushothaman Iyer, S., Narasimha, M.: Probabilistic temporal logics via the modal μ-calculus. Theor. Comput. Sci. **342**(2–3), 316–350 (2005)
8. Castro, P., Kilmurray, C., Piterman, N.: Tractable probabilistic μ-calculus that expresses probabilistic temporal logics. In: 32nd Symposium on Theoretical Aspects of Computer Science. Schloss Dagstuhl (2015)
9. Chatterjee, K., Piterman, N.: Obligation Blackwell games and p-Automata. CoRR, abs/1206.5174 (2013)
10. Emerson, E.A., Jutla S.: Tree automata, μ-calculus and determinacy. In: Proceedings of 32nd Annual Symposium on Foundations of Computer Science, pp. 368–377. IEEE (1991)
11. Emerson, E.A., Lei, C.-L.: Efficient model checking in fragments of the propositional μ-calculus. In: Proceedings of the First Annual IEEE Symposium on Logic in Computer Science, LICS, pp. 267–278 (1986)
12. Grädel, E., Thomas, W., Wilke, T.: Automata Logics, and Infinite Games: A Guide to Current Research. Springer, New York (2002)
13. Huth, M., Kwiatkowska, M.: Quantitative analysis and model checking. In: Proceedings of 12th Annual IEEE Symposium on Logic in Computer Science, Warsaw, Poland, 29 June– 2 July, pp. 111–122 (1997)
14. Janin, D., Walukiewicz, I.: Automata for the modal μ-calculus and related results. Mathematical Foundations of Computer Science, pp. 552–562 (1995)
15. Kozen, D.: Results on the propositional μ-calculus. Theor. Comput. Sci. **27**(3), 333–354 (1983)
16. Kupferman, O., Vardi, M.Y., Wolper, P.: An automata-theoretic approach to branching-time model checking. J. ACM **47**(2), 312–360 (2000)
17. Mio, M.: Game semantics for probabilistic modal μ-calculi. Ph.D. thesis, University of Edinburgh (2012)
18. Mio, M.: Probabilistic modal μ-calculus with independent product. Logical Methods Comput. Sci. **8**(4), 1–36 (2012)
19. Mio, M., Simpson, A.K.: Lukasiewicz μ-calculus. CoRR, abs/1510.00797 (2015)
20. Niwiński, D.: Fixed points vs. infinite generation. In: Proceedings of the Third Annual IEEE Symposium on Logic in Computer Science, LICS, pp. 402–409 (1988)
21. Niwiński, D.: Fixed point characterization of infinite behavior of finite-state systems. Theor. Comput. Sci. **189**(1–2), 1–69 (1997)
22. Schneider, K.: Verification of Reactive Systems: Formal Methods and Algorithms. Texts in Theoretical Computer Science. Springer, Heidelberg (2004)
23. Wilke, T.: Alternating tree automata, parity games, and modal μ-calculus. Bull. Soc. Math. Belg. **8**(2), 359–391 (2001)

Complexity of Bifix-Free Regular Languages

Robert Ferens and Marek Szykuła[✉]

Institute of Computer Science, University of Wrocław, Wrocław, Poland
robert.ferens@interia.pl, msz@cs.uni.wroc.pl

Abstract. We study descriptive complexity properties of the class of regular bifix-free languages, which is the intersection of prefix-free and suffix-free regular languages. We show that there exist universal bifix-free languages that meet all the bounds for the state complexity of basic operations (Boolean operations, product, star, and reversal). This is in contrast with suffix-free languages, where it is known that there does not exist such languages. Then we present a stream of bifix-free languages that is most complex in terms of all basic operations, syntactic complexity, and the number of atoms and their complexities, which requires a superexponential alphabet. We also complete the previous results by characterizing state complexity of product, star, and reversal, and establishing tight upper bounds for atom complexities of bifix-free languages. Moreover, we consider the problem of the minimal size of an alphabet required to meet the bounds, and the problem of attainable values of state complexities (magic numbers).

Keywords: Bifix-free · Most complex · Prefix-free · State complexity · Suffix-free · Transition semigroup

1 Introduction

A language is *prefix-free* or *suffix-free* if no word in the language is a proper prefix or suffix, respectively, of another word from the language. If a language is prefix-free and suffix-free then it is *bifix-free*. Languages with these properties have been studied extensively. They form important classes of codes, whose applications can be found in such fields as cryptography, data compression, information transmission, and error correction methods. In particular, *prefix* and *suffix codes* are prefix-free and suffix-free languages, respectively, while bifix-free languages can serve as both kinds of codes. For a survey about codes see [1,19]. Moreover, they are special cases of *convex languages* (see e.g. [7] for the related algorithmic problems). Here we are interested how the descriptive complexity properties of prefix-free and suffix-free languages are shared in their common subclass.

There are three natural measures of complexity of a regular language that are related to the Myhill (Myhill-Nerode) congruence on words. The usual *state*

This work was supported in part by the National Science Centre, Poland under project number 2014/15/B/ST6/00615.

A. Carayol and C. Nicaud (Eds.): CIAA 2017, LNCS 10329, pp. 76–88, 2017.
DOI: 10.1007/978-3-319-60134-2_7

complexity or *quotient complexity* is the number of states in a minimal DFA recognizing the language. Therefore, state complexity measures how much memory we need to store the language in the form of a DFA, or how much time we need to perform an operation that depends on the size of the DFA. Therefore, we are interested in finding upper bounds for complexities of the resulting languages obtained as a result of some operation (e.g. union, intersection, product, or reversal). *Syntactic complexity* measures the number of transformations in the transition semigroup or, equivalently, the number of classes of words that act differently on the states [21]; this provides a natural bound on the time and space complexity of algorithms working on the transition semigroup (for example, a simple algorithm checking whether a language is *star-free* just enumerates all transformations and verifies whether no one of them contains a non-trivial cycle [20]). The third measure is called the *complexity of atoms* [11], which is the number and state complexities of the languages of words that distinguish exactly the same subset of states (quotients).

Most complex languages and universal witnesses were proposed by Brzozowski in [3]. The point here is that, it is more suitable to have a single witness that is most complex in the given subclass of regular languages, instead of having separate witnesses meeting the upper bound for each particular measure and operation. Besides theoretical aspects, this concept has also a practical motivation: To test efficiency of various algorithms or systems operating on automata (e.g. computational package GAP [15]), it is natural to use worst-case examples, that is, languages with maximal complexities. Therefore, it is preferred to have just one universal most complex example than a set of separate examples for every particular case. Of course, it is also better to use a smallest possible alphabet.

It may be surprising that such a single witness exists for most of the natural subclasses of regular languages: the class of all regular languages [3], right-, left-, and two-sided ideals [4], and prefix-convex languages [8]. However, there does not exist a single witness for the class of suffix-free languages [10], where two different witnesses must be used.

In this paper we continue the studies concerning the class of regular bifix-free languages [5,6,23]. In [5] the tight bound on the state complexity of basic operations on bifix-free languages were established; however, the witnesses were different for particular cases. The syntactic complexity of bifix-free languages was first studied in [6], where a lower bound was established, and then the formula was shown to be an upper bound in [23].

Our main contributions are as follows:

1. We show a single ternary witness of bifix-free languages that meets the upper bounds for all basic operations. This is in contrast with the class of suffix-free languages, where such most complex languages do not exist.
2. We show that there exist most complex languages in terms of state complexity of all basic operations, syntactic complexity, and number of atoms and their complexities. It uses a superexponential alphabet, which cannot be reduced.

3. We prove a tight upper bound on the number of atoms and the quotient complexities of atoms of bifix-free languages.
4. We provide a complete characterization of state complexity for product and star, and show the exact ranges for the possible state complexities for product, star, and reversal of bifix-free languages.
5. We prove that at least a ternary alphabet must be used to meet the bound for reversal, and at an $(n+1)$-ary alphabet must be used to meet the bounds for atom complexities.

The full version of this paper is available at [14].

2   Preliminaries

2.1   Regular Languages and Complexities

Let Σ be a non-empty finite alphabet. In this paper we deal with regular languages $L \subseteq \Sigma^*$. For a word $w \in L$, the *(left) quotient* of L is the set $\{u \mid wu \in L\}$, which is also denoted by $L.w$. Left quotients are related to the Myhill-Nerode congruence on words, where two words $u, v \in \Sigma^*$ are equivalent if for every $x \in \Sigma^*$, we have $ux \in L$ if and only if $vx \in L$. Thus the number of quotients is the number of equivalence classes in this relation. The number of quotients of L is the *quotient complexity* $\kappa(L)$ of this language [2]. A language is regular if it has a finite number of quotients.

Let $L, K \subseteq \Sigma^*$ be regular languages over the same alphabet Σ. By *Boolean operations* on these languages we mean *union* $L \cup K$, *intersection* $L \cap K$, *difference* $L \setminus K$, and *symmetric difference* $L \oplus K$. The reverse language L^R of L is the language $\{a_k \ldots a_1 \mid a_1 \ldots a_k \in L, a_1, \ldots, a_k \in \Sigma\}$. By the *basic operations* on regular languages we mean the Boolean operations, the product (concatenation), the star, and the reversal operation. By the *complexity* of an operation we mean the maximum possible quotient complexity of the resulted language, given as a function of the quotient complexities of the operands.

The *syntactic complexity* $\sigma(L)$ of L is the number of equivalence classes of the Myhill equivalence relation on Σ^+, where two words $u, v \in \Sigma^+$ are equivalent if for any words $x, y \in \Sigma^*$, we have $xuy \in L$ if and only if $xvy \in L$.

The third measure of complexity of a regular language L is the number and quotient complexities of *atoms* [11]. Atoms arise from the left congruence of words refined by Myhill equivalence relation: two words $u, v \in \Sigma^*$ are equivalent if for any word $x \in \Sigma^*$, we have $xu \in L$ if and only if $xv \in L$ [16]. Thus u and v are equivalent if they belong exactly to the same left quotients of L. An equivalence class of this relation is an *atom* [11] of L. It is known that (see [11]) an atom is a non-empty intersection of quotients and their complements, and the quotients of a language are unions of its atoms. Therefore, we can write A_S for an atom, where S is the set of quotients of L; then A_S is the intersection of the quotients of L from S together with the complements of the quotients of L outside S.

2.2 Finite Automata and Transformations

A *deterministic finite automaton* (*DFA*) is a tuple $\mathcal{D} = (Q, \Sigma, \delta, q_0, F)$, where Q is a finite non-empty set of *states*, Σ is a finite non-empty *alphabet*, $\delta \colon Q \times \Sigma \to Q$ is the *transition function*, $q_0 \subset Q$ is the *initial* state, and $F \subseteq Q$ is the set of *final* states. We extend δ to a function $\delta \colon Q \times \Sigma^* \to Q$ as usual: for $q \in Q$, $w \in \Sigma^*$, and $a \in \Sigma$, we have $\delta(q, \varepsilon) = q$ and $\delta(q, wa) = \delta(\delta(q, w), a)$, where ε denotes the empty word.

A state $q \in Q$ is *reachable* if there exists a word $w \in \Sigma^*$ such that $\delta(q_0, w) = q$. Two states $p, q \in Q$ are *distinguishable* if there exists a word $w \in \Sigma^*$ such that either $\delta(p, w) \in F$ and $\delta(q, w) \notin F$ or $\delta(p, w) \notin F$ and $\delta(q, w) \in F$.

A DFA is *minimal* if there is no DFA with a smaller number of states that recognizes the same language. It is well known that this is equivalent to that every state is reachable and every pair of distinct states is distinguishable. Given a regular language L, all its minimal DFAs are isomorphic, and their number of states is equal to the number of left quotients $\kappa(L)$ (see e.g. [2]). Hence, the quotient complexity $\kappa(L)$ is also called the *state complexity* of L. If a DFA is minimal then every state q corresponds to a quotient of the language, which is the set of words w such that $\delta(q, w) \in F$. We denote this quotient by K_q. We also write A_S, where S is a subset of states, for

$$A_S = \bigcap_{q \in S} K_q \cap \bigcap_{q \in \overline{S}} \overline{K_q},$$

which is an atom if A_S is non-empty.

A state q is *empty* if $K_q = \emptyset$.

Throughout the paper, by $\mathcal{D}_n$ we denote a DFA with n states, and without loss of generality we always assume that its set of states $Q = \{0, \dots, n-1\}$ and that the initial state is 0.

In any DFA $\mathcal{D}_n$, every letter $a \in \Sigma$ induces a transformation δ_a on the set Q of n states. By $\mathcal{T}_n$ we denote the set of all n^n transformations of Q; then $\mathcal{T}_n$ is a monoid under composition. For two transformations t_1, t_2 of Q, we denote its composition as $t_1 t_2$. The transformation induced by a word $w \in \Sigma^*$ is denoted by δ_w. The *image* of $q \in Q$ under a transformation δ_w is denoted by $q\delta_w$, and the *image* of a subset $S \subseteq Q$ is $S\delta_w = \{q\delta_w \mid q \in S\}$. The *preimage* of a subset $S \subset Q$ under a transformation δ_w^{-1} is $S\delta_w^{-1} = \{q \in Q \mid q\delta_w \in S\}$. Note that if $w = a_1 \dots a_k$, then $\delta_{a_1 \dots a_k}^{-1} = \delta_{a_k}^{-1} \dots \delta_{a_1}^{-1}$. The *identity transformation* is denoted by $\mathbf{1}$, which is also the same as δ_ε, and we have $q\mathbf{1} = q$ for all $q \in Q$.

The *transition semigroup* $T(n)$ of $\mathcal{D}_n$ is the semigroup of all transformations generated by the transformations induced by Σ. Since the transition semigroup of a minimal DFA of a language L is isomorphic to the syntactic semigroup of L [21], syntactic complexity $\sigma(L)$ is equal to the cardinality $|T(n)|$ of the transition semigroup $T(n)$.

Since a transformation t of Q can be viewed as a directed graph with regular out-degree equal to 1 and possibly with loops, we transfer well known graph terminology to transformations: The *in-degree* of a state $q \in Q$ is the cardinality

$|\{p \in Q \mid pt = q\}|$. A *cycle* in t is a sequence of states $q_1, \ldots, q_k$ for $k \geq 2$ such that $q_i t = q_{i+1}$ for $i = 1, \ldots, k - 1$, and $q_k t = q_1$. A *fixed point* in t is a state q such that $qt = q$; we therefore do not call fixed points cycles.

A transformation that maps a subset S to a state q and fixes all the other states is denoted by $(S \to q)$. If S is a singleton $\{p\}$ then we write shortly $(p \to q)$. A transformation that acts cyclically on states $q_1, \ldots, q_k$ for $k \geq 2$, that is, $q_1 t = q_2$, $q_2 t = q_3$, $\ldots$, $q_k t = q_1$, and fixes all the other states is denoted by $(q_1, \ldots, q_k)$.

A *nondeterministic finite automaton* (*NFA*) is a tuple $\mathcal{N} = (Q, \Sigma, \delta, I, F)$, where Q, Σ, and F are defined as in a DFA, I is the set of *initial states*, and $\delta \colon Q \times \Sigma \cup \{\varepsilon\} \to 2^Q$ is the transition function.

2.3   Most Complex Languages

A *stream* is a sequence $(L_k, L_{k+1}, \ldots)$ of regular languages in some class, where n is the state complexity of L_n. A *dialect* L'_n of a language L_n is a language that differs only slightly from L_n. There are various types of dialects, depending what changes are allowed. A *permutational dialect* (or *permutationally equivalent dialect*) is a language in which letters may be permuted or deleted. Let $\pi \colon \Sigma \to \Sigma$ be a partial permutation. If $L_n(a_1, \ldots, a_k)$ is a language over the alphabet $\Sigma = \{a_1, \ldots, a_k\}$, then we write $L_n(\pi(a_1), \ldots, \pi(a_k))$ for a language in which a letter a_i is replaced by $\pi(a_i)$. In the case a letter a_i is removed, so not defined by $\pi(a_i)$, we write $\pi(a_i) = \_$. For example, if $L = \{a, ab, abc\}$, then $L(b, a, \_) = \{b, ba\}$.

A stream is *most complex* in its class if all the languages and all pairs of the languages from the stream together with the dialects of these languages meet all the bounds for the state complexities of basic operations, the syntactic complexity, the number and the complexities of atoms. Note that binary operations were defined for languages with the same alphabets. Therefore, if the alphabet is not constant in the stream, to meet the bounds for binary Boolean operations, for every pair of languages we must use their dialects that restrict the alphabet to be the same.

Sometimes we restrict only to some of these measures. In some cases, this allows us to provide an essentially simpler stream over a smaller alphabet when we are interested only in those measures. In particular, if a syntactic complexity requires a large alphabet and for basic operations it is enough to use a constant number of letters, it is desirable to provide a separate stream which is most complex just for basic operations.

Dialects are necessary for most complex streams of languages, since otherwise they would not be able to meet upper bounds in most classes. In particular, since $L_n \cup L_n = L_n$, the state complexity of union would be at most n in this case. Other kinds of dialects are possible (e.g. [8]), though permutational dialects are the most restricted.

2.4   Bifix-Free Languages

A language L is *prefix-free* if there are no words $u, v \in \Sigma^+$ such that $uv \in L$ and $u \in L$. A language L is *suffix-free* if there are no words $u, v \in \Sigma^+$ such that $uv \subset L$ and $v \in L$. A language is *bifix-free* if it is both prefix-free and suffix-free.

The following properties of minimal DFAs recognizing prefix-free, suffix-free, and bifix-free languages, adapted to our terminology, are well known (see e.g. [5, 6, 12, 23]):

Lemma 1. *Let $\mathcal{D}_n(Q, \Sigma, \delta, 0, F)$ be a minimal DFA recognizing a non-empty language L. Then L is bifix-free if and only if:*

1. *There is an empty state, which is $n - 1$ by convention (that is, state $n - 1$ is not final and $(n - 1)\delta_a = n - 1$ for all $a \in \Sigma$).*
2. *There exists exactly one final state, which is $n - 2$ by convention, and its quotient is $\{\varepsilon\}$; thus $(n - 2)\delta_a = n - 1$ for all $a \in \Sigma$.*
3. *For $u \in \Sigma^+$ and $q \in Q \setminus \{0\}$, if $q\delta_u \neq n - 1$, then $0\delta_u \neq q\delta_u$.*

The conditions (1) and (2) are sufficient and necessary for a prefix-free language, and the conditions (1) and (3) are sufficient and necessary for a suffix-free language.

It follows that a minimal DFA recognizing a non-empty bifix-free language must have at least $n \geq 3$ states.

Since states 0, $n - 2$, and $n - 1$ are special in the case of DFAs of bifix-free languages, we denote the remaining "middle" states by $Q_M = \{1, \ldots, n - 3\}$. Condition 3 implies that suffix-free and so bifix-free are *non-returning* (see [13]), that is, there is no non-empty word $w \in \Sigma^+$ such that $L.w = L$.

Note that in the case of unary languages, there is exactly one bifix-free language for every state complexity $n \geq 3$, which is $\{a^{n-2}\}$. The classes of unary prefix-free, unary suffix-free, and unary bifix-free languages coincide and we refer to it as *unary free* languages.

The state complexity of basic operations on bifix-free languages was studied in [5], where different witness languages were shown for particular operations.

The syntactic complexity of bifix-free languages was shown to be $(n-1)^{n-3} + (n-2)^{n-3} + (n-3)2^{n-3}$ for $n \geq 6$ [23]. Moreover, the transition semigroup of a minimal DFA $\mathcal{D}_n$ of a witness language meeting the bound must be $\mathbf{W}_{\mathrm{bf}}^{\geq 6}(n)$, which is a transition semigroup containing three types of transformations and can be defined as follows:

Definition 2 (The Largest Bifix-Free Semigroup)

$\mathbf{W}_{\mathrm{bf}}^{\geq 6}(n) = \{t \in T(n) \mid$

(type 1) $\{0, n - 2, n - 1\}t = \{n - 1\}$ *and* $Q_M t \subset Q_M \cup \{n - 2, n - 1\}$ *, or*

(type 2) $0t = n - 2$ *and* $\{n - 2, n - 1\}t = \{n - 1\}$ *and* $Q_M t \subset Q_M \cup \{n - 1\}$ *, or*

(type 3) $0t \in Q_M$ *and* $\{n - 2, n - 1\}t = \{n - 1\}$ *and* $Q_M t \subseteq \{n - 2, n - 1\}$ $\}$.

Following [23], we say that an unordered pair $\{p, q\}$ of distinct states from Q_M is *colliding* in $T(n)$ if there is a transformation $t \in T(n)$ such that $0t = p$ and $rt = q$ for some $r \in Q_M$. A pair of states is *focused* by a transformation $u \in T(n)$ if u maps both states of the pair to a single state $r \in Q_M \cup \{n - 2\}$. It is known that ([23]) in semigroup $\mathbf{W}_{\text{bf}}^{\geq 6}(n)$ there are no colliding pairs and every possible pair of states is focused by some transformation, and it is the unique maximal transition semigroup of a minimal DFA of a bifix-free language with this property.

3   Complexity of Bifix-Free Languages

In this section we summarize and complete known results concerning state complexity of bifix-free regular languages. We start from the obvious upper bound for the maximal complexity of quotients.

Proposition 3. *Let L be a bifix-free language with state complexity n. Each (left) quotient of L has state complexity at most $n - 1$, except L, $\{\varepsilon\}$, and $\emptyset$, which always have state complexities n, 2, and 1, respectively.*

In [5] it was shown that $mn - (m + n)$ (for $m, n \geq 4$) is a tight upper bound for the state complexity of union and symmetric difference of bifix-free languages, and that to meet this bound a ternary alphabet is required. It was also shown there that $mn - 3(m + n - 4)$ and $mn - (2m + 3n - 9)$ (for $m, n \geq 4$) are tight upper bounds for intersection and difference, respectively, and that a binary alphabet is sufficient to meet these bounds. Since the tight bound is smaller for unary free languages, the size of the alphabet cannot be reduced.

It may be interesting to observe that the alphabet must be essentially larger to meet the bounds in the case when $m = 3$.

Remark 4. For $n \geq 3$, to meet the bound $mn - (m + n)$ for union or symmetric difference with minimal DFAs $\mathcal{D}_3'$ and $\mathcal{D}_n$ at least $n - 2$ letters are required.

The tight upper bound for the product is $m + n - 2$, which is met by unary free languages. We show that there is no other possibility for the product of bifix-free languages, that is, $L_m L_n$ has always state complexity $m + n - 2$.

Theorem 5. *For $m \geq 3$, $n \geq 3$, for every bifix-free languages L_m' and L_n, the product $L_m' L_n$ meets the bound $m + n - 2$.*

The tight upper bound for the star is $n - 1$, which is met by binary bifix-free languages [5]. Here we provide a complete characterization for the state complexity of L_n^* and show that there are exactly two possibilities for its state complexity: $n - 1$ and $n - 2$. This may be compared with prefix-free languages, where there are exactly three possibilities for the state complexity L_n^*: n, $n - 1$, and $n - 2$ [18].

Theorem 6. *Let $n \geq 3$ and let $\mathcal{D}_n = (Q, \Sigma, \delta, \{n-2\}, 0)$ be a minimal DFA of a bifix-free language L_n. If the transformation of some $a \in \Sigma$ maps some state from $\{0, \ldots, n-3\}$ to $n-1$, then L_n^* has state complexity $n-1$. Otherwise it has state complexity $n-2$.*

For the state complexity of the reversal of a bifix-free language, it was shown in [5, Theorem 6] that for $n \geq 3$ the tight upper bound is $2^{n-3} + 2$, and that a ternary alphabet is sufficient. We show that the alphabet size cannot be reduced, and characterize the transition semigroup of the DFAs of witness languages.

Theorem 7. *For $n \geq 6$, to meet the bound $2^{n-3} + 2$ for reversal, a witness language must have at least three letters. Moreover, for $n \geq 5$ the transition semigroup $T(n)$ of a minimal DFA $\mathcal{D}_n(Q, \Sigma, \delta, 0, \{n-2\})$ accepting a witness language must be a subsemigroup of $\mathbf{W}_{\mathrm{bf}}^{\geq 6}(n)$.*

It is known that in the case of the class of all regular languages the resulting language of the reversal operation can have any state complexity in the range of integers $[\log_2 n, 2^n]$ [17,22], thus there are no gaps (*magic numbers*) in the interval of possible state complexities. The next theorem states that the situation is similar for the case of bifix-free languages.

Theorem 8. *If L_n is a bifix-free language with state complexity $n \geq 3$, then the state complexity of L_n^R is in $[3 + \log_2(n-2), 2 + 2^{n-3}]$. Moreover, all values in this range are attainable by L_n^R for some bifix-free language L_n, whose minimal DFA has transition semigroup that is a subsemigroup of $\mathbf{W}_{\mathrm{bf}}^{\geq 6}(n)$.*

3.1 Atom Complexities

Here we prove tight upper bounds on the number and the state complexities of atoms of a bifix-free language, and that an alphabet of size $n+1$ is sufficient and necessary to meet the bounds.

Theorem 9. *Suppose that L_n is a bifix-free language recognized by a minimal DFA $\mathcal{D}_n(Q, \Sigma, \delta, 0, \{n-2\})$. Then there are at most $2^{n-3} + 2$ atoms of L_n and the quotient complexity of $\kappa(A_S)$ of atom A_S satisfies:*

$$\kappa(A_S) \begin{cases} \leq 2^{n-2} + 1 & \text{if } S = \emptyset; \\ = n & \text{if } S = \{0\}; \\ = 2 & \text{if } S = \{n-2\}; \\ \leq 3 + \sum_{x=1}^{|S|} \sum_{y=0}^{n-3-|S|} \binom{n-3}{x} \binom{n-3-x}{y} & \text{if } \emptyset \neq S \subseteq \{1, \ldots, n-3\}. \end{cases}$$

Theorem 10. *Let $n \geq 6$, and let L_n be the language recognized by the DFA $\mathcal{D}(Q, \Sigma, \delta, 0, \{n-2\})$, where $\Sigma = \{a, b, c, d, e_1 \ldots, e_{n-3}\}$ and δ is defined as follows: $\delta_a \colon (0 \to 1)((Q \setminus \{0\}) \to n-1)$, $\delta_b \colon (\{0, n-2\} \to n-1)(1,2)$, $\delta_c \colon (\{0, n-2\} \to n-1)(1, \ldots, n-3)$, $\delta_d \colon (\{0, n-2\} \to n-1)(2 \to 1)$, $\delta_{e_q} \colon (\{0, n-2\} \to n-1)(q \to n-2)$ for $q \in Q_M$. Then $\mathcal{D}$ is minimal, L_n is bifix-free and it meets the upper bounds for the number and complexities of atoms from Theorem 9.*

Theorem 11. *For $n \geq 7$, to meet the upper bounds for the atom complexities from Theorem 9 by the language of a minimal DFA $\mathcal{D}_n(Q, \Sigma, \delta, 0, \{n-2\})$, the size of the alphabet Σ must be at least $n+1$. Moreover, the transition semigroup of $\mathcal{D}_n$ must be a subsemigroup of $\mathbf{W}_{\mathrm{bf}}^{\geq 6}(n)$.*

4   Most Complex Bifix-Free Languages

First we show a most complex stream of bifix-free languages for basic operations which uses only a ternary alphabet. The size of this alphabet is the smallest possible, because for union, symmetric difference, and reversal we require at least three letters to meet the bounds.

Definition 12 (Most complex stream for operations). *For $n \geq 7$, we define the DFA $\mathcal{D}_n = (Q, \Sigma, \delta, 0, \{n-2\})$, where $Q = \{0, \ldots, n-1\}$, $\Sigma = \{a, b, c\}$, $h = \lfloor (n-1)/2 \rfloor$ and δ is defined as follows:*

- δ_a: $(0 \to 1)(\{1, \ldots, n-3\} \to n-2)(\{n-2, n-1\} \to n-1)$,
- δ_b: $(\{0, n-2, n-1\} \to n-1)(1, \ldots, n-3)$,
- δ_c: $(\{0, n-2, n-1\} \to n-1)(1 \to h)(h \to n-2)(n-3, \ldots, h+1, h-1, \ldots, 2)$.

The DFA $\mathcal{D}_n$ is illustrated in Fig. 1.

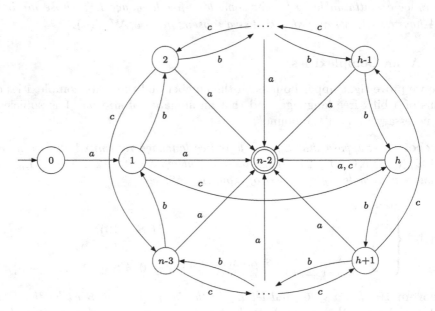

Fig. 1. Automaton $\mathcal{D}_n$ from Definition 12; empty state $n-1$ and the transitions going to $n-1$ are omitted

Theorem 13. *The DFA $\mathcal{D}_n$ from Definition 12 is minimal, recognizes a bifix-free language $L_n(a, b, c)$, has most complex quotients, and its transition semigroup is a subsemigroup of $\mathbf{W}_{\mathrm{bf}}^{\geq 6}(n)$. The stream $(L_n(a, b, c) \mid n \geq 9)$ with some permutationally equivalent dialects meets all the bounds for basic operations as follows:*

- *$L_m(a, b, c)$ and $L_n(a, c, b)$ meet the bound $mn - (m + n)$ for union and symmetric difference, the bound $mn - 3(m + n - 4)$ for intersection and the bound $mn - (2m + 3n - 9)$ for difference.*
- *$L_m(a, b, c)$ and $L_m(a, b, c)$ meet the bound $m + n - 2$ for product.*
- *$L_m(a, b, c)$ meets the bound $n - 1$ for star.*
- *$L_m(a, b, c)$ meets the bound $2^{n-3} + 2$ for reversal.*

Here we define a most complex stream for all three measures of complexity. To meet the bound for syntactic complexity an alphabet of size at least $(n - 3) + ((n - 2)^{n-3} - 1) + (n - 3)(2^{n-3} - 1) = (n - 2)^{n-3} + (n - 3)2^{n-3} - 1$ is required, and so a witness stream cannot have a smaller number of letters. Our stream contains the DFAs from [23, Definition 4], which have the transition semigroup $\mathbf{W}_{\mathrm{bf}}^{\geq 6}(n)$.

Definition 14 (Most complex stream, [23, Definition 4]). *For $n \geq 6$, we define the language W_n which is recognized by the DFA $\mathcal{W}_n$ with $Q = \{0, \ldots, n - 1\}$ and Σ containing the following letters:*

1. *b_i, for $1 \leq i \leq n - 3$, inducing the transformations $(0 \to n - 1)(i \to n - 2)(n - 2 \to n - 1)$,*
2. *c_i, for every transformation of type (2) from Definition 2 that is different from $(0 \to n - 2)(Q_M \to n - 1)(n - 2 \to n - 1)$,*
3. *d_i, for every transformation of type (3) from Definition 2 that is different from $(0 \to q)(Q_M \to n - 1)(n - 2 \to n - 1)$ for some state $q \in Q_M$.*

Theorem 15. *The stream $(W_n \mid n \geq 9)$ is most complex in the class of bifix-free languages:*

1. *The quotients of W_n have maximal state complexity (Proposition 3).*
2. *W_m and W_n' meet the bounds for union, intersection, difference, symmetric difference, where W_n' is a permutationally equivalent dialect of W_n.*
3. *W_m and W_n meet the bound for product.*
4. *W_n meets the bounds for reversal and star.*
5. *W_n meets the bound for the syntactic complexity.*
6. *W_n meets the bounds for the number of atoms and the quotient complexities of atoms (see Theorem 9).*

Moreover, the size of its alphabet is the smallest possible.

Table 1. A summary of complexity of bifix-free languages for $n \geq 6$ with the minimal sizes of the alphabet required to meet the bounds

Measure	Tight upper bound	Min. alphabet
Union $L_m \cup L_n$	$mn - (m + n)$	3
Symmetric difference $L_m \oplus L_n$	$mn - (m + n)$	3
Intersection $L_m \cap L_n$	$mn - 3(m + n - 4)$	2
Difference $L_m \setminus L_n$	$mn - (2m + 3n - 9)$	2
Product $L_m L_n$	$m + n - 2$	1
Star L_n^*	$n - 1$	2
Reversal L_n^R	$2^{n-3} + 2$	3
Syntactic complexity of L_n	$(n-1)^{n-3} + (n-2)^{n-3} +$ $(n-3)2^{n-3}$	$(n-2)^{n-3} +$ $(n-3)2^{n-3} - 1$
Atom complexities $\kappa(A_S)$	The bounds from Theorem 9	$n + 1$

Table 2. The minimal sizes of the alphabet in a universal most complex stream(s) for some of the studied subclasses of regular languages

Class	Min. alphabet	Class	Min. alphabet
Regular languages [3]	3	Prefix-free [8]	$n + 2$
Right ideals [4]	4	Prefix-closed [8]	4
Left ideals [4]	5	k-proper prefix-convex [8]	7
Two-sided ideals [4]	6	Suffix-free [10]	≤ 3 and 5
Bifix-free (Theorem 15)	$(n-2)^{n-3} +$ $(n-3)2^{n-3} - 1$	Non-returning [9]	$n(n-1)/2$

5   Conclusions

We completed the previous results concerning complexity of bifix-free languages. The bounds for each considered measure are summarized in Table 1. Our particular contribution is exhibition of a single ternary stream that meets all the bounds on basic operations. Then we showed a most complex stream that meets all the upper bounds of all three complexity measures.

It is worth noting how the properties of prefix-free and suffix-free languages are shared in the class of bifix-free languages. It is known that there does not exist such a stream in the class of suffix-free languages, even considering only basic operations. Hence, although the classes of bifix-free and suffix-free languages share many properties, such as a similar structure of the largest semigroups, the existence of most complex languages distinguishes them. This is because the bounds for star and product are much smaller for bifix-free languages and are very easily met. Additionally, a most complex stream of bifix-free languages requires a superexponential alphabet, which is much larger than in most complex streams of the other studied subclasses; see Table 2.

References

1. Berstel, J., Perrin, D., Reutenauer, C.: Codes and Automata. Cambridge University Press, Cambridge (2009)
2. Brzozowski, J.A.: Quotient complexity of regular languages. J. Autom. Lang. Comb. **15**(1/2), 71–89 (2010)
3. Brzozowski, J.A.: In search of the most complex regular languages. Int. J. Found. Comput. Sc. **24**(6), 691–708 (2013)
4. Brzozowski, J.A., Davies, S., Liu, B.Y.V.: Most complex regular ideals (2015). http://arxiv.org/abs/1511.00157
5. Brzozowski, J.A., Jirásková, G., Li, B., Smith, J.: Quotient complexity of bifix-, factor-, and subword-free regular languages. Acta Cyber. **21**(4), 507–527 (2014)
6. Brzozowski, J.A., Li, B., Ye, Y.: Syntactic complexity of prefix-, suffix-, bifix-, and factor-free regular languages. Theoret. Comput. Sci. **449**, 37–53 (2012)
7. Brzozowski, J.A., Shallit, J., Xu, Z.: Decision problems for convex languages. Inf. Comput. **209**, 353–367 (2011)
8. Brzozowski, J.A., Sinnamon, C.: Complexity of Prefix-Convex Regular Languages (2017, to appear). http://arxiv.org/abs/1605.06697
9. Brzozowski, J.A., Sinnamon, C.: Most Complex Non-Returning Regular Languages (2017). http://arxiv.org/abs/1701.03944
10. Brzozowski, J., Szykuła, M.: Complexity of suffix free regular languages. In: Kosowski, A., Walukiewicz, I. (eds.) FCT 2015. LNCS, vol. 9210, pp. 146–159. Springer, Cham (2015). doi:10.1007/978-3-319-22177-9_12
11. Brzozowski, J.A., Tamm, H.: Theory of átomata. Theoret. Comput. Sci. **539**, 13–27 (2014)
12. Cmorik, R., Jirásková, G.: Basic operations on binary suffix-free languages. In: Kotásek, Z., Bouda, J., Černá, I., Sekanina, L., Vojnar, T., Antoš, D. (eds.) MEMICS 2011. LNCS, vol. 7119, pp. 94–102. Springer, Heidelberg (2012). doi:10.1007/978-3-642-25929-6_9
13. Eom, H.S., Han, Y.S., Jirásková, G.: State complexity of basic operations on non-returning regular languages. Fundam. Informaticae **144**(2), 161–182 (2016)
14. Ferens, R., Szykuła, M.: Complexity of bifix-free regular languages (2017). http://arxiv.org/abs/1701.03768
15. The GAP Group: GAP - Groups, Algorithms, and Programming (2016). http://www.gap-system.org
16. Iván, S.: Complexity of atoms, combinatorially. Inf. Process. Lett. **116**(5), 356–360 (2016)
17. Jirásková, G.: On the state complexity of complements, stars, and reversals of regular languages. In: Ito, M., Toyama, M. (eds.) DLT 2008. LNCS, vol. 5257, pp. 431–442. Springer, Heidelberg (2008). doi:10.1007/978-3-540-85780-8_34
18. Jirásková, G., Palmovský, M., Šebej, J.: Kleene closure on regular and prefix-free languages. In: Holzer, M., Kutrib, M. (eds.) CIAA 2014. LNCS, vol. 8587, pp. 226–237. Springer, Cham (2014). doi:10.1007/978-3-319-08846-4_17
19. Jürgensen, H., Konstantinidis, S.: Codes. In: Rozenberg, G., Salomaa, A. (eds.) Handbook of Formal Languages. Word, Language, Grammar, vol. 1, pp. 511–607. Springer, Heidelberg (1997)

20. McNaughton, R., Papert, S.A.: Counter-Free Automata. The MIT Press, Cambridge (1971). (M.I.T. Research Monograph No. 65)
21. Pin, J.E.: Syntactic semigroups. In: Rozenberg, G., Salomaa, A. (eds.) Handbook of Formal Languages. Word, Language, Grammar, vol. 1, pp. 679–746. Springer, New York, USA (1997)
22. Šebej, J.: Reversal on regular languages and descriptional complexity. In: Jurgensen, H., Reis, R. (eds.) DCFS 2013. LNCS, vol. 8031, pp. 265–276. Springer, Heidelberg (2013). doi:10.1007/978-3-642-39310-5_25
23. Szykuła, M., Wittnebel, J.: Syntactic complexity of bifix-free languages. In: Carayol, A., Nicaud, C. (eds.) CIAA 2017. LNCS, vol. 10329, pp. 201–212. Springer, Cham (2017)

Computational Completeness of Path-Structured Graph-Controlled Insertion-Deletion Systems

Henning Fernau[1], Lakshmanan Kuppusamy[2], and Indhumathi Raman[3(✉)]

[1] Fachbereich 4 – CIRT, Universität Trier, 54286 Trier, Germany
fernau@uni-trier.de
[2] SCOPE, VIT University, Vellore 632 014, India
klakshma@vit.ac.in
[3] SITE, VIT University, Vellore 632 014, India
indhumathi.r@vit.ac.in

Abstract. A graph-controlled insertion-deletion (GCID) system is a regulated extension of an insertion-deletion system. It has several components and each component contains some insertion-deletion rules. These components are the vertices of a directed control graph. A rule is applied to a string in a component and the resultant string is moved to the target component specified in the rule, describing the arcs of the control graph. We investigate which combinations of size parameters (the maximum number of components, the maximal length of the insertion string, the maximal length of the left context for insertion, the maximal length of the right context for insertion; a similar three restrictions with respect to deletion) are sufficient to maintain the computational completeness of such restricted systems with the additional restriction that the control graph is a path, thus, these results also hold for ins-del P systems.

Keywords: Graph-controlled ins-del systems · Path-structured control graph · Computational completeness · Descriptional complexity measures

1 Introduction

The motivation for insertion-deletion system comes from both linguistics [11] and also from biology, more specifically from DNA processing [14] and RNA editing [1]. Insertion and deletion operations together were introduced into formal language theory in [9]. The corresponding grammatical mechanism is called *insertion-deletion system* (abbreviated as ins-del system). Informally, the insertion operation means inserting a string η in between the strings w_1 and w_2, whereas the deletion operation means deleting a substring δ from the string $w_1\delta w_2$. Several variants of ins-del systems have been considered in the literature. We refer to the survey article [16] for details.

One of the important variants of ins-del systems is *graph-controlled ins-del systems* (abbreviated as GCID systems), introduced in [6] and further studied in [8]. In such a system, the concept of components is introduced, which are associated with insertion or deletion rules. The transition is performed by choosing

© Springer International Publishing AG 2017
A. Carayol and C. Nicaud (Eds.): CIAA 2017, LNCS 10329, pp. 89–100, 2017.
DOI: 10.1007/978-3-319-60134-2_8

any applicable rule from the set of rules of the current component and by moving the resultant string to the target component specified in the rule.

If the underlying graph of a GCID system establishes a path structure (loops, multiple edges and directions are ignored), then such a GCID system can be seen as a special form of a *P system*, namely, an *ins-del P system*. As P systems (a model for *membrane computing*) draw their origins from modeling computations of biological systems, considering insertions and deletions in this context is particularly meaningful. There is one small technical issue, namely, in a P system, usually there is no specific initial membrane where the computation begins, since the membranes evolve in a so-called maximally parallel way. But if the collection of axioms in each membrane (except of one) is empty, then this exceptional membrane can be viewed as an initial membrane to begin with, so that such a system works in the same way as a GCID system where the membranes of a P system correspond to the components of a GCID system; see [13].

The mentioned connections motivate to study GCID systems. Much research has then be devoted to restricting the computational resources as far as possible while still maintaining computational completeness. To be more concrete, typical questions are: To what extent can we limit the context of the insertion or of the deletion rules? How many components are needed? Are there kind of trade-offs between these questions? All this is formalized in the following.

The descriptional complexity of a GCID system is measured by its size $(k; n, i', i''; m, j', j'')$ where the parameters from left to right denote (i) number of components (ii) the maximal length of the insertion string (iii) the maximal length of the left context used in insertion rules (iv) the maximal length of the right context used in insertion rules and the last three parameters follow a similar representation with respect to deletion. The generative power of GCID systems for insertion/deletion lengths satisfying $n + m \in \{2, 3\}$ has also been studied in [4,5,8]. However, the control graph is not a path for many cases.

The main objective of this paper is to characterize recursively enumerable languages (denoted as RE) by GCID systems with bounded sizes, whose underlying (undirected) control graph is a path, as this special case also relates to ins-del P systems [13]. Also, this objective can be seen as a sort of syntactic restriction on GCID systems, on top of the usually considered numerical values limiting the descriptional complexity. We are interested in the question which type of resources of path-structured GCID systems are still powerful enough to characterize RE. We prove that GCID system of sizes $(k; n, i', i''; 1, j', j'')$ with $i', i'', j', j'' \in \{0, 1\}$, $i' + i'' = 1$ and (i) $k = 3, n = 1$, $j' + j'' = 2$, (ii) $k = 4, n = 1$, $j' + j'' = 1$, (iii) $k = 3, n = 2$, $j' + j'' = 1$, all characterize RE with a path as a control graph. Previously, such results were only known for GCID systems with arbitrary control graphs [5]. Our results may also revive interest in the conjecture of Ivanov and Verlan [8] which states that RE $\neq$ GCID(s) if $k = 2$ in $s = (k; 1, i', i''; 1, j', j'')$, with $i', i'', j', j'' \in \{0, 1\}$ and $i' + i'' + j' + j'' \leq 3$. In the same situation, this statement is known to be true if $k = 1$. If the conjecture were true, then our results for $k = 3$ would be optimal.

2   Preliminaries

We assume that the readers are familiar with the standard notations used in formal language theory. We recall a few notations here. Let $\mathbb{N}$ denote the set of positive integers, and $[1 \ldots k] = \{i \in \mathbb{N} : 1 \leq i \leq k\}$. Given an *alphabet* (finite set) Σ, Σ^* denotes the free monoid generated by Σ. The elements of Σ^* are called *strings* or *words*; λ denotes the empty string. For a string $w \in \Sigma^*$, $|w|$ is the length of w and w^R denotes the reversal (mirror image) of w. L^R and $\mathcal{L}^R$ are understood for languages L and language families $\mathcal{L}$. For the computational completeness results, we are using as our main tool the fact that type-0 grammars in Special Geffert Normal Form (SGNF) that characterize RE.

Definition 1. *A type-0 grammar $G = (N, T, P, S)$ is said to be in SGNF if*

- *N decomposes as $N = N' \cup N''$, where $N'' = \{A_1, B_1, A_2, B_2\}$ and N' contains at least the two nonterminals S and S';*
- *the only non-context-free rules in P are $AB \rightarrow \lambda$, where $AB \in \{A_1 B_1, A_2 B_2\}$;*
- *the context-free rules are of the form (i) $S' \rightarrow \lambda$, or (ii) $X \rightarrow Y_1 Y_2$, where $X \in N'$ and $Y_1 Y_2 \in ((N' \setminus \{X\})(T \cup N'')) \cup ((T \cup N'')(N' \setminus \{X\}))$.*

The way the normal form is constructed is described in [6], based on [7]. We assume in this paper that the context-free rules $r : X \rightarrow Y_1 Y_2$ either satisfy $Y_1 \in \{A_1, A_2\}$ and $Y_2 \in N'$, or $Y_1 \in N'$ and $Y_2 \in \{B_1, B_2\} \cup T$. This also means that the derivation in G undergoes two phases: in phase I, only context-free rules are applied. This phase ends with applying the context-free deletion rule $S' \rightarrow \lambda$. Then, only non-context-free deletion rules are applied in phase II. Notice that the symbol from N', as long as present, separates A_1 and A_2 from B_1 and B_2; this prevents a premature start of phase II. We write $\Rightarrow_r$ to denote a single derivation step using rule r, and $\Rightarrow_G$ (or $\Rightarrow$ if no confusion arises) denotes a single derivation step using any rule of G. Then, $L(G) = \{w \in T^* \mid S \Rightarrow^* w\}$, where $\Rightarrow^*$ is the reflexive transitive closure of $\Rightarrow$.

Definition 2. *A graph-controlled insertion-deletion system (GCID for short) with k components is a construct $\Pi = (k, V, T, A, H, i_0, i_f, R)$, where (i) k is the number of components, (ii) V is an alphabet, (iii) $T \subseteq V$ is the terminal alphabet, (iv) $A \subset V^*$ is a finite set of strings, called axiom, (v) H is a set of labels associated (in a one-to-one manner) to the rules in R, (vi) $i_0 \in [1 \ldots k]$ is the initial component, (vii) $i_f \in [1 \ldots k]$ is the final component and (viii) R is a finite set of rules of the form $l : (i, r, j)$, where l is the label of the rule, r is an insertion rule of the form $(u, \eta, v)_I$ or deletion rule of the form $(u, \delta, v)_D$, where $u, v \in V^*$, $\eta, \delta \in V^+$ and $i, j \in [1 \ldots k]$.*

If the initial component itself is the final component, then we call the system *returning*. The pair (u, v) is called the *context*, η is called the *insertion string*, δ is called the *deletion string* and $x \in A$ is called an *axiom*. We write rules in R in the form $l : (i, r, j)$, where $l \in H$ is the label associated to the rule. Often, the component is part of the label name. This will also (implicitly) define H. We shall omit the label l of the rule wherever it is not necessary for the discussion.

We now describe how GCID systems work. Applying an insertion rule of the form $(u, \eta, v)_I$ means that the string η is inserted between u and v; this corresponds to the rewriting rule $uv \to u\eta v$. Similarly, applying a deletion rule of the form $(u, \delta, v)_D$ means that the string δ is deleted between u and v; this corresponds to the rewriting rule $u\delta v \to uv$. A *configuration* of Π is represented by $(w)_i$, where $i \in [1 \ldots k]$ is the number of the current component and $w \in V^*$ is the current string. We also say that w has entered component Ci. We write $(w)_i \Rightarrow_l (w')_j$ or $(w')_j \Leftarrow_l (w)_i$ if there is a rule l: (i, r, j) in R, and w' is obtained by applying the insertion or deletion rule r to w. By $(w)_i \overset{\Rightarrow_l}{\underset{\Leftarrow_{l'}}{}} (w')_j$, we mean that $(w')_j$ is derivable from $(w)_i$ using rule l and $(w)_i$ is derivable from $(w')_j$ using rule l'. For brevity, we write $(w)_i \Rightarrow (w')_j$ if there is some rule l in R such that $(w)_i \Rightarrow_l (w')_j$. To avoid confusion with traditional grammars, we write $\Rightarrow_*$ for the transitive reflexive closure of $\Rightarrow$ between configurations. The language $L(\Pi)$ generated by Π is defined as $\{w \in T^* \mid (x)_{i_0} \Rightarrow_* (w)_{i_f}$ for some $x \in A\}$. For returning GCID systems Π with initial component $C1$, we also write $(w)_1 \Rightarrow' (w')_1$, meaning that there is a sequence of derivation steps $(w)_1 \Rightarrow (w_1)_{c_1} \Rightarrow \cdots \Rightarrow (w_k)_{c_k} \Rightarrow (w')_1$ such that, for all $i = 1, \ldots, k$, $c_i \neq 1$.

The *underlying control graph* of a GCID system Π with k components is defined to be a graph with k nodes labelled $C1$ through Ck and there exists a directed edge from Ci to Cj if there exists a rule of the form (i, r, j) in R of Π. We also associate a simple undirected graph on k nodes to a GCID system of k components as follows: there is an undirected edge from a node Ci to Cj ($i \neq j$) if there exists a rule of the form (i, r_1, j) or (j, r_2, i) in R of Π (hence, loops and multi-edges are excluded). We call a returning GCID system with k components *path-structured* if its underlying undirected control graph has the edge set $\{\{Ci, C(i+1)\} \mid i \in [1 \ldots k - 1]\}$.

The *descriptional complexity* of a GCID system is measured by its *size* $s = (k; n, i', i''; m, j', j'')$, where the parameters represent resource bounds as given below. Slightly abusing notation, the language class that can be generated by GCID systems of size s is denoted by $\text{GCID}(s)$ and the class of languages describable by path-structured GCID systems of size s is denoted by $\text{GCID}_P(s)$.

k = the number of components	
$n = \max\{\|\eta\|: (i, (u, \eta, v)_I, j) \in R\}$	$m = \max\{\|\delta\|: (i, (u, \delta, v)_D, j) \in R\}$
$i' = \max\{\|u\|: (i, (u, \eta, v)_I, j) \in R\}$	$j' = \max\{\|u\|: (i, (u, \delta, v)_D, j) \in R\}$
$i'' = \max\{\|v\|: (i, (u, \eta, v)_I, j) \in R\}$	$j'' = max\{\|v\|: (i, (u, \delta, v)_D, j) \in R\}$

3   Computational Completeness

In this section, to prove the computational completeness of GCID system of certain sizes, we start with a type-0 grammar $G = (N, T, P, S)$ in SGNF as defined in Definition 1. The rules of P are labelled injectively with labels from $[1 \ldots |P|]$. We will use these labels and primed variants thereof as nonterminals in the simulating GCID system. Their purpose is to mark positions in the string and also to enforce a certain sequence of rule applications. As per the definition of SGNF, there are, apart from the easy-to-handle context-free deletion rule, context-free rules $r : X \to Y_1 Y_2$ and non-context-free deletion rules $f : AB \to \lambda$. For these types of rules, we present the simulations in the form of a table, for instance, as in Table 1. A detailed discussion of the working of this simulation will follow in the proof of the next theorem.

To simplify our further results, the following observations from [5] are used.

Proposition 1 [5]. *Let k, n, i', i'', m, j, j'' be non-negative integers.*

1. $\text{GCID}_P(k; n, i', i''; m, j', j'') = [\text{GCID}_P(k; n, i'', i'; m, j'', j')]^R$
2. $\text{RE} = \text{GCID}_P(k; n, i', i''; m, j', j'')$ *iff* $\text{RE} = \text{GCID}_P(k; n, i'', i'; m, j'', j')$

3.1   GCID Systems with Insertion and Deletion Length One

In [15], it has been proved that ins-del systems with size (1,1,1;1,1,1) characterize RE. Notice that it is proved in [10,12] that ins-del systems of size $(1, 1, 1; 1, 1, 0)$ or $(1, 1, 0; 1, 1, 1)$ cannot characterize RE. It is therefore obvious that we need at least 2 components in a graph-controlled ins-del system of sizes $(1, 1, 1; 1, 1, 0)$ and $(1, 1, 0; 1, 1, 1)$ to characterize RE. In [5], we characterized RE by path-structured GCID systems of size $(3; 1, 1, 1; 1, 1, 0)$. Also, in [8], it was shown that $\text{GCID}_P(3; 1, 2, 0; 1, 1, 0) = \text{RE}$ and $\text{GCID}_P(3; 1, 1, 0; 1, 2, 0) = \text{RE}$. We now complement these results.

Table 1. Path-structured GCID systems of size $(3; 1, 1, 0; 1, 1, 1)$ simulating type-0 grammars G in SGNF. In the table, $c' \in \{A_1, A_2, \kappa'\}$ and $c \in \{B_1, B_2, \kappa\} \cup T$, f, r are rule markers, while Δ is a dummy symbol that was not part of the alphabet of G.

Component C1	Component C2	Component C3
$r1.1 : (1, (X, r, \lambda)_I, 2)$	$r2.1 : (2, (\lambda, X, r)_D, 1)$	$r3.1 : (3, (r', Y_1, \lambda)_I, 2)$
$r1.2 : (1, (r, r', \lambda)_I, 2)$	$r2.2 : (2, (\lambda, r, r')_D, 1)$	
$r1.3 : (1, (r', \Delta, \lambda)_I, 1)$	$r2.3.c : (2, (Y_2, \Delta, c)_D, 3)$	
$r1.4 : (1, (r', Y_2, \lambda)_I, 2)$	$r2.4.c' : (2, (c', r', Y_1)_D, 1)$	
$f1.1 : (1, (\lambda, f, \lambda)_I, 2)$	$f2.1 : (2, (f, A, B)_D, 3)$	$f3.1 : (3, (f, B, \lambda)_D, 2)$
	$f2.2 : (2, (\lambda, f, \lambda)_D, 1)$	
$h1.1 : (1, (\lambda, S', \lambda)_D, 1)$		
$\kappa1.1 : (1, (\lambda, \kappa, \lambda)_D, 1)$		
$\kappa'1.1 : (1, (\lambda, \kappa', \lambda)_D, 1)$		

Theorem 1. $\text{RE} = \text{GCID}_P(3; 1, 1, 0; 1, 1, 1) = \text{GCID}_P(3; 1, 0, 1; 1, 1, 1)$.

At a first glance, the reader might wonder that the simulation would be straightforward (as initially thought by the authors themselves, as there are many resources available). However, this is not the case. The problem is that any rule of a component could be applied whenever a string enters that component. Since insertion is only left-context-sensitive, the insertion string can be adjoined any number of times on the right of this context, similar to context-free insertion.

This issue is handled by inserting some markers and then inserting Y_1 and Y_2 (from rule $X \to Y_1Y_2$) after the markers. We have to be careful, since a back-and-forth transition may insert many Y_1's and/or Y_2's after the marker.

Proof. Consider a type-0 grammar $G = (N, T, P, S)$ in SGNF as in Definition 1. We construct a GCID$_P$ system Π such that $L(\Pi) = L(G)$: $\Pi = (3, V, T, \{\kappa'S\kappa\}, H, 1, 1, R)$. The alphabet of Π is $V \subset N \cup T \cup \{r, r' : r \in [1 \dots |P|]\} \cup \{\kappa', \kappa\}$. The simulation is explained in Table 1, which completes the description of R and V. Clearly, Π has size $(3; 1, 1, 0; 1, 1, 1)$.

With the rules of Table 1, we prove $L(G) \subseteq L(\Pi)$ by showing how the different types of rules are simulated. Let us look into the context-free rules first. The simulation of the deletion rule h is obvious and hence omitted. Applying some rule $r : X \to Y_1Y_2$, with $X \in N'$, to $w = \alpha X \beta$, where $\alpha, \beta \in (N'' \cup T)^*$, yields $w' = \alpha Y_1 Y_2 \beta$ in G. In Π, we can find the following simulation, with $\alpha'c' = \kappa'\alpha$ and $c\beta' = \beta\kappa$ where $\alpha'\kappa, \kappa'c\kappa, \kappa'c'\kappa, \kappa'\beta' \in \{\kappa'\}(N'' \cup T)^*\{\kappa\}$:

$$(\kappa'w\kappa)_1 \Rightarrow_{r1.1} (\alpha'c'Xrc\beta')_2 \Rightarrow_{r2.1} (\alpha'c'rc\beta')_1 \Rightarrow_{r1.2} (\alpha'c'rr'c\beta')_2 \Rightarrow_{r2.2} (\alpha'c'r'c\beta')_1$$
$$\Rightarrow_{r1.3} (\alpha'c'r'\Delta c\beta')_1 \Rightarrow_{r1.4} (\alpha'c'r'Y_2\Delta c\beta')_2 \Rightarrow_{r2.3.c} (\alpha'c'r'Y_2c\beta')_3 \Rightarrow_{r3.1}$$
$$(\alpha'c'r'Y_1Y_2c\beta')_2 \Rightarrow_{r2.4.c'} (\alpha'c'Y_1Y_2c\beta')_1 = (\kappa'\alpha Y_1Y_2\beta\kappa)_1 = (\kappa'w'\kappa)_1 \,.$$

For the non-context-free case, the simulation of $f : AB \to \lambda$ is straightforward; hence, details are omitted. By induction, this proves that whenever $S \Rightarrow^* w$ in G, then there is a derivation $(\kappa'S\kappa)_1 \Rightarrow'_* (\kappa'w\kappa)_1$ in Π, and finally $(\kappa'w\kappa)_1 \Rightarrow' (w)_1$ is possible.

In the following we show the converse $L(\Pi) \subseteq L(G)$ and this is important since it also proves that Π not only produces intended strings as above but also does not produce any unintended strings as well.

Conversely, consider a configuration $(w)_1$, with $(\kappa'S\kappa)_1 \Rightarrow'_* (w)_1$. We assume now that w starts with κ' and ends with κ, and that these are the only occurrences of these special letters in w, as no malicious derivations are possible when prematurely deleting κ or κ'. We now discuss five situations for w and prove in each case that, whenever $(w) \Rightarrow' (w')$, then w' satisfies one of these five situations, or from $(w')_1$ no final configuration can be reached. As $S \in N'$, the base case $\kappa'S\kappa$ is covered in case (iii) which is presented below. Hence, by induction, the case distinction presented in the following considers all possibilities.

(i) Assume that w contains one occurrence of r' (the primed marker of some context-free rule r), but no occurrence of unprimed markers of context-free rules, and no occurrence of any nonterminal from N', neither an occurrence of Δ. Hence, $w = \kappa'\alpha r'\beta\kappa$ for appropriate strings $\alpha, \beta \in (N'' \cup T)^*$. Then, the rules (i.a) $r1.3$, (i.b) $r1.4$, as well as the simulation initiation rules like (i.c) $f1.1$ are applicable. Let us discuss these possibilities now. Subcase (i.c): If $f1.1$ is applied, then, say, f is introduced to the right of some occurrence of A. In $C2$, one can then try to apply (i.c.1) $f2.1$, (i.c.2) $f2, 2$, or (i.c.3) $r2.4.c'$ for an appropriate c'. However, as we are still simulating phase I of G, B cannot be to the right of A, so that Subcase (i.c.1) cannot occur. Subcase (i.c.2) simply undoes the effect of previously applying $f1.1$, so that we can ignore its discussion. In Subcase (i.c.3), we are back in $C1$ with a string that contains no symbols from N', nor any variants of context-free rule markers, nor any Δ, but one non-context-free rule marker. We will discuss this in Case (v) below and show that such a derivation cannot terminate. Subcase (i.b): If we apply $r1.4$ to w immediately, we are stuck in $C2$. Hence, consider finally Subcase (i.a): we apply $r1.3$ first once. Now, we are in a very similar situation as before, but one Δ is added to the right of r'. This means that continuing with $f1.1$ will get stuck again in $C2$. In order to make progress, we should finally apply $r1.4$. Now, we are in the configuration $(\kappa'\alpha r'Y_2\Delta^n\beta\kappa)_2$ for some $n \geq 1$. As $Y_1 \neq Y_2$, $r2.4.c'$ is not applicable for any c', so the derivation is stuck in $C2$. If we apply $r.2.3.c$, then we can only proceed if $n = 1$, which means that we applied $r1.3$ exactly once before. Hence, $(\kappa'\alpha r'Y_2\Delta\beta\kappa)_2 \Rightarrow (\kappa'\alpha r'Y_2\beta\kappa)_3 \Rightarrow (\kappa'\alpha r'Y_1Y_2\beta\kappa)_2 \Rightarrow (\kappa'\alpha Y_1Y_2\beta\kappa)_1$ is enforced. This corresponds to the intended derivation; the assumed occurrence of r' in the string was replaced by Y_1Y_2; this corresponds to the situation of Case (iii).

(ii) Assume that w contains one occurrence of r (the unprimed marker of some context-free rule r), but no occurrence of primed markers of context-free rules, and no occurrence of any nonterminal from N', neither an occurrence of Δ. Hence, $w = \kappa'\alpha r\beta\kappa$ for appropriate strings $\alpha, \beta \in (N'' \cup T')^*$. Similarly as discussed in Case (i), trying to start a simulation of some non-context-free rule gets stuck in $C2$, in particular, as we are simulating phase I of G and there is no nonterminal from N' in the current string. Hence, we are now forced to apply $r1.2$. This means that in $C2$, we have to apply $r2.2$, leading us to $(w')_1$ with $w' = \alpha r'\beta$, a situation previously discussed in Case (i).

(iii) Assume that w contains one occurrence $X \in N'$, but no occurrence of unprimed or primed markers of context-free rules, and no occurrence of Δ. Hence, $w = \kappa'\alpha X\beta\kappa$ for appropriate strings $\alpha, \beta \in (N'' \cup T)^*$. As we are still simulating phase I of G, we are now forced to apply $r1.1$ or simulate the context-free deletion rule (which gives a trivial discussion that is omitted; the important point is that this switches to phase II of the simulation of G). This means that in $C2$, we have to apply $r2.1$, leading us to $(w')_1$ with $w' = \kappa'\alpha r\beta\kappa$ for some context-free rule $r : X \to Y_1Y_2$, a situation already discussed in Case (ii).

(iv) Assume that $w \in \{\kappa'\}(N'' \cup T)^*\{\kappa\}$. Now, it is straightforward to analyze that we have to follow the simulation of one of the non-context-free deletion rules, or finally apply the rule deleting the special symbols κ, κ'.

(v) Assume that w contains no primed or unprimed markers of context-free rules, nor a symbol from N', nor any Δ but contains a non-context-free rule marker. This means we have to apply some rule $f1.1$, but although this might successfully simulate a non-context-free deletion rule, it will bring us back to $C1$ with a non-context-free rule marker in the string. Hence, we are back in Case (v), so that this type of derivation can never terminate.

The second claim follows by Proposition 1. The underlying graph of the simulation is shown in Fig. 1(a). The corresponding undirected graph is a path and hence the presented GCID system is path-structured.   □

In [6], it was shown that GCID systems of sizes $(4; 1, 1, 0; 1, 1, 0)$ and $(4; 1, 1, 0; 1, 0, 1)$ describe RE, with the underlying control graph not being a

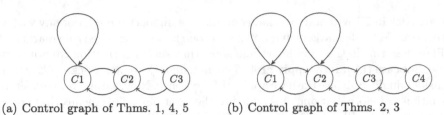

(a) Control graph of Thms. 1, 4, 5   (b) Control graph of Thms. 2, 3

Fig. 1. Control graphs underlying the GCID systems (characterizing RE) in this paper

path. In [5], the number of components was reduced from 4 to 3, however, with the underlying graph still not being a path. In the next two theorems we characterize RE by path-structured GCID systems of sizes $(4; 1, 1, 0; 1, 1, 0)$ and $(4; 1, 1, 0; 1, 0, 1)$. The former result also complements an earlier result of [8], which stated that $\mathrm{GCID}_P(3; 1, 2, 0; 1, 1, 0) = \mathrm{GCID}_P(3; 1, 1, 0; 1, 2, 0) = \mathrm{RE}$. We trade-off the number of components against the length of the left context of the insertion/deletion.

Theorem 2. $\mathrm{RE} = \mathrm{GCID}_P(4; 1, 1, 0; 1, 1, 0) = \mathrm{GCID}_P(4; 1, 0, 1; 1, 0, 1)$.

Proof. Consider a type-0 grammar $G = (N, T, P, S)$ in SGNF as in Definition 1. We construct a GCID_P system $\Pi = (4, V, T, \{\kappa S\}, H, 1, 1, R)$ such that $L(\Pi) = L(G)$. The four columns of the table correspond to the four components of Π. The rows correspond to the simulation of $r : X \to Y_1 Y_2$, $f : AB \to \lambda$ and of the context-free deletion rule $h : S' \to \lambda$. The last row deletes the left-end marker κ introduced in the axiom. The alphabet of Π is $V \subset N \cup T \cup \{p, p', p'', p''' : p \in [1 \ldots |P|]\} \cup \{\kappa\}$. R is defined as shown in Table 2, depending on G. Clearly, Π has size $(4; 1, 1, 0; 1, 1, 0)$. We now prove that $L(G) \subseteq L(\Pi)$. To this end, we show that if $w \Rightarrow w'$ in G, with $w, w' \in (N \cup T)^*$, then $(\kappa w)_1 \Rightarrow' (\kappa w')_1$ according to Π. From this fact, the claim follows by a simple induction argument. As the claim is evident for rule h, we only need to discuss $w \Rightarrow w'$ due to using a context-free rule (Case CF) or due to using a non-context-free rule (Case $\overline{\mathrm{CF}}$).

Case CF: The intended simulation works as follows:

$$(\kappa \alpha X \beta)_1 \Rightarrow_{r1.1} (\kappa \alpha r X \beta)_2 \Rightarrow_{r2.1} (\kappa \alpha r X r' \beta)_3 \Rightarrow_{r3.1} (\kappa \alpha r r' \beta)_4 \Rightarrow_{r4.1}$$
$$(\kappa \alpha r r' r'' \beta)_3 \Rightarrow_{r3.2} (\kappa \alpha r r' r'' r''' \beta)_2 \Rightarrow_{r2.2} (\kappa \alpha r r'' r''' \beta)_2 \Rightarrow_{r2.3} (\kappa \alpha r r''' \beta)_3 \Rightarrow_{r3.3}$$
$$(\kappa \alpha r r''' Y_2 \beta)_4 \Rightarrow_{r4.2} (\kappa \alpha r''' Y_2 \beta)_3 \Rightarrow_{r3.4} (\kappa \alpha r''' Y_1 Y_2 \beta)_2 \Rightarrow_{r2.4.c} (\kappa \alpha Y_1 Y_2 \beta)_1.$$

Table 2. GCID rules of size $(4; 1, 1, 0; 1, 1, 0)$ with axiom κS and $c \in N'' \cup T \cup \{\kappa\}$.

Component C1	Component C2	Component C3	Component C4
$r1.1 : (1, (\lambda, r, \lambda)_I, 2)$	$r2.1 : (2, (X, r', \lambda)_I, 3)$	$r3.1 : (3, (r, X, \lambda)_D, 4)$	$r4.1 : (4, (r', r'', \lambda)_I, 3)$
	$r2.2 : (2, (r, r', \lambda)_D, 2)$	$r3.2 : (3, (r'', r''', \lambda)_I, 2)$	$r4.2 : (4, (\lambda, r, \lambda)_D, 3)$
	$r2.3 : (2, (r, r'', \lambda)_D, 3)$	$r3.3 : (3, (r''', Y_2, \lambda)_I, 4)$	
	$r2.4.c : (2, (c, r''', \lambda)_D, 1)$	$r3.4 : (3, (r''', Y_1, \lambda)_I, 2)$	
$f1.1 : (1, (\lambda, f, \lambda)_I, 2)$	$f2.1 : (2, (A, f', \lambda)_I, 3)$	$f3.1 : (3, (f', B, \lambda)_D, 4)$	$f4.1 : (4, (f, A, \lambda)_D, 3)$
	$f2.2 : (2, (\lambda, f, \lambda)_D, 1)$	$f3.2 : (3, (f, f', \lambda)_D, 2)$	
$h1.1 : (1, (\lambda, S', \lambda)_D, 1)$			
$\kappa 1.1 : (1, (\lambda, \kappa, \lambda)_D, 1)$			

Here, c is the last symbol of $\kappa\alpha$, possibly κ.

Case $\overline{\text{CF}}$: Let us consider $f : AB \to \lambda$. This means that $w = \alpha AB\beta$ and $w' = \alpha\beta$ for some $\alpha, \beta \in (N \cup T)^*$. Within Π, this can be simulated as follows.

$$(\kappa w)_1 = (\kappa\alpha AB\beta)_1 \Rightarrow_{f1.1} (\kappa\alpha fAB\beta)_2 \Rightarrow_{f2.1} (\kappa\alpha fAf'B\beta)_3$$
$$\Rightarrow_{f3.1} (\kappa\alpha fAf'\beta)_4 \Rightarrow_{f4.1} (\kappa\alpha ff'\beta)_3 \Rightarrow_{f3.2} (\kappa\alpha f\beta)_2 \Rightarrow_{f2.2} (\kappa w')_1.$$

The converse inclusion $L(\Pi) \subseteq L(G)$ is following an inductive argument as in the previous theorem and hence is omitted here. The second claim follows by Proposition 1. The underlying graph of the simulation is shown in Fig. 1(b). $\square$

Theorem 3. $\text{RE} = \text{GCID}_P(4; 1, 1, 0; 1, 0, 1) = \text{GCID}_P(4; 1, 0, 1; 1, 1, 0)$.

Proof. Consider a type-0 grammar $G = (N, T, P, S)$ in SGNF. The rules of P are labelled injectively with labels from $[1 \ldots |P|]$. We construct a GCID_P system Π such that $L(\Pi) = L(G)$, with $\Pi = (4, V, T, \{S\}, H, 1, 1, R)$. The alphabet of Π is $V \subset N \cup T \cup \{p, p', p'', p''' : p \in [1 \ldots |P|]\}$. R is defined as shown in Table 3. Π has the claimed size. The intended simulation of a context-free rule is as follows.

$$(\alpha X\beta)_1 \Rightarrow_{r1.1} (\alpha Xr\beta)_2 \Rightarrow_{r2.1} (\alpha r\beta)_1 \Rightarrow_{r1.2} (\alpha rr'\beta)_2 \Rightarrow_{r2.2}$$
$$(\alpha r'\beta)_1 \Rightarrow_{r1.3} (\alpha r'r''\beta)_2 \Rightarrow_{r2.3} (\alpha r'r''Y_2\beta)_3 \Rightarrow_{r3.1} (\alpha r'Y_2\beta)_4 \Rightarrow_{r4.1}$$
$$(\alpha r'r'''Y_2\beta)_3 \Rightarrow_{r3.2} (\alpha r'r'''Y_1Y_2\beta)_2 \to_{r2.4} (\alpha r'Y_1Y_2\beta)_2 \Rightarrow_{r2.5} (\alpha Y_1Y_2\beta)_1.$$

The intended simulation of a non-context-free rule is as follows.

$$(\alpha AB\beta)_1 \Rightarrow_{f1.1} (\alpha ABf\beta)_2 \Rightarrow_{f2.1} (\alpha Af'Bf\beta)_3 \Rightarrow_{f3.1}$$
$$(\alpha f'Bf\beta)_4 \Rightarrow_{r4.1} (\alpha f'f\beta)_3 \Rightarrow_{r3.2} (\alpha f\beta)_2 \Rightarrow_{r2.2} (\alpha\beta)_1.$$

This shows that $L(G) \subseteq L(\Pi)$. The main complication for the correctness proof is the fact that we may return to $C1$ with strings containing rule markers. This brings along a detailed discussion of four different situations for w when considering $(S)_1 \Rightarrow'_* (w)_1 \Rightarrow' (w')_1$ according to Π. A detailed explanation of these different situations follows a similar argument as in Theorem 1 and is omitted here in view of page constraint. $\square$

Table 3. GCID rules of size $(4; 1, 1, 0; 1, 0, 1)$ simulating a type-0 grammar in SGNF

Component C1	Component C2	Component C3	Component C4
$r1.1 : (1, (X, r, \lambda)_I, 2)$	$r2.1 : (2, (\lambda, X, r)_D, 1)$	$r3.1 : (3, (\lambda, r'', Y_2)_D, 4)$	$r4.1 : (4, (r', r''', \lambda)_I, 3)$
$r1.2 : (1, (r, r', \lambda)_I, 2)$	$r2.2 : (2, (\lambda, r, r')_D, 1)$	$r3.2 : (3, (r''', Y_1, \lambda)_I, 2)$	
$r1.3 : (1, (r', r'', \lambda)_I, 2)$	$r2.3 : (2, (r'', Y_2, \lambda)_I, 3)$		
	$r2.4 : (2, (\lambda, r''', Y_1)_D, 2)$		
	$r2.5 : (2, (\lambda, r', Y_1)_D, 1)$		
$f1.1 : (1, (\lambda, f, \lambda)_I, 2)$	$f2.1 : (2, (A, f', \lambda)_I, 3)$	$f3.1 : (3, (\lambda, A, f')_D, 4)$	$f4.1 : (4, (\lambda, B, f)_D, 3)$
	$f2.2 : (2, (\lambda, f, \lambda)_D, 1)$	$f3.2 : (3, (\lambda, f', f)_D, 2)$	
$h1.1 : (1, (\lambda, S', \lambda)_D, 1)$			

3.2   GCID Systems with Insertion Length Two

In [6], it is shown that $GCID_P(4; 2, 0, 0; 1, 1, 0) = RE$. Here, we show that, if we allow a context (either left or right) for insertion, then we can still describe RE while decreasing the number of components from 4 to 3, yet obtaining path-structured GCID systems.

Theorem 4. $RE = GCID_P(3; 2, 1, 0; 1, 0, 1) = GCID_P(3; 2, 0, 1; 1, 1, 0)$.

Table 4. GCID rules of size $(3; 2, 1, 0; 1, 0, 1)$ simulating a type-0 grammar in SGNF.

Component C1	Component C2	Component C3
$r1.1 : (1, (X, r, \lambda)_I, 2)$	$r2.1 : (2, (\lambda, X, r)_D, 3)$ $r2.2 : (2, (\lambda, r, \lambda)_D, 1)$	$r3.1 : (3, (r, Y_1Y_2, \lambda)_I, 2)$
$f1.1 : (1, (B, f, \lambda)_I, 2)$	$f2.1 : (2, (\lambda, B, f)_D, 3)$ $f2.2 : (2, (\lambda, f, \lambda)_D, 1)$	$f3.1 : (3, (\lambda, A, f)_D, 2)$
$h1.1 : (1, (\lambda, S', \lambda)_D, 1)$	.	

Proof. Consider a type-0 grammar $G = (N, T, P, S)$ in SGNF as in Definition 1. We construct a $GCID_P$ system $\Pi = (3, V, T, \{S\}, H, 1, 1, R)$ of size $(3; 2, 1, 0; 1, 0, 1)$ such that $L(\Pi) = L(G)$. Here, let $V \subset N \cup T \cup [1 \ldots |P|]$ contain in particular those rule labels used in the rules listed in Table 4. Π is of size $(3; 2, 1, 0; 1, 0, 1)$. We now prove that $L(G) \subseteq L(\Pi)$. As the claim is evident for $h : S' \to \lambda$, we show that if $w \Rightarrow w'$ in G, then $(w)_1 \Rightarrow' (w')_1$ according to Π in two more cases.

<u>Case CF</u>: Here, $w = \alpha X \beta$ and $w' = \alpha Y_1 Y_2 \beta$ for some $\alpha, \beta \in (N'' \cup T)^*$. The simulation of $r : X \to Y_1 Y_2$ performs as follows:

$$(\alpha X \beta)_1 \overset{r2.2}{\underset{r1.1}{\Leftrightarrow}} (\alpha X r \beta)_2 \Rightarrow_{r2.1} (\alpha r \beta)_3 \Rightarrow_{r3.1} (\alpha r Y_1 Y_2 \beta)_2 \Rightarrow_{r2.2} (\alpha Y_1 Y_2 \beta)_1 .$$

Note the role of the right context r in $r2.1$. If the marker r is not present for the deletion, then after applying $r3.1$, when we come back to $C2$, we can apply $r2.1$ again and could end-up with a malicious derivation.

<u>Case $\overline{CF}$</u>: Here $w = \alpha A B \beta$ and $w' = \alpha \beta$ for some $\alpha, \beta \in (N \cup T)^*$. The rules $f : AB \to \lambda$ can be simulated as follows.

$$(\alpha A B \beta)_1 \overset{f2.2}{\underset{f1.1}{\Leftrightarrow}} (\alpha A B f \beta)_2 \Rightarrow_{f2.1} (\alpha A f \beta)_3 \Rightarrow_{f3.1} (\alpha f \beta)_2 \Rightarrow_{f2.2} (\alpha \beta)_1 .$$

We leave it to the reader to verify that no malicious derivations are possible. Proposition 1 shows that also GCID systems of size $(3; 2, 0, 1; 1, 1, 0)$ are computationally complete. Figure 1(a) shows the control graph of the simulation.   □

Theorem 5. $RE = GCID_P(3; 2, 1, 0; 1, 1, 0) = GCID_P(3; 2, 0, 1; 1, 0, 1)$.

The simulation is very similar to Theorem 4 and hence we provide only the simulating rules in Table 5.   □

Table 5. GCID rules of size $(3; 2, 1, 0; 1, 1, 0)$ simulating a type-0 grammar in SGNF.

Component C1	Component C2	Component C3
$r1.1 : (1, (\lambda, r, \lambda)_I, 2)$	$p2.1 : (2, (r, X, \lambda)_D, 3)$ $r2.2 : (2, (\lambda, r, \lambda)_D, 1)$	$r3.1 : (3, (r, Y_1 Y_2, \lambda)_I, 2)$
$f1.1 : (1, (\lambda, f, \lambda)_I, 2)$	$f2.1 : (2, (f, A, \lambda)_D, 3)$ $f2.2 : (2, (\lambda, f, \lambda)_D, 1)$	$f3.1 : (3, (f, B, \lambda)_D, 2)$
$h1.1 : (1, (\lambda, S', \lambda)_D, 1)$		

3.3 Consequences for ins-del P Systems

Representing the family of languages generated by ins-del P system with k membranes and size (n, i', i'', m, j', j''), where the size parameters have the same meaning as in GCID system by $\mathrm{ELSP}_k(\mathrm{INS}_n^{i',i''}\mathrm{DEL}_m^{j',j''})$ (this notation was used in [8], based on [13]), we know that $\mathrm{ELSP}_4(\mathrm{INS}_1^{1,0}\mathrm{DEL}_2^{0,0})$, $\mathrm{ELSP}_4(\mathrm{INS}_2^{0,0}\mathrm{DEL}_1^{1,0})$ ([6]) and $\mathrm{ELSP}_3(\mathrm{INS}_1^{2,0}\mathrm{DEL}_1^{1,0})$, $\mathrm{ELSP}_3(\mathrm{INS}_1^{1,0}\mathrm{DEL}_1^{2,0})$ ([8]) are computationally complete. Since the underlying control graph of all the GCID systems (characterizing RE) in this paper has a path structure, the results that we obtained correspond to ins-del P systems in the following way, complementing [6,8].

Corollary 1. *For $i', i'', j', j'' \in \{0, 1\}$ with $i' + i'' - j' + j'' = 1$, the following ins-del P systems are computationally complete.*

1. $\mathrm{RE} = \mathrm{ELSP}_3(\mathrm{INS}_2^{i',i''}\mathrm{DEL}_1^{j',j''}) = \mathrm{ELSP}_4(\mathrm{INS}_1^{i',i''}\mathrm{DEL}_1^{j',j''})$.
2. $\mathrm{RE} = \mathrm{ELSP}_3(\mathrm{INS}_1^{1,0}\mathrm{DEL}_1^{1,1}) = \mathrm{ELSP}_3(\mathrm{INS}_1^{0,1}\mathrm{DEL}_1^{1,1})$. $\square$

4 Summary and Open Problems

In this paper, we focused on examining the computational power of graph-controlled ins-del systems with paths as control graphs, which naturally correspond to variants of P systems. We lowered the resource needs to describe RE. However, we still do not know if these resource bounds are optimal.

Here we considered the underlying graph of GCID systems to be path-structured only. One may also consider also tree structure, which may give additional power, especially to ins-del P systems. The resources used in the results of ins-del P systems need not be optimal since in ins-del P systems, each membrane can have initial strings and they all evolve in parallel which may reduce the size.

The reader may have noticed that we discussed in detail the case of insertion strings of length two, but a similar discussion for the case of deletion strings of length two is missing. More precisely, to state one concrete question, it is open whether $\mathrm{RE} = \mathrm{GCID}_P(3; 1, 1, 0; 2, 1, 0) = \mathrm{GCID}_P(3; 1, 1, 0; 2, 0, 1)$.

In view of the connections with P systems, it would be also interesting to study Parikh images of (restricted) graph-controlled ins-del systems, as started out for matrix-controlled ins-del systems in [3]. This also relates to the macroset GCID systems considered in [2].

Acknowledgement. This work was supported by overhead money from the DFG grant FE 560/6-1.

References

1. Benne, R. (ed.): RNA Editing: The Alteration of Protein Coding Sequences of RNA. Molecular Biology. Ellis Horwood, Chichester (1993)
2. Fernau, H.: An essay on general grammars. J. Automata Lang. Comb. **21**, 69–92 (2016)
3. Fernau, H., Kuppusamy, L.: Parikh images of matrix ins-del systems. In: Gopal, T.V., Jäger, G., Steila, S. (eds.) TAMC 2017. LNCS, vol. 10185, pp. 201–215. Springer, Cham (2017). doi:10.1007/978-3-319-55911-7_15
4. Fernau, H., Kuppusamy, L., Raman, I.: Generative power of graph-controlled ins-del systems with small sizes. Accepted with J. Automata Lang. Comb. (2017)
5. Fernau, H., Kuppusamy, L., Raman, I.: On the computational completeness of graph-controlled insertion-deletion systems with binary sizes. Accepted with Theor. Comput. Sci. (2017). http://dx.doi.org/10.1016/j.tcs.2017.01.019
6. Freund, R., Kogler, M., Rogozhin, Y., Verlan, S.: Graph-controlled insertion-deletion systems. In: McQuillan, I., Pighizzini, G. (eds.) Proceedings Twelfth Annual Workshop on Descriptional Complexity of Formal Systems, DCFS. EPTCS, vol. 31, pp. 88–98 (2010)
7. Geffert, V.: Normal forms for phrase-structure grammars. RAIRO Informatique Théorique Appl. / Theor. Inf. Appl. **25**, 473–498 (1991)
8. Ivanov, S., Verlan, S.: About one-sided one-symbol insertion-deletion P systems. In: Alhazov, A., Cojocaru, S., Gheorghe, M., Rogozhin, Y., Rozenberg, G., Salomaa, A. (eds.) CMC 2013. LNCS, vol. 8340, pp. 225–237. Springer, Heidelberg (2014). doi:10.1007/978-3-642-54239-8_16
9. Kari, L., Thierrin, G.: Contextual insertions/deletions and computability. Inf. Comput. **131**(1), 47–61 (1996)
10. Krassovitskiy, A., Rogozhin, Y., Verlan, S.: Further results on insertion-deletion systems with one-sided contexts. In: Martín-Vide, C., Otto, F., Fernau, H. (eds.) LATA 2008. LNCS, vol. 5196, pp. 333–344. Springer, Heidelberg (2008). doi:10.1007/978-3-540-88282-4_31
11. Marcus, S.: Contextual grammars. Rev. Roum. Mathématiques Pures Appliquées **14**, 1525–1534 (1969)
12. Matveevici, A., Rogozhin, Y., Verlan, S.: Insertion-deletion systems with one-sided contexts. In: Durand-Lose, J., Margenstern, M. (eds.) MCU 2007. LNCS, vol. 4664, pp. 205–217. Springer, Heidelberg (2007). doi:10.1007/978-3-540-74593-8_18
13. Păun, Gh.: Membrane Computing: An Introduction. Springer, Heidelberg (2002)
14. Păun, Gh., Rozenberg, G., Salomaa, A.: DNA Computing: New Computing Paradigms. Springer, Heidelberg (1998)
15. Takahara, A., Yokomori, T.: On the computational power of insertion-deletion systems. Nat. Comput. **2**(4), 321–336 (2003)
16. Verlan, S.: Recent developments on insertion-deletion systems. Comput. Sci. J. Moldova **18**(2), 210–245 (2010)

Stamina: Stabilisation Monoids in Automata Theory

Nathanaël Fijalkow[1]([✉]), Hugo Gimbert[2], Edon Kelmendi[3],
and Denis Kuperberg[4]

[1] University of Warwick, Warwick, UK
nathanael.fijalkow@gmail.com
[2] LaBRI, Bordeaux, France
[3] TU Munich, Munich, Germany
[4] CNRS, ÉNS Lyon, Lyon, France

Abstract. We present Stamina, a tool solving three algorithmic problems in automata theory. First, compute the star height of a regular language, i.e. the minimal number of nested Kleene stars needed for expressing the language with a complement-free regular expression. Second, decide limitedness for regular cost functions. Third, decide whether a probabilistic leaktight automaton has value 1, i.e. whether a probabilistic leaktight automaton accepts words with probability arbitrarily close to 1.

All three problems reduce to the computation of the stabilisation monoid associated with an automaton, which is computationally challenging because the monoid is exponentially larger than the automaton. The compact data structures used in Stamina, together with optimisations and heuristics, allow us to handle automata with several hundreds of states. This radically improves upon the performances of ACME, a similar tool solving a subset of these problems.

The tool Stamina is open source and available from Github, details are given on the webpage http://stamina.labri.fr.

1 Introduction

Stamina is a tool for deciding properties of automata, through the construction of an algebraic structure called stabilisation monoid. It solves three problems:

- compute the star height of a regular language,
- decide limitedness for regular cost functions,
- decide whether a probabilistic leaktight automaton has value 1.

The star height problem, introduced by Eggan in 1963 [Egg63], takes as input a regular language L and an integer h and decides whether there exists

This work was supported by The Alan Turing Institute under the EPSRC grant EP/N510129/1. H. Gimbert and E. Kelmendi are supported by the French ANR project "Stoch-MC" and "LaBEX CPU" of Université de Bordeaux. This work has been partly funded by the grant Palse Impulsion.

© Springer International Publishing AG 2017
A. Carayol and C. Nicaud (Eds.): CIAA 2017, LNCS 10329, pp. 101–112, 2017.
DOI: 10.1007/978-3-319-60134-2_9

a regular expression for L with at most h nested Kleene stars. The minimal h having this property is called the star height of L. An excellent introduction to the star height problem is given in [Kir05], which mentions some of the important industrial applications such as speech recognition, database theory and image compression. This problem was considered as one of the most difficult problems in the theory of recognizable languages and it took 25 years before being solved by Hashiguchi [Has88]. Implementing Hashiguchi's algorithm is hopeless: even for a language L given by an automaton with 4 states, a "very low minorant" of the number of languages to be tested with L for equality is $c^{(c^c)}$ with $c = 10^{10^{10}}$ [LS02].

It took another 22 years before an algorithm with a better algorithmic complexity was given by Kirsten in [Kir05]. Kirsten's algorithm takes as input an automaton recognising a language L and an integer h and constructs an automaton with counters (nowadays called a B-automaton) inducing a function $f : A^* \rightarrow \mathbb{N} \cup \{\infty\}$ with the following property: f is limited if, and only if, the star height of L is at most h. Kirsten's solution was later adapted to trees [CL08a] using the framework of regular cost functions.

Stamina aims at solving the star height problem for practical applications, albeit the doubly exponential space complexity of Kirsten's algorithm is a challenge to tackle. To our best knowledge, this is the first time a solution to the star height problem is implemented.

The limitedness problem for regular cost functions takes as input a B-automaton inducing a function $f : A^* \rightarrow \mathbb{N} \cup \{\infty\}$, and checks whether the function f is bounded on its domain (words with a finite value). The theory of regular cost functions has been introduced by Colcombet [Col09, Col13], as a general formalism to express limitedness problems. A number of problems have been solved thanks to this theory (see e.g. [CL08a, CL08b, CKLB13]), and Stamina includes a general-purpose cost functions library.

The value 1 problem takes as input a probabilistic automaton and checks whether there are words accepted with probability arbitrarily close to 1. Probabilistic automata are a versatile tool widely used in speech recognition as well as a modelling tool for the control of systems with partial observations. They extend classical automata with probabilistic transitions, see [Rab63] for an introduction, and [FGO12] for the value 1 problem. This problem is a reformulation of a natural controller synthesis problem: assume a blackbox finite state system with random events is controlled by a blind controller who inputs actions to the blackbox but has absolutely no feedback on the state of the system. Then the synthesis of controllers with arbitraily high reliability is equivalent to solving the value 1 problem.

Stabilisation monoids are the key mathematical object behind the solutions to those three problems. For both B-automata and probabilistic automata, one can associate a stabilisation monoid generalising the notion of transition monoid. This monoid carries precise information about the behaviour of the automaton.

A seminal paper by Simon [Sim94] provides a combinatorial tool called the forest factorization theorem, at the heart of the solution of the limitedness problem for stabilisation monoids associated to B-automata. These algebraic techniques were adapted to solve the value 1 problem for probabilistic leaktight automata [FGO12, FGKO15].

Related work. Stamina is written in C++ and improves over a previous tool called Acme [FK14] implemented in OCaml, which was a first proof-of-concept tool using stabilisation monoids as an algorithmic back-end to solve the limitedness problem for regular cost functions. We provide quantitative experiments showing that Stamina performs much better than Acme, thanks to several optimisations. This improvement allows us to provide a new functionality: solving the star height problem, which was unrealistic with Acme as it could not handle large automata.

2   Computing the Stabilisation Monoid

The core computation performed by Stamina is the construction of the stabilisation monoid generated by a finite set of matrices.

2.1   Stabilisation Monoids in a Nutshell

Stabilisation monoids are sets of square matrices of fixed dimension n over a finite semiring $(\mathbb{S}, +, \cdot, 0, 1)$. When solving problems related to probabilistic automata, $\mathbb{S}$ is the boolean semiring $(\{0, 1\}, \vee, \wedge, 0, 1)$. When solving problems related to B-automata, including the star height problem, $\mathbb{S}$ is the semiring of sets of counter actions, see Subsect. 4.1.

The set of square matrices of dimension n over $\mathbb{S}$ inherits from $\mathbb{S}$ a monoid structure, where the product of two matrices is defined as usual:

$$(M \cdot N)[i, j] = \sum_{k=1}^{n} M[i, k] \cdot N[k, j] \ .$$

To obtain a stabilisation monoid one furthermore defines a unary operation on matrices called the *stabilisation* and denoted $\sharp$, which satisfies some axioms:

$$(M^{\sharp})^{\sharp} = M^{\sharp} \tag{1}$$

$$(MN)^{\sharp}M = M(NM)^{\sharp} \tag{2}$$

The intuition is that every matrix M is the abstraction of a matrix $\mathbf{M}$ with coefficients in an infinite monoid (e.g. for probabilistic automata, the reals with addition and multiplication) and $M^{\sharp}$ represents the asymptotic behaviour of the sequence $(\mathbf{M}^n)_{n \in \mathbb{N}}$. Some more details are provided in Sect. 4. The formal definition of a stabilisation monoid involves an order as well [Col09], which plays no role in Stamina.

2.2   Efficient Computation of Stabilisation Monoids

We report on our implementation of the following algorithmic task: Given a set of matrices S, compute the stabilisation monoid it generates, which is the smallest set of matrices containing S and stable under product and stabilisation.

Since the semiring $\mathbb{S}$ is finite then the set of $n \times n$ matrices on $\mathbb{S}$ is finite as well and the stabilisation monoid generated by S is computable as follows:

Repeat
    Add to S every product $M \cdot N$ for $M, N \in S$
    Add to S every $M^\sharp$ for $M \in S$
Until no new elements are added to S

Stamina implements this naïve algorithm with two main optimisations, one saves space and the other saves time.

Saving space: unique identifiers for matrices and vectors. The generated monoid can be exponential in the size of the matrices, so the crucial aspect here is space optimisation.

An $n \times n$ matrix is not represented as a list of n^2 coefficients but as a list of $2n$ pointers to vectors representing the rows and columns of the matrix: The vectors themselves are stored in a compact way, for example on a 64 bit architecture a single integer is used to store up to 64 coefficients of the boolean semiring.

To save even more space, all vectors and matrices are stored uniquely in global hashmaps. This induces a constant time comparison for matrices and vectors, as they are equal if, and only if, their pointers are equal. This allows Stamina to handle monoids with several billions of elements, and in practice Stamina computes monoids with several millions of elements with a small memory footprint.

Saving time: rewrite rules. In our application, the initial set of matrices is given by matrices M_a for $a \in A$, where A is the finite alphabet of the automaton. Hence we naturally associate to every element of the stabilisation monoid a $\sharp$-expression, which is a term on two operations: product and stabilisation. For instance $(M_a \cdot M_b^\sharp \cdot M_a)^\sharp$ is associated to $(ab^\sharp a)^\sharp$. There are infinitely many $\sharp$-expressions and finitely many matrices thus most $\sharp$-expressions rewrite in an equivalent and shorter way. Along with the computation of the vectors and matrices of the monoid, Stamina stores a list of rewrite rules of $\sharp$-expressions to a set of minimal non-equivalent expressions.

These rewrite rules are used in conjunction with the axioms (1) and (2) in order to minimise the number of iterations of the algorithm. For example, if $MN = M^\sharp$ then $(MN)^\sharp = M^\sharp$ according to (1), so once the rewrite rule $MN \to M^\sharp$ is known, Stamina avoids the computation of $(MN)^\sharp$.

Stamina implement the inner loop of the naïve algorithm as follows. It alternates between closure by product and closure by stabilisation. In both cases,

Stamina keeps a pending list of candidates for new elements. The computation of the generated monoid is over when the list of candidates is empty. For each candidate, Stamina checks whether it can be simplified by rewrite rules and axioms and in this case the candidate is dropped. Otherwise Stamina computes the corresponding matrix and checks whether this matrix is already known. If yes, Stamina creates a new rewrite rule. If not, Stamina adds a new element to the monoid.

3   Benchmarks

We compared the running times of Stamina and its predecessor Acme [FK14].

For the benchmarks we draw random automata which produce larger stabilisation monoids in order to observe the difference in performances between the two versions. The point of comparison is the size of the computed monoid rather than the number of states in the automaton, since some large automata can produce small monoids, and vice-versa, some small automata can produce large monoids.

To obtain random automata we proceed as follows. First, for each state s we pick a state t with uniform probability on the set of states and add a transition between s and t, ensuring that each state has an outgoing transition for each letter. After this we pick a number $p \in [0, 1]$ at random, and for all other states t' different from t, we add a transition between s and t' with probability p.

The results have been plotted in Fig. 1. One can observe that there is a threshold in the size of the Markov monoid after Acme will not be useful, *i.e.* either takes too much time or has a stack overflow. This threshold is depicted by the vertical line in the graph below (it hovers around 3500 elements).

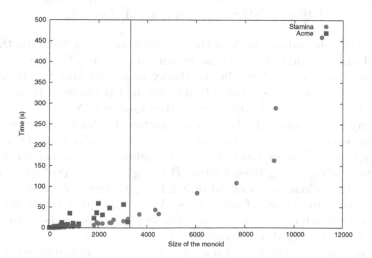

Fig. 1. Random automata of size 10.

4   Stabilisation Monoids for B- and Probabilistic Automata

The notion of stabilisation monoids appears in two distinct contexts. It has first been developed in the theory of regular cost functions, introduced by Colcombet [Col09, Col13]. The underlying ideas have then been transferred to the setting of probabilistic automata [FGO12].

4.1   Stabilisation Monoids in the Theory of Regular Cost Functions

At the heart of the theory of regular cost functions lies the equivalence between different formalisms: a logical formalism, cost MSO, two automata model, B- and S-automata, and an algebraic counterpart, stabilisation monoids.

Here we briefly describe the model of B-automata, and their transformations to stabilisation monoids. This automaton model generalises non-deterministic automata by adding a finite set of counters; instead of accepting or rejecting a word, a B-automaton associates an integer value to each input word. Formally, a B-automaton is a tuple $\mathcal{A} = \langle A, Q, \Gamma, I, F, \Delta \rangle$, where A is a finite alphabet, Q is a finite set of states, Γ is a finite set of counters, $I \subseteq Q$ is the set of initial states, $F \subseteq Q$ is the set of final states, and $\Delta \subseteq Q \times A \times \{\mathbf{r}, \mathbf{e}, \mathbf{ic}\}^{\Gamma} \times Q$ is the set of transitions. A transition (p, a, τ, q) allows the automaton to go from state p to state q while reading letter a and performing action $\tau(\gamma)$ on counter γ. The action $\mathbf{ic}$ increments the current counter value by 1, $\mathbf{e}$ leaves the counter unchanged, and $\mathbf{r}$ resets the counter to 0.

The value of a run is the maximal value assumed by any of the counters during the run. The semantics of a B-automaton $\mathcal{A}$ is defined on a word w by

$$[\![\mathcal{A}]\!](w) = \inf\{\mathrm{val}(\rho) \mid \rho \text{ is a run of } \mathcal{A} \text{ on } w\}.$$

In other words, the automaton uses the non determinism to minimise the value among all runs. In particular, if $\mathcal{A}$ has no run on w, then $[\![\mathcal{A}]\!](w) = \infty$.

The main decision problem in the theory of regular cost functions is the limitedness problem. We say that a B-automaton $\mathcal{A}$ is *limited* if there exists N such that for all words w, if $[\![\mathcal{A}]\!](w) < \infty$, then $[\![\mathcal{A}]\!](w) < N$.

One way to determine whether a B-automaton $\mathcal{A}$ is limited is by computing its stabilisation monoid. It contains matrices over the semiring of sets of counter actions $\{\mathbf{r}, \mathbf{e}, \mathbf{ic}, \omega\}^{\Gamma}$; more precisely it is the stabilisation monoid generated by the matrices corresponding to each letter. Defining the semiring of sets of counter actions is a bit tedious (see [Col09, Col13]); for the sake of explanations we will restrict ourselves to the case of one counter. As we will explain for the star height problem it is enough to work with a subclass of B-automata called hierarchical, for which this semiring also considerably simplifies.

Assuming the B-automaton $\mathcal{A}$ has only one counter, its stabilisation monoid is a set of matrices over the semiring of counter actions $\{\mathbf{r}, \mathbf{e}, \mathbf{ic}, \omega\}$ defined as follows: the addition of the semiring is the minimum for the order $\mathbf{r} < \mathbf{e} < \mathbf{ic} < \omega$, and the multiplication is the maximum for the order $\mathbf{e} \prec \mathbf{ic} \prec \mathbf{r} \prec \omega$.

This semiring structure induces a product operation on matrices. See [Col09] for a formal definition of the stabilisation operation on these matrices.

We now give some intuitions about the stabilisation monoid of $\mathcal{A}$. Consider a $\sharp$-expression e, as for instance $a(ba)^\sharp$. It induces a sequence of words, in the example $(a(ba)^n)_{n\in\mathbb{N}}$. The goal is to associate to every $\sharp$-expression e a matrix M_e such that M_e summarises the action of $\mathcal{A}$ on the sequence of words induced by e. More precisely, $M_e[i,j]$ is a counter action describing the runs from i to j on the sequence of words. To illustrate, assume that for each word $a(ba)^n$ there are two runs from i to j, performing on the counter the actions $\mathbf{e}(\mathbf{ic\ e})^n$ and $\mathbf{r}(\mathbf{ic\ r})^n$, respectively. The first run gives rise to $\max(\mathbf{e}, (\max(\mathbf{ic}, \mathbf{e}))^\sharp) = \max(\mathbf{e}, \omega) = \omega$, and the second to $\max(\mathbf{r}, (\max(\mathbf{ic}, \mathbf{r})^\sharp) = \max(\mathbf{r}, \mathbf{r}) = \mathbf{r}$. The summary of these two runs is $\min(\omega, \mathbf{r}) = \mathbf{r}$. The use of min and max matches the definition of a value of a word as the infimum over all runs of the maximum values of the counter.

An unlimited witness is a $\sharp$-expression inducing a sequence of words $(u_n)_{n\in\mathbb{N}}$ such that $\lim_n [\![\mathcal{A}]\!](u_n) = \infty$. As shown in [Col09, Col13], the stabilisation monoid of a B-automaton $\mathcal{A}$ contains an unlimited witness if, and only if, it is not limited. This gives a conceptually simple solution to the limitedness problem: compute the stabilisation monoid and check for the existence of unlimited witnesses.

We briefly discuss the case of hierarchical actions, as it is used for the solution to the star height problem, and correspond to the nested distance automata in [Kir05]. We have $k + 1$ counters numbered from 0 to k. The hierarchical actions are the following, for $j \in [0, k]$:

- R_j resets all counters p with $p \geq j$, the others remain unchanged;
- I_j increments the counter j, resets the counters p with $p > j$, the others remain unchanged;
- $\mathbf{e}$ leaves all counters unchanged;
- ω means that some counter reached very high values.

The addition of the semiring is the minimum for the order $R_0 < R_1 < \cdots < R_k < \mathbf{e} < I_0 < I_1 < \cdots < I_k < \omega$. The multiplication of the semiring is the maximum for the order $\mathbf{e} \prec I_k \prec R_k \prec I_{k-1} \prec R_{k-1} \prec \cdots \prec I_0 \prec R_0 \prec \omega$.

4.2 Stabilisation Monoids for Probabilistic Automata

The notion of stabilisation monoids also appeared for probabilistic automata, for the Markov Monoid Algorithm. This algorithm was introduced in [FGO12] to partially solve the value 1 problem: given a probabilistic automaton $\mathcal{A}$, does there exist $(u_n)_{n\in\mathbb{N}}$ a sequence of words such that $\lim_n \mathbb{P}_\mathcal{A}(u_n) = 1$?

Although the value 1 problem is undecidable, it has been shown that the Markov Monoid Algorithm correctly determines whether a probabilistic automaton has value 1 under the *leaktight* restriction. It has been recently shown that all classes of probabilistic automata for which the value 1 problem has been shown decidable are included in the class of leaktight automata [FGKO15], hence the Markov Monoid Algorithm is the *most correct* algorithm known to (partially) solve the value 1 problem.

As for the case of B-automata, the stabilisation monoid of a probabilistic automaton is the stabilisation monoid generated by the set of matrices corresponding to each letter. The underlying semiring is the Boolean semiring; the definition of the stabilisation is specific to probabilistic automata, we refer to [FGO12,FGKO15] for details.

5   The Star Height Algorithm

The latest algorithm in the literature for computing star height is designed for tree automata [CL08a], but we will use it here in the special case of words. The main improvement over the previous algorithm from [Kir05] is the identification of the structure of Subset Automata, which allows minimisation. We discuss the main ideas of the algorithm.

5.1   Subset Automata

We consider deterministic automata with ϵ-transitions, $i.e.$ such that the transition relation is of the form $\Delta \subseteq Q \times (A \cup \{\epsilon\}) \times Q$. One can see the ϵ-transitions as defining a partial order on states.

Definition 1 ([CL08a]). *A subset automaton $\mathcal{A}$ is a deterministic automaton with ϵ-transitions such that:*

- *The ϵ-transitions induce a sup-semi-lattice, i.e. every subset P of Q has a least upper bound $\bigvee P$. In particular, there is a minimum element $\bigvee \emptyset$ and a maximal element $\bigvee Q$.*
- *The transition function of $\mathcal{A}$ is compatible with the sup-semi-lattice structure, i.e. for all $P \subseteq Q$ and $a \in A$, we have $\delta(\bigvee P, a) = \bigvee\{\delta(p,a) \mid p \in P\}$.*

It is proved in [CL08a] that any regular language can be recognized by a subset automaton, which can be obtained by a powerset construction from a non-deterministic automaton for the complement language. Note however that this subset automaton is of exponential size in the original automaton.

An interesting property of subset automata is that they can be minimised. The states of the minimal subset automaton are intersection of residuals of the language [CL08a]. We implemented the minimisation algorithm, which turns out to be a precious optimisation.

5.2   Reduction to the Limitedness Problem for B-Automata

We start from a subset automaton recognising the language L and an integer k, and want to determine whether L has star height at most k. We construct a hierarchical B-automaton $\mathcal{B}$ with $k + 1$ counters such that L has star height at most k if, and only if, $\mathcal{B}$ is limited.

The set of states is $Q' = \bigcup_{i=1}^{k+1} Q^i$, which we view as a subset of Q^*. The initial state is q_0. A state $\rho \cdot p$ is final if, and only if, $p \in F$. We now define the transitions:

- If $(p, a, q) \in \Delta$ and $\rho \in Q^{\leq k}$, we add the transition $(\rho \cdot p, a, I_{|\rho|}, \rho \cdot q)$. If $a = \varepsilon$, the action may equivalently be replaced by $\mathbf{e}$, as we do in the implementation.
- If $\rho \in Q^{\leq k-1}$ and $p \in Q$, we add the transition $(\rho \cdot p, \epsilon, R_{|\rho \cdot p|}, \rho \cdot p \cdot p)$.
- If $\rho \in Q^{\leq k-1}$ and $p, q \in Q$, we add the transition $(\rho \cdot p \cdot q, \epsilon, R_{|\rho \cdot p|}, \rho \cdot q)$.

Example 1. We apply the construction to the following automaton $\mathcal{A}$, and want to determine whether it has star height at most 1. The minimal subset automaton of $\mathcal{A}$ happens to be isomorphic to $\mathcal{A}$ in this case.

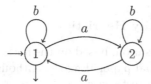

We construct the following B-automaton $\mathcal{B}$, where the ε-transitions are the dashed transitions.

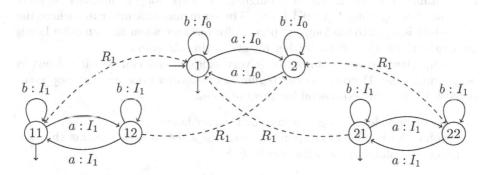

Therefore, for any fixed k, we can decide whether a regular language given by a deterministic automaton has star height at most k. The algorithm is the following:

- first construct a subset automaton recognising the same language by a powerset construction, yielding an exponentially bigger automaton,
- minimise the subset automaton,
- construct the B-automaton $\mathcal{B}$ as above,
- check $\mathcal{B}$ for limitedness using the stabilisation monoid algorithm, which means constructing the stabilisation monoid of $\mathcal{B}$, of exponential size in $\mathcal{B}$.

The best theoretical computational complexity uses exponential space, which requires to perform the computation of the stabilisation monoid on the fly using polynomial space. Note that Kirsten's algorithm uses doubly exponential space because it takes a non-deterministic automaton as input.

The algorithmic task that we want to perform is the following: given a regular language L, compute its star height. The section above describes how, given a language L and an integer k, we can test whether L has star height at most k, by constructing a B-automaton $\mathcal{B}(k)$ such that L has star height at most k if, and only if, $\mathcal{B}(k)$ is limited. One may thus simply apply this algorithm for increasing values of k. Unfortunately, the automaton $\mathcal{B}(k)$ becomes rather quickly very large. This means that checking it for limitedness may be intractable. We know that there are short witnesses that $\mathcal{B}(k)$ is not limited, given by unlimited witnesses. We will show in the next section how the loop complexity heuristic provides us with potential such witnesses.

5.3   The Loop Complexity Heuristic

We present a decisive optimisation, based on the notion of loop complexity introduced by Eggan in his seminal paper [Egg63]. Although it is only a heuristic, it led to huge improvements in test cases.

The *loop complexity* of an automaton $\mathcal{A}$, denoted $LC(\mathcal{A})$, is the star height of an expression obtained from the automaton via a standard algorithm. It has been extensively studied, and many properties of the loop complexity are known. For instance, the star height of a language L is the loop complexity of *some* automaton recognising L [Egg63,LS02]. There are many natural cases where the star height is equal to the loop complexity, for instance when all transition labels are distinct, see [Coh70] for further results in this direction.

Computing the loop complexity is very efficient and can be carried out in polynomial time. Denote e_{LC} the regular expression witnessing the loop complexity. We use this expression for two purposes:

- First, it provides an upper bound for the star height.
- Second, the regular expression e_{LC} induces a list of $\sharp$-expressions that are potential unlimitedness witnesses in $\mathcal{B}(k)$.

The point is that computing both e_{LC} and the potential witnesses is very fast compared to actually checking whether $\mathcal{B}(k)$ is limited. Hence this gives fast means to observe that $\mathcal{B}(k)$ is unlimited without having to compute its stabilisation monoid.

Starting from a regular expression, we construct a list of $\sharp$-expressions in the following way.

- First, we say that a regular expression is in normal form if the sums appear only at the root or directly below Kleene stars, *i.e.* not under a product. One can easily rewrite a regular expression into one in normal form by distributing sums over products.
- Given a regular expression in normal form, one obtains a $\sharp$-expression by inductively transforming $(\sum_i e_i)^*$ into $(\prod_i e_i^\sharp)^\sharp$. For instance, $(a+b)^*$ becomes $(a^\sharp b^\sharp)^\sharp$. The idea behind this translation if to make the most of loops in the automaton.
- A regular expression e in normal form is a sum of regular expressions e_i, each in normal form. The list of $\sharp$-expressions for e is obtained by applying the previous transformation to each e_i.

Let us return to the example presented above, Example 1. Its loop complexity is 2, and the expression computed by the algorithm is $e_{LC} = (b + (ab^*a))^*$. This regular expression is turned into the $\sharp$-expression $(b^\sharp(ab^\sharp a)^\sharp)^\sharp$ by our heuristic. It turns out that this $\sharp$-expression is an unlimited witness for $\mathcal{B}(1)$. The simplest such witness is $(b^\sharp ab^\sharp a)^\sharp$. This shows that in this example the loop complexity heuristic allows us to instantly pinpoint the unlimited behaviour of $\mathcal{B}(1)$, circumventing the hefty price of computing the stabilisation monoid.

5.4   The Algorithm

Compute the regular expression e_{LC} of star height $LC(\mathcal{A})$

Compute a subset automaton, and minimise it

$k = 0$

Repeat

    Construct $\mathcal{B}(k)$

    Check whether the $\sharp$-expressions induced by e_{LC} are witnesses of $\mathcal{B}(k)$

        If an unlimited witness is found, increment k

        Otherwise, check $\mathcal{B}(k)$ for limitedness

            If $\mathcal{B}(k)$ is not limited, increment k

Until $k = LC(\mathcal{A})$ or $\mathcal{B}(k)$ is limited

Return k

One may wonder whether the two optimisations, namely the loop complexity heuristic and minimising the subset automaton, indeed provide a speed-up. As an evidence that it does, we report on the following experiment. We enumerated 200 automata with three states and computed their star height. The computation was considered an overflow when the number of pending matrix products was >5 billions.

Settings	Overflows	AvgTime(s)	Avg monoid dim - size
No optimisation	5	12.5	62.1–1328.0
Loop complexity (LC)	4	10.2	
Minimisation	0	6.4	45.7–489.1
Minimisation + LC	0	3.5	

6   Conclusions

After more than 50 years of research, the star height problem still had the reputation to be intractable, even for very small automata. By implementing state-of-the-art algorithms together with new heuristics and optimisations, we reached a new step in the understanding of this problem. In particular, we discovered a relationship between expressions of optimal loop complexity and unlimited witnesses, which could be of theoretical interest. Our tool Stamina shows that one can compute the star height in non-trivial cases, as it has been successfully tested on several examples of different nature. It is also a drastic improvement over its previous version ACME for computing limitedness of B-automata and value 1 for leaktight probabilistic automata.

References

[CKLB13] Colcombet, T., Kuperberg, D., Löding, C., Vanden Boom, M.: Deciding the weak definability of Büchi definable tree languages. In: CSL, pp. 215–230 (2013)

[CL08a] Colcombet, T., Löding, C.: The nesting-depth of disjunctive μ-calculus for tree languages and the limitedness problem. In: CSL, pp. 416–430 (2008)

[CL08b] Colcombet, T., Löding, C.: The non-deterministic Mostowski hierarchy and distance-parity automata. In: Aceto, L., Damgård, I., Goldberg, L.A., Halldórsson, M.M., Ingólfsdóttir, A., Walukiewicz, I. (eds.) ICALP 2008. LNCS, vol. 5126, pp. 398–409. Springer, Heidelberg (2008). doi:10.1007/978-3-540-70583-3_33

[Coh70] Cohen, R.S.: Star height of certain families of regular events. J. Comput. Syst. Sci. **4**(3), 281–297 (1970)

[Col09] Colcombet, T.: The theory of stabilisation monoids and regular cost functions. In: Albers, S., Marchetti-Spaccamela, A., Matias, Y., Nikoletseas, S., Thomas, W. (eds.) ICALP 2009. LNCS, vol. 5556, pp. 139–150. Springer, Heidelberg (2009). doi:10.1007/978-3-642-02930-1_12

[Col13] Colcombet, T.: Regular cost-functions Part I: logic and algebra over words. Logical Meth. Comput. Sci. **9**(3), 1–47 (2013)

[Egg63] Eggan, L.C.: Transition graphs and the star-height of regular events. Mich. Math. J. **10**, 385–397 (1963)

[FGKO15] Fijalkow, N., Gimbert, H., Kelmendi, E., Oualhadj, Y.: Deciding the value 1 problem for probabilistic leaktight automata. Logical Meth. Comput. Sci. **11**(1) (2015). http://www.lmcs-online.org/ojs/viewarticle.php?id=1588

[FGO12] Fijalkow, N., Gimbert, H., Oualhadj, Y.: Deciding the value 1 problem for probabilistic leaktight automata. In: LICS, pp. 295–304 (2012)

[FK14] Fijalkow, N., Kuperberg, A.D.: Automata with counters, monoids and equivalence. In: ATVA, pp. 163–167 (2014)

[Has88] Hashiguchi, K.: Algorithms for determining relative star height and star height. Inf. Comput. **78**(2), 124–169 (1988)

[Kir05] Kirsten, D.: Distance desert automata and the star height problem. Theor. Inf. Appl. **39**(3), 455–509 (2005)

[LS02] Lombardy, S., Sakarovitch, J.: Star height of reversible languages and universal automata. In: Rajsbaum, S. (ed.) LATIN 2002. LNCS, vol. 2286, pp. 76–90. Springer, Heidelberg (2002). doi:10.1007/3-540-45995-2_12

[Rab63] Rabin, M.O.: Probabilistic automata. Inf. Control **6**(3), 230–245 (1963)

[Sim94] Simon, I.: On semigroups of matrices over the tropical semiring. Theor. Inf. Appl. **28**(3–4), 277–294 (1994)

A Simple Method for Building Bimachines from Functional Finite-State Transducers

Stefan Gerdjikov[1,2], Stoyan Mihov[2(✉)], and Klaus U. Schulz[3]

[1] Faculty of Mathematics and Informatics, Sofia University,
5, James Borchier Blvd., 1164 Sofia, Bulgaria
stefangerdzhikov@fmi.uni-sofia.bg
[2] Institute of Information and Communication Technologies,
Bulgarian Academy of Sciences, 25A, Acad. G. Bonchev Street, 1113 Sofia, Bulgaria
stoyan@lml.bas.bg
[3] Centrum für Informations-und Sprachverarbeitung (CIS),
Ludwig-Maximilians-Universität München,
Oettingenstr. 67, 80538 München, Germany
schulz@cis.uni-muenchen.de

Abstract. The standard construction of a bimachine from a functional transducer involves a preparation step for converting the transducer into an unambiguous transducer (A transducer is unambiguous if there exists at most one successful path for each label.). The conversion involves a specialized determinization. We introduce a new construction principle where the transducer is directly translated into a bimachine. For any input word accepted by the transducer the bimachine exactly imitates one successful path of the transducer. For some classes of transducers the new construction can build a bimachine with an exponentially lower number of states compared to the standard construction. We first present a simple and generic variant of the construction. A second specialized version leads to better complexity bounds in terms of the size of the bimachine.

Keywords: Bimachines · Transducers · Rational functions

1 Introduction

Finite-state transducers are used for a large spectrum of translation tasks in text analysis and natural language processing [4–7]. Many practical translation tasks are functional in the sense that a given input needs to be transformed into a unique output. While (non-deterministic versions of) finite-state transducers can model arbitrary "regular" (s.b.) functions between strings, many regular functions cannot be recognized by deterministic finite-state transducers. In contrast, bimachines as a more powerful type of finite-state device enable a fully deterministic processing of arbitrary regular string functions [11].

© Springer International Publishing AG 2017
A. Carayol and C. Nicaud (Eds.): CIAA 2017, LNCS 10329, pp. 113–125, 2017.
DOI: 10.1007/978-3-319-60134-2_10

For a given regular string function f it is often simple to find a non-deterministic finite-state transducer that represents f. Since a deterministic processing via bimachines is more efficient, there is an obvious interest in general methods for converting functional finite-state transducers into bimachines or equivalent devices [10,12]. The classical algorithm, described in [7], starts with a preparation step for converting the transducer into an unambiguous transducer. The conversion requires that the source transducer is "pseudo-deterministic". Afterwards it uses a specialized determinization for discarding unwanted paths. Essentially, only the least accepting paths under some lexicographical order are left. This construction can be applied to arbitrary output monoids after introducing a linear order on the outputs of single transitions.

Here we introduce a new single-step method that can be applied to any functional real-time transducer with output (codomain) in an arbitrary monoid. States of the right deterministic automaton of the bimachine are sets R of active states obtained when using inversed transitions of the functional input transducer $\mathcal{T}$, starting from final states. States of the left deterministic automaton of the bimachine are sets L of active states of $\mathcal{T}$ that are enhanced by a special function. Using this enhancement the bimachine satisfies the "path reconstruction" principle: (i) At each step, the bimachine output m represents the output of a single transducer transition step $\langle q, \langle a, m \rangle, q' \rangle$ for some $q \in L \cap R$. (ii) for any input w: the sequence of bimachine outputs w is given by the sequence of outputs of $\mathcal{T}$ for w on a specific path.

After formal preliminaries in Sect. 2 the new construction is described in Sect. 3. We start with a generic and flexible version that is conceptually simple. Afterwards a specialized version is added which leads to better complexity bounds for the number of states of the left and right deterministic automata of the bimachine. Correctness proofs are given. For the sake of comparison we sketch the classical bimachine construction in Sect. 4. A class of examples is given where the new construction leads to an exponentially lower number of states. A conclusion is presented in Sect. 5.

2   Formal Preliminaries

We assume that the reader is familiar with the basic notions of words over an alphabet and monoids (see e.g. [2]). The set Σ^* with concatenation as monoid operation and the empty word ε as unit element is called the *free monoid* over Σ. We list notions needed for the discussion of the paper. A *monoidal finite-state automaton* is a tuple of the form $\mathcal{A} = \langle \mathcal{M}, Q, I, F, \Delta \rangle$ where

- $\mathcal{M} = \langle M, \circ, e \rangle$ is a monoid,
- Q is a finite set called the set of states,
- $I \subseteq Q$ is the set of initial states,
- $F \subseteq Q$ is the set of final states, and
- $\Delta \subseteq Q \times M \times Q$ is a finite set of transitions called the transition relation.

A *proper path* in $\mathcal{A}$ is a finite sequence of $k > 0$ transitions, denoted

$$\pi = q_0 \to^{a_1} q_1 \ldots \to^{a_k} q_k$$

where $\langle q_{i-1}, a_i, q_i \rangle \subset \Delta$ for $i = 1 \ldots k$. The monoid element $w = a_1 \circ \ldots \circ a_k$ is called the *label* of π. A *successful path* is a path starting in an initial state and ending in a final state.

The *generalized transition relation* Δ^* is defined as the smallest subset of $Q \times M \times Q$ with the following closure properties:

- for all $q \in Q$ we have $\langle q, e, q \rangle \in \Delta^*$.
- For all $q_1, q_2, q_3 \in Q$ and $w, a \in M$: if $\langle q_1, w, q_2 \rangle \in \Delta^*$ and $\langle q_2, a, q_3 \rangle \in \Delta$, then also $\langle q_1, w \circ a, q_3 \rangle \in \Delta^*$.

The monoidal language *accepted* (or *recognized*) by $\mathcal{A}$ is defined as $L(\mathcal{A}) := \{w \in M \mid \exists p \in I\, \exists q \in F : \langle p, w, q \rangle \in \Delta^*\}$.
A monoidal finite-state automaton $\mathcal{A}$ is *unambiguous* iff for every element $m \in M$ there exists at most one successful path in $\mathcal{A}$ with label m.
A state $q \in Q$ is *accessible* if q is the ending of a path of $\mathcal{A}$ starting from an initial state. A state $q \in Q$ is *co-accessible* if q is the starting of a path of $\mathcal{A}$ ending in a final state. A monoidal finite-state automaton $\mathcal{A}$ is *trimmed* iff each state $q \in Q$ is accessible and co-accessible.
A *deterministic finite-state automaton* is a monoidal finite-state automaton over the free monoid $\mathcal{A} = \langle \Sigma^*, Q, I, F, \Delta \rangle$, such that $|I| = 1$ and Δ is a graph of a (partial) function with domain $dom(\Delta) \subseteq Q \times \Sigma$. In this case we identify Δ with the function $\Delta : Q \times \Sigma \to Q$ that it represents. The *reversed finite-state automaton* for $\mathcal{A}$ is $\mathcal{A}^{rev} = \langle \Sigma^*, Q, F, I, \Delta^{rev} \rangle$, where $\Delta^{rev} = \{\langle q, a^{rev}, p \rangle \mid \langle p, a, q \rangle \in \Delta\}$.

Definition 1. *A monoidal finite-state automaton T over a monoid $\mathcal{M}$ is a monoidal finite-state transducer iff $\mathcal{M}$ can be represented as the Cartesian product of a free monoid Σ^* with another monoid $\mathcal{M}'$, i.e. $\mathcal{M} = \Sigma^* \times \mathcal{M}'$. For a monoidal finite-state transducer $T = \langle \Sigma^* \times \mathcal{M}, Q, I, F, \Delta \rangle$ the underlying finite-state automaton is the monoidal finite-state automaton $\mathcal{A}_T = \langle \Sigma^*, Q, I, F, \Delta_\Sigma \rangle$ where $\Delta_\Sigma = \{\langle p, a, q \rangle \mid \exists m \in M(\langle p, \langle a, m \rangle, q \rangle \in \Delta\}$. A monoidal finite-state transducer $T = \langle \Sigma^* \times \mathcal{M}', Q, I, F, \Delta \rangle$ is said to be real-time if $\Delta \subseteq Q \times (\Sigma \times \mathcal{M}') \times Q$.*

Let $\mathcal{M}$ be a monoid. A set $L \subseteq M$ is *rational* iff it is accepted by a monoidal finite-state automaton. If M is a Cartesian product, then rational sets are relations. A *rational function* is a rational set that is a function.

Definition 2. *A* bimachine *is a tuple $\mathcal{B} = \langle \mathcal{M}, \mathcal{A}_L, \mathcal{A}_R, \psi \rangle$, where:*

- *$\mathcal{A}_L = \langle \Sigma, L, s_L, L, \delta_L \rangle$ and $\mathcal{A}_R = \langle \Sigma, R, s_R, R, \delta_R \rangle$ are deterministic finite-state automata called the* left *and* right automaton *of the bimachine;*
- *$\mathcal{M} = \langle M, \circ, e \rangle$ is the* output monoid *and $\psi : (L \times \Sigma \times R) \to M$ is a partial function called the* output function.

Note that all states of A_L and A_L are final. The function ψ is naturally extended to the generalized output function ψ^* as follows:

- $\psi^*(l, \varepsilon, r) = e$ *for all* $l \in L, r \in R$;
- $\psi^*(l, t\sigma, r) = \psi^*(l, t, \delta_R(r, \sigma)) \circ \psi(\delta_L^*(l, t), \sigma, r)$ *for* $l \in L, r \in R, t \in \Sigma^*, \sigma \in \Sigma$.

The function represented by the bimachine is

$$O_\mathcal{B} : \Sigma^* \to M : t \mapsto \psi^*(s_L, t, s_R).$$

If $O_\mathcal{B}(t) = t'$ we say that the bimachine $\mathcal{B}$ translates t into t'.

Note that for any states $p, q \in Q$ of a monoidal finite-state transducer $\mathcal{T} = \langle \Sigma^* \times \mathcal{M}, Q, I, F, \Delta \rangle$ and word $w \in \Sigma^*$ holds $\exists m \in M : \langle p, \langle w, m \rangle, q \rangle \in \Delta^* \iff \langle p, w, q \rangle \in \Delta_\Sigma^*$, where Δ_Σ is the transition relation of its underlying automaton.

If $\mathcal{A}^{rev} = \langle \Sigma^*, Q, F, I, \Delta^{rev} \rangle$ is the reversed finite-state automaton of $\mathcal{A} = \langle \Sigma^*, Q, I, F, \Delta \rangle$, then for any states $q, p \in Q$ and any word $w \in \Sigma^*$ we have $\langle p, w, q \rangle \in \Delta^* \iff \langle q, w^{rev}, p \rangle \in \Delta^{rev*}$.

After applying the power-set construction to transform a nondeterministic automaton $\mathcal{A} = \langle \Sigma^*, Q, I, F, \Delta \rangle$ into an equivalent deterministic one $\mathcal{A}_D = \langle \Sigma^*, Q_D, \{I\}, F_D, \delta_D \rangle$ with states $Q_D \subseteq 2^Q$ the following holds:

$$\forall w \in \Sigma^* \; \forall P \in Q_D : \delta_D^*(P, w) = \{q \mid \exists p \in P : \langle p, w, q \rangle \in \Delta^*\}.$$

Proposition 1. *(Cf. e.g. [7]) Let $\mathcal{A} = \langle \Sigma^* \times \mathcal{M}, Q, I, F, \Delta \rangle$ be a trimmed monoidal transducer. If $\mathcal{A}$ does not contain any cycle of the form $\langle p, \langle \varepsilon, m \rangle, p \rangle \in \Delta^*$ with $m \neq e$, then $\mathcal{A}$ can be effectively transformed into a real-time transducer $\mathcal{A}'$ such that $L(\mathcal{A}) \cap (\Sigma^+ \times M) = L(\mathcal{A}') \cap (\Sigma^+ \times M)$. Furthermore, we can effectively compute the set $\{m \mid \langle \varepsilon, m \rangle \in L(\mathcal{A})\}$.*

3   New Bimachine Construction

From now on we assume that $\mathcal{T} = \langle \Sigma^* \times \mathcal{M}, Q, I, F, \Delta \rangle$ is any trimmed real-time functional monoidal transducer. We assume that $\langle \varepsilon, e \rangle \in L(\mathcal{T})$. Let $\mathcal{A}_\mathcal{T} = \langle \Sigma^*, Q, I, F, \Delta_\Sigma \rangle$ be the underlying finite-state automaton of $\mathcal{T}$ and $\mathcal{A}_\mathcal{T}^{rev} = \langle \Sigma^*, Q, F, I, \Delta_\Sigma^{rev} \rangle$ be the reverse finite-state automaton of $\mathcal{A}_\mathcal{T}$. Let $\mathcal{A}_{\mathcal{T}D} = \langle \Sigma^*, 2^Q, \{I\}, F_D, \delta_{\Sigma D} \rangle$ and $\mathcal{A}_\mathcal{T}^{rev}{}_D = \langle \Sigma^*, 2^Q, \{F\}, I_D, \delta_{\Sigma}^{rev}{}_D \rangle$ be the deterministic finite-state automata for $\mathcal{A}_\mathcal{T}$ and $\mathcal{A}_\mathcal{T}^{rev}$, respectively.

For each set of states $P \subseteq Q$ and $w \in \Sigma^*$, we define the set of w-successors and w-predecessors of P as

$$Succ_w(P) := \delta_{\Sigma D}^*(P, w) = \{q \in Q \mid \exists p \in P, m \in M : \langle p, \langle w, m \rangle, q \rangle \in \Delta^*\}$$
$$Pred_w(P) := \delta_\Sigma^{rev*}{}_D(P, w) = \{q \in Q \mid \exists p \in P, m \in M : \langle q, \langle w^{rev}, m \rangle, p \rangle \in \Delta^*\}.$$

Note that the first (second) clause is based on a left-to-right (right-to-left) reading order.

Lemma 1 (Butterfly Lemma). *Let $\mathcal{T}$ be as above. Let $u, v \in \Sigma^*$, $a \in \Sigma$, let $L := Succ_u(I)$, $L' := Succ_{ua}(I)$, $R' := Pred_v(F)$ and $R := Pred_{av}(F)$. Then*

1. *for all $q \in L \cap R$ there is $q' \in L' \cap R'$ and $m \in M$ such that $\langle q, \langle a, m \rangle, q' \rangle \in \Delta$,*
2. *for all $q' \in L' \cap R'$ there is $q \in L \cap R$ and $m \in M$ such that $\langle q, \langle a, m \rangle, q' \rangle \in \Delta$,*
3. *$L \cap R \neq \emptyset$ iff $L' \cap R' \neq \emptyset$.*

Proof. As to 1, let $q \in L \cap R$. Since $R = Pred_a(R')$ there exists a transition of the form $\langle q, \langle a, m \rangle, q' \rangle \in \Delta$ such that $q' \in R'$. Since $q \in L$ we have $q' \in L'$. 2 follows by a symmetric argument. 3 directly follows from 1 and 2.   □

3.1 Generic Construction

We now show how to build an equivalent bimachine $\mathcal{B} = \langle \mathcal{M}, \mathcal{A}_L, \mathcal{A}_R, \psi \rangle$, given the transducer $\mathcal{T}$ as input. First, we construct the **right automaton** $\mathcal{A}_R$ applying a determinization procedure to the reversed underlying automaton of $\mathcal{T}$. Let

$$\mathcal{A}_R = \mathcal{A}_{\mathcal{T}}^{rev}{}_D = \langle \Sigma^*, Q_R, s_R, F_R, \delta_R \rangle.$$

By definition $s_R = \{F\}$ and $\delta_R(R, a) = \delta_{\Sigma}^{rev}{}_D(R, a) = Pred_a(R)$ for $R \in Q_R$ and $a \in \Sigma$. The idea for the **left automaton** is to use the accessible sets in $\mathcal{A}_{\mathcal{T}D}$

$$Q'_L := \{ \delta_{\Sigma D}^*(I, w) \mid w \in \Sigma^* \} = \{ Succ_w(I) \mid w \in \Sigma^* \}$$

as a "core" part of the states, but to enrich this core part by additional information that enables the reconstruction of successful paths in $\mathcal{T}$. Let $L \in Q'_L$. An *L-centered state selector function* is a partial function $\phi : Q_R \rightarrow Q$ such that the following conditions hold for any state of the right automaton $R \in Q_R$:

1. $\phi(R)$ is defined iff $R \cap L \neq \emptyset$ and
2. if $\phi(R)$ is defined, then $\phi(R) \in R \cap L$.

A state of the left automaton $\mathcal{A}_L = \langle \Sigma, Q_L, s_L, Q_L, \delta_L \rangle$ is a pair $\langle L, \phi \rangle$ where $L \in Q'_L$ and ϕ is an L-centered state selector function. The following induction defines s_L, the set of states Q_L, and the transition function δ_L.

- $s_L := \langle I, \phi_0 \rangle$ where $\phi_0(R) := \begin{cases} \text{any element of } R \cap I \text{ if } R \cap I \neq \emptyset \\ \text{undefined} \qquad\qquad\quad \text{otherwise.} \end{cases}$
- For $\langle L, \phi \rangle \in Q_L$ and $a \in \Sigma$ we define $\delta_L(\langle L, \phi \rangle, a) := \langle L', \phi' \rangle$ where
  - $L' := Succ_a(L)$.
  - $\phi'(R') := \begin{cases} \text{any element of } \{q' \mid \exists m \in M : \langle q, \langle a, m \rangle, q' \rangle \in \Delta\} \\ \qquad\qquad \text{if } q = \phi(Pred_a(R')) \text{ is defined} \\ \text{undefined} \qquad \text{otherwise.} \end{cases}$

In the above notions we show that

1. for each state $\langle L, \phi \rangle$ always ϕ is an L-centered state selection function, and
2. if $\phi(Pred_a(R'))$ is defined, then $q' = \phi'(R')$ is also defined.

The proof is by induction. For $s_L := \langle I, \phi_0 \rangle$ clearly ϕ_0 is defined as an I-centered state selection function. For the induction step, given state $\langle L, \phi \rangle$ assume that ϕ is an L-centered state selection function. Let $R' \in Q_R$ and $R := Pred_a(R')$. First, if $q = \phi(R)$ is defined, then (ϕ is L-centered) $L \cap R \neq \emptyset$ and $q \in L \cap R$. By the Butterfly Lemma we have that $L' \cap R' \neq \emptyset$ and further there exists a transition $\langle q, \langle a, m \rangle, q' \rangle \in \Delta$ such that $q' \in L' \cap R'$. Therefore $q' = \phi'(R')$ is defined and $\phi'(R') \in L' \cap R'$. On the other hand, if $\phi(R)$ is undefined, then (ϕ is L-centered) $L \cap R = \emptyset$ and (Butterfly Lemma) $L' \cap R' = \emptyset$. It follows that ϕ' is L'-centered.

It remains to define the **output function** ψ of the bimachine. Given a pair of states $\langle L, \phi \rangle$ and R' of the left and right automaton and $a \in \Sigma$, let $\langle L', \phi' \rangle := \delta_L(\langle L, \phi \rangle, a)$ and $R := Pred_a(R') = \delta_R(R', a)$. Then

$$\psi(\langle L, \phi \rangle, a, R') := \begin{cases} \text{any element of } \{m \mid \langle \phi(R), \langle a, m \rangle, \phi'(R') \rangle \in \Delta\} & \text{if } !\phi(R) \\ \text{undefined} & \text{otherwise} \end{cases}$$

(We have shown above that there always exists a transition of the above form.)

Correctness. We now show that the function defined by the bimachine $\mathcal{B} = \langle \mathcal{A}_L, \mathcal{A}_R, \psi \rangle$ coincides with the language of the transducer $\mathcal{T}$.

Theorem 1. *Let* $u = a_1 \ldots a_k \in dom(\mathcal{T})$. *For* $i \in \{0, 1, \ldots, k\}$ *let* $\langle L_i, \phi_i \rangle := \delta_L^*(s_L, a_1 \ldots a_i)$ *and* $R_i := \delta_R^*(s_R, a_k, \ldots, a_{i+1})$. *Then for any* $i \leq k$ *the following hold:*

1. $q_i := \phi_i(R_i)$ *is defined.*
2. $m_{i+1} := \psi(L_i, a_{i+1}, R_{i+1})$ *is defined and* $\langle q_i, \langle a_{i+1}, m_{i+1} \rangle, q_{i+1} \rangle \in \Delta$.

Furthermore $O_\mathcal{B} = L(\mathcal{T})$.

Proof. Let $u_i = a_1 \ldots a_i$ and $v_i = a_{i+1} \ldots a_k$. Then we have that $L_i = Succ_{u_i}(I)$ and $R_i = Pred_{v_i}(F)$. Since $u_i v_i = u \in dom(\mathcal{T})$ it follows that $L_i \cap R_i \neq \emptyset$. Thus, since ϕ_i is L_i-centered we deduce that $q_i = \phi_i(R_i)$ is defined. Further, since $q_{i+1} = \phi_{i+1}(R_{i+1})$ is well-defined it follows that there is a transition $\langle q_i, \langle a_{i+1}, m_{i+1} \rangle, q_{i+1} \rangle \in \Delta$. As a consequence we obtain

$$\langle q_0, \langle u, m_1 \ldots m_k \rangle, q_k \rangle \in \Delta^*.$$

Since $q_0 = \phi_0(R_0) \in L_0 = I$ and $q_k = \phi_k(R_k) \in R_k = F$ we have $\langle u, m_1 \ldots m_k \rangle \in L(\mathcal{T})$. Furthermore in this case $O_\mathcal{B}(u) = m_1 \ldots m_k = L(\mathcal{T})(u)$. This proves that if $u \in dom(\mathcal{T})$, then $u \in dom(\mathcal{B})$ and $L(\mathcal{T})(u) = O_\mathcal{B}(u)$.

Finally, if $u \notin dom(\mathcal{T})$, then $R_0 \cap I = \emptyset$ and therefore $\phi_0(R_0)$ is not defined. In particular, $O_\mathcal{B}(u)$ is not defined. Hence both functions have the same domain and coincide.

Remark 1. The construction can be applied to a non-functional transducer $\mathcal{T}$ and in this case for the output function of the bimachine we have $O_\mathcal{B} \subseteq L(\mathcal{T})$.

Applying the standard conversion of a bimachine to transducer we obtain the following corollary.

Corollary 1. *For any functional monoidal finite-state transducer T there exists an unambiguous monoidal finite-state transducer T' such that $L(T) = L(T')$.*

Proof. After constructing the bimachine $\mathcal{B}$ we define the monoidal finite-state transducer $T' = \langle \Sigma^* \times \mathcal{M}, Q_L \times Q_R, \{s_L\} \times Q_R, Q_L \times \{s_R\}, \Delta' \rangle$, where

$$\Delta := \{\langle \langle l, r \rangle, \langle a, m \rangle, \langle l', r' \rangle \rangle \mid l' = \delta_L(l, a), r = \delta_R(r', a), m = \psi(l, a, r')\}.$$

It can be shown that $L(T) = L(T')$.

3.2   Complexity Analysis and Specialized Construction

When using the generic construction presented above we obtain the bound $|Q_R| \leq |2^Q|$ for the number of states of the right automaton $\mathcal{A}_R$. The number of (partial) functions mapping Q_R to Q is $(|Q| + 1)^{|Q_R|}$. Hence the number of states of $\mathcal{A}_L$ satisfies

$$|Q_L| \leq 2^{|Q|}(|Q| + 1)^{|Q_R|} \leq 2^{|Q|}(|Q| + 1)^{2^{|Q|}} = 2^{|Q| + 2^{|Q|} \log(|Q| + 1)}.$$

A characteristics of the above generic construction is the arbitrariness of the selection of a state q' in the second clause of the inductive definition of the states of the left automaton. Since each new state selection function introduced during the construction produces its own swarm of followers the question arises if a more principled approach to select q' helps to avoid any unnecessary blow-up and to reduce the upper bound on the number of states of $\mathcal{A}_L$.

To this end we apply the idea to compare paths of transducers using the lexicographic ordering. It has been successfully used in different uniformization problems related to transducers [3,8,9,12]. In the context of bimachines, we use the idea to specialize the generic selection mechanism described in the previous section.

First, we define the states of the left automaton $\mathcal{A}_L$ as pairs $p = \langle L, <_p \rangle$, see also Algorithm 1. As before, the left component L is always an element of $Q'_L := \{Succ_w(I) \mid w \in \Sigma^*\}$. The second component $<_p$ is a strict linear order on L. The ordering $<_p$ induces a *canonical* state selector function $\phi_{<_p}(R)$: if $L \cap R \neq \emptyset$, then $\phi_{<_p}(R)$ is defined as the $<_p$-minimal element of $L \cap R$. Otherwise $\phi_{<_p}(R)$ is undefined. Note that in this way state selector functions are always L-centered. Still, in order to follow this line, we need a method for defining the a-successor $q = \langle L', <_q \rangle$ of a state $p = \langle L, <_p \rangle$ in such a way that the $<_q$-minimal element of $L' \cap R$ always represents a state q' with $\langle q, \langle a, . \rangle, q' \rangle \in \Delta$.

Given $\langle L, <_p \rangle$ and a state $r' \in L' := Succ_a(L)$ the set of a-predecessors of r' in L is defined as $Pred_{a,L}(r') := L \cap Pred_a(\{r'\})$. Note that, by the definition of L', each set $Pred_{a,L}(r')$ where $r' \in L'$ is non-empty. The $<_p$-*minimal a-predecessor of r' in L*, denoted $min\_pred_{a,L}(r')$, is the minimal element of $Pred_{a,L}(r')$ with respect to the ordering $<_p$.

We define the initial state, s_L, the set of states, Q_L, and the new transition function, δ_L, for the new definition of the left automaton, $\mathcal{A}_L$, as follows:

Algorithm 1. Direct construction of a bimachine. SeqTrans computes the transition of the left automaton; SelectMinimal determines the least element in the left state that is an element of the right state. Out computes the output produced by a left state, input character, and a right state.

Project(Δ)
01 return$\{\langle p,a,q\rangle | \exists m\langle p,\langle a,m\rangle,q\rangle \in \Delta\}$

Reverse(Δ)
01 return $\{\langle q,a,p\rangle \mid \langle p,a,q\rangle \in \Delta\}$

SetTrans(Δ,P,a)
01 return $\{q \mid \exists p \in P(\langle p,a,q\rangle \in \Delta)\}$

SeqTrans(Δ,P,a)
01 $S \leftarrow \langle\rangle$; $i \leftarrow 0$
02 for $j=0$ to $|P|-1$ do
03   for $\langle P[j],a,q\rangle \in \Delta$ do
04   if $q \notin S[0..i-1]$ then
05       $S[i] \leftarrow q$
06       $i \leftarrow i+1$
07   fi
08 return S

DetGeneric($\mathcal{A}, CmpTrans, i\_state$)
01 $\langle \Sigma,Q,I,F,\Delta\rangle \leftarrow \mathcal{A}$
02 $Q_D^{(-1)} \leftarrow \emptyset$; $Q_D^{(0)} \leftarrow \{i\_state\}$
03 $\delta_D \leftarrow \emptyset$; $i \leftarrow 0$;
03 while $Q_D^{(i)} \neq Q_D^{(i-1)}$ do
04   $Q_D^{(i+1)} \leftarrow Q_D^{(i)}$
05   for $P \in Q_D^{(i)} \setminus Q_D^{(i-1)}$ do
06   for $a \in \Sigma$ do
07       $\delta_D(P,a) \leftarrow CmpTrans(\Delta,P,a)$
08       $Q_D^{(i+1)} \leftarrow Q_D^{(i+1)} \cup \{\delta_D(P,a)\}$
09   $i \leftarrow i+1$
010 return $\langle \Sigma, Q_D^{(i)}, \{I\}, Q_D^{(i)}, \delta_D\rangle$

SelectMinimal(L,R)
01 for $i=0$ to $|L|-1$ do
02   if $L[i] \in R$ then
03   return L[i]
04   fi
05 done
06 return $\perp$

Out($L,\delta_L,a,R,\delta_R,\Delta$)
01 $p \leftarrow SelectMinimal(L,\delta_R(R,a))$
02 $q \leftarrow SelectMinimal(\delta_L(L,a),R)$
03 if $p=\perp$ or $q=\perp$ then
04   return $\perp$
05 else
06   let $\langle p,\langle a,m\rangle,q\rangle \in \Delta$
07 return m

ComputeBimachine($\mathcal{T}$)
01 $\langle \Sigma \times \mathcal{M},Q,I,F,\Delta\rangle \leftarrow \mathcal{T}$
02 $\Delta_\Sigma \leftarrow Project(\Delta)$
03 $\mathcal{A} \leftarrow \langle \Sigma,Q,I,F,\Delta_\Sigma\rangle$
04 $\mathcal{A}^r \leftarrow \langle \Sigma,Q,F,I,Reverse(\Delta_\Sigma)\rangle$
05 $\mathcal{A}_R \leftarrow DetGeneric(\mathcal{A}^r, SetTrans, F)$
06 $I' \leftarrow$ sequence of I
06 $\mathcal{A}_L \leftarrow DetGeneric(\mathcal{A}, SeqTrans, I')$
07 $\langle \Sigma,Q_L,s_L,Q_L,\delta_L\rangle \leftarrow \mathcal{A}_L$
08 $\langle \Sigma,Q_R,s_R,Q_R,\delta_R\rangle \leftarrow \mathcal{A}_R$
09 for $\langle L,a,R\rangle \in Q_L \times \Sigma \times Q_R$ do
010   $\psi(L,a,R) \leftarrow Out(L,\delta_L,a,R,\delta_R,\Delta)$
011 return $\langle \mathcal{M}, \mathcal{A}_L, \mathcal{A}_R, \psi\rangle$

- $s_L := \langle I, <_0\rangle$ where $<_0$ is any fixed linear order of I.
- For $\langle L,<\rangle \in Q_L$ and $a \in \Sigma$ we define $\delta_L(\langle L,<\rangle,a) := (L',<')$ where $L' := Succ_a(L)$ and $<'$ is any linear order on L' satisfying the condition

$$\forall p',r' \in L': p' \leq' r' \Rightarrow min\_pred_{a,L}(p') \leq min\_pred_{a,L}(r').$$

A linear order $<'$ of this form is obtained by starting with the elements of L' that have the $<$-minimal element q_{min} of L as their $<$-minimal a-predecessor (the ordering between these elements of L' is arbitrary). We then continue with the elements of L' that have the $<$-minimal element of $L \setminus \{q_{min}\}$ as their $<$-minimal a-predecessor, etc.

The following lemma shows that the new construction is a specialized version of the former construction described above.

Lemma 2. *Let $(L, <)$ and $(L', <')$ be as above. Let $\phi_<$ and $\phi_{<'}$ denote the canonical state selector functions corresponding to $<$ and $<'$, respectively. Let $R' \in Q_R$ and $R := Pred_a(R')$. Then $\phi_{<'}(R')$ is defined iff $\phi_<(R)$ is defined. Furthermore, if $q = \phi_<(R)$ and $q' = \phi'(R')$ are defined, then $\langle q, \langle a, m \rangle, q' \rangle \in \Delta$ for some $m \in M$.*

Proof. The Butterfly Lemma shows that

$$\phi_<(R) \text{ is defined} \overset{def}{\Longleftrightarrow} L \cap R \neq \emptyset \overset{\text{Butterfly}}{\underset{\text{Lemma}}{\Longleftrightarrow}} L' \cap R' \neq \emptyset \overset{def}{\Longleftrightarrow} \phi_{<'}(R') \text{ is defined}$$

If $\phi_<(R)$ and $\phi_{<'}(R')$ are defined, then $q := \phi_<(R)$ is a $<$-minimal state of $L \cap R$ and $q' := \phi_{<'}(R')$ is a $<'$-minimal state of $L' \cap R'$. The Butterfly Lemma shows that there exist $p \in L \cap R$, $m \in M$, and a transition $\langle p, \langle a, m \rangle, q' \rangle \in \Delta$. Let p_0 be a $<$-minimal element of $L \cap R$ with this property. We claim that $p_0 = q$. The Butterfly Lemma shows that there exist $p' \in L' \cap R'$ and $m' \in M$ with $\langle q, \langle a, m' \rangle, p' \rangle \in \Delta$. From the minimality of q' we obtain $q' \leq' p'$, the definition of $\leq'$ shows that $p_0 \leq q$. Minimality of q implies that in fact $p_0 = q$. It follows that there exists a transition $\langle q, \langle a, m \rangle, q' \rangle \in \Delta$.

Theorem 2. *Given a functional real-time transducer $\mathcal{T} = \langle \Sigma, \mathcal{M}, Q, I, \Delta, F \rangle$ we can construct an equivalent bimachine $\mathcal{B} = \langle \mathcal{A}_L, \mathcal{A}_R, \psi \rangle$ such that the number of states of $\mathcal{A}_L$ is $O(|Q|!)$ and the number of states of $\mathcal{A}_R$ is $O(2^{|Q|})$.*

Proof. Clearly, the number of states of $\mathcal{A}_R$ is $O(2^{|Q|})$. Let $Seq(Q)$ denote the set of linearly ordered subsets of Q. In the specialized construction, the states of $\mathcal{A}_L$ can be represented as elements of $Seq(Q)$. We have

$$|Seq(Q)| = \sum_{k=0}^{|Q|} \binom{|Q|}{k} k! = \sum_{k=0}^{|Q|} \frac{|Q|!}{(|Q| - k)!} = 2|Q|! + \sum_{k=0}^{|Q|-2} \frac{|Q|!}{(|Q| - k)!}.$$

Taking into account that $(|Q| - k)! \geq 2^{|Q|-k}$ for $k \leq |Q| - 2$ we obtain:

$$|Seq(Q)| = 2|Q|! + \sum_{k=0}^{|Q|-2} \frac{|Q|!}{(|Q| - k)!} \leq 2|Q|! + \sum_{k=0}^{|Q|-2} \frac{|Q|!}{2^{|Q|-k}} \leq 3|Q|!$$

thus showing that $|Q'_L| \leq |Seq(Q)| \leq 3|Q|!$. $\qquad\square$

4   Remark on the Classical Bimachine Construction

The classical construction of bimachines [2] refers to the special case where $\mathcal{M} = \langle \Omega^*, \circ, \varepsilon \rangle$ is the free monoid generated by an alphabet Ω. As described in [7], but see also the proofs in [1,2,8], it departs from a pseudo-deterministic transducer, i.e. a transducer $\mathcal{T} = \langle \Sigma \times \Omega^*, Q, I, F, \Delta \rangle$ that can be considered as a deterministic finite-state automaton over the new alphabet $\Sigma \times \Omega^*$. This means that I contains a single state i and Δ is a finite graph of a function $Q \times (\Sigma \times \Omega^*) \to Q$.

The next step is the core of the construction. The goal is to construct an unambiguous transducer $\mathcal{T}'$ equivalent to $\mathcal{T}$. This is achieved by specializing the standard determinization construction for finite-state automata: the sets generated by the determinization procedure are split into two parts, a single *guessed positive state* – this is our positive hypothesis for the successful path to be followed, and a set of *negative states* – these are the alternative hypotheses that must all fail in order for our positive hypothesis to be confirmed. Formally, the states in the resulting transducer are pairs $\langle p, N \rangle \in Q \times 2^Q$. The initial state is $i' = \langle i, \emptyset \rangle$. The algorithm inductively defines transitions in Δ' and states in Q'. Let $\prec_{lex}$ denote the lexicographic order on Σ^*. For a generated state $\langle p, N \rangle$ and each transition $\langle p, \langle a, v \rangle, p' \rangle \in \Delta$ we obtain a transition

$$\langle \langle p, N \rangle, \langle a, v \rangle, \langle p', N' \rangle \rangle \in \Delta', \text{ where}$$
$$N' = Succ_a(N) \cup \{q \mid \exists v' \prec_{lex} v(\langle p, \langle a, v' \rangle, q \rangle \in \Delta\}.$$

The pair $\langle p', N' \rangle$ is added to Q'. Intuitively, this transition makes a guess about the lexicographically smallest continuation of the output that can be followed to a final state $f \in F$. Accordingly, all transitions that have the same input character, a, but lexicographically smaller output, are implicitly assumed to fail. To reflect this, we add those states to the set of negative hypotheses, N'. To maintain the previously accumulated negative hypotheses along the path to $\langle p, N \rangle$ the a-successors of N are added to N'. Following these lines, the set of final states of $\mathcal{T}'$ is defined as:

$$F' = \{\langle f, N \rangle \mid f \in F \text{ and } N \cap F = \emptyset\}.$$

Note, that $\langle f, N \rangle$ becomes final only if $f \in F$ and there is no final state $n \in N$ reached with smaller output on a parallel path. It can be formally shown [7], that this construction indeed leads to an unambiguous transducer:

$$\mathcal{T}' = \langle \Sigma \times \Omega^*, Q', \{i'\}, F', \Delta' \rangle$$

equivalent to $\mathcal{T}$.

The final step is to convert the (trimmed part of) $\mathcal{T}'$ in an equivalent bimachine. This can be easily done by a determinization of $\mathcal{A}_L = \mathcal{A}_{\mathcal{T}',D}$ and $\mathcal{A}_R = \mathcal{A}_{\mathcal{T}'}^{rev}{}_D$ and defining an appropriate output function $\psi : Q_L \times \Sigma \times Q_R \to \Omega^*$. The following points have to be stressed about this construction.

Remark 2. The states of the left automaton are sets $L \subseteq 2^{Q \times 2^Q}$. Yet, these sets have an inner structure that enables a non-trivial upper bound on their number, $|Q_L| = O(|Q|! \exp(|Q| + 1))$. We sketch the main points of the proof:

- First, if $q = \langle p', N' \rangle \in L$, then, since q is co-accessible in $\mathcal{T}'$, it follows that $p' \notin N'$. Assume now that $\langle p', N' \rangle, \langle p'', N'' \rangle \in L$.
- Let $\langle p', N' \rangle \neq \langle p'', N'' \rangle \in \mathcal{T}'$ be distinct states accessible via the same input word $u \in \Sigma^*$. Then either $\{p'\} \cup N' \subseteq N''$ or $\{p''\} \cup N'' \subseteq N'$ (the proof uses a simple induction on $|u|$).

- Let $\langle p', N' \rangle \neq \langle p'', N'' \rangle \in L$ be distinct. Then, $\langle p', N' \rangle$ and $\langle p'', N'' \rangle$ are all accessible in $\mathcal{T}$ via a common word $u \in \Sigma$. By the above argument we can assume that $\{p'\} \cup N' \subseteq N''$. By the first argument we have that $p'' \notin N''$ and therefore $\{p'\} \cup N' \subsetneq \{p''\} \cup N''$.
- This proves that every left state $L = \{\langle p_i, N_i \rangle \mid i \leq |L|\}$ induces a linear order on $\{p_1, \ldots, p_{|L|}\}$ by defining $p_i < p_j$ if and only if $\{p_i\} \cup N_i \subsetneq \{p_j\} \cup N_j$. This shows that the left states L arise as linear orders of the states $\{p_1, \ldots, p_{|L|}\}$ and some additional elements $q \in Q \setminus \{p_1, \ldots, p_{|L|}\}$ that belong to some N_i. By the third point we can assign each such state q to the least N_i with $q \in N_i$. By the linear order it will belong to all the bigger sets $\{p_j\} \cup N_j$.
- With this remarks, the problem becomes a combinatorial one and using ideas similar to those in the proof of Theorem 2 one can prove that

$$|Q_L| \leq \sum_{k=1}^{|Q|} \binom{|Q|}{k} k! (k+1)^{|Q|-k} = |Q|! \sum_{k=1}^{|Q|} \frac{(k+1)^{|Q|-k}}{(|Q|-k)!}.$$

Looking at the term for $k = |Q|$, one sees that the upper bound for Q_L is at least $Q!$. On the other hand, since $k \leq |Q|$, substituting $k + 1$ with $|Q| + 1$ we easily get that: $|Q_L| \leq |Q|! \sum_{k=1}^{|Q|} \frac{(|Q|+1)^{|Q|-k}}{(|Q|-k)!} \leq |Q|! \exp(|Q| + 1)$.

Remark 3. Since the transducer $\mathcal{T}'$ is unambiguous any two states $L \in Q_L$ and $R \in Q_R$ have at most one common element. This shows that for each $L \in Q_L$, there is a unique L-centered function ϕ_L and therefore our construction would find exactly this function if run on $\mathcal{T}'$. Thus in this case the output function $\psi : Q_L \times \Sigma \times Q_R \to \Omega^*$ will be defined in exactly the same way.

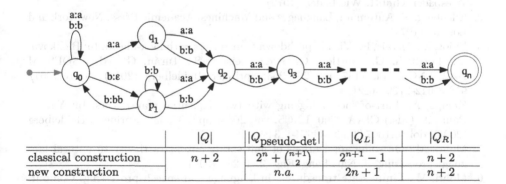

	$|Q|$	$|Q_{\text{pseudo-det}}|$	$|Q_L|$	$|Q_R|$
classical construction	$n+2$	$2^n + \binom{n+1}{2}$	$2^{n+1} - 1$	$n+2$
new construction		n.a.	$2n+1$	$n+2$

Fig. 1. A class of ambiguous finite-state transducers representing the rational functions $\{\langle a, a \rangle, \langle b, b \rangle\}^* \{\langle a, a \rangle, \langle b, \varepsilon \rangle\} \{\langle a, a \rangle, \langle b, b \rangle\}^{n-1}$, which deletes the n-th character from right-to-left if it is a b. The table shows the number of states of the source transducer, the pseudo-deterministic transducer, the left and the right automaton of the bimachine built by the standard and the new constructions.

Remark 4. The classical construction is starting from a pseudo-deterministic transducer. However, if $\mathcal{T}$ is an arbitrary real-time transducer the initial conversion to a pseudo-deterministic transducer may cause an exponential blow-up. In contrast, our constructions can be applied directly to arbitrary real-time transducers and thus avoids this blow-up. See Fig. 1 for an example.

5   Conclusion

In this paper we introduced a new generic algorithm and a specialization for building bimachines from functional finite-state transducers. The generic procedure is conceptually simple. Both constructions avoid the preparatory steps used in the classical construction, namely pseudodeterminization and disambiguation.

For the specialized construction we derived an upper bound on the size of the bimachine. We showed that this construction is asymptotically not worse than the classical construction. Moreover we presented a class of transducers for which the classical construction generates a bimachine with exponentially more states than the new construction.

The generic construction described in Subsect. 3.1 is not based on any order of the successful paths. It provides a simple and general algorithmic scheme for bimachine constructions, leaving room for other specialization, with new path selection strategies that might lead to even smaller bimachines. The study of optimal path selection strategies is a point for future research.

References

1. Berstel, J.: Transductions and Context-Free Languages. Springer Fachmedien Wiesbaden GmbH, Wiesbaden (1979)
2. Eilenberg, S.: Automata, Languages and Machines. Academic Press, New York and London (1974)
3. Filiot, E., Servais, F.: Visibly pushdown transducers with look-ahead. In: Bieliková, M., Friedrich, G., Gottlob, G., Katzenbeisser, S., Turán, G. (eds.) SOFSEM 2012. LNCS, vol. 7147, pp. 251–263. Springer, Heidelberg (2012). doi:10.1007/978-3-642-27660-6_21
4. Kempe, A.: Part-of-speech tagging with two sequential transducers. In: Yu, S., Păun, A. (eds.) CIAA 2000. LNCS, vol. 2088, pp. 337–339. Springer, Heidelberg (2001). doi:10.1007/3-540-44674-5_34
5. Mohri, M.: On some applications of finite-state automata theory to natural language processing. J. Nat. Lang. Eng. **2**, 1–20 (1996)
6. Mohri, M.: Finite-state transducers in language and speech processing. Comput. Linguist. **23**(2), 269–311 (1997)
7. Roche, E., Schabes, Y.: Finite-State Language Processing. MIT Press, Cambridge (1997)
8. Sakarovitch, J.: Elements of Automata Theory. Cambridge University Press, Cambridge (2009)
9. Sakarovitch, J., de Souza, R.: Lexicographic decomposition of k-valued transducers. Theor. Comp. Sys. **47**(3), 758–785 (2010). http://dx.doi.org/10.1007/s00224-009-9206-6

10. Santean, N.: Bimachines and structurally-reversed automata. J. Automata Lang. Comb. **9**(1), 121–146 (2004)
11. Schützenberger, M.P.: A remark on finite transducers. Inf. Control **4**, 185–196 (1961)
12. Souza, R.: A note on bimachines. In: 1a Escola de Informática Teórica e Métodos Formais, Natal - RN, pp. 83–92, November 2016

Alignment Distance of Regular Tree Languages

Yo-Sub Han[1] and Sang-Ki Ko[2(✉)]

[1] Department of Computer Science, Yonsei University, 50 Yonsei-Ro,
Seodaemun-Gu, Seoul 120-749, Republic of Korea
emmous@yonsei.ac.kr
[2] Department of Computer Science, University of Liverpool, Liverpool L69 3BX, UK
sangkiko@liverpool.ac.uk

Abstract. We consider the tree alignment distance problem between a tree and a regular tree language. The tree alignment distance is an alternative of the tree edit-distance, in which we construct an optimal alignment between two trees and compute its cost instead of directly computing the minimum cost of tree edits. The alignment distance is crucial for understanding the structural similarity between trees.

We, in particular, consider the following problem: given a tree t and a tree automaton recognizing a regular tree language L, find the most similar tree from L with respect to t under the tree alignment metric. Regular tree languages are commonly used in practice such as XML schema or bioinformatics. We propose an $O(mn)$ time algorithm for computing the (ordered) alignment distance between t and L when the maximum degree of t and trees in L is bounded by a constant, and $O(mn^2)$ time algorithm when the maximum degree of trees in L is not bounded, where m is the size of t and n is the size of finite tree automaton for L. We also study the case where a tree is not necessarily ordered, and show that the time complexity remains $O(mn)$ if the maximum degree is bounded and MAX SNP-hard otherwise.

Keywords: Tree alignment · Alignment edit-distance · Regular tree languages · Tree automata

1 Introduction

Measuring the similarity or dissimilarity between tree-structured data is essential in many fields such as XML document processing [14], RNA secondary structure alignment [6], pattern recognition [11]. In particular, much attention has been paid to research on various metrics for defining the similarity or dissimilarity of trees [7,15,20]. For example, the *tree edit-distance* between two ordered trees is the cost of the optimal edit script required to transform one tree into the other and is a natural extension of the Levenshtein distance [10]—often called the *edit-distance* in the literature—defined for strings.

The tree edit-distance problem have been extensively studied by many researchers [4,8,15]. Given two trees t and t' of size m and n (namely, there

© Springer International Publishing AG 2017
A. Carayol and C. Nicaud (Eds.): CIAA 2017, LNCS 10329, pp. 126–137, 2017.
DOI: 10.1007/978-3-319-60134-2_11

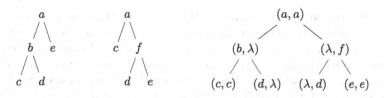

Fig. 1. Two trees t and t' and its optimal alignment $\mathcal{A}$

are m nodes in t and n nodes in t'), the currently best known algorithm for computing the tree edit-distance between t and t' has been suggested by Demaine et al. [4] and runs in $O(m^2 n(1 + \log \frac{n}{m}))$ time, for $n \geq m$, using an optimal decomposition strategy. Similar questions for unordered trees also have been studied [18,20]. Zhang et al. [20] showed that computing the tree edit-distance between unordered trees is NP-complete (in fact, MAX SNP-hard [19]).

Jiang et al. [7] introduced the *alignment distance* as an alternative to the tree edit-distance. Instead of considering the minimum number of tree editing operations, they considered the cost of an optimal tree alignment between two trees. They presented an $O(mnk^2)$ time algorithm for computing the alignment distance of two trees t and t', where m is the size of t, n is the size of t', and k is the maximum degree of t and t'. They also proved that computing the unordered alignment distance between two trees is MAX SNP hard if the degree of one of the trees is not bounded. Lu et al. [13] proposed another constrained variant called the *less-constrained edit-distance* but Kuboyama et al. [9] proved that the less-constrained edit-distance is, in fact, equivalent to the alignment distance.

The alignment distance is useful in terms of visualization since we can obtain visualizable alignments for multiple trees whereas the tree edit-distance only cares optimal sequence of tree edits. See Fig. 1 for example. Höchsmann et al. [6] suggested a systematic approach for comparing RNA secondary structures based on the alignment distance since we can represent RNA secondary structures as trees by preserving their structural properties.

The problems of computing the tree edit-distance and its related variants have been extended to the case when we are given a tree t and a set L of trees— a regular tree language [2,12]. Here we search for the most similar tree from L with respect to t under the considered distance metric. Note that in general L may be infinite and we need an efficient representation for such infinite L. Researchers suggested a regular tree grammar (RTG) and a tree automaton (TA) for recognizing a (infinite) set of trees preserving a certain regularity [3]. RTGs and TAs are widely used for denoting regular tree languages in several applications including XML schema [2], bioinformatics [16] and image recognition [11]. For example, we can formally define a set of RNA secondary structures excluding pseudoknots with a regular tree language. Xing [17] proposed an $O(mn \log n)$ time algorithm for computing the alignment distance between a tree and a regular tree grammar which recognizes a regular set of unranked trees. Unfortunately, the proposed algorithm cannot compute optimal alignments in all cases.

We extend the alignment distance problem to the alignment distance between a single tree and a regular tree language described as a TA. We separately consider two problems: the ranked case and the unranked case. For the ranked case where we fix the maximum degree of t and the maximum rank of A, we design an $O(mn)$ time algorithm for computing the alignment distance between a tree of size m and a ranked TA of size n. We also establish an $O(mn^2)$ time algorithm for unranked TAs.

We furthermore examine the unordered alignment distance between a tree and a regular tree language where the linear ordering of children is ignored. We show that the time complexity still remains polynomial by fixing the maximum degree of t and the maximum rank of A and otherwise, becomes MAX SNP-hard. The basic idea behind our algorithms is that we extend the classical dynamic programming algorithm [7] to operate with tree automata which can recognize regular sets of trees by their finite-state control. In order to employ the dynamic programming, we analyze the possible cases of alignments between a tree and a tree automaton and break the whole alignment problem into subproblems.

2   Preliminaries

A ranked alphabet Σ is a pair of a finite set of characters and a function $r : \Sigma \to rN \cup \{0\}$. We denote the set of elements of rank $m \geq 0$ by $\Sigma_m \subseteq \Sigma$. The set F_Σ consists of Σ-labelled trees, where a node labelled by $\sigma \in \Sigma_m$ for $m \geq 0$, always has m children. We denote the set of trees over Σ by F_Σ, which is the smallest set S satisfying the following condition: if $m \geq 0, \sigma \in \Sigma_m$ and $t, \ldots, t_m \in S$, then $\sigma(t, \ldots, t_m) \in S$.

A *nondeterministic bottom-up TA* A over a ranked alphabet Σ is specified by a tuple $A = (Q, \Sigma, F, \delta)$, where Q is a finite set of states, $F \subseteq Q$ is a set of final states, and δ associates to each $\sigma \in \Sigma_m$ a mapping $\sigma_\delta : Q^m \to 2^Q, m \geq 0$. For each tree $t = \sigma(t, \ldots, t_m) \in F_\Sigma$, we define inductively the set $t_\delta \subseteq Q$ by setting $q \in t_g$ if and only if there exist $q_i \in (t_i)_\delta$, for $1 \leq i \leq m$, such that $q \in \sigma_\delta(q_1, \ldots, q_m)$. Intuitively, t_δ consists of the states of Q that A may reach by reading the tree t. Thus, the tree language accepted by A is defined as follows: $L(A) = \{t \in F_\Sigma \mid t_\delta \cap F \neq \emptyset\}$. Given a state q of A, $A[q]$ denotes a new TA obtained from A by making $F = \{q\}$. We define the size $|A|$ of a ranked TA A to be $|Q| + \sum_{q \in \sigma_\delta(q_1, \ldots, q_m)} (r(\sigma) + 1)$.

Many modern applications of tree automata use automata operating on trees where the label of a node does not determine the number of children. For this reason we consider also unranked TAs.

A *nondeterministic unranked TA* is specified by a tuple $A = (\Sigma, Q, F, \delta)$, where Σ is an (unranked) alphabet, Q is a finite set of states, $F \subseteq Q$ is a set of final states, and δ is a transition relation defined in terms of horizontal languages that consist of regular sets of strings over Q. For each $q \in Q$ and $\sigma \in \Sigma$, we define $\delta(q, \sigma)$ to be the horizontal language associated with q and σ. We denote a finite-state automaton (FA) for the horizontal language $\delta(q, \sigma)$ of A by $H^A_{q,\sigma}$, which is called a *horizontal FA*. Note that an FA is specified by $A = (P, \Sigma, s, F, \delta)$,

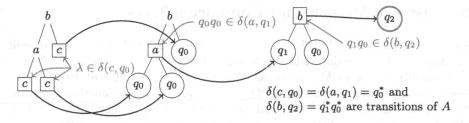

Fig. 2. An accepting run of an unranked TA $A = (\{q_0, q_1, q_2\}, \{a, b, c\}, \{q_2\}, \delta)$ for the tree t on the left-hand side. Note that horizontal languages are described as regular expressions.

where P is a set of states, Σ is the input alphabet, s is the start state, $F \subseteq P$ is a set of final states, and δ is the transition function. Remind that horizontal FAs of the unranked TA $A = (\Sigma, Q, F, \delta)$ is defined over Q—the state set of A.

We denote an FA $H_{q,\sigma}^A[s_1, s_2] = (S_{q,\sigma}, Q, s_1, \{s_2\}, \gamma_{q,\sigma})$ obtained from $H_{q,\sigma}^A$ by having the initial state s_1 and the only final state s_2, where $s_1, s_2 \in S_{q,\sigma}$. Then, according to the transition relation δ, each $\sigma \in \Sigma$ defines a partial function $\sigma_\delta : Q^* \to Q$, where, for $w \in Q^*$, $q \in Q$, $q \in \sigma_\delta(w)$ if $w \in L(H_{q,\sigma}^A)$. The transition relation is, in a natural way, extended as a binary relation on Σ-trees where some of the leaves can be labelled by elements of Q [3]. The tree language accepted by A is defined as follows: $L(A) = \{t \in T_\Sigma \mid t \xrightarrow{*} q_f \in F\}$. An accepting run of an unranked TA is described in Fig. 2. We define the size $|A|$ of an unranked TA A to be $|Q| + \sum_{q \in Q, \sigma \in \Sigma}(|H_{q,\sigma}^A| + 1)$. Naturally a ranked TA is a special case of an unranked TA, where for $\sigma \in \Sigma_m$ and $q \in Q$ we always have $L(H_{q,\sigma}^A) \subseteq Q^m$.

For a tree t, the *postorder traversal* of t is obtained by visiting all children in a left-to-right order and recursively visiting the subtrees rooted at the children, and then $\mathsf{root}(t)$. For a tree t, $t[i]$ denotes the ith node of t in postorder. When an ordering is specified for all nodes in a tree, the tree is called *ordered tree*. A *hedge* is a sequence of trees. We assume that all trees we discuss are ordered, unless explicitly stated otherwise. We denote a subhedge of a tree t that consists of the nodes from i to j by $t[i \ldots j]$ where $i \leq j$. Here the nodes from i to j should satisfy one of the following two conditions: (1) a leaf or (2) all of its descendants are between i and j. We denote a hedge—a sequence $t_i, \ldots, t_j$ of trees for $i \leq j$— by $h[t_i \ldots t_j]$. A hedge formed from t by deleting the root node is denoted by $\hat{t}$. We denote the leftmost leaf descendant of node $t[i]$ by $l(i)$. Similarly, we denote the leftmost leaf descendant of a tree t by $l(t)$. We define $\mathsf{par}(t[i])$ to be the parent node of $t[i]$. Let $\mathsf{des}(t[i])$ be the set of all descendants of $t[i]$ including $t[i]$ itself. Thus, $t[l(i) \ldots i]$ is the subtree rooted at $t[i]$, that is the subtree consisting of node i and all its descendants. Similarly, we define $\mathsf{anc}(t[i])$ to be the set of all ancestors of $t[i]$ including $t[i]$. We also denote the lowest common ancestor of $t[i]$ and $t[j]$ by $\mathsf{lca}(t[i], t[j])$. The size $|t|$ of t is the number of nodes in t and the degree $\mathsf{deg}(t)$ of t is the maximum number of children a node t has. Let θ be the empty tree. We denote the character labelling a node $t[i]$ by $\sigma(i)$.

3   Distance Measures for Comparing Trees

Given an alphabet Σ, let $\Omega = \{(a \rightarrow b) \mid a, b \in \Sigma \cup \{\lambda\}\}$ be a set of edit operations. There are three edit operations: *deletion* $(a \rightarrow \lambda)$, *insertion* $(\lambda \rightarrow a)$ and *substitution* $(a \rightarrow b)$. We associate a non-negative edit cost to each edit operation $\omega_i \in \Omega$ as a function $c : \Omega \rightarrow \mathbb{R}_+$. Note that the function c returns zero for the edit operations of trivial substitution $(a \rightarrow a)$, where $a \in \Sigma \cup \{\lambda\}$. We assume that c is a distance metric satisfying the following conditions:

1. $c(a \rightarrow b) = 0$ if and only if $a = b$,
2. $c(a \rightarrow b) = c(b \rightarrow a)$, and
3. $c(a \rightarrow c) \leq c(a \rightarrow b) + c(b \rightarrow c)$,

where $a, b, c \in \Sigma \cup \{\lambda\}$.

An *edit script* $S \in \Omega^*$ between two trees t and t' is a sequence of edit operations transforming t into t'. The cost $c(S)$ of $S = s_1 s_2 \cdots s_n$ is $c(S) = \sum_{i=1}^{n} c(s_i)$. An *optimal edit script* between t and t' is an edit script of minimum cost and the minimum cost is the *tree edit-distance* between t and t'.

Definition 1. *We define the tree edit-distance $d(t, t')$ of two trees t and t' to be $d(t, t') = \min\{c(S) \mid S \text{ is an edit script transforming } t \text{ into } t'\}$. Namely, if S is an optimal edit script that transforms t into t', then $c(S) = d(t, t')$.*

Let T and T' be sets of nodes in t and t', respectively. Define a triple (M, T, T') to be a mapping from t to t', where $M \subseteq T \times T'$ is a set of pairs of nodes (i, j) for $1 \leq i \leq |T|$ and $1 \leq j \leq |T'|$. We use M instead of (M, T, T') for simplicity when there is no confusion. We assume that trees are ordered in postorder. For any pair of (i_1, j_1) and (i_2, j_2) in M, the mapping M has the following restrictions:

1. $i_1 = i_2$ if and only if $j_1 = j_2$ (one-to-one)
2. $i_1 < i_2$ if and only if $j_1 < j_2$ (sibling order preserved)
3. $t[i_1] \in \text{anc}(t[i_2])$ if and only if $t'[j_1] \in \text{anc}(t'[j_2])$ (ancestor order preserved).

We consider the *alignment distance* between trees. Let t and t' be two labelled trees. We define an *alignment* $\mathcal{A}$ to be a tree where each node has a label from the set of edit operations. Let $\text{left}(\mathcal{A})$ ($\text{right}(\mathcal{A})$, resp.) be the left (right, resp.) projection of the alignment $\mathcal{A}$. Then, $\mathcal{A}$ is the alignment of t and t' if $\text{left}(\mathcal{A}) = t$ and $\text{right}(\mathcal{A}) = t'$. See Fig. 1 for example. We define the cost $c(\mathcal{A})$ of an alignment $\mathcal{A}$ to be the sum of the costs of all pairs of labels in the alignment. In Fig. 1, the cost $c(\mathcal{A})$ is 4 if we assume unit cost for all pairs in which two labels are different. We say that an alignment is optimal if the cost of the alignment is minimum over all possible alignments. Now we define the alignment distance between two trees as follows:

Definition 2. *We define the alignment distance $ad(t, t')$ of two trees t and t' to be $ad(t, t') = \min\{c(\mathcal{A}) \mid \mathcal{A} \text{ is an alignment of } t \text{ and } t'\}$. Note that the distance is symmetric $ad(t, t') = ad(t', t)$.*

We call a mapping corresponding to the alignment an *alignment mapping*. Now we formally define the additional restrictions required a mapping M to be an alignment mapping. For any triple of $(i_1, j_1), (i_2, j_2)$, and (i_3, j_3) in M, the alignment mapping M has the following additional restriction:

if $\mathsf{lca}(t[i_1], t[i_3]) \in \mathsf{anc}(\mathsf{lca}(t[i_1], t[i_2]))$, then $\mathsf{lca}(t'[j_1], t'[j_3]) = \mathsf{lca}(t'[j_2], t'[j_3])$.

Next we extend the alignment distance between trees to the distance between a tree and a set of trees—a tree language.

Definition 3. *We define the alignment distance $ad(t, L)$ between a tree t and a tree language L to be $ad(t, L) = \inf\{ad(t, t') \mid t' \in L\}$.*

We also consider an unordered variant for which we ignore the linear ordering of children called the *unordered alignment distance* and denote the distance between two trees t and t' by $uad(t, t')$.

4   Alignment Distance Problem

We study the alignment distance between a tree and a regular tree language. We tackle the following two cases separately: the ranked case and the unranked case. In the ranked case, we assume that the language is given by a ranked TA such that the number of children is fixed for every symbol in Σ. For the unranked case, the language is given by an unranked TA such that there is no restriction on the number of children. Our approach to these problems is based on the dynamic programming.

4.1   Ranked Case

We first establish the basis for our dynamic programming algorithm. For a tree t, we define the cost of a tree $\mathsf{c}(t)$ to be the minimum cost of inserting all nodes of the tree t. We denote the smallest cost among the costs of all trees in $L(A)$ by $\mathsf{mintree}(A) = \min\{\mathsf{c}(t) \mid t \in L(A)\}$. Then, given a tree t and a ranked TA $A = (\Sigma, Q, F, \Delta)$, we have the following equations for the basis:

1. $ad(\theta, \theta) = 0$,
2. $ad(t[1 \ldots i], \theta) = ad(t[1 \ldots i-1], \theta) + \mathsf{c}(\sigma(i), \lambda)$,
3. $ad(\theta, q_1 \ldots q_k) = \displaystyle\sum_{1 \leq i \leq k} \mathsf{mintree}(A[q_i])$, where $q_i \in Q$ for $1 \leq i \leq k$.

It is straightforward to verify that the first two equations hold: The first case is when no edit operation is required and the second case is when we insert a node in a hedge $t[1 \ldots i-1]$ to transform into $t[1 \ldots i]$. Notice that $ad(\theta, t[1 \ldots i]) = i$ if we assume unit cost for all edit-operations. For the third case, $ad(q_1 \ldots q_k, \theta)$ is the alignment distance between an empty tree and the smallest hedge accepted by the sequence of states. Now we are ready to present a recursive formula of the distance between a sequence of states and a subhedge.

Lemma 4. *Given a tree t and a state q of a ranked TA $A = (\Sigma, Q, F, \delta)$, the alignment distance $ad(t, q)$ can be computed as follows:*

$$ad(t, q) = \min_{\substack{1 \leq i_1 \leq l; \\ 1 \leq i_2 \leq k; \\ q \in \sigma_\delta(q_1, \ldots, q_k)}} \begin{cases} ad(t, \theta) + ad(t_{i_1}, q) - ad(t_{i_1}, \theta), \\ ad(\theta, q) + ad(t, q_{i_2}) - ad(\theta, q_{i_2}), \\ ad(h[t_1 \ldots t_l], q_1 \ldots q_k) + \mathsf{c}(\mathsf{root}(t_l) \rightarrow \sigma), \end{cases} \tag{1}$$

where $q_n \in Q$ for $1 \leq n \leq k$ and $\hat{t} = h[t_1 \ldots t_l]$.

Proof. We prove the recurrence by considering an optimal alignment $\mathcal{A}_{t,t'}$ between two trees t and t', where t' is a tree accepted by reaching the state q in A. Especially, we consider the possible root node cases of the optimal alignment $\mathcal{A}_{t,t'}$ between t and t'. There are three possible cases to consider:

Case 1: The root node of $\mathcal{A}_{t,t'}$ is $(\mathsf{root}(t), \lambda)$. Then, the root node $\mathsf{root}(t')$ of t' is aligned with a descendant of t. Otherwise, $\mathcal{A}_{t,t'}$ has a node $(\lambda, \mathsf{root}(t'))$ and we can always have a better alignment by replacing $(\mathsf{root}(t), \lambda)$ and $(\lambda, \mathsf{root}(t'))$ with $(\mathsf{root}(t), \mathsf{root}(t'))$, which is considered in **Case 3**. Suppose that $\mathsf{root}(t')$ is aligned with a node in the ith subtree of t. Then the cost of the alignment can be written as follows: $\min_{1 \leq i \leq l}\{ad(t, \theta) + ad(t_i, t') - ad(t_i, \theta)\}$.

Since t' is accepted by reaching the state q in A, the first term in the recurrence captures this case.

Case 2: The optimal alignment $\mathcal{A}_{t,t'}$ has $(\lambda, \mathsf{root}(t'))$ as a root node. This case is completely symmetric with **Case 1** and described in the second term.

Case 3: The root node of $\mathcal{A}_{t,t'}$ is $(\mathsf{root}(t), \mathsf{root}(t'))$. Since the root nodes of two trees are aligned, it remains to compute an optimal alignment between two ordered sequences of trees under the root nodes. This also implies that we need to compute the alignment distance $ad(h[t_1 \ldots t_l], h[t'_1 \ldots t'_k])$ between two subhedges obtained from t and t' by removing the root nodes.

Now we define the alignment distance between two subhedges—two ordered sequences of trees. Since we are considering the alignment distance between a tree and a regular tree language, we use a sequence of states on the right-hand side in the distance function.

Lemma 5. *Given a subhedge $h[t_1 \ldots t_l]$ of t and a sequence $q_1, \ldots, q_k$ of states of a ranked TA $A = (\Sigma, Q, F, \delta)$, we can compute $ad(h[t_1 \ldots t_l], q_1 \ldots q_k)$ as follows:*

$$ad(h[t_1 \ldots t_l], q_1 \ldots q_k) =$$

$$\min_{\substack{1 \leq i_1 \leq l; \\ 1 \leq i_2 \leq k; \\ q_k \in \sigma_\delta(q'_1, \ldots, q'_j)}} \begin{cases} ad(h[t_1 \ldots t_l], q_1 \ldots q_{k-1}) + ad(\theta, q_k), \\ ad(h[t_1 \ldots t_{l-1}], q_1 \ldots q_k) + ad(t_l, \theta), \\ ad(f[t_1 \ldots t_{l-1}], q_1 \ldots q_{i_2-1}) + ad(\hat{t}_l, q_{i_2} \ldots q_k) + \mathsf{c}(\mathsf{root}(t_l) \rightarrow \lambda), \\ ad(h[t_1 \ldots t_{i_1-1}], q_1 \ldots q_{k-1}) + ad(h[t_{i_1} \ldots t_l], q'_1 \ldots q'_j) + \mathsf{c}(\lambda \rightarrow \sigma), \\ ad(h[t_1 \ldots t_{l-1}], q_1 \ldots q_{k-1}) + ad(\hat{t}_l, q'_1 \ldots q'_j) + \mathsf{c}(\mathsf{root}(t_l) \rightarrow \sigma), \end{cases}$$

$$\tag{2}$$

where $q_n, q'_m \in Q$ for $1 \leq n \leq k$ and $1 \leq m \leq j$.

Now we are ready to present an efficient algorithm for computing the alignment distance between a tree t and a regular tree language $L(A)$ described by a ranked TA A.

Theorem 6. *Given a tree t and a ranked TA $A = (\Sigma, Q, F, \delta)$, we can compute $ad(t, L(A))$ in $O(mnk^2)$ in the worst-case, where $m = |t|$, $n = |A|$ and $k = \deg(t) + \max\{r(\sigma) \mid \sigma \in \Sigma\}$.*

Proof. Notice that we need to compute the alignment distance for each subhedge $t[l(i) \ldots i - 1]$ of t and transition $q \in \sigma_g(q_1, \ldots, q_l)$ of A. Let m_i be the number of children of a node $t[i]$ and denote the subhedge $t[l(i) \ldots i - 1]$ by $h[t_1 \ldots t_{m_i}]$ for notational convenience.

Let us analyze the time complexity for computing $ad(h[t_1 \ldots t_{m_i}], q_1 \ldots q_l)$, which is the alignment distance between a sequence of states of length l and a hedge that consists of m_i trees. There are in total $m_i^2 l + m_i l^2$ values to compute and computing each ad value takes $O(m_i n_\delta + l)$ time in the worst-case, where n_δ is the number of transitions of A. Since $m_i + l \leq k$, the time complexity required to compute each ad value is bounded by $O(n)$, where n is the size of A.

Hence, the total time complexity is bounded by

$$\sum_{i=1}^{m} O((m_i l) \cdot (m_i + l) \cdot n) \leq \sum_{i=1}^{m} O(m_i k^2 n) \leq O(mnk^2).$$

Note that if both the degree of t and the rank of A are bounded by a constant, the time complexity for computing $ad(t, L(A))$ is $O(mn)$. $\qquad \square$

4.2 Unranked Case

We consider the case when we have an unranked TA for a regular tree language of unranked trees. Contrary to the ranked TAs where we consider a sequence of states in each bottom-up computation, we instead consider a horizontal language that contains a set of sequences of states. Let $A = (\Sigma, Q, F, \delta)$ be an unranked TA, $q \in Q$ and $\sigma \in \Sigma$. We define the alignment distance between a horizontal language $\delta(q, \sigma)$ and a subhedge $h[t_1 \ldots t_l]$ of t as follows:

$$ad(h[t_1 \ldots t_l], \delta(q, \sigma)) = \min\{\delta(h[t_1 \ldots t_l], w) \mid w \in \delta(q, \sigma)\}.$$

Note that we use the definition for the alignment distance between a sequence of states and a subhedge given in Lemma 5.

We also define the following notation that is essential for computing the alignment distance $ad(h[t_1 \ldots t_l], \delta(q, \sigma))$ between a subhedge and a horizontal language. Let $H_{q,\sigma}^A = (S_{q,\sigma}, Q, s_{q,\sigma}, F_{q,\sigma}, \gamma_{q,\sigma})$ be a horizontal FA that accepts $\delta(q, \sigma)$, namely, $L(H_{q,\sigma}^A) = \delta(q, \sigma)$. We define the alignment distance between a subhedge $h[t_1 \ldots t_l]$ and two horizontal states $s_1, s_2 \in S_{q,\sigma}$ as follows:

$$ad(h[t_1 \ldots t_l], [s_1, s_2]) = \min\{ad(h[t_1 \ldots t_l], w) \mid w \in L(H_{q,\sigma}^A[s_1, s_2])\}.$$

Let $H_{q,\sigma}^A = (S_{q,\sigma}, Q, s_{q,\sigma}, F_{q,\sigma}, \gamma_{q,\sigma})$ be a horizontal FA. Then, the following holds: $ad(h[t_1 \ldots t_l], \delta(q,\sigma)) = \min\{ad(h[t_1 \ldots t_l], [s_{q,\sigma}, f_{q,\sigma}]) \mid f_{q,\sigma} \in F_{q,\sigma}\}$. Now we are ready to establish the alignment distance between a tree t and a state q of an unranked TA A as follows:

Lemma 7. *Given a tree t and a state q of an unranked TA $A = (\Sigma, Q, F, \delta)$, the alignment distance $ad(t,q)$ can be computed as follows:*

$$ad(t,q) = \min_{\substack{w \in \delta(q,\sigma); \\ 1 \le i_1 \le l; \\ 1 \le i_2 \le |w|;}} \begin{cases} ad(t, \theta) + ad(t_{i_1}, q) - ad(t_{i_1}, \theta), \\ ad(\theta, q) + ad(t, w_{i_2}) - ad(t_{i_1}, w_{i_2}), \\ ad(h[t_1 \ldots t_l], w) + \mathsf{c}(\mathsf{root}(t_l) \to \sigma), \end{cases} \quad (3)$$

where $\hat{t} = h[t_1 \ldots t_l]$.

We can see that the computation of Eq. (3) requires the computation of the alignment distance between a subhedge of t and a horizontal language $\delta(q,\sigma)$.

Lemma 8. *Let $A = (\Sigma, Q, F, \delta)$ be an unranked TA and $H_{q,\sigma}^A = (S_{q,\sigma}, Q, s_{q,\sigma}, F_{q,\sigma}, \gamma_{q,\sigma})$ be a horizontal FA of A associated with a state $q \in Q$ and $\sigma \in \Sigma$. Given a subhedge $h[t_1 \ldots t_l]$ of t and two horizontal states s_1, s_2 of $H_{q,\sigma}^A$, the alignment distance $ad(h[t_1 \ldots t_l], [s_1, s_2])$ can be computed as follows:*

$$ad(h[t_1 \ldots t_l], [s_1, s_2]) =$$

$$\min_{\substack{1 \le i \le l; \\ w \in \delta(q', \sigma); \\ s_2 \in \gamma_{q,\sigma}(s', q')}} \begin{cases} ad(h[t_1 \ldots t_l], [s_1, s']) + ad(\theta, q'), \\ ad(h[t_1 \ldots t_{l-1}], [s_1, s_2]) + ad(t_l, \theta), \\ ad(f[t_1 \ldots t_{l-1}], [s_1, r]) + ad(\hat{t_l}, [r, s_2]) + \mathsf{c}(\mathsf{root}(t_l) \to \lambda), \\ ad(h[t_1 \ldots t_{i-1}], [s_1, s']) + ad(h[t_i \ldots t_l], w) + \mathsf{c}(\lambda \to \sigma), \\ ad(h[t_1 \ldots t_{l-1}], [s_1, s']) + ad(\hat{t_l}, w) + \mathsf{c}(\mathsf{root}(t_l) \to \sigma), \end{cases}$$

where $s', r \in S_{q,\sigma}$ and $q' \in Q$.

Now we describe how we compute the alignment distance for the unranked case. We use the weighted directed graph for computing $ad(h[t_1 \ldots t_l], \delta(q,\sigma))$ between a hedge $h[t_1 \ldots t_l]$ and a horizontal language $\delta(q,\sigma)$.

Let $H_{q,\sigma}^A = (S_{q,\sigma}, Q, s_{q,\sigma}, F_{q,\sigma}, \gamma_{q,\sigma})$ be a horizontal FA recognizing $\delta(q,\sigma)$. We construct a weighted directed graph $\mathcal{W}(h[t_1 \ldots t_l], H_{q,\sigma}^A) = (V, E)$ where $V = S_{q,\sigma} \times \{0, 1, \ldots, l\}$ is a set of vertices and $E \subseteq V \times \mathbb{N}_0 \times V$ is a set of weighted directed edges. For each transition $s_2 \in \gamma_{q,\sigma}(s_1, q)$ of $H_{q,\sigma}^A$, we define E to contain the following edges:

- $((s_1, i), ad(\theta, q), (s_2, i))$ for $0 \le i \le l$,
- $((s_1, i), ad(h[t_{i+1} \ldots t_j], \delta(q,\sigma)) + \mathsf{c}(\lambda \to \sigma), (s_2, j))$ for $0 \le i < j \le l$, and
- $((s_1, i), ad(\hat{t}_{i+1}, \delta(q,\sigma)) + \mathsf{c}(\mathsf{root}(t_{i+1}) \to \sigma), (s_2, i+1))$ for $0 \le i \le l - 1$.

For each state $s \in S_{q,\sigma}$, we also define E to contain the following edges:

- $((s, i), ad(t_{i+1}, \theta), (s, i+1))$ for $0 \le i \le l - 1$.

Finally, for each pair of states $s_1, s_2 \in S_{q,\sigma}$, we add the following edges to E:

- $((s_1, i), ad(\hat{t}_{i+1}, [s_1, s_2]) + c(\text{root}(t_{i+1}) \to \lambda), (s_2, i+1))$ for $0 \leq i \leq l-1$.

By the construction, we know that the cost of the minimum cost path from (s_1, i) to (s_2, j), where $1 \leq i \leq j \leq l$, in $\mathcal{W}(h[t_1 \ldots t_l], H_{q,\sigma}^A)$ implies $ad(h[t_{i+1} \ldots t_j], [s_1, s_2])$. Now we are ready to present a polynomial time algorithm in the unranked case.

Theorem 9. *Given a tree t and an unranked TA $A = (\Sigma, Q, F, \delta)$, we can compute $ad(t, L(A))$ in $O(mn^2k^2)$ in the worst-case, where $m = |t|$, $n = |A|$, and $k = \deg(t)$.*

Proof. We can compute the alignment distance between a horizontal language and a hedge by constructing a weighted directed graph and computing the minimum cost path from $(s_{q,\sigma}, 0)$ to $(f_{q,\sigma}, l)$ where $f_{q,\sigma} \in F_{q,\sigma}$.

Given that the size of $H_{q,\sigma}^A$ has x states and y transitions, the construction of the weighted directed graph $\mathcal{W}(h[t_1 \ldots t_l], H_{q,\sigma}^A)$ yields $O(xl)$ vertices and $O(x^2l^2)$ edges. Note that Dijkstra's algorithm based on a min-priority queue for finding the minimum cost path runs in $O(|V| \log |V| + |E|)$ time [5] for a graph $G = (V, E)$ where V is a set of vertices and E is a set of edges. Therefore, we can find the minimum cost path in $\mathcal{W}(h[t_1 \ldots t_l], H_{q,\sigma}^A)$ in $O(x^2l^2)$ time. Since we construct $\mathcal{W}(h[t_i \ldots t_l], H_{q,\sigma}^A)$ for all $q \in Q, 1 \leq i \leq l$ and compute the minimum cost path, the total time complexity is upper bounded by

$$\sum_{i=1}^{m} \sum_{q \subset Q} O(m_i \cdot x^2 m_i^2) \leq \sum_{i=1}^{m} \sum_{q \in Q} O(m_i \cdot x^2 k^2) \leq \sum_{q \in Q} O(mx^2k^2) \leq O(mn^2k^2).$$

Note that if the degree of t is bounded by a constant, the time complexity is upper bounded by $O(mn^2)$. □

5   Unordered Alignment Distance Problem

We study the unordered version of the alignment distance problem. The main difference from the ordered case is that here we treat sequences of trees (resp., sequences of states) as sets of trees (resp., multisets of states) because we do not care about the order of nodes.

Lemma 10. *Given a set $T_{1,l}$ of subtrees of t and a multiset $Q_{1,k}$ of states of a ranked TA $A = (\Sigma, Q, F, \delta)$, the unordered alignment distance $uad(T_{1,l}, Q_{1,k})$ can be computed as follows:*

$$uad(T_{1,l}, Q_{1,k}) =$$

$$\min_{\substack{1 \leq i_1 \leq l; \\ 1 \leq i_2 \leq k; \\ q_{i_2} \in \sigma_\delta(q_1', \ldots, q_j')}} \begin{cases} uad(T_{1,l} \setminus \{t_{i_1}\}, Q_{1,k} \setminus Q') + uad(\hat{t}_{i_1}, Q') + c(\text{root}(t_{i_1}) \to \lambda), \\ uad(T_{1,l} \setminus T, Q_{1,k} \setminus \{q_{i_2}\}) + uad(T, P) + c(\lambda \to \sigma), \\ uad(T_{1,l} \setminus \{t_{i_1}\}, Q_{1,k} \setminus \{q_{i_2}\}) + uad(\hat{t}_{i_1}, P) + c(\text{root}(t_{i_1}) \to \sigma), \end{cases}$$

where $T \subseteq T_{1,l}, Q' \subseteq Q_{1,k}$, and $P = \{q_1', \ldots, q_j'\}$.

Proof. This lemma is an unordered extension of Lemma 5. The main difference between the ordered and unordered versions is that we treat sequences of subtrees (resp., sequences of states) as sets of trees (resp., multisets of states). Notice that a multiset (or bag) is a generalization of a set in which multiple instances of elements are allowed. Consider a transition $q \in \sigma_\delta(q_1, \ldots, q_k)$ of A. We cannot convert the sequence $q_1, \ldots, q_k$ of states into the set $\{q_1, \ldots, q_k\}$ as we may have multiple instances of a state. Therefore, we replace a sequence $q_1, \ldots, q_k$ of states by a multiset $\{q_1, \ldots, q_k\}$ of states and a hedge $h[t_1 \ldots t_l]$ by a set $\{t_1, \ldots, t_l\}$ of trees. For the sake of simplicity, we denote $\{q_1, \ldots, q_k\}$ by $Q_{1,k}$ and $\{t_1, \ldots, t_l\}$ by $T_{1,l}$.

For sequences of trees, it is enough to use sets as there is no chance of containing multiple instances of the same subtree. We also mention that the hedge $\hat{t}_{i_1}$ used in the equation also denotes the set of subtrees of t_{i_1}, not the sequence of subtrees of t_{i_1}. □

Based on Lemma 10, we design an algorithm that computes the unordered alignment distance $uad(T_{1,l}, Q_{1,k})$ between a set of subtrees of t and a multiset of states.

Theorem 11. *Given a tree t and a ranked TA $A = (\Sigma, Q, F, \delta)$, we can compute $uad(t, L(A))$ in $O(mn2^k)$ in the worst-case, where $m = |t|$, $n = |A|$ and $k = \deg(t) + \max\{r(\sigma) \mid \sigma \in \Sigma\}$.*

Proof. Note that the algorithm for computing the unordered alignment distance follows almost the same procedure except that we use the recurrence given in Lemma 10 instead of Lemma 5. This gives rise to the following time complexity:

$$\sum_{i=1}^{m} O(m_i n \cdot 2^{m_i + l}) \leq \sum_{i=1}^{m} O(m_i n 2^k) \leq O(mn2^k).$$

Note that the time complexity remains polynomial if we fix k to be a constant. □

Given two trees t and t', it is known that computing $uad(t, t')$ is MAX SNP-hard [7] if the degree of one of the two trees is not bounded by a constant. This means that unless $P = NP$ there is no polynomial-time approximation scheme for the problem [1]. We can immediately obtain the following results.

Corollary 12. *Let t be a tree and A be a ranked TA. Then, we can compute the unordered alignment distance $uad(t, L(A))$ in $O(mn)$ time if $\deg(t) = k$ for some $k < \infty$, otherwise, the problem is MAX SNP-hard.*

Corollary 13. *Let t be a tree and A be an unranked TA. Then, the problem of computing the unordered alignment distance $uad(t, L(A))$ is MAX SNP-hard.*

References

1. Arora, S., Lund, C., Motwani, R., Sudan, M., Szegedy, M.: Proof verification and the hardness of approximation problems. J. ACM **45**(3), 501–555 (1998)
2. Canfield, E.R., Xing, G.: Approximate matching of XML document with regular hedge grammar. Int. J. Comput. Math. **82**(10), 1191–1198 (2005)
3. Comon, H., Dauchet, M., Jacquemard, F., Lugiez, D., Tison, S., Tommasi, M.: Tree Automata Techniques and Applications (2007)
4. Demaine, E.D., Mozes, S., Rossman, B., Weimann, O.: An optimal decomposition algorithm for tree edit distance. ACM Trans. Algorithms **6**(1), 2:1–2:19 (2009)
5. Fredman, M.L., Tarjan, R.E.: Fibonacci heaps and their uses in improved network optimization algorithms. J. ACM **34**(3), 596–615 (1987)
6. Höchsmann, M., Töller, T., Giegerich, R., Kurtz, S.: Local similarity in RNA secondary structures. In: Proceedings of the 2nd IEEE Computer Society Conference on Bioinformatics, pp. 159–168 (2003)
7. Jiang, T., Wang, L., Zhang, K.: Alignment of trees – an alternative to tree edit. Theoret. Comput. Sci. **143**(1), 137–148 (1995)
8. Klein, P.N.: Computing the edit-distance between unrooted ordered trees. In: Proceedings of the 6th Annual European Symposium on Algorithms, pp. 91–102 (1998)
9. Kuboyama, T., Shin, K., Miyahara, T., Yasuda, H.: A theoretical analysis of alignment and edit problems for trees. In: Proceedings of the 9th Italian Conference on Theoretical Computer Science, pp. 323–337 (2005)
10. Levenshtein, V.I.: Binary codes capable of correcting deletions, insertions, and reversals. Sov. Phys. Dokl. **10**(8), 707 710 (1966)
11. López, D., España, S.: Error-correcting tree language inference. Pattern Recogn. Lett. **23**(1–3), 1–12 (2002)
12. López, D., Sempere, J.M., García, P.: Error correcting analysis for tree languages. Int. J. Pattern Recogn. Artif. Intell. **14**(03), 357–368 (2000)
13. Lu, C.L., Su, Z.-Y., Tang, C.Y.: A new measure of edit distance between labeled trees. In: Proceedings of the 7th Annual International Conference on Computing and Combinatorics, pp. 338–348 (2001)
14. Nierman, A., Jagadish, H.V.: Evaluating structural similarity in XML documents. In: Proceedings of the 5th International Workshop on the Web and Databases, pp. 61–66 (2002)
15. Tai, K.-C.: The tree-to-tree correction problem. J. ACM **26**(3), 422–433 (1979)
16. Voß, B., Giegerich, R., Rehmsmeier, M.: Complete probabilistic analysis of RNA shapes. BMC Biol. **4**(1), 1–23 (2006)
17. Xing, G.: Approximate matching of XML documents with schemata using tree alignment. In: Proceedings of the 2014 ACM Southeast Regional Conference, pp. 43:1–43:4 (2014)
18. Zhang, K.: A constrained edit distance between unordered labeled trees. Algorithmica **15**(3), 205–222 (1996)
19. Zhang, K., Jiang, T.: Some MAX SNP-hard results concerning unordered labeled trees. Inf. Process. Lett. **49**(5), 249–254 (1994)
20. Zhang, K., Statman, R., Shasha, D.: On the editing distance between unordered labeled trees. Inf. Process. Lett. **42**(3), 133–139 (1992)

Nondeterministic Complexity of Operations on Free and Convex Languages

Michal Hospodár[✉], Galina Jirásková, and Peter Mlynárčik

Mathematical Institute, Slovak Academy of Sciences,
Grešákova 6, 040 01 Košice, Slovakia
hosmich@gmail.com, jiraskov@saske.sk, mlynarcik1972@gmail.com

Abstract. We study the nondeterministic state complexity of basic regular operations on the classes of prefix-, suffix-, factor-, and subword-free and -convex regular languages. For the operations of intersection, union, concatenation, square, star, reversal, and complementation, we get the tight upper bounds for all considered classes except for complementation on factor- and subword-convex languages. Most of our witnesses are described over optimal alphabets. The most interesting result is the describing of a proper suffix-convex language over a five-letter alphabet meeting the upper bound 2^n for complementation.

1 Introduction

The nondeterministic state complexity of a regular language L, $\mathrm{nsc}(L)$, is the smallest number of states in any nondeterministic finite automaton (NFA) with a single initial state accepting the language L. The nondeterministic state complexity of a regular operation is defined as the maximal nondeterministic state complexity of languages resulting from the operation, considered as a function of nondeterministic state complexities of the operands. The languages that meet this maximal complexity for an operation are called witnesses for the operation. The (deterministic) state complexity of a regular language and a regular operation are defined analogously.

If operands for an operation satisfy some additional properties, the resulting complexity may be smaller than in the general case. In this paper we focus on the classes of prefix-, suffix-, factor-, subword-free and -convex languages. In the deterministic case, the complexity of basic regular operations on the classes of closed, ideal, and free languages was examined by Brzozowski *et al.* [2,4,5]. Some partial results in the classes of convex languages can be found in [3].

The nondeterministic state complexity of basic operations on regular languages was investigated by Holzer and Kutrib [9], and binary witnesses for reversal and complementation were presented in [11]. Han *et al.* [7,8] studied

Research supported by VEGA grant 2/0084/15 and grant APVV-15-0091. This work was conducted as a part of PhD study of Michal Hospodár and Peter Mlynárčik at the Faculty of Mathematics, Physics and Informatics of the Comenius University.

© Springer International Publishing AG 2017
A. Carayol and C. Nicaud (Eds.): CIAA 2017, LNCS 10329, pp. 138–150, 2017.
DOI: 10.1007/978-3-319-60134-2_12

the nondeterministic complexity of operations on prefix-free and suffix-free languages; some of their results were improved in [13]. Mlynárčik [15] examined the nondeterministic complexity of complementation on the classes of free and ideal languages. The remaining operations on ideal languages as well as all basic operations on closed languages were investigated in [10].

In this paper we continue this research and study the nondeterministic complexity of operations of intersection, union, concatenation, square, star, reversal, and complementation on the classes of prefix-, suffix-, factor-, subword-free and -convex languages. Except for complementation on factor- and subword-convex languages, we provide tight upper bounds, and to prove tightness, we use a small fixed alphabet in most cases. In some cases, we improve the known results by decreasing the size of alphabet for witness languages. We fix a small bug from the literature [8, Theorem 3.2] concerning union on prefix-free languages.

2   Preliminaries

We use a standard model of a nondeterministic finite automaton (NFA), as explained, for example, in [16]. An NFA $A = (Q, \Sigma, \cdot, s, F)$ is a (complete) *deterministic finite automaton* (DFA) if for each state q in Q and each input symbol a in Σ, the set $q \cdot a$ has exactly one element. If $|q \cdot a| \le 1$ for each q and a, then A is an *incomplete* DFA. In an ε-NFA, we also allow the transitions on the empty string. It is known that for each ε-NFA there exists an equivalent NFA with the same number of states [17, Theorem 2.3]. Sometimes, we allow an NFA to have multiple initial states and use the shortcut NNFA for this model.

A state q of an NFA A is called a *dead state* if no string is accepted by A from q, that is, if $q \cdot w \cap F = \emptyset$ for each string w. An NFA A is a *trim* NFA if each its state q is reachable, that is, there is a string u in Σ^* such that $q \in s \cdot u$, and, moreover, no state of A is dead. We say that (p, a, q) is a transition in NFA A if $q \in p \cdot a$. We also say that the state q has an *in-transition* on symbol a, and the state p has an *out-transition* on symbol a. An NFA is *non-returning* if its initial state does not have any in-transitions, and it is *non-exiting* if each final state of A does not have any out-transitions.

Definition 1. *A set of pairs of strings* $\{(u_1, v_1), (u_2, v_2), \ldots, (u_n, v_n)\}$ *is called a* fooling set *for a language L if for all i, j in $\{1, 2, \ldots, n\}$,*

(F1) $u_i v_i \in L$, *and*
(F2) *if $i \ne j$, then $u_i v_j \notin L$ or $u_j v_i \notin L$.*

Lemma 2 ([1, Lemma 1]). *Let $\mathcal{F}$ be a fooling set for a language L. Then every NNFA for the language L has at least $|\mathcal{F}|$ states.*   □

Let us emphasize that the size of a fooling set for L provides a lower bound on the number of states in any NNFA for L. If we insist on having just one initial state, then the following modification of a fooling set method can be used.

Lemma 3 ([12, Lemma 4]). *Let A and B be sets of pairs of strings and let u and v be two strings such that $A \cup B$, $A \cup \{(\varepsilon, u)\}$, and $B \cup \{(\varepsilon, v)\}$ are fooling sets for a language L. Then every NFA for L has at least $|A| + |B| + 1$ states.* □

Let $A = (Q, \Sigma, \cdot, I, F)$ be an NNFA and $S, T \subseteq Q$. We say that S is *reachable* in A if there is a string w in Σ^* such that $S = I \cdot w$. Next, we say that T is *co-reachable* in A if T is reachable in A^R obtained from A by swapping the role of initial and final states and by reversing all the transitions. The next two observations are used throughout this paper.

Lemma 4. *Let A be an NNFA. Let for each state q of A, the singleton set $\{q\}$ be reachable as well as co-reachable in A. Then A is minimal.*

Proof. Let $A = (Q, \Sigma, \cdot, I, F)$. Since $\{q\}$ is reachable in A, there is a string u_q such that $I \cdot u_q = \{q\}$. Since $\{q\}$ is co-reachable in A, there is a string v_q accepted by A from and only from the state q. Then $\{(u_q, v_q) \mid q \in Q\}$ is a fooling set for $L(A)$. By Lemma 2, the NNFA A is minimal.   □

Lemma 5. *Let A be a trim NFA. If both A and A^R are incomplete DFAs, then A and A^R are minimal NFAs.*

Proof. If A is a trim incomplete DFA, then for each state q of A, the singleton set $\{q\}$ is reachable. If moreover A^R is an incomplete DFA, then $\{q\}$ is co-reachable in A. By Lemma 4, A and A^R are minimal NFAs.   □

If $u, v, w, x \in \Sigma^*$ and $w = uxv$, then u is a *prefix* of w, x is a *factor* of w, and v is a *suffix* of w. If $w = u_0 v_1 u_1 \cdots v_n u_n$, where $u_i, v_i \in \Sigma^*$, then $v_1 v_2 \cdots v_n$ is a *subword* of w. A prefix v (suffix, factor, subword) of w is *proper* if $v \neq w$.

A language L is *prefix-free* if $w \in L$ implies that no proper prefix of w is in L; it is *prefix-closed* if $w \in L$ implies that each prefix of w is in L; and it is *prefix-convex* if $u, w \in L$ and u is a prefix of w imply that each string v such that u is a prefix of v and v is a prefix of w is in L. Suffix-, factor-, and subword-free, -closed, and -convex languages are defined analogously. It is known that a minimal NFA for a prefix-free (suffix-free) language is non-exiting (non-returning) [7,8]. The next lemma gives a sufficient condition for an incomplete DFA accepting a suffix-free language.

Lemma 6. ([6, Lemma 1]). *Let A be a non-returning incomplete DFA that has a unique final state. If each state of A has at most one in-transition on every input symbol, then $L(A)$ is suffix-free.*   □

3   Unary Convex Languages

We start with examination of unary free and unary convex languages. Notice that if $i \leq j$, then a^i is a prefix, suffix, factor, and subword of a^j. It follows that in the unary case, all free classes and all convex classes coincide. Moreover, if $n \geq 2$ then $L = \{a^{n-1}\}$ is the only unary free language with $\mathrm{nsc}(L) = n$.

Let L be a unary convex language and k be the length of the shortest string in L. If L is infinite, then $L = \{a^i \mid i \geq k\}$. If L is finite and ℓ is the length of the longest string in L, then $L = \{a^i \mid k \leq i \leq \ell\}$. The set $\{(a^i, a^{t-i}) \mid 0 \leq i \leq t\}$ is a fooling set for L, where $t = k$ for infinite L and $t = \ell$ for finite L. Thus the minimal incomplete DFA for L, which has $t + 1$ states, is a minimal NFA for L.

The next theorem provides tight upper bounds for unary convex languages. All the results, except for the intersection and complementation, hold true for free languages too. On unary free languages, the complexity of intersection is n if $m = n$ and 1 if $m \neq n$, and the complexity of complementation is $\Theta(\sqrt{n})$ [13].

Theorem 7 (Unary Convex Languages). *Let $m, n \geq 2$. Let K and L be unary convex languages with $\mathrm{nsc}(K) = m$ and $\mathrm{nsc}(L) = n$. Then*

(a) $\mathrm{nsc}(K \cap L), \mathrm{nsc}(K \cup L) \leq \max\{m, n\}$,
(b) $\mathrm{nsc}(KL) \leq m + n - 1$ and $\mathrm{nsc}(L^2) \leq 2n - 1$,
(c) $\mathrm{nsc}(L^*) \leq n - 1$, $\mathrm{nsc}(L^R) \leq n$, and $\mathrm{nsc}(L^c) \leq n + 1$,

and all these upper bounds are tight.

Proof. The upper bound for intersection and union can be verified by the case analysis, where K and L can be finite or infinite. The upper bounds for concatenation, square, and complementation follow from the fact that the minimal NFAs can be incomplete deterministic. The upper bound for reversal follows from the fact that $L^R = L$.

Now we prove an upper bound for star. Let L be a unary convex language with $\mathrm{nsc}(L) = n$. If L is infinite, then $L = a^{n-1}a^*$, and the language L^* is accepted by the $(n-1)$-state NFA $N = (\{0, 1, \ldots, n-2\}, \{a\}, \cdot, 0, \{0\})$ where $i \cdot a = \{i + 1\}$ if $i < n - 2$ and $i \cdot a = \{0, n - 2\}$ if $i = n - 2$.

If L is finite, then there is an integer k such that $L = \{a^i \mid k \leq i \leq n - 1\}$. Then the $(n-1)$-state NFA for L^* can be constructed from a minimal incomplete DFA $(\{0, 1, \ldots, n - 1\}, \{a\}, \cdot, 0, \{k, k+1, \ldots, n-1\})$ for L by making the state $n - 1$ initial, adding the transition $(n - 1, a, 1)$, and removing the state 0.

The languages $a^{m-1}a^*$ and $a^{n-1}a^*$ meet the upper bound for intersection, the languages a^{m-1} and a^{n-1} meet the upper bound for union and concatenation, the language a^{n-1} meets the upper bound for square, star, and reversal, and the language $\{a^i \mid i \leq n - 1\}$ meets the upper bound for complementation.   □

Table 1 summarizes our results on unary convex languages and compares them to the known results on unary regular and free languages [9, 13].

Table 1. The nondeterministic complexity of operations on unary classes; the results are from [13] (first row), Theorem 7 (second row), and [9] (third row).

	$K \cap L$	$K \cup L$	KL	L^2	L^*	L^c
Unary free	$n; m = n$	$\max\{m,n\}$	$m+n-1$	$2n-1$	$n-1$	$\Theta(\sqrt{n})$
Unary convex	$\max\{m,n\}$	$\max\{m,n\}$	$m+n-1$	$2n-1$	$n-1$	$n+1$
Unary regular	$mn; \gcd(m,n) = 1$	$m+n+1;$ $\gcd(m,n)=1$	$\geq m+n-1$ $\leq m+n$	$\geq 2n-1$ $\leq 2n$	$n+1$	$2^{\Theta(\sqrt{n \log n})}$

4   Prefix-, Suffix-, Factor-, Subword-Free Languages

The nondeterministic complexity of operations on prefix- and suffix-free languages was studied by Han *et al.* [7,8], where tight upper bounds were obtained for basic regular operations. Some of their results were improved by decreasing the size of the alphabet for witness languages in [14]. The aim of this section is to get tight upper bounds on the nondeterministic state complexity of basic regular operations on factor- and subword-free languages as they are shown in Table 2. We also fix a small bug in [8] concerning union on prefix-free languages. For tightness, we use a unary or binary alphabet in all cases except for intersection on subword-free languages, and these alphabets are always optimal. The size of alphabet is shown in the right part of each column. The dot denotes the same complexity as in the previous column. The results for complementation are from [13], and the ternary alphabet is also optimal here. We start with intersection.

Theorem 8 (Intersection). *Let K and L be regular languages over an alphabet Σ such that $\mathrm{nsc}(K) = m$ and $\mathrm{nsc}(L) = n$.*

(a) *If K and L are prefix-free (suffix-free) then $\mathrm{nsc}(K \cap L) \leq mn - (m+n-2)$, and the bound is tight if $m \geq 4$, $n \geq 2$, and $|\Sigma| \geq 2$.*
(b) *If K and L are factor-free, then $\mathrm{nsc}(K \cap L) \leq mn - 2(m+n-3)$, and the bound is tight if $m \geq 5$, $n \geq 3$, and $|\Sigma| \geq 2$.*
(c) *If $m, n \geq 3$, then there exist subword-free regular languages K and L over an $(m+n-5)$-letter alphabet such that $\mathrm{nsc}(K) = m$, $\mathrm{nsc}(L) = n$, and $\mathrm{nsc}(K \cap L) = mn - 2(m+n-3)$.*

Proof. We first prove the upper bounds. Let A and B be minimal NFAs for K and L, respectively. We may assume that the state sets of A and B are $\{0, 1, \ldots, m-1\}$ and $\{0, 1, \ldots, n-1\}$, respectively, with the initial state 0 in both automata. Construct the product automaton $A \times B$ for $K \cap L$.

If K and L are prefix-free with the final states $m-1$ and $n-1$ respectively, then all states in the last row and last column, except for $(m-1, n-1)$, are dead, so we can omit them. If K and L are suffix-free, then A and B are non-returning, so all states in the first row and first column, except for $(0,0)$, are unreachable. Since every factor-free language is both prefix-free and suffix-free, all the three upper bounds follow from these observations.

Table 2. The nondeterministic state complexity of operations on free classes; complementation is from [13]. The dot means that the complexity is the same as in the previous column.

	Regular	$|\Sigma|$	Prefix-free	$|\Sigma|$	Suffix-free	$|\Sigma|$	Factor-free	$|\Sigma|$	Subword-tree	$|\Sigma|$
$K \cap L$	mn	2	$mn-(m+n-2)$	2	·	2	$mn-2(m+n-3)$	2	·	$m+n-5$
$K \cup L$	$m+n+1$	2	$m+n$	2	$m+n-1$	2	$m+n-2$	2	·	2
KL	$m+n$	2	$m+n-1$	1	·	1	·	1	·	1
L^2	$2n$	2	$2n-1$	1	·	1	·	1	·	1
L^*	$n+1$	1	n	2	·	2	$n-1$	1	·	1
L^R	$n+1$	2	n	1	$n+1$	2	n	1	·	1
L^c	2^n	2	2^{n-1}	3	·	3	$2^{n-2}+1$	3	·	2^{n-2}

To prove tightness, we first consider factor-free languages. Let $m \geq 5$, $n \geq 3$. Let K and L be the languages accepted by the NFAs A and B shown in Fig. 1.

Every string w in K begins and ends with a, and $|w|_b \bmod (m-2) = (m-3)$. Every proper factor v of w which begins and ends with a has a computation in A which either starts in the state 0 and ends in the state 2, or starts and ends in 2, or starts in 2 and ends in $m-1$. However, in all three cases, $|v|_b \bmod (m-2) \neq (m-3)$, so $v \notin L$. Hence the language K is factor-free. Next, every string in L has exactly $n-1$ a's, but every proper factor of every string in L has less than $n-1$ a's. Hence L is factor-free.

Construct the product automaton $A \times B$ and remove all the unreachable and dead states to get a trim NFA N for $K \cap L$. Since the NFA N and its reverse N^R are incomplete DFAs, the NFA N is minimal by Lemma 4. So we have $\mathrm{nsc}(K \cap L) = mn - 2(m+n-3)$. Notice that there is no need to prove that NFAs A and B are minimal because the upper bound cannot be met by languages of a smaller complexity. For this reason we do not prove the minimality of witnesses in what follows.

Next, the left quotients of K and L by the string a, that is, the languages $a\backslash K$ and $a\backslash L$, are prefix-free and meet the upper bound $mn - (m+n-2)$. Similarly, the right quotients K/a and L/a are suffix-free witnesses.

Finally, we consider the complexity of intersection on subword-free languages. Let $\Sigma = \{a\} \cup \{b_k \mid 2 \leq k \leq m-2\} \cup \{c_\ell \mid 2 \leq \ell \leq n-2\}$. Let K and L be

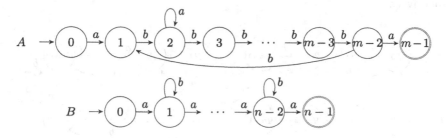

Fig. 1. Binary factor-free witnesses for intersection.

languages accepted by incomplete DFAs $A = (\{0, 1, \ldots, m-1\}, \Sigma, \cdot, 0, \{m-1\})$ and $B = (\{0, 1, \ldots, n-1\}, \Sigma, \circ, 0, \{n-1\})$, where for each i $(0 \leq i \leq m-2)$, j $(0 \leq j \leq n-2)$, k $(2 \leq k \leq m-2)$, and ℓ $(2 \leq \ell \leq n-2)$, we have

$$i \cdot a = i+1, \qquad\qquad j \circ a = j+1,$$
$$0 \cdot b_k = k \text{ and } (k-1) \cdot b_k = m-1, \qquad 0 \circ b_k = 1 \text{ and } (n-2) \circ b_k = n-1,$$
$$0 \cdot c_\ell = 1 \text{ and } (m-2) \cdot c_\ell = m-1, \qquad 0 \circ c_\ell = \ell \text{ and } (\ell-1) \circ c_\ell = n-1.$$

We can prove that K and L are subword-free and meet the upper bound for intersection.   □

As a result of the previous theorem, we get the nondeterministic state complexity of intersection on each of the four classes of free languages, as it is shown in the corresponding row of Table 2.

Now we consider the union operation. In [8] it is claimed that the upper bound $m + n$ is met by the union of prefix-free languages $K = (a^{m-1})^*b$ and $L = (c^{n-1})^*d$, and a set P of pairs of strings of size $m+n$ is described in [8, Proof of Theorem 3.2]. The authors claimed that P is a fooling set for $K \cup L$. However, the language $K \cup L$ is accepted by an NNFA of $m + n - 1$ states. Therefore P cannot be a fooling set for $K \cup L$. Here we prove the tightness of the upper bound $m + n$ for union of prefix-free languages using a binary alphabet and a modified fooling set method given by Lemma 3. Next we get the tight upper bound for union of suffix-, factor-, and subword-free languages. To get tightness, we always use a binary alphabet which is optimal for all four classes.

Theorem 9 (Union). *Let K and L be regular languages over an alphabet Σ such that $\mathrm{nsc}(K) = m$ and $\mathrm{nsc}(L) = n$.*

(a) *If K and L are prefix-free then $\mathrm{nsc}(K \cup L) \leq m + n$, and the bound is tight if $m \geq 3, n \geq 3$, and $\Sigma \geq 2$.*
(b) *If K and L are suffix-free then $\mathrm{nsc}(K \cup L) \leq m + n - 1$, and the bound is tight if $m \geq 3, n \geq 3$, and $\Sigma \geq 2$.*
(c) *If K and L are factor-free, then $\mathrm{nsc}(K \cup L) \leq m + n - 2$, and the bound is met by binary subword-free languages if $m \geq 2$ and $n \geq 2$.*

Proof. We first prove the upper bounds. Let A and B be minimal NFAs for K and L, respectively, with disjoint state sets, and the initial states s_A and s_B, respectively.

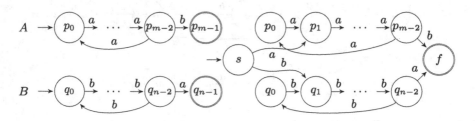

Fig. 2. Binary prefix-free witnesses for union meeting the upper bound $m + n$.

(a) If K and L are prefix-free, then NFAs A and B are non-exiting and have a unique final state. To get an $(m + n)$-state NFA for $K \cup L$ from A and B, add a new initial (non-final) state connected through ε-transitions to s_A and s_B, make the states s_A and s_B non-initial, and merge the final states of A and B.

(b) If K and L are suffix-free, then A and B are non-returning. We can get an $(m + n - 1)$-state NFA for $K \cup L$ from A and B by merging their initial states.

(c) If K and L are factor-free, then they are both prefix- and suffix-free. To get an $(m + n - 2)$-state NFA for $K \cup L$ from A and B, we merge their initial states, and then we merge their final states.

To prove tightness, consider languages K and L accepted by an m-state and n-state NFAs A and B, respectively, shown in Fig. 2 (left). Notice that K is prefix-free since every string in K ends with b while every proper prefix of every string in K is in a^*. Similarly, L is prefix-free.

Construct the $(m + n)$-state NFA for their union by adding a new initial state s, by adding transitions (s, a, p_1) and (s, b, q_1), by making states p_0 and q_0 non-initial, and by merging their final states as shown in Fig. 2 (right). The resulting trim NFA is an incomplete DFA, and its reverse is an incomplete DFA as well. By Lemma 5, this NFA is minimal. It follows that $\operatorname{nsc}(K \cup L) \geq m + n$.

Next, the languages K^R and L^R are suffix-free, and they are accepted by m-state and n-state NFAs A^R and B^R, respectively. To get an NFA for $K^R \cup L^R$, we merge the initial states of A^R and B^R. For each state q of the resulting automaton, the singleton set $\{q\}$ is reachable, as well as co-reachable. By Lemma 4, this NFA is minimal. Hence we get $\operatorname{nsc}(K^R \cup L^R) \geq m + n - 1$. Finally, we again use Lemma 5 to show that the union of binary subword-free languages $\{a^{m-1}\}$ and $\{b^{n-1}\}$ meets the upper bound $m + n - 2$. □

The theorem above gives the nondeterministic state complexity of union on free languages, as it is shown in the corresponding row of Table 2.

The nondeterministic state complexity of concatenation on regular languages is $m + n$ with binary witnesses [9, Theorem 7]. For prefix-free and suffix-free languages, the upper bound is $m + n - 1$ [7,8], and to prove tightness, a binary alphabet was used in [8, Theorem 3.1] and [7, Theorem 4]. In this section, we show that this upper bound is tight for all four classes of free languages, and to prove tightness, we use a unary alphabet.

Theorem 10 (Concatenation, Square). *Let K and L be prefix-free (suffix-free) languages with $\operatorname{nsc}(K) = m$ and $\operatorname{nsc}(L) = n$. Then $\operatorname{nsc}(KL) \leq m + n - 1$, $\operatorname{nsc}(L^2) \leq 2n - 1$, and these bounds are met by unary subword-free languages.*

Proof. Let A and B be minimal NFAs for K and L, respectively. In the prefix-free case, we can merge the final state of A and the initial state of B to get an NFA for KL. In the suffix-free case, automata A and B are non-returning. To get an NFA for KL, we add the transition (p, a, q) for each final state p of A and each transition (s_B, a, q) of B. Next, we make final states of A non-final, and remove the unreachable state s_B. As a result, we get an NFA for KL of $m + n - 1$ states in both cases. This upper bound is met by the concatenation of unary subword-free languages $\{a^{m-1}\}$ and $\{a^{n-1}\}$. Since the witnesses have the same structure, the complexity $2n - 1$ for square follows.   □

Using the theorem above, we obtain the nondeterministic state complexity of concatenation and square on free languages, as shown in Table 2.

We next consider the Kleene star and reversal operations. Both operations have nondeterministic complexity $n + 1$ on regular languages with a unary witness for star [9, Theorem 9] and a binary witness for reversal [11, Theorem 2]. The following theorem provides tight upper bounds for star on all four classes of free languages, as shown in Table 2. To get tightness, we use an optimal binary alphabet in the prefix- and suffix-free case, and a unary alphabet otherwise.

Theorem 11 (Star). *Let L be a language over an alphabet Σ with $\mathrm{nsc}(L) = n$.*

(a) *If L is prefix- or suffix-free then $\mathrm{nsc}(L^*) \leq n$. These upper bounds are tight if $|\Sigma| \geq 2$, and the size of alphabet cannot be decreased.*
(b) *If L is factor-free, then $\mathrm{nsc}(L^*) \leq n - 1$, and the bound is met by a unary subword-free language.*

Proof. Let $A = (Q, \Sigma, \cdot, s, F)$ be a minimal NFA for L.

(a) If L is prefix-free, then A is non-exiting and has a unique final state q_f. We can construct an n-state ε-NFA for the language L^* from A by making state q_f initial and state s non-initial, and by adding the ε-transition from q_f to s. If L is suffix-free, then A is non-returning. Now we construct an n-state ε-NFA for L^* from A by making the initial state s final, and by adding the ε-transition from every final state to the initial state s. Suffix-free language $a^{n-1}b^*$ and prefix-free language b^*a^{n-1} meet the upper bound n.

(b) If L is factor-free, then A is non-returning, non-exiting, and it has a unique final state q_f. We construct an NFA for L^* by making state q_f initial, by adding transition (q_f, a, q) for each transition (s, a, q), and by omitting the state s. The unary subword-free language $\{a^{n-1}\}$ meets this upper bound.   □

Now we turn our attention to the reversal operation. Han *et al.* obtained tight upper bounds for reversal on prefix-free and suffix-free languages and they provided a binary prefix-free witness [8, Theorem 3.4] and a ternary suffix-free witness [7, Theorem 9]. As shown in the next theorem, the upper bound for reversal on prefix-free languages is n, so it is met by any unary language. In the suffix-free case, we provide a binary witness meeting the upper bound $n + 1$. Notice that the reverse of a language accepted by an n-state NFA is accepted by an n-state NNFA. This means that we cannot use a fooling set method to prove the tightness of the bound $n + 1$. However, a modified fooling set method described in Lemma 3 can be successfully used here. As a result of this theorem, we get the corresponding row of Table 2.

Theorem 12 (Reversal).

(a) Let L be a prefix-free language with $\mathrm{nsc}(L) = n$. Then $\mathrm{nsc}(L^R) \leq n$, and this bound is met by a unary subword-free language.

(b) If $n \geq 5$, then there exists a binary suffix-free regular language L such that $\mathrm{nsc}(L) = n$ and $\mathrm{nsc}(L^R) = n + 1$.

Proof.

(a) If L is prefix-free, then every minimal NFA for L has a unique final state. Thus $\mathrm{nsc}(L^R) \leq n$. The bound is met by the language $\{a^{n-1}\}$.

(b) Set $L = ba^{n-4}(a^{n-3})^* + ab(bb)^*$. Since every string in L contain both a and b, but every proper suffix of every string in L is in $a^* \cup b^*$, the language L is suffix-free. Let

$\mathcal{A} = \{(a^{n-3}, a^{n-4}b)\} \cup \{(a^i, a^{n-4-i}b) \mid 1 \leq i \leq n-4\} \cup \{(a^{n-4}b, \varepsilon)\}$,
$\mathcal{B} = \{(bb, ba), (b, a)\}$,
$u = ba$, and $v = a^{n-4}b$.

Using Lemma 3, we show that every NFA for L^R needs at least $n+1$ states. □

5 Convex Languages

In this section, we examine the nondeterministic state complexity of basic regular operations on convex languages. Recall that prefix-closed and right ideal languages are prefix-convex, and similar inclusions exist for suffix-, factor-, and subword-closed, and left, two-sided, and all-sided ideal classes.

The complexity of operations on closed and ideal languages was studied in [10], where for each operation, except for complementation, and for each of the four convex classes, a closed or an ideal witness, meeting the complexity of the operation in the class of regular languages, is described: binary subword-closed languages meeting the upper bound mn for intersection, and binary subword-closed witnesses meeting the upper bound $m + n + 1$ for union are given in Theorems 4 and 5, ternary subword-closed languages meeting the bound $m + n$ for concatenation and $2n$ for square, are described in Theorem 6 and Corollary 7, the binary all-sided ideal meeting the upper bound $n + 1$ for star is provided in Theorem 16, and for reversal, the binary prefix-closed, ternary factor-closed, and subword-closed witness defined over an alphabet of size $2n-2$ are described in Theorem 9. Therefore, as shown in Table 3, the complexity of operations on convex languages, except for complementation, is the same as for regular languages, although, to get tightness, larger alphabets are used in some cases.

The nondeterministic state complexity of complementation on regular languages is 2^n with a binary witness [9,11]. The upper bound 2^n is met by binary prefix-closed languages [10, Theorem 10]. On the other hand, this upper bound cannot be met by suffix-closed, suffix-free, or left ideal languages [10,13,15].

Our last result shows that the upper bound 2^n for complementation is tight on suffix-convex languages. We describe a proper suffix-convex language, that is, a suffix-convex languages which is neither suffix-free, nor suffix-closed, nor left ideal, that meets this upper bound for complementation.

Table 3. The nondeterministic state complexity of operations on convex classes. The results for regular languages are from [9]. All the remaining results, except for complementation on suffix-convex languages, follow from [9,10].

	Regular	$|\Sigma|$	Prefix-convex	$|\Sigma|$	Suffix-convex	$|\Sigma|$	Factor-convex	$|\Sigma|$	Subword-convex	$|\Sigma|$
$K \cap L$	mn	2	·	2	·	2	·	2	·	2
$K \cup L$	$m+n+1$	2	·	2	·	2	·	2	·	2
KL	$m+n$	2	·	3	·	3	·	3	·	3
L^2	$2n$	2	·	3	·	3	·	3	·	3
L^*	$n+1$	1	·	2	·	2	·	2	·	2
L^R	$n+1$	2	·	2	·	3	·	3	·	$2n-2$
L^c	2^n	2	·	2	·	5	$\geq 2^{n-1}+1 \leq 2^n$	2	$\geq 2^{n-1}+1 \leq 2^n$	2^n

Theorem 13 (Complementation on Suffix-Convex Languages). *Let $n \geq 3$. There exists a suffix-convex regular language L over a 5-letter alphabet such that* $\mathrm{nsc}(L) = n$ *and* $\mathrm{nsc}(L^c) = 2^n$.

Proof. Let L be the language accepted by the nondeterministic finite automaton $A = (\{0, 1, \ldots, n-1\}, \{a, b, c, d, e\}, \cdot, 0, \{1, 2, \ldots, n-1\})$, where the transitions on a and b are shown in Fig. 3, the transitions on c, d, e are as follows: $0 \cdot c = \{0, 1, \ldots, n-1\}$, $0 \cdot d = \{1, 2, \ldots, n-1\}$, $q \cdot e = \{n-1\}$ for each state q of A, and all the remaining transitions go to the empty set. In the NFA A^R, the final state 0 goes to itself on a, b, c and to the empty set on d and e. Next, every other state of A^R goes to 0 on d, and the state $n-1$ goes to $\{0, 1, \ldots, n-1\}$ on e. Thus in the subset automaton of A^R, each final subset, that is, a subset containing the state 0, goes either to a final subset containing 0 or to the empty set on each input symbol. It follows that the language L^R is prefix-convex, so L is suffix-convex. We can show that each subset of the state set of A is reachable and co-reachable. Hence for each subset S, there exists a string u_S in Σ^* such that $s \cdot u_S = S$. Next, S^c is co-reachable, so there is a string v_S which is accepted by A from each state in S^c, but rejected from each state in S. Thus $\{(u_S, v_S) \mid S \subseteq Q\}$ is a fooling set for L^c of size 2^n, so $\mathrm{nsc}(L^c) \geq 2^n$ by Lemma 2. $\qquad\square$

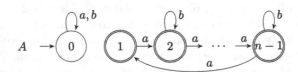

Fig. 3. Transitions on a and b in suffix-convex witness for complementation.

6   Conclusions

We investigated the nondeterministic state complexity of basic operations on the classes of prefix-, suffix-, factor-, subword-free and -convex languages. For each class and for each operation, except for complementation on factor- and subword-convex languages, we obtained the tight upper bounds.

Our results are summarized in Tables 1, 2, and 3. For complementation on factor- and subword-convex languages we do not know whether or not the upper bound 2^n is tight. All the remaining upper bounds are tight. Whenever we used a binary alphabet, it is always optimal in the sense that the upper bound is not tight for any smaller alphabet. In any other case, we do not know whether the upper bounds are tight for a smaller alphabet. The complexity of complementation on factor- and subword-convex languages remains open as well.

Acknowledgment. We would like to thank Jozef Jirásek, Jr., for his help with finding the suffix-convex witness for complementation and for fruitful discussions on the topic.

References

1. Birget, J.: Intersection and union of regular languages and state complexity. Inform. Process. Lett. **43**(4), 185–190 (1992). doi:10.1016/0020-0190(92)90198-5
2. Brzozowski, J., Jirásková, G., Li, B., Smith, J.: Quotient complexity of bifix-, factor-, and subword-free regular languages. Acta Cybernetica **21**(4), 507–527 (2014)
3. Brzozowski, J.: Complexity in convex languages. In: Dediu, A.-H., Fernau, H., Martín-Vide, C. (eds.) LATA 2010. LNCS, vol. 6031, pp. 1–15. Springer, Heidelberg (2010). doi:10.1007/978-3-642-13089-2_1
4. Brzozowski, J.A., Jirásková, G., Li, B.: Quotient complexity of ideal languages. Theoret. Comput. Sci. **470**, 36–52 (2013). doi:10.1016/j.tcs.2012.10.055
5. Brzozowski, J.A., Jirásková, G., Zou, C.: Quotient complexity of closed languages. Theory Comput. Syst. **54**(2), 277–292 (2014). doi:10.1007/s00224-013-9515-7
6. Cmorik, R., Jirásková, G.: Basic operations on binary suffix-free languages. In: Kotásek, Z., Bouda, J., Černá, I., Sekanina, L., Vojnar, T., Antoš, D. (eds.) MEMICS 2011. LNCS, vol. 7119, pp. 94–102. Springer, Heidelberg (2012). doi:10.1007/978-3-642-25929-6_9
7. Han, Y., Salomaa, K.: Nondeterministic state complexity for suffix-free regular languages. In: McQuillan, I., Pighizzini, G. (eds.) DCFS 2010. EPTCS, vol. 31, pp. 189–196 (2010). doi:10.4204/EPTCS.31.21
8. Han, Y., Salomaa, K., Wood, D.: Nondeterministic state complexity of basic operations for prefix-free regular languages. Fundam. Inform. **90**(1–2), 93–106 (2009). doi:10.3233/FI-2009-0008
9. Holzer, M., Kutrib, M.: Nondeterministic descriptional complexity of regular languages. Int. J. Found. Comput. Sci. **14**(6), 1087–1102 (2003). doi:10.1142/S0129054103002199
10. Hospodár, M., Jirásková, G., Mlynárčik, P.: Nondeterministic complexity of operations on closed and ideal languages. In: Han, Y.-S., Salomaa, K. (eds.) CIAA 2016. LNCS, vol. 9705, pp. 125–137. Springer, Cham (2016). doi:10.1007/978-3-319-40946-7_11

11. Jirásková, G.: State complexity of some operations on binary regular languages. Theoret. Comput. Sci. **330**(2), 287–298 (2005). doi:10.1016/j.tcs.2004.04.011
12. Jirásková, G., Masopust, T.: Complexity in union-free regular languages. Internat. J. Found. Comput. Sci. **22**(7), 1639–1653 (2011). doi:10.1142/S0129054111008933
13. Jirásková, G., Mlynárčik, P.: Complement on prefix-free, suffix-free, and non-returning NFA languages. In: Jürgensen, H., Karhumäki, J., Okhotin, A. (eds.) DCFS 2014. LNCS, vol. 8614, pp. 222–233. Springer, Cham (2014). doi:10.1007/978-3-319-09704-6_20
14. Jirásková, G., Olejár, P.: State complexity of intersection and union of suffix-free languages and descriptional complexity. In: Bordihn, H., et al. (eds.) NCMA 2009, vol. 256, pp. 151–166. Austrian Computer Society (2009). books.ocg.at
15. Mlynárčik, P.: Complement on free and ideal languages. In: Shallit, J., Okhotin, A. (eds.) DCFS 2015. LNCS, vol. 9118, pp. 185–196. Springer, Cham (2015). doi:10.1007/978-3-319-19225-3_16
16. Sipser, M.: Introduction to the Theory of Computation. PWS Publishing Company, Boston (1997)
17. Yu, S.: Regular languages. In: Rozenberg, G., Salomaa, A. (eds.) Handbook of Formal Languages, vol. 1, pp. 41–110. Springer, Heidelberg (1997)

Transducing Reversibly with Finite State Machines

Martin Kutrib[⊠], Andreas Malcher, and Matthias Wendlandt

Institut für Informatik, Universität Giessen, Arndtstr. 2, 35392 Giessen, Germany
{kutrib,malcher,matthias.wendlandt}@informatik.uni-giessen.de

Abstract. Finite state machines are investigated towards their ability to reversibly compute transductions, that is, to transform inputs into outputs in a reversible way. This means that the transducers are backward deterministic and hence are able to uniquely step the computation back and forth. The families of transductions computed are classified with regard to three types of length-preserving transductions as well as to the property of working reversibly. It is possible to settle all inclusion relations between the families of transductions. Finally, the standard closure properties are investigated and the non-closure under almost all operations can be shown.

1 Introduction

One main motivation for the study of computational devices performing reversible computations is the physical observation that a loss of information results in heat dissipation [13]. It is therefore of great interest to avoid such situations and to privilege computations in which every configuration has a unique successor configuration as well as a unique predecessor configuration so that at every point of the computation no information gets lost. Reversibility has been studied for many computational devices starting with Lecerf's [15] and Bennett's [5] investigations for Turing machines, where it is shown that for every (possibly irreversible) Turing machine an equivalent reversible Turing machine can be constructed. This result has been achieved also for deterministic space-bounded Turing machines in [14]. For deterministic multi-head finite automata, the results depend on whether or not two-way motion of the heads is allowed. It is shown in [16] that the general model and the reversible model coincide for two-way multi-head finite automata, whereas the reversible model is weaker than the general model in case of one-way motion [12]. A similar result has been obtained in [10] for deterministic pushdown automata. In both cases, the loss of information in computations is inevitable. Reversible computations in deterministic finite automata (DFA) have been introduced in [3] and it is shown in [17] that there are regular languages which cannot be accepted by any (one-way) reversible deterministic finite automaton. On the other hand, it is known due to [9] that the general model and the reversible model coincide if the input head is two-way. Recent results on reversible regular languages are given in [8],

© Springer International Publishing AG 2017
A. Carayol and C. Nicaud (Eds.): CIAA 2017, LNCS 10329, pp. 151–162, 2017.
DOI: 10.1007/978-3-319-60134-2_13

where it is shown that it is NL-complete to decide whether a given one-way DFA accepts a reversible language. Additionally, exponential upper and lower bounds for the conversion of one-way DFAs to equivalent reversible DFAs are given.

Computational models are not only interesting from the vantage point of accepting some input, but also from the viewpoint of transforming some input into some output. For example, a parser for a formal language should not only return the information whether or not the input word can be parsed, but also the parse tree in the positive case. The simplest model in this context is the finite state transducer which is a finite automaton with an output alphabet that assigns to each input accepted at least one output word. Transductions computed by different variants of such transducers are studied in detail in [7]. Deterministic and nondeterministic pushdown transducers are investigated in [2]. Furthermore, characterizations of pushdown transductions as well as applications to the parsing of context-free languages are given. A more general theory of transducing devices has been outlined already 1969 in [1]. More recently, transducing variants of stack automata have been considered in [6], whereas the parallel model of cellular automata has been investigated in [11] towards its transducing capabilities.

Here, we study *reversible* deterministic finite state transducers (DFST). Since reversible devices should be able to preserve information and DFSTs use and produce information concerning the input *and* the output, the transition function in DFSTs will be defined depending on the input and the output. Thus, reversible DFSTs may be considered as reversible Turing machines (see, for example, [4,5]) with a one-way input tape and a one-way output tape. To start with a weak form of transductions and, again, from the viewpoint of information preserving computations, we are here considering essentially *length-preserving* transductions. In Sect. 2 we give the formal definition of a reversible DFST (REV-DFST) and define Mealy, strongly, and weakly length-preserving DFSTs which basically differ by the fact whether or not both heads have to move synchronously. In Sect. 3, we compare the three notions of length-preserving transducers. It turns out that the Mealy DFSTs are equivalent to strongly length-preserving DFSTs, but weaker than weakly length-preserving DFSTs. These results hold for the reversible case as well. Moreover, the reversible models turn out to be weaker than the general model. In addition, we obtain the decidability of the question whether or not the transduction realized by an arbitrary Mealy DFST can be realized by a Mealy REV-DFST as well. In the affirmative case, the Mealy REV-DFST can effectively be constructed. Finally, we discuss in Sect. 4 the usually investigated closure properties for reversible and length-preserving DFSTs. We obtain closure under intersection, but non-closure under union, complementation, composition, inversion, concatenation, iteration, and reversal.

2   Preliminaries

We write Σ^* for the set of all words over the finite alphabet Σ. The empty word is denoted by λ, and we set $\Sigma^+ = \Sigma^* \setminus \{\lambda\}$. The reversal of a word w is denoted by w^R, and for the length of w we write $|w|$. We use $\subseteq$ for inclusions and $\subset$ for strict inclusions.

First, we define reversible deterministic finite state transducers. We define this model as usual with two tapes, namely, an input and an output tape. The model can be seen as a restricted variant of a Turing machine having a one-way read-only input tape and a one-way output tape. In the forward computation the transducer decides its operation depending on the current state, the current input symbol, and the symbol at the current square of the output tape. It may perform a right move on the input tape and may rewrite the current tape square on the output tape and afterwards may perform a right move on the output tape as well. The output tape is initially filled with blank symbols.

Formally, we define a *deterministic finite state transducer* (DFST) as a system $M = \langle Q, \Sigma, \Delta, q_0, \delta, F \rangle$, where Q is the set of *internal states*, Σ is the set of *input symbols*, Δ is the set of *output symbols* containing the blank symbol $\sqcup$, q_0 is the initial state, $F \subseteq Q$ is the set of *accepting states*, and

$$\delta \colon Q \times \Sigma \times \Delta \to Q \times (\Delta \setminus \{\sqcup\}) \times \{0,1\} \times \{0,1\}$$

is the partial *transition function*.

A *configuration* of DFST M at some time $t \geq 0$ is a quadruple (v, p, w, z), where $v \in \Sigma^*$ is the already read part of the input to the left of the input head, $p \in Q$ is the current state, $w \in \Sigma^*$ is the still unread part of the input to the right of the input head, and $z \in \Delta^+$ is the already written part of the output, the rightmost symbol of z being the currently scanned symbol on the output tape. The *initial configuration* for input w is set to $(\lambda, q_0, w, \sqcup)$. During the course of its computation, M runs through a sequence of configurations. One step from a configuration to its *successor configuration* is denoted by $\vdash$ and defined as follows. For $p \in Q$, $a \in \Sigma$, $v, w \in \Sigma^*$, $z \in \Delta^*$, and $b \in \Delta$, let (v, p, aw, zb) be a configuration. Then we define

$$\begin{aligned}
(v, p, aw, zb) &\vdash (va, q, w, zc), &&\text{if } \delta(p, a, b) = (q, c, 1, 0), \\
(v, p, aw, zb) &\vdash (v, q, aw, zc), &&\text{if } \delta(p, a, b) = (q, c, 0, 0), \\
(v, p, aw, zb) &\vdash (va, q, w, zc\sqcup), &&\text{if } \delta(p, a, b) = (q, c, 1, 1), \\
(v, p, aw, zb) &\vdash (v, q, aw, zc\sqcup), &&\text{if } \delta(p, a, b) = (q, c, 0, 1).
\end{aligned}$$

The reflexive transitive closure of $\vdash$ is denoted by $\vdash^*$.

A DFST *halts* if the transition function is undefined for the current configuration. The *output* written by a DFST M on input $w \in \Sigma^*$ is denoted by $M(w) \in (\Delta \setminus \{\sqcup\})^*$ and is defined as $M(w) = v$, if $(\lambda, q_0, w, \sqcup) \vdash^* (w, q, \lambda, v')$ with $q \in F$, v is the non-blank part of v', and M halts. Otherwise, $M(w)$ is defined to be the empty set. Now, the *transduction* defined by M is the set $T(M) = \{ (w, M(w)) \mid w \in \Sigma^* \text{ and } M(w) \neq \emptyset \}$. We remark that M may also be considered as a partial function mapping some $w \in \Sigma^*$ to $v \in (\Delta \setminus \{\sqcup\})^*$. If we build the projection on the first components of $T(M)$, denoted by $L(M)$, then the transducer degenerates to a deterministic language acceptor.

In general, the family of all transductions performed by some device of type X is denoted by $\mathscr{T}(X)$.

Now, we turn to *reversible* DFST. Basically, reversibility is meant with respect to the possibility of stepping the computation back and forth.

So, the machines have also to be backward deterministic. In particular, the machines reread the symbols which they have read in a preceding forward computation step. So, for reverse computation steps each head is either moved to the *left* or stays stationary. Figuratively, one can imagine that in a forward step, first the current symbols are read and then the heads are moved, whereas in a backward step first the heads are moved and then the symbols are read.

A DFST is said to be *reversible*, abbreviated as REV-DFST, if for any two *distinct* transitions

$$\delta(p, x_0, x_1) = (q, y_1, d_0, d_1) \quad \text{and}$$
$$\delta(p', x_0', x_1') = (q', y_1', d_0', d_1'),$$

if $q = q'$, then $(d_0, d_1) = (d_0', d_1')$ and $(x_0, y_1) \neq (x_0', y_1')$. The first condition means that transitions reaching the same state have to move both heads in the same way. The second condition ensures that for any configuration the predecessor state can uniquely be determined from the state (which then implies the head movements), the input symbol read and the output symbol written.

A consequence of the definition of reversibility is the following property usually required for reversible devices.

Lemma 1. *For any REV-DFST holds that any configuration has at most one predecessor configuration.*

In this paper, we consider in particular length-preserving DFST and differentiate between three notions. We call a DFST a *Mealy* transducer (M-DFST) if the transition function δ maps from $Q \times \Sigma \times \Delta$ to $Q \times (\Delta \setminus \{\sqcup\}) \times \{1\} \times \{1\}$. That is, in every time step an input symbol is read, an output symbol is written, and both heads proceed one position to the right. We call a DFST *strongly length-preserving* (s-DFST) if the transition function δ maps from $Q \times \Sigma \times \Delta$ to $Q \times (\Delta \setminus \{\sqcup\}) \times \{(1,1), (0,0)\}$. That is, both heads are moved synchronously. Finally, we call a DFST M *weakly length-preserving* (w-DFST), if $|w| = |M(w)|$, for all $(w, M(w)) \in T(M)$. That is, the length of the input word read and the length of the output word written is equal at the end of the transduction.

In order to clarify the definitions we present an example.

Example 2. The transduction $\{(a^n b^m, a^n b c^{m-1}) \mid m \geq 1, n \geq 0\}$ can be computed by some Mealy REV-DFST $M = \langle \{q_0, q_1\}, \{a, b\}, \{\sqcup, a, b, c\}, q_0, \delta, \{q_1\}\rangle$. For every a, the transducer writes an a on the output tape and makes a right move. When the first b appears in the input, it changes its state, emits b and makes a right move. Subsequently, M writes for every b a c in the output and makes a right move. Formally, the transition function δ is defined as

$$\delta(q_0, a, \sqcup) = (q_0, a, 1, 1), \qquad \delta(q_0, b, \sqcup) = (q_1, b, 1, 1), \qquad \delta(q_1, b, \sqcup) = (q_1, c, 1, 1).$$

The reversibility of M is easily verified by inspecting the transition function and checking the two conditions of the definition. Thus, the transduction defined by M belongs to $\mathscr{T}(\text{M-REV-DFST})$. We note that the projection of $T(M)$ to the first component $L(M)$ is the regular language $\{a^n b^m \mid m \geq 1, n \geq 0\}$ which is known to be irreversible. ∎

3   Computational Capacity

We turn to consider the computational capacity of reversible DFSTs. In particular, whenever two types of devices have different language acceptance power, then trivial transductions applied to a language from their symmetric difference would be a witness for separating also the power of the transducers. However, in the following we consider transductions of languages that are accepted by both types of devices in question. In this way, we are separating in fact the capabilities of computing transductions. We start with a normalization result stating that every length-preserving DFST can be transformed into an equivalent one that moves at least one head in every step of its computation. Moreover, the construction preserves reversibility.

Lemma 3. *Every w-DFST (s-DFST, M-DFST) M can be converted into an equivalent w-DFST (s-DFST, M-DFST) M' such that in any computation step of M' at least one head is moved. Moreover, if M is reversible then M' is reversible as well.*

The construction given in Lemma 3 leads to the following corollary.

Corollary 4. *The families $\mathscr{T}(M\text{-}DFST)$ and $\mathscr{T}(s\text{-}DFST)$ as well as the families $\mathscr{T}(M\text{-}REV\text{-}DFST)$ and $\mathscr{T}(s\text{-}REV\text{-}DFST)$ are equal.*

Proof. Both inclusions $\mathscr{T}(\text{M-DFST}) \subseteq \mathscr{T}(\text{s-DFST})$ and $\mathscr{T}(\text{M-REV-DFST}) \subseteq \mathscr{T}(\text{s-REV-DFST})$ follow from the definition. On the other hand, the construction in the proof of Lemma 3 leads to an equivalent M-DFST (M-REV-DFST) for a given s-DFST (s-REV-DFST). □

Theorem 5. *Let M be a Mealy transducer. Then it is NL-complete to decide whether $T(M)$ can be realized by a reversible Mealy transducer. If the question is answered in the affirmative, an equivalent reversible Mealy transducer can effectively be constructed.*

Proof. Given a Mealy transducer $M = \langle Q, \Sigma, \Delta, q_0, \delta, F \rangle$, we construct a deterministic finite automaton $M' = \langle Q, \Sigma \times \Delta, q_0, \delta', F \rangle$, where for $q, q' \in Q$, $x \in \Sigma$ and $y \in \Delta$, $\delta'(q, (x, y)) = q'$ if and only if $\delta(q, x, \sqcup) = (q', y, 1, 1)$. Since a Mealy machine moves its heads in every step, it sees in every computation step a blank symbol on the output tape and, thus, no other situations have to be considered. Both machines work deterministically, so for each pair $(w, w') \in T(M)$ there is a word $(w, w') \in L(M')$ and vice versa. In particular, the construction reveals that there are no two distinct transitions $\delta'(q, (x, y))$ and $\delta'(q, (x, y'))$. Moreover, the construction preserves reversibility: If M is reversible, then for any two distinct transitions $\delta(p, x_0, x_1) = (q, y, 1, 1)$ and $\delta(p', x_0', x_1') = (q', y', 1, 1)$ we have that $q = q'$ implies $(x_0, y) \neq (x_0', y')$. So, for the constructed transitions $\delta'(p, (x_0, y)) = q$ and $\delta'(p', (x_0', y')) = q'$ the equality $q = q'$ implies $(x_0, y) \neq (x_0', y')$ as well, which means that M' is reversible.

Conversely, given a deterministic finite automaton $M' = \langle Q, \Sigma \times \Delta, q_0, \delta', F \rangle$ with no two distinct transitions $\delta'(q, (x, y))$ and $\delta'(q, (x, y'))$, we construct a

Mealy transducer $M = \langle Q, \Sigma, \Delta, q_0, \delta, F \rangle$, where for $q, q' \in Q$, $x \in \Sigma$ and $y \in \Delta$, $\delta(q, x, \sqcup) = (q', y, 1, 1)$ if and only if $\delta'(q, (x, y)) = q'$. Since M' is deterministic and meets the property there are not two distinct transitions $\delta'(q, (x, y))$ and $\delta'(q, (x, y'))$, M is deterministic as well. So, by construction, for each word $(w, w') \in L(M')$ there is a pair $(w, w') \in T(M)$ and vice versa. Again, the construction preserves reversibility: Let M' be reversible. Since Mealy machines move both heads in each computation step, for M the first condition of working reversibly is fulfilled. For every pair of a state and an input symbol, M' has a unique predecessor state, since it is reversible. Thus the second condition of reversibility of M can be concluded. So, M is reversible as well.

Now, let $L(M')$ be the language of a deterministic finite automaton M' that has been constructed from a Mealy transducer M. For each transduction $M(zxz') = uyu'$ with $|z| = |u|$, $x \in \Sigma$, and $y \in \Delta$, there is no transduction $M(zxz'') = uy'u''$ with $y \neq y'$ since M works deterministically. It can be concluded that the property that there are no two distinct transitions $\delta'(q, (x, y))$ and $\delta'(q, (x, y'))$ is met by any automaton accepting $L(M')$.

So far, we have shown that given a Mealy transducer M there exists an equivalent reversible Mealy transducer $\hat{M}$ if and only if the DFA M' constructed from M accepts a language that can be accepted by some reversible DFA $\hat{M}'$, where a DFA is reversible, if every input letter a induces an *injective partial mapping* from the state set to itself *via* the mapping $\delta_a : Q \to Q$ with $p \mapsto \delta(p, a)$. In [8] it has been shown that the regular language reversibility problem – given a DFA M', decide whether $L(M')$ is accepted by any reversible DFA – is NL-complete. If the question is answered in the affirmative, an equivalent reversible DFA can effectively be constructed.

These results together with the constructions shown above prove the assertion.   □

We turn to show that the condition to work reversibly strictly weakens the computational capacity of Mealy transducers, thus, separating the families $\mathscr{T}$(M-REV-DFST) and $\mathscr{T}$(M-DFST). Note that the witness transduction relies on an input language that is accepted by the weaker devices.

Theorem 6. *The family $\mathscr{T}$(M-REV-DFST) is strictly included in the family $\mathscr{T}$(M-DFST).*

Proof. We consider the Mealy transducer $M = \langle Q, \Sigma, \Delta, q_0, \delta, F \rangle$ depicted in Fig. 1 which is irreversible due to the transitions $\delta(q_1, b, \sqcup) = (q_3, b, 1, 1)$ and $\delta(q_2, b, \sqcup) = (q_3, b, 1, 1)$.

In order to show that there is no equivalent reversible Mealy transducer we apply the constructions of the proof of Theorem 5. The minimal deterministic finite automaton $M' = \langle Q, \Sigma \times \Delta, q_0, \delta', F \rangle$ constructed from M is obtained by merging the two accepting states q_5 and q_6 in Fig. 1. In [8] it has been shown that the language $L(M')$ can be accepted by a reversible DFA if and only if there do not exist useful states $p, q \in Q$, a pair $(x, y) \in \Sigma \times \Delta$, and a word $w \in (\Sigma \times \Delta)^*$ such that $p \neq q$, $\delta'(p, (x, y)) = \delta'(q, (x, y))$, and $\delta'(q, (x, y)w) = q$.

Due to the two transitions $\delta'(q_1, (b, b)) = \delta'(q_2, (b, b))$, and the computation path $\delta'(q_1, (b, b)(a', a)) = q_1$, it follows that there is no equivalent reversible DFA and, thus, there is no reversible Mealy transducer realizing the transduction $T(M)$.   □

Our next result separates the families of reversible weakly and reversible strongly length-preserving finite state transducers. We define the transduction $\tau_1 = \{ (aab^m\$b^n, ab^m\$b^{n+1}) \mid m, n \geq 0 \}$ that is realized by a w-REV-DFST as shown in the following example.

Example 7. The transduction τ_1 is realized by the w-REV-DFST

$$M = \langle \{q_0, q_1, \ldots, q_4\}, \{a, b, \$\}, \{a, b, \$, \sqcup\}, q_0, \delta, \{q_4\}\rangle,$$

where the transition function δ is as follows.

$$\delta(q_0, a, \sqcup) = (q_1, b, 1, 0), \quad \delta(q_2, b, \sqcup) = (q_2, b, 1, 1), \quad \delta(q_3, \$, \sqcup) = (q_4, b, 1, 1),$$
$$\delta(q_1, a, b) = (q_2, a, 1, 1), \quad \delta(q_2, \$, \sqcup) = (q_3, \$, 0, 1), \quad \delta(q_4, b, \sqcup) = (q_4, b, 1, 1).$$

The reversibility of M is easily verified by inspecting the transition function.   ∎

Theorem 8. *The transduction τ_1 is a witness for the strictness of the inclusion $\mathscr{T}(s\text{-}REV\text{-}DFST) \subset \mathscr{T}(w\text{-}REV\text{-}DFST)$. Moreover, transduction τ_1 belongs to $\mathscr{T}(w\text{-}REV\text{-}DFST) \setminus \mathscr{T}(s\text{-}DFST)$.*

Proof. By Example 7, transduction τ_1 belongs to $\mathscr{T}(w\text{-}REV\text{-}DFST)$. The inclusion itself follows for structural reasons. It remains to be shown that τ_1 does not belong to the family $\mathscr{T}(s\text{-}DFST)$. In contrast to the assertion assume τ_1 is realized by the s-DFST $M = \langle Q, \Sigma, \Delta, q_0, \delta, F\rangle$.

We consider input prefixes and let $(\lambda, q_0, aab^m, \sqcup) \vdash^* (aab^m, q_1, \lambda, ab^{m+1}\sqcup)$ be the computation on the input prefix aab^m (since both heads of M must move synchronously, the output head scans the $\sqcup$ after ab^{m+1}). Now, the computation is extended by a further input symbol b as $(aab^m, q_1, b, ab^{m+1}\sqcup) \vdash^*$

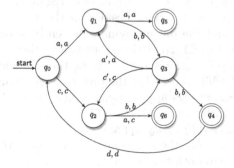

Fig. 1. A Mealy transducer for which no equivalent reversible Mealy transducer exists, though the input language is reversible regular.

$(aab^mb, q_2, \lambda, ab^{m+1}x\sqcup)$ with $x \in \Delta$. Since x cannot be rewritten anymore, it must be either b or \$.

If $x = b$, then the computation cannot be the beginning of a computation realizing τ_1, since on input aab^{m+1} the output ab^{m+2} has been written, but the input $aab^{m+1}\$b^n$ has to be transformed into $ab^{m+1}\$b^{n+1}$. On the other hand, if $x = \$$ then the computation cannot be the beginning of a computation realizing τ_1 either, since on input aab^{m+1} the output $ab^{m+1}\$$ has been written, but the input $aab^{m+2}\$b^n$ has to be transformed into $ab^{m+2}\$b^{n+1}$. The contradiction shows the assertion. □

For the next separation, again, the witness transduction relies on an input language that is accepted by the weaker devices. We define the transduction $\tau_2 = \{ (a^m\$b^n, a^{m-1}\$b^{n+1}) \mid m \geq 1, n \geq 0 \}$ that is realized by a w-DFST as shown in the following example.

Example 9. The transduction τ_2 is realized by the w-DFST

$$M = \langle\{q_0, q_1, \ldots, q_3\}, \{a, b, \$\}, \{a, b, \$, \sqcup\}, q_0, \delta, \{q_3\}\rangle,$$

where the transition function δ is as follows.

$$\delta(q_0, a, \sqcup) = (q_1, b, 1, 0), \quad \delta(q_1, a, \sqcup) = (q_1, b, 1, 0), \quad \delta(q_2, \$, \sqcup) = (q_3, b, 1, 1),$$
$$\delta(q_1, a, b) = (q_1, a, 0, 1), \quad \delta(q_1, \$, b) = (q_2, \$, 0, 1), \quad \delta(q_3, b, \sqcup) = (q_3, b, 1, 1).$$

Transducer M is not reversible due to, for example, the first two rules.   ∎

Theorem 10. *The transduction τ_2 is a witness for the strictness of the inclusion $\mathscr{T}(\text{w-REV-DFST}) \subset \mathscr{T}(\text{w-DFST})$.*

Proof. By Example 9, transduction τ_2 belongs to $\mathscr{T}(\text{w-DFST})$. The inclusion itself follows for structural reasons. It remains to be shown that τ_2 does not belong to the family $\mathscr{T}(\text{w-REV-DFST})$. In contrast to the assertion assume τ_2 is realized by the w-REV-DFST $M = \langle Q, \Sigma, \Delta, q_0, \delta, F \rangle$.

We consider input prefixes a^m, for m large enough. While M processes these prefixes, its input head always sees the symbol a, regardless of the moves of the input head. The transition function, besides on the input symbol a, depends on the current state and the output symbol currently scanned by the output head. Within at most $|Q| \cdot |\Delta|$ transitions, one pair of these parameters appears twice. Let $c_0 \vdash c_1 \vdash \cdots \vdash c_t$, for some $t \geq 0$, be the sequence of configurations passed through by M while processing the prefix a^m. Assume that the first time where such pairs of parameters appear twice is in c_i and c_{i+j} with $i, j \geq 1$. Let $c_i = (u_i, q_i, v_i, w_ix_i)$ with $u_iv_i \in a^*$, $q_i \in Q$, $x_i \in \Delta$, and $w_i \in \Delta^*$. Then we conclude $\delta(q_{i-1}, a, x_{i-1}) = (q_i, y, d_0, d_1)$ and $\delta(q_{i+j-1}, a, x_{i+j-1}) = (q_i, y, d_0, d_1)$. Since on the right-hand sides the states are identical and M is reversible, d_0 as well as d_1 are the same in both transitions. If $d_1 = 1$ then in both configurations the output head scans a blank. If $d_1 = 0$ then in both configurations the output head scans the currently written symbol $y \in \Delta$. However, the two transitions

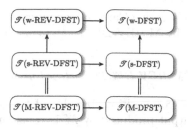

Fig. 2. Relations between the families of transductions discussed, where an arrow denotes a proper inclusion.

violate the reversibility of M. The contradiction shows that the assumption $i \geq 1$ was wrong.

Now let $i = 0$. Then M runs through cycles of length j, that is, the sequence of configurations passed through is $c_0 \vdash c_1 \vdash \cdots \vdash c_j \vdash \cdots$, with $c_0 = (\lambda, q_0, a^m, \sqcup)$, $c_j = (a^k, q_0, a^{m-k}, a^\ell \sqcup)$, and $c_{2j} = (a^{2k}, q_0, a^{m-2k}, a^{2\ell} \sqcup)$, for some $k, \ell \geq 0$ (since the computation is in a cycle, state and currently scanned output symbol are identical, that is, q_0 and $\sqcup$). If $k \neq \ell$ and M transduces $a^m \$ b^n$ to $a^{m-1} \$ b^{n+1}$, then it also transduces $a^{m+k} \$ b^n$ to $a^{m-1+\ell} \$ b^{n+1}$ which does not belong to τ_2. Therefore, we derive $k = \ell$. But this implies $(\lambda, q_0, a^{k \cdot m} \$ b^n, \sqcup) \vdash^* (a^{k \cdot m}, q_0, \$ b^n, a^{k \cdot m} \sqcup)$ which cannot be the beginning of a computation realizing τ_2, since the number of a's written is already too large by one. So, we have a contradiction to the assumption that τ_2 is realized by some w-REV-DFST. $\qquad \square$

The relations between the families of transductions shown in this section are summarized in Fig. 2.

4   Closure Properties

In this section, we will essentially show that the families $\mathscr{T}(\text{w-REV-DFST})$ and $\mathscr{T}(\text{M-REV-DFST})$ (hence also $\mathscr{T}(\text{s-REV-DFST})$) are not closed under the usually studied operations for transductions. We start with the easy observation that any transduction realized by some DFST M has to be functional, that is, any input w is transduced into at most one output $M(w)$. This fact will be used in the following lemma.

Lemma 11. *The families $\mathscr{T}(w\text{-}REV\text{-}DFST)$ and $\mathscr{T}(M\text{-}REV\text{-}DFST)$ are neither closed under union nor under complementation.*

Proof. Consider the two transductions $\tau_1 = \{ (a^m \$ b^n, a^m \$ b^n) \mid m, n \geq 0 \}$ and $\tau_2 = \{ (a^m \$ b^n, c^m \$ d^n) \mid m, n \geq 0 \}$, that can be realized by some M-REV-DFST (w-REV-DFST). But the transduction $\tau_1 \cup \tau_2$ is no longer functional, since some inputs have to be transduced to at least two different words. Thus, transduction $\tau_1 \cup \tau_2$ cannot be computed by any M-REV-DFST (w-REV-DFST).

Since the complement of a transduction realized by a DFST is in general not functional, we obtain the non-closure under complementation for the families $\mathscr{T}(\text{w-REV-DFST})$ and $\mathscr{T}(\text{M-REV-DFST})$ as well. $\qquad \square$

However, using the well-known Cartesian product construction for the family of transductions realized by M-REV-DFSTs the closure under intersection can be shown.

Lemma 12. *Family $\mathscr{T}(M\text{-}REV\text{-}DFST)$ is closed under intersection.*

Next, we consider the composition $M \circ M'$ of two transducers M and M' which means that the output produced by M is considered as input for M'.

Lemma 13. *The family $\mathscr{T}(M\text{-}REV\text{-}DFST)$ is not closed under composition.*

Proof. We consider the M-DFST M depicted in Fig. 1. It has been shown in Theorem 6 that $T(M)$ cannot be computed by any M-REV-DFST. Now, M is reconstructed to M' in such a way that every edge e labeled with (x, y) is changed to (x, y_i) where i is a unique number for the edge e. Clearly, M' is an M-REV-DFST, since the output symbol uniquely indicates the predecessor state. Next, we construct another M-REV-DFST M'' with a single state that translates every symbol x_i to x. So, $M''(M'(w)) = M(w)$, for every word w. Since $T(M)$ cannot be computed by any M-REV-DFST, it can be concluded that the composition $M' \circ M''$ cannot be computed by any M-REV-DFST. $\square$

Theorem 14. *The family $\mathscr{T}(w\text{-}REV\text{-}DFST)$ is not closed under composition.*

Proof. Let $M = \langle\{q_0, q_1, q_2, q_3\}, \{a, b, \$\}, \{a, b, c, \$, \$_0, \sqcup\}, q_0, \delta, \{q_3\}\rangle$ with

$$\delta(q_0, a, \sqcup) = (q_1, c, 1, 1), \quad \delta(q_1, \$, \sqcup) = (q_3, \$_0, 1, 1), \quad \delta(q_2, \$, \sqcup) = (q_3, \$, 1, 1),$$
$$\delta(q_1, a, \sqcup) = (q_2, c, 1, 1), \quad \delta(q_2, a, \sqcup) = (q_2, a, 1, 1), \quad \delta(q_3, b, \sqcup) = (q_3, b, 1, 1),$$

be an M-REV-DFST that computes the transduction

$$\tau_1 = \{ (a^m\$b^n, cca^{m-2}\$b^n) \mid m \geq 2, n \geq 0 \} \cup \{ (a\$b^n, c\$_0b^n) \mid n \geq 0 \}.$$

Let $M' = \langle\{q_0, q_1, \ldots, q_4\}, \{a, b, c, \$, \$_0\}, \{a, b, \$, \sqcup\}, q_0, \delta', \{q_4\}\rangle$ with

$$\delta'(q_0, c, \sqcup) = (q_1, c, 1, 0), \quad \delta'(q_2, a, \sqcup) = (q_2, a, 1, 1), \quad \delta'(q_4, b, \sqcup) = (q_4, b, 1, 1),$$
$$\delta'(q_1, c, c) = (q_2, a, 1, 1), \quad \delta'(q_2, \$, \sqcup) = (q_3, \$, 0, 1), \quad \delta'(q_5, \$_0, \sqcup) = (q_4, b, 1, 1),$$
$$\delta'(q_1, \$_0, c) = (q_5, \$, 0, 1), \quad \delta'(q_3, \$, \sqcup) = (q_4, b, 1, 1),$$

be a w-REV-DFST that realizes

$$\tau_2 = \{ (cca^m\$b^n, a^{m+1}\$b^{n+1}) \mid m, n \geq 0 \} \cup \{ (c\$_0b^n, \$b^{n+1}) \mid m, n \geq 0 \}.$$

The transduction realized by the composition $M \circ M'$ is

$$\{ (a^m\$b^n, a^{m-1}\$b^{n+1}) \mid m \geq 1, n \geq 0 \}$$

which cannot be computed by any w-REV-DFST due to Theorem 10. $\square$

Let $T(M)$ be a transduction computed by some DFST M. Then the inverse transduction $T^{-1}(M)$ is defined as $\{ (w, w') \mid (w', w) \in T(M) \}$.

Lemma 15. *The families $\mathscr{T}(w\text{-REV-DFST})$ and $\mathscr{T}(M\text{-REV-DFST})$ are not closed under inversion.*

Proof. Let M be a M-REV-DFST computing $\{\,(w, a^{|w|}) \mid w \in \{a, b\}^*\,\}$. For any $n \geq 0$, M transduces 2^n words to the same image a^n. Thus, the inverse transduction is no longer functional and hence cannot be computed by any M-REV-DFST or w-REV-DFST. $\qquad\square$

For the non-closure under reversal we need the following lemma stating that in length-preserving transductions the distance between input head and output head is always bounded by some constant.

Lemma 16. *Let M be a w-DFST with state set Q and w be any input such that $M(w) \neq \emptyset$. Then the length difference between the words on the input tape and the output tape during the transduction of w is at most $|Q|$.*

Lemma 17. *The families $\mathscr{T}(w\text{-REV-DFST})$ and $\mathscr{T}(M\text{-REV-DFST})$ are not closed under reversal.*

Lemma 18. *The families $\mathscr{T}(w\text{-REV-DFST})$ and $\mathscr{T}(M\text{-REV-DFST})$ are neither closed under concatenation nor under iteration.*

Proof. We consider two transductions $\{\,(\$b^m ea^n, \$b^m ea^n) \mid m, n \geq 0\,\} \cup \{(\lambda, \lambda)\}$ and $\{\,(\#b^m ea^n, \#d^m cc^n) \mid m, n \geq 0\,\} \cup \{(\lambda, \lambda)\}$ that can be computed by some M-REV-DFSTs M and M'. Since the transductions $T(M)$ and $T(M')$, hence also $T(M) \cup T(M')$, are contained in the concatenation $T(M)T(M')$, we can apply a similar argumentation as in Lemma 17 and obtain that $T(M)T(M')$ cannot be computed by any w-REV-DFST which gives the non-closure under concatenation.

For the non-closure under iteration we consider the transduction

$$\{\,(a^n \$b^m \$a^l, a^n \$b^m \$c^l) \mid m, n, l \geq 0\,\}$$

that can be computed by some M-REV-DFST M. Let us consider an input word $w = a^n \$b^m \$a^l \$b^{m'} \$a^{l'}$ with $l > 2$ and $m, n, m', l' \geq 0$ for the transduction $T(M)^*$.

Since $l > 2$, we always can find four non-negative integers l_1, l_2, l'_1, l'_2 such that $l = l_1 + l_2 = l'_1 + l'_2$ with $(l_1, l_2) \neq (l'_1, l'_2)$. Then both $(w, a^n \$b^m \$c^{l_1} a^{l_2} \$b^{m'} \$c^{l'})$ and $(w, a^n \$b^m \$c^{l'_1} a^{l'_2} \$b^{m'} \$c^{l'})$ belong to $T(M)^*$. So, the transduction is no longer functional and cannot be realized by any w-REV-DFST. $\qquad\square$

The closure properties obtained in this section are summarized in Table 1.

Table 1. Closure properties of the transduction families discussed.

Family	$-$	$\cup$	$\cap$	$\circ$	$^{-1}$	$\cdot$	$*$	R
$\mathscr{L}$(M-REV-DFST)	No	No	Yes	No	No	No	No	No
$\mathscr{L}$(w-REV-DFST)	No	No	?	No	No	No	No	No

References

1. Aho, A.V., Hopcroft, J.E., Ullman, J.D.: A general theory of translation. Math. Syst. Theor. **3**, 193–221 (1969)
2. Aho, A.V., Ullman, J.D.: The theory of parsing, translation, and compiling. Parsing, vol. I. Prentice-Hall (1972)
3. Angluin, D.: Inference of reversible languages. J. ACM **29**, 741–765 (1982)
4. Axelsen, H.B., Jakobi, S., Kutrib, M., Malcher, A.: A hierarchy of fast reversible turing machines. In: Krivine, J., Stefani, J.-B. (eds.) RC 2015. LNCS, vol. 9138, pp. 29–44. Springer, Cham (2015). doi:10.1007/978-3-319-20860-2_2
5. Bennett, C.H.: Logical reversibility of computation. IBM J. Res. Dev. **17**, 525–532 (1973)
6. Bensch, S., Björklund, J., Kutrib, M.: Deterministic stack transducers. In: Han, Y.-S., Salomaa, K. (eds.) CIAA 2016. LNCS, vol. 9705, pp. 27–38. Springer, Cham (2016). doi:10.1007/978-3-319-40946-7_3
7. Berstel, J.: Transductions and Context-Free-Languages. Teubner (1979)
8. Holzer, M., Jakobi, S., Kutrib, M.: Minimal reversible deterministic finite automata. In: Potapov, I. (ed.) DLT 2015. LNCS, vol. 9168, pp. 276–287. Springer, Cham (2015). doi:10.1007/978-3-319-21500-6_22
9. Kondacs, A., Watrous, J.: On the power of quantum finite state automata. In: Foundations of Computer Science (FOCS 1997), pp. 66–75. IEEE Computer Society (1997)
10. Kutrib, M., Malcher, A.: Reversible pushdown automata. J. Comput. System Sci. **78**, 1814–1827 (2012)
11. Kutrib, M., Malcher, A.: One-dimensional cellular automaton transducers. Fundam. Inform. **126**, 201–224 (2013)
12. Kutrib, M., Malcher, A.: One-way reversible multi-head finite automata. Theor. Comput. Sci., to appear
13. Landauer, R.: Irreversibility and heat generation in the computing process. IBM J. Res. Dev. **5**, 183–191 (1961)
14. Lange, K.J., McKenzie, P., Tapp, A.: Reversible space equals deterministic space. J. Comput. Syst. Sci. **60**, 354–367 (2000)
15. Lecerf, Y.: Logique mathématique: machines de Turing réversible. C.R. Séances Acad. Sci. **257**, 2597–2600 (1963)
16. Morita, K.: Two-way reversible multi-head finite automata. Fund. Inform. **110**, 241–254 (2011)
17. Pin, J.-E.: On reversible automata. In: Simon, I. (ed.) LATIN 1992. LNCS, vol. 583, pp. 401–416. Springer, Heidelberg (1992). doi:10.1007/BFb0023844

From Hadamard Expressions to Weighted Rotating Automata and Back

Louis-Marie Dando and Sylvain Lombardy[✉]

LaBRI UMR 5800, Université de Bordeaux INP Bordeaux, CNRS, Bordeaux, France
{louis-marie.dando,sylvain.lombardy}@labri.fr

Abstract. This paper deals with the conversion of expressions denoting Hadamard series into weighted rotating automata. We prove that any algorithm converting rational series into one-way weighted automata can be extended to provide an algorithm which achieves our goal. We apply this to define the derivation and the follow automata of a Hadamard expression. Our method is also used to extend algorithms which perform the inverse conversion, up to some adjustment in order to fulfill some constraints.

1 Introduction

Rotating automata are a natural extension of (one-way) automata. They have been introduced in [11]. Such an automaton can read its input several time as if this input is a cyclic word endowed with a marker to separate the last and the first letters. In the Boolean case, *i.e.* for unweighted rotating automata, accepted languages are regular languages, but they have been studied (*cf. e.g.* [6,9]) since they can be much more succint than NFA, and simpler than two-way automata. In particular, the intersection of two languages recognised by such automata can be realised with a linear number of states. These automata are sometimes introduced as restrictions of two-way automata, but we present them here as an extension of one-way automata, endowed with *rewinding* transitions that allow to come back at the beginning of the input.

Like two-way automata, rotating automata may have an infinite number of computations accepting a given finite word. This may lead to some issues in the definition of the behaviour of weighted rotating automata, since the weight of a word accepted by a weighted automaton is the sum of the weights of its accepting computations. In this paper, we focus on rotating automata with weights in *rationally additive semirings* [3]. In this framework, the behaviour of rotating automata is always defined.

Moreover, the series realised by these automata are exactly the Hadamard series [4,7]. The set of Hadamard series is the closure of rational series under sum, Hadamard product – entrywise product – and Hadamard iteration – sum of Hadamard powers. If the semiring of coefficients is commutative, the Hadamard product of two rational series is rational, but it is no more the case if the coefficients are not commutative, and, even in the commutative case, the Hadamard iteration does not preserve the rationality of series (*cf.* [7]).

© Springer International Publishing AG 2017
A. Carayol and C. Nicaud (Eds.): CIAA 2017, LNCS 10329, pp. 163–174, 2017.
DOI: 10.1007/978-3-319-60134-2_14

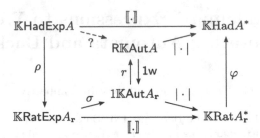

Fig. 1. The transformation of Hadamard expressions into rotating automata.

This paper presents a generic framework to extend any algorithm that converts a rational expression to a (weighted) one-way automaton, into an algorithm that converts a Hadamard expression to a rotating automaton. More precisely, we show that every Hadamard expression E can be rewritten into a rational expression $\rho(E)$ such that the conversion of $\rho(E)$ into a (one-way) automaton $\mathcal{A}$ by some algorithm σ can be interpreted as a rotating automaton $\mathcal{A}^r$ that realises the series denoted by the original Hadamard expression E. These transformations are presented in Fig. 1. The proof of our main theorem amounts to prove that this diagram – where $[\![.]\!]$ is the interpretation of expressions and $|\cdot|$ is the *behaviour* of automata – is actually commutative. We then apply this result to two methods of automata synthesis: the *derivation automaton* and the *follow automaton*, and prove rules that allow in each of these cases to directly handle Hadamard expressions.

The inverse conversion can also be extended, even if some extra conditions are required on the algorithm. A variant of the well-known State Elimination method is described; this variant is used in the core of an algorithm converting weighted rotating automata into Hadamard expressions.

The results stated in this paper are generic and can be applied to any semiring, commutative or not. If the semiring of weight is not rationally additive, the same methods can be applied, but the fact that the interpretation of expressions and the behaviour of automata are defined, as well as the validity of the transformations, depend on specific properties of the expressions or automata.

2   Rational and Hadamard Formal Power Series

Let A be a finite alphabet and let A^* be the set of words over A, where ε denotes the empty word. A language over A is a subset of A^*. Let $(\mathbb{K}, +, .)$ be a semiring. In this paper, we assume that $\mathbb{K}$ is a *rationally additive semiring* [3]. Two important axioms of these semirings are: for every element x of $\mathbb{K}$, the family of powers of x is summable and this sum is denoted x^* (the *star* of x; for every partition of a family, if the sum over each part is defined, as well as the sum s of these sums, then the family is summable with sum s. This later property is used in the proof of Lemma 1. For instance, the Boolean semiring $\mathbb{B}$, every complete lattice, $\mathbb{Q}_+\cup\{\infty\}$, the rational languages over a given alphabet, $([0;1], \max, .)$ are all rationally additive semirings.

We consider the set $\mathbb{K}\langle\langle A^*\rangle\rangle$ of formal power series over A^* with coefficients in $\mathbb{K}$. A series s in $\mathbb{K}\langle\langle A^*\rangle\rangle$ is a mapping from A^* into $\mathbb{K}$; the coefficient of a word w in s is denoted $\langle s, w\rangle$, and s itself is denoted as a formal sum. The support of s is the language of words with a coefficient different from 0. If it is finite, s is a polynomial. Different products can be defined for series:

$$\text{Cauchy product}: s \cdot t = \sum_{w\in A^*}\ \sum_{\substack{u,v\in A^* \\ uv=w}} (\langle s, u\rangle.\langle t, v\rangle)\, w;$$

$$\text{Hadamard product}: s \odot t = \sum_{w\in A^*} (\langle s, w\rangle.\langle t, w\rangle)\, w. \tag{1}$$

The Hadamard and the Cauchy products are both associative operations which distribute over the sum. From [3], if $\mathbb{K}$ is a rationally additive semiring, so are the semirings $(\mathbb{K}\langle\langle A^*\rangle\rangle, +, \cdot)$ and $(\mathbb{K}\langle\langle A^*\rangle\rangle, +, \odot)$; the star of a series s in each of these semirings is respectively called the *Kleene star* denoted s^* and the *Hadamard iteration* denoted $s^{\circledR}$. Notice that, for every word w, $\langle s^{\circledR}, w\rangle = \langle s, w\rangle^*$.

Definition 1. *The set $\mathbb{K}\mathrm{Rat}A^*$ of rational series is the closure of polynomials in $\mathbb{K}\langle\langle A^*\rangle\rangle$ under the rational operations: sum, Cauchy product, and Kleene star. The set $\mathbb{K}\mathrm{Had}A^*$ of Hadamard series is the closure of $\mathbb{K}\mathrm{Rat}A^*$ under the entrywise operations: sum, Hadamard product, and Hadamard iteration.*

3 Weighted Rotating Automata

Definition 2. *Let $\mathbb{K}$ be a semiring and A an alphabet. A rotating $\mathbb{K}$-automaton over A is a tuple (Q, E, R, I, T), where*

- *Q is a finite set of states;*
- *$E : Q \times A \times Q \longrightarrow \mathbb{K}$ is the transition function, and $R : Q \times Q \longrightarrow \mathbb{K}$ is the rewinding function;*
- *$I : Q \longrightarrow \mathbb{K}$ is the initial function, and $T : Q \longrightarrow \mathbb{K}$ is the final function.*

The set of rotating $\mathbb{K}$-automata over A is denoted $\mathrm{R}\mathbb{K}\mathrm{Aut}A$.

The rewinding function allows the head of the automaton to return to the beginning of the input when the end of the input is reached.

A state p is initial if $I(p) \neq 0$; it is final if $T(p) \neq 0$. In order to define the labels of computations and the behaviour of the automaton, we assume that there exists a special letter $\mathbf{r}$ which does not belong to A. In the sequel we denote $A_{\mathbf{r}} = A \cup \{\mathbf{r}\}$. A transition is a triple (p, a, q) in $Q \times A_{\mathbf{r}} \times Q$ such that either a is in A and $E(p, a, q) \neq 0$, or $a = \mathbf{r}$ and $R(p, q) \neq 0$. The letter a in $A_{\mathbf{r}}$ is the *label* of such a transition, $E(p, a, q)$ is the *weight* of the transition.

Like in graphs, a path is a sequence of consecutive transitions. The label of a path is the concatenation of labels of its transitions. A computation over a word

w in A^* is a path which starts in an initial state and ends in a final state, with a label in $(w\mathbf{r})^*w$.

The weight of a computation is the product of the initial weight of the starting state, the weight of each transition, and the final weight of the ending state. The weight of a word w in a rotating $\mathbb{K}$-automaton $\mathcal{A}$, denoted $\langle \mathcal{A}, w \rangle$, is defined if and only if the family of weights of computations over w is summable. In this case, $\langle \mathcal{A}, w \rangle$ is equal to this sum.

Definition 3. *An automaton $\mathcal{A}$ is valid if for every word w, the weight of w in the automaton exists. In this case, the behaviour of $\mathcal{A}$ is the series*

$$|\mathcal{A}| = \sum_{w \in A^*} \langle \mathcal{A}, w \rangle w.$$

It is proved in [7] that, if $\mathbb{K}$ is a rationally additive semiring, then every two-way $\mathbb{K}$-automaton is valid. This result naturally translates to the rotating automata considered in this paper.

In our setting, one-way automata are rotating $\mathbb{K}$-automata without any rewinding transition. $1\mathbb{K}\mathrm{Aut}A$ is the set of one-way $\mathbb{K}$-automata over A, and every automaton in $1\mathbb{K}\mathrm{Aut}A$ is characterised by a tuple (Q, E, I, T). Moreover, an automaton $\mathcal{A} = (Q, E, R, I, T)$ in $\mathbb{R}\mathbb{K}\mathrm{Aut}A$ can be considered as a one-way $\mathbb{K}$-automaton $1\mathrm{w}(\mathcal{A}) = (Q, E', I, T)$, over the alphabet $A_\mathbf{r}$, with $E' = E \cup \{(p, \mathbf{r}, q) \mapsto R(p, q) \mid (p, q) \in Q^2\}$. Conversely, if $\mathcal{A}$ is in $1\mathbb{K}\mathrm{Aut}A_\mathbf{r}$, $\mathcal{A}^r$ is the corresponding automaton in $\mathbb{R}\mathbb{K}\mathrm{Aut}A$, obtained by replacing every transition with label $\mathbf{r}$ by a rewinding transition.

The canonical bijection between transitions of $\mathcal{A}$ and $1\mathrm{w}(\mathcal{A})$ extends to paths, and every pair of corresponding paths has the same label and the same weight. In particular, for every word w in A^*, every computation in $\mathcal{A}$ over w corresponds to a computation in the automaton $1\mathrm{w}(\mathcal{A})$ over a word u in $(w\mathbf{r})^*w$. To characterise the behaviour of the rotating $\mathbb{K}$-automaton $\mathcal{A}$ with respect to the behaviour of the one-way $\mathbb{K}$-automaton $1\mathrm{w}(\mathcal{A})$, we define a linear function from $\mathbb{K}\langle\langle A_\mathbf{r}^* \rangle\rangle$ to $\mathbb{K}\langle\langle A^* \rangle\rangle$:

$$\forall s \in \mathbb{K}\langle\langle A_\mathbf{r}^* \rangle\rangle, \qquad \varphi\left(\sum_{u \in A_\mathbf{r}^*} \langle s, u \rangle u \right) = \sum_{w \in A^*} \left(\sum_{u \in w(\mathbf{r}w)^*} \langle s, u \rangle \right) w. \qquad (2)$$

Notice that φ is partially defined; for every series s, $\varphi(s)$ is defined if and only if, for every word w, the family $(\langle s, u \rangle)_{u \in w(\mathbf{r}w)^*}$ is summable.

The following proposition naturally follows:

Proposition 1. *Let $\mathbb{K}$ be a rationally additive semiring. For every automaton $\mathcal{A}$ in $\mathbb{R}\mathbb{K}\mathrm{Aut}A$, $\varphi(|1\mathrm{w}(\mathcal{A})|)$ is defined and equal to $|\mathcal{A}|$.*

Since every rational series is the behaviour of a one-way automaton, and every Hadamard series is the behaviour of a rotating automaton (*cf.* [7]), the following corollary holds.

Corollary 1. *The image of φ restricted to $\mathbb{K}\mathrm{Rat}A_\mathbf{r}^*$ is the set $\mathbb{K}\mathrm{Had}A^*$.*

4   Hadamard Expressions

Like rational series, Hadamard series are naturally denoted by expressions. In the following grammar, where A is an alphabet, R generates $\mathbb{K}$-rational expressions in $\mathbb{K}\mathsf{RatExp}A$, while H generates $\mathbb{K}$-Hadamard expressions in $\mathbb{K}\mathsf{HadExp}A$.

$$R \to 0 \mid 1 \mid a \in A \mid kR, k \in \mathbb{K} \mid R + R \mid RR \mid R^*,$$
$$H \to R \mid kH, k \in \mathbb{K} \mid H + H \mid H \odot H \mid H \circledast H. \tag{3}$$

As usual, parentheses can be added to prevent ambiguity. In the following, the classical rules of priority apply. Notice that we use in the Hadamard expressions a binary iteration operator that appears to be more suitable with the definitions below (definition of ρ in particular). It is straightforward that the expressiveness of this operator is equivalent to a unary star operator: if E denotes the series s, $s^{\circledast}$ is denoted by $\mathsf{E} \circledast (a_1 + \ldots + a_n)^*$, where $A = \{a_1, \ldots a_n\}$.

Definition 4. *The interpretation of an expression in* $\mathbb{K}\mathsf{HadExp}A$ *is a series in* $\mathbb{K}\mathsf{Had}A^*$ *inductively defined by :*

$$[\![0]\!] = 0_\mathbb{K}, \quad [\![1]\!] = 1_\mathbb{K}, \quad \forall a \in A, \ [\![a]\!] = a, \quad \forall k \in \mathbb{K}, \ [\![k\mathsf{F}]\!] = k[\![\mathsf{F}]\!],$$
$$[\![\mathsf{F} + \mathsf{G}]\!] = [\![\mathsf{F}]\!] + [\![\mathsf{G}]\!], \quad [\![\mathsf{FG}]\!] = [\![\mathsf{F}]\!] \cdot [\![\mathsf{G}]\!], \quad [\![\mathsf{F}^*]\!] = [\![\mathsf{F}]\!]^*, \tag{4}$$
$$[\![\mathsf{F} \odot \mathsf{G}]\!] = [\![\mathsf{F}]\!] \odot [\![\mathsf{G}]\!], \quad [\![\mathsf{F} \circledast \mathsf{G}]\!] = [\![\mathsf{F}]\!]^{\circledast} \odot [\![\mathsf{G}]\!].$$

In Sect. 3, we showed that every Hadamard series is the image by φ of a rational series. In this section, we describe a formal inverse of φ: this is a syntactic transformation ρ which turns an expression E in $\mathbb{K}\mathsf{HadExp}A$ into an expression in $\mathbb{K}\mathsf{RatExp}A_\mathbf{r}$, inductively defined by:

$$\rho(\mathsf{E}) = \mathsf{E} \text{ if } \mathsf{E} \in \mathbb{K}\mathsf{RatExp}A, \qquad \forall k \in \mathbb{K}, \ \rho(k\mathsf{E}) = k\rho(\mathsf{E}),$$
$$\rho(\mathsf{F} + \mathsf{G}) = \rho(\mathsf{F}) + \rho(\mathsf{G}), \ \rho(\mathsf{F} \odot \mathsf{G}) = \rho(\mathsf{F})\mathbf{r}\rho(\mathsf{G}), \ \rho(\mathsf{F} \circledast \mathsf{G}) = (\rho(\mathsf{F})\mathbf{r})^*\rho(\mathsf{G}). \tag{5}$$

Proposition 2. *Let* E *be a Hadamard expression. It holds* $[\![\mathsf{E}]\!] = \varphi([\![\rho(\mathsf{E})]\!])$.

Proposition 2 is based on the following lemma. The proof involves some summation exchanges which are licit in rationally additive semirings; using this result in other semirings may require a new proof.

Lemma 1. *Let* E *be an expression in* $\mathbb{K}\mathsf{HadExp}A$. *Then, for every word w in A^*,*

$$\langle \mathsf{E}, w \rangle = \sum_{i=0}^{\infty} \langle \rho(\mathsf{E}), w(\mathbf{r}w)^i \rangle. \tag{6}$$

The following proposition characterises the images of Hadamard expressions by ρ, on which $\rho^{-1}(\mathsf{E})$ can be computed in reversing identities in Eq. (5).

Proposition 3. *The image of ρ is the set* $\mathbb{K}\mathsf{PreHadExp}A$ *of* $\mathbb{K}$-pre-Hadamard *expressions over A generated by the following grammar:*

$$\mathsf{P} \to \mathsf{E} \in \mathbb{K}\mathsf{RatExp}A \mid k\mathsf{P}, k \in \mathbb{K} \mid \mathsf{P} + \mathsf{P} \mid \mathsf{P}\mathbf{r}\mathsf{P} \mid (\mathsf{P}\mathbf{r})^*\mathsf{P}. \tag{7}$$

5   From Hadamard Expressions to Weighted Rotating Automata

5.1   A Generic Extension of Automata Synthesis

An algorithm which turns a rational expression into a (one-way) automaton realises a mapping σ from rational expressions to automata which is consistent with the interpretation of expressions and the behaviour of automata.

This property, as well as Propositions 1 and 2, can be summarised by the commutative diagram of Fig. 1, which proves the following theorem. In the diagram as in the theorem, r is the reverse function of 1w; it converts a one-way automaton in $1\mathbb{K}\mathrm{Aut}A_r$ into a rotating automaton in $\mathbb{R}\mathbb{K}\mathrm{Aut}A$.

Theorem 1. *If σ is an algorithm that converts a rational expression into an equivalent one-way automaton, then $r \circ \sigma \circ \rho$ converts a Hadamard expression to an equivalent rotating automaton.*

The complexity of the transformation of a Hadamard expression into a rational expression by ρ is linear, and the complexity of r is constant, since it is only a different interpretation of the same object. Therefore, since the complexity of the conversion σ of a rational expression to an automaton is at least linear, the complexity of $r \circ \sigma \circ \rho$ is equal to the complexity of σ.

Notice that when the number of letters in the rational expression is a parameter of the complexity of the conversion, this paramater must also count the number of Hadamard operators to get the complexity of the extension of the conversion from Hadamard expressions to rotating automata.

5.2   Derivation

We first apply Theorem 1 to the derivation of weighted rational expressions defined in [8].

Definition 5. *The derivatives of an expression E in $\mathbb{K}\mathrm{RatExp}A$ by a letter is a polynomial[1] of expressions inductively defined for all a in A as:*

$$\frac{\partial}{\partial a}0 = \frac{\partial}{\partial a}1 = 0, \; \forall b \in A, \frac{\partial}{\partial a}b = \begin{cases} 1 \; if \; a = b, \\ 0 \; otherwise \, , \end{cases} \quad \forall k \in \mathbb{K}, \; \frac{\partial}{\partial a}k\mathsf{E} = k\frac{\partial}{\partial a}\mathsf{E},$$

$$\frac{\partial}{\partial a}(\mathsf{E} + \mathsf{F}) = \frac{\partial}{\partial a}\mathsf{E} \boxplus \frac{\partial}{\partial a}\mathsf{F}, \qquad \frac{\partial}{\partial a}(\mathsf{E}\mathsf{F}) = \left[\frac{\partial}{\partial a}\mathsf{E}\right].\mathsf{F} \boxplus \mathrm{Null}(\mathsf{E})\frac{\partial}{\partial a}\mathsf{F},$$

$$\frac{\partial}{\partial a}(\mathsf{E}^*) = \mathrm{Null}(\mathsf{E}^*)\left[\frac{\partial}{\partial a}\mathsf{E}\right].\mathsf{E}^*.$$

$$(8)$$

The definition of derivatives involves the function Null such that $\mathrm{Null}(\mathsf{E}) = \langle E, \varepsilon \rangle$.

---

[1]   The formal sum in polynomials of expressions (like in polynomials of *positions* in the next part) is denoted $\boxplus$ to avoid any confusion with the sum in expressions or with Hadamard operators.

Proposition 4. *If* E *is a rational expression, the weight of the empty word in* $[\![E]\!]$ *is given by the function* Null *from* $\mathbb{K}\mathsf{RatExp}A$ *into* $\mathbb{K}$ *inductively defined as*

$$\forall a \in A, \ \mathsf{Null}(a) = \mathsf{Null}(0) = 0, \qquad \mathsf{Null}(1) = 1,$$
$$\mathsf{Null}(F + G) = \mathsf{Null}(F) + \mathsf{Null}(G), \qquad \forall k \in \mathbb{K}, \ \mathsf{Null}(kF) = k\,\mathsf{Null}(F), \qquad (9)$$
$$\mathsf{Null}(F.G) = \mathsf{Null}(F)\,\mathsf{Null}(G), \qquad \mathsf{Null}(F^*) = \mathsf{Null}(F)^*.$$

By linearity, the interpretation of rational expressions extends to polynomials of expressions. The derivation is defined in such a way that, for every expression E and every letter a, $[\![\frac{\partial}{\partial a}E]\!] = a^{-1}[\![E]\!]$. Moreover, there is only a finite number of expressions that arise in the iterated derivation of an expression E. Therefore, a weighted (one-way) automaton can be built, where each state is an expression, the initial state is E itself, there is a transition from F to G with label a and weight k if $\langle \frac{\partial}{\partial a}F, G \rangle = k$, and the final weight of a state F is $\langle F, \varepsilon \rangle$.

Example 1. Let $E_0 = ((\frac{1}{2}(a+b))^*b(a+b)^*) \circledast (ab)^*$. We set $F_1 = (\frac{1}{2}(a+b))^*b(a+b)^*$, then $E_1 = \rho(E_0) = (F_1 r)^*(ab)^*$. The derivatives of E_1, as well as the derivation automaton of E_1 are shown on Fig. 2. By Theorem 1, this automaton can be interpreted as the rotating derivation automaton of E_0.

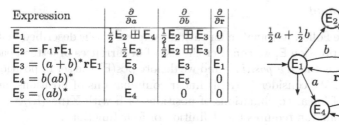

Expression	$\frac{\partial}{\partial a}$	$\frac{\partial}{\partial b}$	$\frac{\partial}{\partial r}$
E_1	$\frac{1}{2}E_2 \boxplus E_4$	$\frac{1}{2}E_2 \boxplus E_3$	0
$E_2 = F_1 r E_1$	$\frac{1}{2}E_2$	$\frac{1}{2}E_2 \boxplus E_3$	0
$E_3 = (a+b)^* r E_1$	E_3	E_3	E_1
$E_4 = b(ab)^*$	0	E_5	0
$E_5 = (ab)^*$	E_4	0	0

Fig. 2. The derivatives of E_1 and the one-way derivation automaton of $E_1 = \rho(E_0)$.

We define now an extension of the derivation rules to directly derive Hadamard expressions. We define first Null(E) which is no more equal to $\langle E, \varepsilon \rangle$, but is forged to be equal to $\langle \rho(E), \varepsilon \rangle$.

Definition 6. *For every Hadamard expression* E, *if* E *is a rational expression,* Null(E) *follows the definition of Proposition 4, otherwise, it is defined as:*

$$\forall k \in \mathbb{K}, \ \mathsf{Null}(kE) = k\,\mathsf{Null}(E), \qquad \mathsf{Null}(E + F) = \mathsf{Null}(E) + \mathsf{Null}(F),$$
$$\mathsf{Null}(E \odot F) = 0, \qquad \mathsf{Null}(E \circledast F) = \mathsf{Null}(F). \qquad (10)$$

Definition 7. *The derivation over Hadamard expressions is extended as follows; for every letter* a, *if* E *is a rational expression, the derivation follows Definition 5, otherwise, the derivation is inductively defined as:*

$$\forall k \in \mathbb{K}, \ \frac{\partial}{\partial a}k\mathsf{E} = k\,\frac{\partial}{\partial a}\mathsf{E}\,, \qquad \frac{\partial}{\partial a}(\mathsf{E}+\mathsf{F}) = \frac{\partial}{\partial a}\mathsf{E}\boxplus\frac{\partial}{\partial a}\mathsf{F},$$

$$\frac{\partial}{\partial a}(\mathsf{E}\odot\mathsf{F}) = \left[\frac{\partial}{\partial a}\mathsf{E}\right]\odot\mathsf{F}, \qquad \frac{\partial}{\partial a}(\mathsf{E}\circledast\mathsf{F}) = \left[\frac{\partial}{\partial a}\mathsf{E}\right]\odot(\mathsf{E}\circledast\mathsf{F})\boxplus\frac{\partial}{\partial a}\mathsf{F}. \qquad (11)$$

A derivation with respect to the Hadamard operators is also defined:

$$\frac{\partial}{\partial\odot}\mathsf{E} = 0 \ \text{if } \mathsf{E} \in \mathbb{K}\mathsf{RatExp}, \qquad \forall k \in \mathbb{K}, \ \frac{\partial}{\partial\odot}(k\mathsf{E}) = k\frac{\partial}{\partial\odot}\mathsf{E},$$

$$\frac{\partial}{\partial\odot}(\mathsf{E}+\mathsf{F}) = \frac{\partial}{\partial\odot}\mathsf{E}\boxplus\frac{\partial}{\partial\odot}\mathsf{E}, \qquad \frac{\partial}{\partial\odot}(\mathsf{E}\odot\mathsf{F}) = \mathsf{Null}(\mathsf{E})\,\mathsf{F}\boxplus\left[\frac{\partial}{\partial\odot}\mathsf{E}\right]\odot\mathsf{F}, \qquad (12)$$

$$\frac{\partial}{\partial\odot}(\mathsf{E}\circledast\mathsf{F}) = \left[\frac{\partial}{\partial\odot}\mathsf{E}\right]\odot(\mathsf{E}\circledast\mathsf{F})\boxplus\mathsf{Null}(\mathsf{E})\,(\mathsf{E}\circledast\mathsf{F})\boxplus\frac{\partial}{\partial\odot}\mathsf{F}.$$

The correctness of this definition comes from Theorem 1 and the following proposition, whose proof is by induction.

Proposition 5. *For every Hadamard expression* E, $\mathsf{Null}(\mathsf{E}) = \mathsf{Null}(\rho(\mathsf{E}))$,

$$\forall a \in A, \ \frac{\partial}{\partial a}\mathsf{E} = \rho^{-1}\left(\frac{\partial}{\partial a}\rho(\mathsf{E})\right), \ \text{and} \ \frac{\partial}{\partial\odot}\mathsf{E} = \rho^{-1}\left(\frac{\partial}{\partial r}\rho(\mathsf{E})\right). \qquad (13)$$

5.3 Follow Automata

The definition of the Follow automaton for rational expressions is described in [5]. In every rational expression E, we consider the list of occurrences of letters; each of these occurrences is called a *position*, and we denote $\mathsf{pos}(\mathsf{E})$ the set of positions of the expression E. We consider (formal) linear combinations of positions, and we denote the set of linear combinations of positions of E with $\mathbb{K}\langle\mathsf{pos}(\mathsf{E})\rangle$.[2]

The Follow automaton requires the definition of four functions:

- $\mathsf{Null}(\mathsf{E})$ in $\mathbb{K}$ is the weight of the empty word in $[\![\mathsf{E}]\!]$ (already defined in Proposition 4);
- $\mathsf{First}(\mathsf{E})$ is in $\mathbb{K}\langle\mathsf{pos}(\mathsf{E})\rangle$: $\langle\mathsf{First}(\mathsf{E}),p\rangle$ shows with which weight the letter at position p can appear as first letter in $[\![\mathsf{E}]\!]$;
- $\mathsf{Last}(\mathsf{E})$ in $\mathbb{K}\langle\mathsf{pos}(\mathsf{E})\rangle$ is similar to $\mathsf{First}(\mathsf{E})$ for last letters in $[\![\mathsf{E}]\!]$;
- $\mathsf{Follow}(\mathsf{E},p)$ is in $\mathbb{K}\langle\mathsf{pos}(\mathsf{E})\rangle$: $\langle\mathsf{Follow}(\mathsf{E},p),q\rangle$ shows with which weight the letter at position q can follow a letter at position p in $[\![\mathsf{E}]\!]$.

As shown in [2], these functions can be inductively computed on rational expressions. It is convenient to extends $\mathsf{pos}(\mathsf{E})$ with an *initial position* i_0 and to extend Follow by $\mathsf{Follow}(\mathsf{E},i_0) = \mathsf{First}(\mathsf{E})$, and to set $\langle\mathsf{Last}(\mathsf{E}),i_0\rangle = \mathsf{Null}(\mathsf{E})$.

The weighted *Position automaton* [2] can then be defined, where the set of states is the set of positions, the initial state is the initial position, there is a

---

[2] Notice that $\mathbb{K}\langle\mathsf{pos}(\mathsf{E})\rangle$ is not a semiring, since $\mathsf{pos}(\mathsf{E})$ is not a monoid; nevertheless, we use the same notations as series for denoting the coefficient of such a linear combination.

position	Follow(E_1, pos)	$\langle$Last(E_1), pos$\rangle$
i_0	$\frac{1}{2}1 \boxplus \frac{1}{2}2 \boxplus 3 \boxplus 7$	1
1 (a)	$\frac{1}{2}1 \boxplus \frac{1}{2}2 \boxplus 3$	0
2 (b)	$\frac{1}{2}1 \boxplus \frac{1}{2}2 \boxplus 3$	0
3 (b)	$4 \boxplus 5 \boxplus 6$	0
4 (a)	$4 \boxplus 5 \boxplus 6$	0
5 (b)	$4 \boxplus 5 \boxplus 6$	0
6 (r)	$\frac{1}{2}1 \boxplus \frac{1}{2}2 \boxplus 3 \boxplus 7$	1
7 (a)	8	0
8 (b)	7	1

Fig. 3. The Follow and Last functions and the Follow automaton of $E_1 = \rho(E_0)$.

transition from p to q with label a and weight k if there is a letter a in position q and $\langle$Follow(E, p), $q\rangle = k$; the final weight of state p is $\langle$Last(E), $p\rangle$.

The *Follow automaton* is a *quotient* of the Position automaton: if Follow and Last coincide on two positions p and q, then the corresponding states can be merged.

Example 2. Let E_1 be the expression with 8 positions defined in Example 1. For convenience, we add indices to identify positions: $((\frac{1}{2}(a_1 + b_2))^*b_3(a_4 + b_5)^*r_6)^*(a_7b_8)^*$. The Follow and Last functions are described on Fig. 3 (left); they induce an equivalence on positions: $\{\{i_0, 6\}, \{1, 2\}, \{3, 4, 5\}, \{7\}, \{8\}\}$; the Follow automaton of E_1 is drawn on Fig. 3 (right); seen as a rotating automaton, this automaton realises $[\![E_0]\!]$.

Like for derivatives, the functions First, Last and Follow can be extended to Hadamard expressions in order to get a direct construction. Notice that, for every Hadamard expression E, an occurrence of letter $\mathbf{r}$ appears in $\rho(E)$ for each Hadamard operator which appears in E. This leads to extend the positions to the occurrences of Hadamard operators. The extension of function Null is done in Definition 6.

Definition 8. *For every Hadamard expression* E, *if* E *is a rational expression,* First, Last *and* Follow *follows definitions of [2], otherwise, they are inductively defined for all k in* $\mathbb{K}$ *by*

$$\text{First}(kF) = k\,\text{First}(F), \qquad\qquad \text{Last}(kF) = \text{Last}(F),$$

$$\text{First}(F + G) = \text{First}(F) \boxplus \text{First}(G), \qquad \text{Last}(F + G) = \text{Last}(F) \boxplus \text{Last}(G),$$

$$\text{First}(F \odot_i G) = \text{First}(F) \boxplus \text{Null}(F)\,i, \qquad \text{Last}(F \odot_i G) = \text{Last}(G) \boxplus \text{Null}(G)\,i,$$

$$\text{First}(F \circledast_i G) = \text{First}(F \odot_i G) \boxplus \text{First}(G), \qquad \text{Last}(F \circledast_i G) = \text{Last}(G) \boxplus \text{Null}(G)\,i,$$

$$\text{Follow}(kF, p) = \text{Follow}(F, p),$$

$$\text{Follow}(F + G, p) = \text{Follow}(F, p) \boxplus \text{Follow}(G, p),$$

$$\text{Follow}(F \odot_i G, p) = \text{Follow}(F + G, p) \boxplus \langle\text{Last}(F), p\rangle\,i \boxplus \langle i, p\rangle\text{First}(G),$$

$$\text{Follow}(F \circledast_i G, p) = \text{Follow}(F + G, p) \boxplus \langle\text{Last}(F), p\rangle\,i \boxplus \langle i, p\rangle\text{First}(F \circledast_i G),$$

$$\tag{14}$$

where $\langle i, p\rangle$ *is equal to 1 if $i = p$, and to 0 otherwise.*

Since a position is assigned to each Hadamard operator of a Hadamard expression E, and each Hadamard operator has a corresponding occurrence of $\mathbf{r}$ in $\rho(\mathsf{E})$, there is a natural bijection between positions of E and positions of $\rho(\mathsf{E})$. The soundness of Definition 8 comes hence from the following proposition.

Proposition 6. *For every Hadamard expression* E, E *and* $\rho(E)$ *have the same images by functions* First, Last *and* Follow.

We have applied Theorem 1 to derivation and follow automata; likewise, it can be applied to any algorithm that converts rational expressions to automata.

6   From Weighted Rotating Automata to Hadamard Expressions

We apply the method used in the previous section to get an algorithm which converts rotating automata to Hadamard expressions. An algorithm that turns a one-way automaton into a rational expression is a function τ from $1\mathbb{K}\mathrm{Aut}A$ to $\mathbb{K}\mathrm{RatExp}A$ which is consistent with the interpretation of expressions and the behaviour of automata. Thus, if an inverse of ρ existed, a commutative diagram similar to Fig. 1 could be drawn, and a result similar to Theorem 1 would be proved. Unfortunately, the inverse of ρ is only defined on pre-Hadamard expressions defined in Proposition 3. Hence, to apply our method, we must ensure that the algorithm τ outputs pre-Hadamard expressions.

Theorem 2. *If* τ *is an algorithm that converts an automaton in* $1\mathbb{K}\mathrm{Aut}A_r$ *to an equivalent pre-Hadamard expression, then* $\rho^{-1} \circ \tau \circ 1\mathrm{w}$ *converts an automaton in* $\mathbb{R}\mathbb{K}\mathrm{Aut}A$ *to an equivalent Hadamard expression.*

6.1   State Elimination on an r-local Automaton

We show in this part that the State Elimination method introduced in [1] can be applied on some particular automata over $A_{\mathbf{r}}$ in such a way that it outputs pre-Hadamard expressions. These automata are $\mathbf{r}$-local automata.

Definition 9. *An automaton* (Q, E, I, T) *in* $1\mathbb{K}\mathrm{Aut}A_r$ *is* $\mathbf{r}$-local *if there is a partition* $\{Q_1, Q_2\}$ *of* Q *with no initial state in* Q_2, *and such that the label of a transition is* $\mathbf{r}$ *if and only if this transition ends in* Q_2.

We briefly recall the principle of the State Elimination method applied to an automaton $\mathcal{A} = (Q, E, I, T)$ in $\mathbb{K}\mathrm{Aut}A$. It requires to convert $\mathcal{A}$ into a slightly different automaton: first, $\mathcal{A}$ is turned to an automaton where labels are expressions: every transition (p, a, q) with weight k is replaced by a transition from p to q with label ka; if there are several transitions between the same pair of states, they are merged into one transition whose label is the sum of the former labels. Second, two fresh states i_0 (pre-initial) and t_0 (post-final) are added, and a transition with the expression $k1$ as label is created from i_0 to every initial state with initial weight k, and a transition with label $k1$ is created from every final state with weight k to t_0.

Then, the elimination method runs as follow. At each step, a state p is considered. For every predecessor q of p, for every successor r of p, the transition from q to r is updated as follow:

Then, the state p is deleted. If the state p has no loop, there is no factor F^* in the resulting expression.

At the end, only states i_0 and t_0 remain, and the label of the transition from i_0 to t_0 denotes the behaviour of $\mathcal{A}$. Notice that the result heavily depends on the ordering on states during the elimination.

We present a variant of this algorithm for **r**-local automata in order to obtain a pre-Hadamard expression. First, the states with incoming transitions with label different from **r** are deleted before the other ones. Second, to get well-formed pre-Hadamard expressions, the following rewriting is applied when two expressions are added: if the expressions are of the form Er and Fr, then $\mathsf{Er} + \mathsf{Fr} = (\mathsf{E} + \mathsf{F})\mathsf{r}$.

Proposition 7. *The variant of the elimination method applied to an **r**-local automaton $\mathcal{A}$ yields a pre-Hadamard expression $\mathsf{E}(\mathcal{A})$ such that $[\![\mathsf{E}(\mathcal{A})]\!] = |\mathcal{A}|$.*

Proof. Let $\mathcal{A} = (Q_1 \cup Q_2, E, I, T)$ be an **r**-local automaton in $1\mathbb{K}\mathsf{Aut}A_{\mathbf{r}}$. Let i_0 and t_0 be respectively the pre-initial and post-final states added to $\mathcal{A}$. Let R be the set of states that remain at each step of the elimination. The first stage is the removing of states in Q_1; the following properties are invariant during this stage :

$$\forall p \in R, \forall q_1 \in R \setminus Q_2, \ p \xrightarrow{\ \mathsf{E}\ } q_1 \implies \mathsf{E} \in \mathbb{K}\mathsf{RatExp}A,$$
$$\forall q_2 \in Q_2 \cap R, \ p \xrightarrow{\ \mathsf{E}\ } q_2 \implies \mathsf{E} = \mathsf{Fr} \text{ with } \mathsf{F} \in \mathbb{K}\mathsf{RatExp}A. \tag{15}$$

The second stage is the removing of states in Q_2, and the invariants are:

$$\forall p \in R, \forall q_2 \in Q_2 \cap R, \ p \xrightarrow{\ \mathsf{E}\ } q_2 \implies \mathsf{E} = \mathsf{Fr} \text{ with } \mathsf{F} \in \mathbb{K}\mathsf{PreHadExp}A,$$
$$p \xrightarrow{\ \mathsf{E}\ } t_0 \implies \mathsf{E} \in \mathbb{K}\mathsf{PreHadExp}A. \tag{16}$$

At the end, the label of the transition from i_0 to t_0 is in $\mathbb{K}\mathsf{PreHadExp}A$. □

6.2 State Elimination Variant in $1\mathbb{K}\mathbf{Aut}A_{\mathbf{r}}$.

If an automaton in $1\mathbb{K}\mathsf{Aut}A_{\mathbf{r}}$ is not **r**-local the algorithm first split states which violate the **r**-local property.

Let $\mathcal{B} = (S, F, J, U)$ be in $1\mathbb{K}\mathsf{Aut}A_{\mathbf{r}}$. We define the automaton $\mathcal{A} = (Q_1 \cup Q_2, E, I, T)$ in $1\mathbb{K}\mathsf{Aut}A_{\mathbf{r}}$. Q_1 and Q_2 are two distinct copies of S; for every state p in S, the corresponding state in Q_1 (*resp.* Q_2) is denoted p_1 (*resp.* p_2). For every p, q in S, for every i in $\{1, 2\}$,

$$I(p_1) = J(p), \qquad I(p_2) = 0, \qquad T(p_i) = U(p),$$
$$\forall a \in A, \ E(p_i, a, q_1) = F(p, a, q), \qquad E(p_i, a, q_2) = 0,$$
$$E(p_i, \mathbf{r}, q_1) = 0, \qquad E(p_i, \mathbf{r}, q_2) = F(p, \mathbf{r}, q).$$

Automaton $\mathcal{A}$ is r-local and is a *covering* (*cf.* [10]) of $\mathcal{B}$: there is a bijection from initial states of $\mathcal{B}$ onto initial states of $\mathcal{A}$, with the same initial weights, every state of $\mathcal{A}$ has the same final weight as the corresponding state in $\mathcal{B}$, and for each state p_i of $\mathcal{A}$, there is a bijection of transitions outgoing from p_i to transitions outgoing from p in $\mathcal{B}$ such that, for every transition (p_i, a, q_j) in $\mathcal{A}$, (p, a, q) is a transition in $\mathcal{B}$ with the same weight.

This implies a bisimulation between automata $\mathcal{A}$ and $\mathcal{B}$: there is one and only one way to lift up every computation of $\mathcal{B}$ in $\mathcal{A}$. Therefore, there is a canonical one-to-one mapping of computations of $\mathcal{B}$ into computations of $\mathcal{A}$ that preserves both the labels and the weights. Hence, automata $\mathcal{A}$ and $\mathcal{B}$ have the same behaviour.

Lemma 2. *Every automaton in* $1\mathbb{K}\mathrm{Aut}A_r$ *admits an r-local covering.*

Finally, we get an algorithm τ that fulfills the hypothesis of Theorem 2, from which an algorithm that converts rotating automata to Hadamard expressions is deduced.

Proposition 8. *Let* $\mathcal{A}$ *be in* $\mathbb{R}\mathbb{K}\mathrm{Aut}A$ *and let* F *be the pre-Hadamard expression computed by the elimination method on a r-local covering of* $1\mathrm{w}(\mathcal{A})$. *Then,* $\rho^{-1}(\mathsf{F})$ *is a Hadamard expression such that* $[\![\rho^{-1}(\mathsf{F})]\!] = |\mathcal{A}|$.

Remark 1. It is possible to design an algorithm h that turns every expression in $\mathbb{K}\mathrm{RatExp}A_r$ to a pre-Hadamard expression. Then for every algorithm τ which converts weighted one-way automata into a rational expressions, the algorithm $\rho^{-1} \circ h \circ \tau \circ 1\mathrm{w}$ converts weighted rotating automata to Hadamard expressions. Nevertheless, it seems that it is more efficient to modify the algorithm τ such that it directly outputs pre-Hadamard expressions.

References

1. Brzozowski, J.A., McCluskey, E.J.: Signal flow graph techniques for sequential circuit state diagrams. IEEE Trans. Electron. Comput. **EC–12**(2), 67–76 (1963)
2. Caron, P., Flouret, M.: Glushkov construction for series: the non commutative case. Int. J. Comput. Math. **80**(4), 457–472 (2003)
3. Ésik, Z., Kuich, W.: Rationally additive semirings. J. UCS **8**(2), 173–183 (2002)
4. Guillon, B.: Two-wayness: automata and transducers. Ph.D. thesis, Université Paris Diderot - Università degli studi di Milano, Paris (2016)
5. Ilie, L., Yu, S.: Follow automata. Inf. Comput. **186**(1), 140–162 (2003)
6. Kapoutsis, C., Královič, R., Mömke, T.: Size complexity of rotating and sweeping automata. J. Comput. Syst. Sci. **78**(2), 537–558 (2012)
7. Lombardy, S.: Two-way representations and weighted automata. RAIRO - Theor. Inf. Appl. **50**(4), 331–350 (2016)
8. Lombardy, S., Sakarovitch, J.: Derivatives of rational expressions with multiplicity. Theor. Comput. Sci. **332**(1–3), 141–177 (2005)
9. Pighizzini, G.: Two-way finite automata: old and recent results. Fundam. Inform. **126**(2–3), 225–246 (2013)
10. Sakarovitch, J.: Elements of Automata Theory. Cambridge University Press, New York (2009)
11. Sakoda, W.J., Sipser, M.: Nondeterminism and the size of two way finite automata. In: Proceedings of STOC, pp. 275–286. ACM (1978)

On the Conjecture $\mathcal{L}_{\mathsf{DFCM}} \subsetneq \mathsf{RCM}$

Paolo Massazza[✉]

Dipartimento di Scienze Teoriche e Applicate - Sezione Informatica,
Università degli Studi dell'Insubria, Via Mazzini 5, 21100 Varese, Italy
paolo.massazza@uninsubria.it

Abstract. We prove that the class of the languages recognized by one-way deterministic 1-reversal bounded 1-counter machines is contained in RCM, a class of languages that has been recently introduced and that admits interesting properties. This is the first step to prove the conjecture $\mathcal{L}_{\mathsf{DFCM}} \subsetneq \mathsf{RCM}$, which says that for any fixed integer k all the languages recognized by one-way deterministic 1-reversal bounded k-counter machines are in RCM. We recall that this conjecture implies that the generating function of a language in $\mathcal{L}_{\mathsf{DFCM}}$ is holonomic.

1 Introduction

A well-known result of Chomsky-Schützenberger [1] states that the generating functions of regular languages are rational whereas the generating functions of unambiguous context-free languages are algebraic. This fact allows us to use analytic methods to determine properties of languages. For example, a method to show that a context-free language L is inherently ambiguous, employed by Flajolet in [2,3], consists of proving that the generating function of L is transcendental. However, the problem of determining the class of functions to which the generating function of a context-free language belongs is still open.

It is then interesting to look for suitable classes of languages having generating functions that belong to particular classes of functions. In this context, the holonomic functions have been widely investigated since the end of 1980s. The class of the holonomic functions in one variable is an extension of the class of the algebraic functions and contains all the functions satisfying a linear differential equation with polynomial coefficients (see [4,5]). A first use of the holonomic functions in the context of formal languages was in [6], where the authors proved that the problem of deciding the holonomicity of the generating function of a context-free language is equivalent to the problem of deciding whether a context-free language is inherently ambiguous. Furthermore, a class of languages with holonomic generating functions, called LCL, was introduced in [7] by means of linear constraints on the number of occurrences of symbols of the alphabet. A particular subclass $\mathsf{LCL}_R \subsetneq \mathsf{LCL}$ was also studied in [6]. The idea of using constraints and finite state automata in order to define languages is also at the basis of a family of automata called Parikh Automata and defined in [8,9]. In particular, the subclass LPA of Parikh Automata on letters has been defined in [10] (actually, as noted in [11], $\mathcal{L}_{\mathsf{LPA}} = \mathsf{LCL}_R$). Recently, in [11] a wider class of

© Springer International Publishing AG 2017
A. Carayol and C. Nicaud (Eds.): CIAA 2017, LNCS 10329, pp. 175–187, 2017.
DOI: 10.1007/978-3-319-60134-2_15

languages with holonomic generating functions, called RCM, has been defined. This class of languages is contained in $\mathcal{L}_{\mathsf{NFCM}}$, the class of languages recognized by nondeterministic one-way reversal bounded counter machines, whereas it is not contained in $\mathcal{L}_{\mathsf{DFCM}}$, the class of languages recognized by deterministic one-way reversal bounded counter machines [12]. Lastly, in [11] the conjecture $\mathcal{L}_{\mathsf{DFCM}} \subsetneq \mathsf{RCM}$ has been stated.

In this paper we prove that the class $\mathcal{L}_{\mathsf{DFCM}(1,0,1)}$ of languages recognized by deterministic counter machines with one-way input tape and one 1-reversal bounded counter is contained in RCM. This result is obtained by introducing particular finite automata that we think can be exploited also in the general case where the deterministic machine has k counters, for any fixed k. In other words, we introduce a possible basis to prove the conjecture $\mathcal{L}_{\mathsf{DFCM}} \subsetneq \mathsf{RCM}$. Furthermore, the relation $\mathcal{L}_{\mathsf{DFCM}(1,0,1)} \subsetneq \mathsf{RCM}$, together with the closure properties of RCM and the results on the left and on the right quotient of languages in $\mathcal{L}_{\mathsf{DFCM}(1,0,1)}$ provided in [13], allows us to show that some interesting subclasses of $\mathcal{L}_{\mathsf{DFCM}}$ are contained in RCM.

We recall that for any class of languages $\mathcal{L}$, the relation $\mathcal{L} \subseteq \mathsf{RCM}$ implies that the generating function of a language in $\mathcal{L}$ is holonomic. This provides a method for proving that a language L is not in $\mathcal{L}$, which resembles in some sense the Flajolet methodology, used when $\mathcal{L}$ is the class of unambiguous context free languages. Notice that for $\mathcal{L} = \mathcal{L}_{\mathsf{DFCM}(1,0,1)}$ the generating function of a language $L \in \mathcal{L}$ is algebraic (hence holonomic) since L is unambiguous context-free [14].

2   Preliminaries

In this section we give some basics about languages, classes of languages and automata of our interest in the paper. Let $\Sigma = \{\sigma_1, \sigma_2, \ldots, \sigma_h\}$ be a finite alphabet and $w \in \Sigma^\star$. For all $\sigma \in \Sigma$ we indicate by $|w|_\sigma$ the number of occurrences of σ in w. The *length* of w is $|w| = \sum_{\sigma \in \Sigma} |w|_\sigma$. Given two finite alphabets Γ and Σ, a morphism $\mu : \Gamma^\star \mapsto \Sigma^\star$ is said to be *length preserving* if for all $w \in \Gamma^\star$ one has $|\mu(w)| = |w|$. In particular, we are interested in length preserving morphisms that are injective on a fixed language $L \subseteq \Gamma^\star$, that is, morphisms μ such that for all $v, w \in L$, if $v \neq w$ then $\mu(v) \neq \mu(w)$. We also define a function $\kappa : \mathbb{N} \mapsto \{0,1\}$ as $\kappa(x) = 0$ if $x = 0$ else 1.

2.1   Classes of Languages

Linear constraints on the number of occurrences of symbols in an alphabet have been used in [7,11] to define two classes of languages with holonomic generating functions, called LCL and RCM, respectively. In those papers, linear constraints were formally defined as follows.

Definition 1 (linear constraint). *A linear constraint on the occurrences of symbols of* $\Gamma = \{\gamma_1, \gamma_2, \ldots, \gamma_h\}$ *in* $w \in \Gamma^\star$ *is an expression of the form*

$$\sum_{i=1}^{h} c_i |w|_{\gamma_i} \,\triangle\, c_{h+1}, \quad \text{with } c_i \in \mathbb{Z}, \triangle \in \{<, \leq, =, \neq, \geq, >\}.$$

Definition 2 (system of linear constraints). *A system of linear constraints C is either a linear constraint, or $C_1 \vee C_2$ or $C_1 \wedge C_2$ or $\neg C_1$, where C_1, C_2 are systems of linear constraints.*

We denote by $[C]$ the language consisting of the words in Γ^* that satisfy the system of linear constraints C. Let L be a language on Γ, C a system of linear constraints on the number of occurrences of symbols in Γ and $\mu : \Gamma^* \mapsto \Sigma^*$ a morphism. We indicate by $\langle L, C, \mu \rangle$ the language $\mu(L \cap [C]) \subseteq \Sigma^*$. In [11] the class of languages RCM has been defined as follows.

Definition 3 (RCM). RCM *is the class of the languages $\langle R, C, \mu \rangle$ where R is a regular language on an alphabet Γ, C a system of linear constraints on Γ and $\mu : \Gamma^* \mapsto \Sigma^*$ a length preserving morphism that is injective on $R \cap [C]$.*

Example 1. Let EQUAL $\subseteq \{a, b, \sharp\}^*$ be the language $\{a, b\}^* \cdot \{a^n \sharp a^n | n \in \mathbb{N}\}$, which is used in [10] to show that the class of languages recognized by deterministic Parikh Automata is strictly included in the class of languages recognized by Parikh Automata. Let $\Gamma = \{a_1, a_2, a_3, b_1, c_1\}$, $R = (a_1 + b_1)^* a_2^* c_1 a_3^*$, and consider the linear constraint C given by $|w|_{a_2} = |w|_{a_3}$, together with the morphism $\mu : \Gamma^* \mapsto \{a, b, \sharp\}^*$ defined by $\mu(a_1) = \mu(a_2) = \mu(a_3) = a$, $\mu(b_1) = b$ and $\mu(c_1) = \sharp$. It is immediate to see that μ is length preserving and injective on $R \cap [C]$ (but not on R). Thus, one has EQUAL $= \langle R, C, \mu \rangle \in$ RCM.

The class RCM admits several interesting properties. Indeed, it is closed under union and intersection, it contains languages with holonomic generating function, and most of the decision problems (i.e. equivalence, inclusion, disjointness, emptiness, universe) are decidable, see [11].

In Sect. 4, the class RCM will be compared to a class of languages recognized by a particular family of counter machines. So, we recall that a two-way k-counter machine is a finite automaton equipped with k counters. The operations admitted on a counter are the increment or the decrement by 1, as well as the comparison with 0. The machine is called l-reversal bounded if the count in each counter alternately increases and decreases at most l times. We refer to [12] for all definitions and for main results concerning the class DFCM(k, m, n) (NFCM(k, m, n)) of *deterministic (non-deterministic) (m, n)-reversal bounded k-counter machines*, that is, n-reversal bounded k-counter machines with a two-way input tape, where the input head reverses direction at most m times. In particular, we are interested in the class DFCM$(k, 0, 1)$ where the input tape is one-way and the counters can change from increasing to decreasing mode at most once. Formally, $M \in$ DFCM$(k, 0, 1)$ is a 7-tuple $M = (k, Q, \Sigma, \$, \delta, \dot{q}, F)$, where k indicates the number of counters, Q is a finite set of states, Σ is the input alphabet, $\$$ is the right end-marker, δ is the transition function, $\dot{q} \in Q$ is the initial state and $F \subseteq Q$ is the set of final states. The transition function is a mapping from $Q \times (\Sigma \cup \{\$\}) \times \{0, 1\}^k$ into $Q \times \{S, R\} \times \{-1, 0, +1\}^k$ such that if $\delta(q, a, c_1, \ldots, c_k) = (p, d, d_1, \ldots, d_k)$ and $c_i = 0$ for some i, then d_i has to be nonnegative to prevent negative values in a counter. The symbols S and R are used to indicate the movement of the input tape head (S = stay, R = right).

A configuration of M is a tuple $(q, x\$, n_1, \ldots, n_k)$ where $q \in Q$, $x \in \Sigma^*$ is the unread suffix of the input word and $n_i \in \mathbb{N}$ represents the value of the i-th counter. The transition relation on the set of configurations is denoted by $\rightarrow$, and its transitive closure by $\stackrel{*}{\rightarrow}$. Hence, we write $(p, v, n_1, \ldots, n_k) \rightarrow (q, z, n_1', \ldots, n_k')$ if and only if $\delta(p, \sigma, n_1, \ldots, n_k) = (q, d, d_1, \ldots, d_k)$, $n_i' = n_i + d_i$ for all i with $1 \leq i \leq k$, and $v = \sigma z$ (if $d = R$) or $z = v$ (if $d = S$). When there is only one counter, we say that a transition $(p, v, c) \rightarrow (q, z, c')$ is *negative* (*positive*, *nonnegative*, *stable*, resp.) if $c' < c$ ($c' > c$, $c' \geq c$, $c' = c$, resp.). In the sequel, we are interested in the relation $\Rightarrow$, called *one-symbol transition*.

Definition 4 ($\Rightarrow$). *Let $A = (1, Q, \Sigma, \$, \delta, \dot{q}, F) \in \mathsf{DFCM}(1, 0, 1)$. For any $x \in \Sigma^*$ and $\sigma \in \Sigma$ we write $(p, \sigma x\$, c) \Rightarrow (q, x\$, c')$ if and only if $p, q \in Q$, and either $\delta(p, \sigma, \kappa(c)) = (q, R, d)$ with $c' = c + d$, or $\delta(p, \sigma, \kappa(c)) = (q_1, S, d_1)$, $\delta(q_1, \sigma, \kappa(c + d_1)) = (q_2, S, d_2), \ldots, \delta(q_h, S, \kappa(c + \sum_{i=1..h} d_i)) = (q, R, d_{h+1})$, with $c' = c + \sum_{i=1..h+1} d_i$.*

Notice that the transition $(p, \sigma x\$, c) \Rightarrow (q, x\$, c')$ uniquely identifies a sequence $\{d_i\}$ of integers in $\{-1, 0, 1\}$ and a sequence $\{q_i\}$ of states in Q. A sequence of $|w|$ one-symbol transitions that reads a word w is shortened as $(p, wx\$, c) \stackrel{|w|}{\Rightarrow} (q, x\$, c')$. A word $w \in \Sigma^*$ is accepted by M if and only if $(\dot{q}, w\$, 0, \ldots, 0) \stackrel{|w|}{\Rightarrow} (p, \$, c_1, \ldots, c_k) \stackrel{*}{\rightarrow} (q, \$, c_1', \ldots, c_k')$, for some $q \in F$, with $c_i, c_i' \geq 0$ for $1 \leq i \leq k$. The language recognized by M, denoted by $L(M)$, is the set of all the words accepted by M. Without loss of generality, we suppose that M always terminates and has only one final state, denoted by $\ddot{q}$, and that a word is accepted with all the counters equal to 0.

3   s-Automata and m-Automata

Let $A = (1, Q, \Sigma, \$, \delta, \dot{q}, \{\ddot{q}\})$ be a counter machine in $\mathsf{DFCM}(1, 0, 1)$. A word $w \in L(A)$ can be uniquely written as $w = vxyz$ where:

- v consists of the longest prefix of w that is read by a sequence of stable transitions (the counter is always zero);
- the first symbol of x is associated with the first positive transition; the remaining symbols of x are read by nonnegative transitions (the counter is always greater than 0);
- the first symbol of y is associated with the first negative transition; the remaining symbols of y are read by a sequence of negative or stable transitions with the counter greater than 0;
- z consists of the symbols read by a sequence of stable transitions occurring on a zero counter.

So, in w we can distinguish between symbols that are not counted (all the symbols in v and z, and possibly some symbols in x, y), symbols that are counted positively (some of the symbols in x) and symbols that are counted negatively (some of the symbols in y). Furthermore, at each step of the computation of A

the counter is exactly in one of four different states, denoted by a value in the set $\{0, 1, 2, 3\}$, called the global state of the counter. More precisely, 0 is the state of a zero counter that has not been increased yet, 1 is the state of a counter that has been increased but not decreased, 2 is the state of a counter that has been increased and decreased and is greater than zero and, finally, 3 is the state of a counter that has been increased and decreased and is equal to zero. The global state of the counter may change from i to $i+1$, for $0 \le i \le 2$, but not vice versa, hence the ordering $0 < 1 < 2 < 3$ naturally arises. A sequence $\{d_i\}$ of integers in $\{-1, 0, 1\}$ is called *1-reversal acceptable* if and only if $d_i = -1$ implies $d_j \le 0$ for all $j > i$. Moreover, $\{d_i\}$ is *compatible* with the global state α of the counter if it is 1-reversal acceptable and:

- if $\alpha = 3$ then $\forall i \ d_i = 0$;
- if $\alpha = 2$ then $\forall i \ d_i \le 0$;
- if $\alpha = 0$ then $|\{i | d_i = -1\}| \le |\{i | d_i = 1\}|$.

Let $0 \le \alpha \le \beta \le 3$ and consider a sequence $s = \{d_i\}$, with $a = |\{i | d_i = -1\}|$ and $b = |\{i | d_i = 1\}|$. We say that s *changes* the global state of the counter from α to β if s is compatible with α and the conditions in the following table hold (a dash indicates a case that can not occur).

	$\beta = 0$	$\beta = 1$	$\beta = 2$	$\beta = 3$
$\alpha = 0$	$a = b = 0$	$b > a = 0$	$b > a > 0$	$a = b$
$\alpha = 1$	–	$a = 0$	$a > 0$	$a > b \ge 0$
$\alpha = 2$	–	–	$a \ge b = 0$	$a > b = 0$
$\alpha = 3$	–	–	–	$a = b = 0$

Let α, β be two global states of the counter, with $\alpha \le \beta$. We say that a transition $t = (p, \sigma x\$, c) \Rightarrow (q, x\$, c')$ *changes* α to β if the associated sequence of increments $\{d_i\}$ is *compatible* with α and changes α to β (the global state of the counter in $(q, x\$, c')$ becomes β). In particular, t is *stable* if it changes α to β and $\alpha = \beta$. (i.e. the global state of the counter in $(q, x\$, c')$ is still α).

In the following we are interested in particular sets of states $Q_\beta \subseteq Q$ associated with the global state β of the counter.

Definition 5 (Q_0, Q_1, Q_2, Q_3). *Let* $(1, Q, \Sigma, \$, \delta, \acute{q}, \{\acute{q}\}) \in \text{DFCM}(1, 0, 1)$. *For any* β, *with* $0 \le \beta \le 3$, *we define the subsets of states* Q_β *by considering only the transitions occurring on symbols* $\sigma \ne \$:$

$(\beta = 0)$ Q_0 *is the set of all* $q \in Q$ *that can be reached from* $\acute{q}$ *by a sequence of stable transitions (in each transition the counter is zero),*

$$Q_0 = \{q \in Q | \exists w \in \Sigma^\star, (\acute{q}, wx\$, 0) \overset{|w|}{\Rightarrow} (q, x\$, 0) \text{ is made of stable transitions}\};$$

$(\beta > 0)$ *Consider the set of states* $Q'_\beta = \{q \in Q | \exists \alpha, p, \sigma, c, 0 \leq \alpha < \beta, p \in Q_\alpha, \sigma \in \Sigma, c \geq 0 \, s.t \, (p, \sigma x\$, c) \Rightarrow (q, x\$, c') \, changes \, \alpha \, to \, \beta\}$. *Then,* $Q_\beta = Q'_\beta \cup Q''_\beta$ *where* $Q''_\beta = \{q \in Q | \exists w \in \Sigma^\star, p \in Q'_\beta, \, s.t. \, (p, wx\$, c) \overset{|w|}{\Rightarrow} (q, x\$, c') \, is \, made \, of \, stable \, transitions\}$.

A *nonnegative cycle* on $\sigma \in \Sigma$ is a sequence of k different states $q_1, \ldots, q_k$ such that $\delta(q_1, \sigma, 0) = (q_2, S, 0), \delta(q_2, \sigma, 0) = (q_3, S, 0), \ldots, \delta(q_k, \sigma, 0) = (q_1, S, 0)$ or $\delta(q_1, \sigma, 1) = (q_2, S, c_1), \delta(q_2, \sigma, 1) = (q_3, S, c_2), \ldots, \delta(q_k, \sigma, 1) = (q_1, S, c_k)$, with $c_e \geq 0$ for $1 \leq e \leq k$. Since A is deterministic and always terminates, we can not find in A a nonnegative cycle. In other words, there is not a sequence of nonnegative transitions that do not consume an input symbol (i.e. the input head always stays) and lead A from a state q to itself. On the contrary, a *negative cycle* may exist. Indeed, a sequence of k different states $q_1, q_2, \ldots, q_k$ such that $\delta(q_1, \sigma, 1) = (q_2, S, c_1)$, $\delta(q_2, \sigma, 1) = (q_3, S, c_2)$, $\ldots$, $\delta(q_k, \sigma, 1) = (q_1, S, c_k)$, with $c_e \leq 0$ for all e and $d = \sum_e c_e < 0$, corresponds to a cycle that resets the counter. The integer d is called the *weight* of the cycle. Once A enters a state q that belongs to a negative cycle (of weight d) on σ then, if the input symbol is σ, the integer r stored in the counter is replaced by 0, and the state that is reached when the counter becomes 0 can be associated with the modulus of the value r by the weight d. This, together with the unread suffix of the input word w, is the only information that A can exploit to accept or to reject w. Since A is deterministic, the number of different negative cycles in A is finite. Every word w is accepted (or rejected) by a computation of A with at most one negative cycle. By recalling the previous decomposition $w = vxyz$ of a word in $L(A)$, if no negative cycle is traversed then the sum C_+ of all the increments caused by symbols (in x) that are counted positively is just the opposite of the sum C_- of all the decrements caused by symbols (in y) that are counted negatively, i.e. $C_+ + C_- = 0$. Otherwise, before entering a negative cycle on a symbol σ of y, the relations $r = C_+ + C_- > 0$ and $r \bmod d = k$ hold, for a suitable k associated with a state of a negative cycle of weight d. In this case the value C_- does not consider the decrement $-r$ caused by the symbol σ (associated with the negative cycle that resets the counter). Thus, let D be the set of the weights of all the negative cycles in A. If $D \neq \emptyset$ we define $\pi = \prod_{d \in D} d$. By the previous remarks, it follows that the exact value r of the counter is not needed when a word is accepted through a negative cycle. Indeed, it is sufficient to know the value $r' = r \bmod \pi$, since $r \bmod d = k$ if and only if $r' \bmod d = k$.

All the previous remarks lead directly to a particular deterministic finite state automaton A', associated with a given $A \in \text{DFCM}(1,0,1)$ and used in Theorem 1 to show that $\mathcal{L}_{\text{DFCM}(1,0,1)} \subsetneq \text{RCM}$. Actually, the construction of A' depends on the occurrence in A of negative cycles of weight less than -1. Thus, we first consider the case of deterministic 1-reversal bounded 1-counter machines without negative cycles of weight less than -1. This leads to the notion of *s-automaton* (s for simple). The construction is based on the definition of a new (larger) alphabet Γ for A', where the symbols are obtained by encoding the possible events that occur during a transition of A on a symbol σ (that is, how the counter is changed and how its global state evolves).

Definition 6 (s-automaton). *Let* $A = (1, Q, \Sigma, \$, \delta, \dot{q}, \{\ddot{q}\}) \in \mathsf{DFCM}(1, 0, 1)$ *be a counter machine without negative cycles of weight less than* -1. *The s-automaton of* A *is the deterministic finite state automaton* $A' = (Q', \Gamma, \delta', \dot{q}_0, F)$ *where*

$$Q' = \{q_\alpha | 0 \leq \alpha \leq 3, q \in Q_\alpha\},$$
$$\Gamma = \{\sigma_i, \sigma'_j, \sigma'' | \sigma \in \Sigma, -|Q| \leq i \leq |Q|, -|Q| \leq j < 0\},$$
$$F = \{q_\alpha | \alpha \in \{0, 3\}, q \in Q_0 \cup Q_3 \text{ and in } A \text{ one has } (q, \$, 0) \overset{*}{\rightarrow} (\ddot{q}, \$, 0)\}.$$

and $\delta' : Q' \times \Gamma \mapsto Q'$ *is defined by setting* $\delta'(p_\alpha, \gamma) = q_\beta$ *if and only if in* A *there exists a transition* $(p, \sigma x\$, c) \Rightarrow (q, x\$, c + d)$, *for a suitable* $c \in \mathbb{N}$, *which changes the global state of the counter from* α *to* β, *and where* γ *(depending on* σ *and* d) *is determined by Table 1-S below.*

Table 1. Table 1-S (left) and Table 1-M (right)

	α	d	β	γ		α	d	β	γ	j
1)	0	0	0	σ_0	1)	0	0	0	σ_0	0
2)	0	> 0	1	σ_d	2)	0	> 0	1	σ_d	d
3)	0	> 0	2	σ_d	3)	0	> 0	2	σ_d	d
4)	0	0	3	σ_0	4)	0	0	3	σ_0	0
5)	1	≥ 0	1	σ_d	5)	1	≥ 0	1	σ_d	$(i + d) \bmod \pi$
6)	1	any	2	σ_d	6)	1	any	2	σ_d	$(i + d) \bmod \pi$
7)	1	< 0	3	σ'_d	7)	1	< 0	3	σ'_d	0 (if $i \equiv d \bmod \pi$)
8)	1	$-c$ (neg. cycle)	3	σ''	8)	1	$-c$ (neg. cycle)	3	σ''	0
9)	2	≤ 0	2	σ_d	9)	2	≤ 0	2	σ_d	$(i + d) \bmod \pi$
10)	2	< 0	3	σ'_d	10)	2	< 0	3	σ'_d	0 (if $i \equiv d \bmod \pi$)
11)	2	$-c$ (neg. cycle)	3	σ''	11)	2	$-c$ (neg. cycle)	3	σ''	0
12)	3	0	3	σ_0	12)	3	0	3	σ_0	0

Notice that Table 1-S defines a deterministic automaton since A is deterministic. For instance, the transitions 2 and 3 are not in conflict since they are associated with sequences $\{d_i\}$ with different properties. Indeed, the former corresponds to a sequence $\{d_i\}$ with $d_i \geq 0$ for all i and $d_e = 1$ for at least one e, which changes the state of the counter from 0 to 1, whereas the latter implies that $|\{d_i = 1\}| > |\{d_i = -1\}| > 0$, and then the state of the counter changes from 0 to 2. Transitions 8 and 11 correspond to negative cycles. Here the decrement d corresponds to the current value c of the counter. Since a computation traverses a negative cycle at most once, a symbol σ'' occurs at most once in a word of A'.

Example 2. Let $\Sigma = \{a, b\}$ and consider the language L of the words $w_1 b b w_2$, with $w_1, w_2 \in \Sigma^+$, such that the factor bb does not occur in w_1 and the number of occurrences of bb in bbw_2 is equal to the number of b's in w_1. It is immediate to see that L is the unambiguos context free language recognized by the automaton $A \in \mathsf{DFCM}(1,0,1)$ at the top of Fig. 1, where each transition consumes an input symbol (i.e. the input head always moves to the right) and an arrow from p to q with label σ, c, d stands for $\delta(p, \sigma, c) = (q, R, d)$. By Definition 5, one has $Q_0 = \{\dot{q}, p, t\}$, $Q_1 = \{\dot{q}, p\}$, $Q_2 = \{r, s\}$ and $Q_3 = \{r, s, t\}$. Since A does not have a negative cycle, by Definition 6 the alphabet and the set of states of the s-automaton A' of A are $\Gamma = \{a_0, a_1, b_{-1}, b_0, b'_{-1}\}$ and $Q' = \{\dot{q}_0, p_0, t_0, \dot{q}_1, p_1, r_2, s_2, r_3, s_3, t_3\}$, respectively. Note that Γ is a proper subset of the alphabet specified in Definition 6, as we consider only symbols associated with existing transitions (e.g. a'', b'' or a'_{-1} are not added to Γ). The automaton A' is shown at the bottom of Fig. 1.

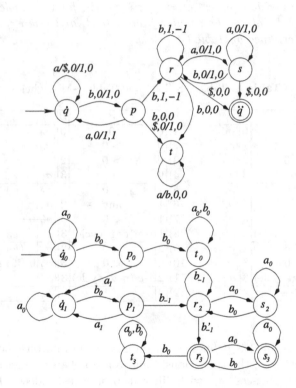

Fig. 1. The reversal bounded automaton A and the associated s-automaton A'.

When a counter machine A has a negative cycle of weight less than -1, the finite state automaton associated with A can be obtained by considering the modulus of the counter as a part of the information represented by a state. Such automaton is called the m-automaton of A (m stands for modulus).

Definition 7 (m-automaton). *Let $A = (1, Q, \Sigma, \$, \delta, \dot{q}, \{\ddot{q}\}) \in \mathsf{DFCM}(1,0,1)$ be a counter machine with at least one negative cycle of weight less than -1 and let $\pi = \prod_{d \in D} |d|$, where D is the set of the weights of the negative cycles of A.*

The m-automaton *of A is the finite state automaton* $A' = (Q', \Gamma, \delta', \dot{q}_0, F)$ *where*

$$Q' = \{p_\alpha(0), q_\beta(i), | \alpha \in \{0,3\}, \beta \in \{1,2\}, p \in Q_\alpha, q \in Q_\beta, 0 \le i < \pi\},$$
$$\Gamma = \{\sigma_i, \sigma'_j, \sigma'' | \sigma \in \Sigma, -|Q| \le i \le |Q|, -|Q| \le j < 0\},$$
$$F = \{p_\alpha(0) | \alpha \in \{0,3\}, p \in Q_0 \cup Q_3 \text{ and in } A \text{ one has}(p, \$, 0) \xrightarrow{*} (\dot{q}, \$, 0)\}.$$

and $\delta' : Q' \times \Gamma \mapsto Q'$ *is defined by setting* $\delta'(p_\alpha(i), \gamma) = q_\beta(j)$ *if and only if in* A *there exists a transition* $(p, \sigma x\$, c) \Rightarrow (q, x\$, c + d)$, *for suitable* $c \in \mathbb{N}$, $p \in Q_\alpha$ *and* $q \in Q_\beta$, *which changes the global state of the counter from* α *to* β, *where* γ *and* j *(depending on* α, β, d*) are given in Table 1-M above.*

We point out that a word accepted by an s-automaton A' (or by an m-automaton) is either a word on the alphabet $\Sigma_0 = \{\sigma_0 | \sigma \in \Sigma\}$ or it contains exactly one occurrence of a symbol in $\Sigma' = \{\sigma'', \sigma'_i | \sigma \in \Sigma, i < 0\}$. Such a symbol is used to guess that the counter of A is zero.

4 $\mathcal{L}_{DFCM(1,0,1)}$ and RCM

In this section we compare RCM to $\mathcal{L}_{DFCM(1,0,1)}$. We recall that RCM is not contained in $\mathcal{L}_{DFCM}$ [11, Theorem 9], whereas it is contained in $\mathcal{L}_{NFCM}$ [11, Theorem 10]. In order to prove that $\mathcal{L}_{DFCM(1,0,1)} \subsetneq$ RCM it is sufficient to show that for any $L \in \mathcal{L}_{DFCM(1,0,1)}$ one can find a regular language R, a set C of linear constraints and a morphism μ (injective on $R \cap [C]$) such that $L = \langle R, C, \mu \rangle$.

Theorem 1. $\mathcal{L}_{DFCM(1,0,1)} \subsetneq$ RCM.

Proof. First, by [11, Theorem 9] one has $\mathcal{L}_{DFCM(1,0,1)} \ne$ RCM. So, let $A \in$ DFCM$(1, 0, 1)$ be a counter machine with at least one negative cycle of weight less than -1, $A = (1, Q, \Sigma, \$, \delta, \dot{q}, \{\dot{q}\})$, and let $A' = (Q', \Gamma, \delta', \dot{q}_0, F)$ be the m-automaton of A (if A does not have a negative cycle of weight less than -1 we construct the s-automaton of A and proceed similarly). We determine a system of linear constraints C such that $L(A) = \langle L(A'), C, \mu \rangle$, where $\mu : \Gamma^* \mapsto \Sigma^*$ is an injective morphism on $L(A') \cap [C]$ defined by $\mu(\sigma'') = \mu(\sigma'_i) = \mu(\sigma_i) = \sigma$.

We associate with each symbol σ_i, σ'_i in Γ its weight $W(\sigma_i) = W(\sigma'_i) = i$. By convention, the weight of $\sigma'' \in \Gamma$ is $W(\sigma'') = 1$. Weights are used to determine the set of constraints C. Indeed, A' has been defined so that it reads a symbol σ_i or σ'_i if and only if A adds i to the counter on reading $\sigma = \mu(\sigma_i) = \mu(\sigma'_i)$. Hence, the weight of a word of n symbols, $w = \gamma_1 \gamma_2 \cdots \gamma_n \in L(A')$, is $W(w) = \sum_{j=1}^{n} W(\gamma_j) = \sum_{\sigma'' \in \Gamma} |w|_{\sigma''} + \sum_{\sigma'_i \in \Gamma} i|w|_{\sigma'_i} + \sum_{\sigma_i \in \Gamma} i|w|_{\sigma_i}$. As observed at the end of Sect. 3, a word $w \in L(A')$ either belongs to Σ_0^* or has exactly one occurrence of a symbol in Σ'. Thus, we consider the system of linear constraints C given by $C_1 \vee C_2 \vee C_3$, where

$$C_1 : \quad \sum_{\sigma_i'} |w|_{\sigma_i'} = 0 \wedge \sum_{\sigma''} |w|_{\sigma''} = 0 \wedge \sum_{i \neq 0} |w|_{\sigma_i} = 0,$$

$$C_2 : \quad \sum_{\sigma_i'} |w|_{\sigma_i'} = 1 \wedge \sum_{\sigma''} |w|_{\sigma''} = 0 \wedge \sum_{\sigma_i, \sigma_i'} (i|w|_{\sigma_i} + i|w|_{\sigma_i'}) = 0,$$

$$C_3 : \quad \sum_{\sigma_i'} |w|_{\sigma_i'} = 0 \wedge \sum_{\sigma''} |w|_{\sigma''} = 1 \wedge \sum_{\sigma_i} i|w|_{\sigma_i} > 0.$$

Now, we prove that μ is injective on $L(A') \cap [C]$. Suppose that there exist $x_1, x_2 \in L(A') \cap [C]$ such that $x_1 = x\tau_1 z_1$ and $x_2 = x\tau_2 z_2$, with $x, z_1, z_2 \in \Gamma^*$, $\tau_1, \tau_2 \in \Gamma$, $\tau_1 \neq \tau_2$, $\mu(\tau_1) = \mu(\tau_2) = \sigma$ and $z = \mu(z_1) = \mu(z_2)$. Let $y = \mu(x)$. Note that no negative cycle is traversed when reading x, otherwise one has $\tau_1 z_1, \tau_2 z_2 \in \Sigma_0^*$ and then $\mu(\tau_1 z_1) = \mu(\tau_2 z_2)$ implies $\tau_1 z_1 = \tau_2 z_2$, hence $x_1 = x_2$ (see Transitions 8, 11 and 12 of Table 1-M). Since A is deterministic, there is only one pair (p, k), with $p \in Q$ and $k \geq 0$, such that $(\dot{q}, y\sigma z\$, 0) \overset{|y|}{\Rightarrow} (p, \sigma z\$, k)$. Furthermore, also $s = (p, \sigma z\$, k) \Rightarrow (\hat{p}, z\$, k+i)$ is uniquely determined, as well as $i \in \mathbb{Z}$. If s contains a negative cycle, Transitions 8 and 11 of Table 1-M imply that $\tau_1 = \tau_2 = \sigma''$. Since τ_1 and τ_2 have to be different, we necessarily have $\tau_1 = \sigma_i$ and $\tau_2 = \sigma_i'$, and this implies $i < 0$. Once A' makes Transition 7 or 10 (the only ones associated with a symbol σ_i'), all the subsequent input symbols have weight zero (see Transition 12), since the transition guesses that the value of the counter is $-i$. Thus, one has $W(x_1) = W(x) + i + W(z_1)$, with $W(z_1) < 0$, whereas $W(x_2) = W(x) + i + W(z_2)$, with $W(z_2) = 0$. In fact, Transitions 6 and 9 with $i < 0$ (corresponding to $\tau_1 = \sigma_i$) imply that all the subsequent input symbols have weight at most 0, and that at least one of them has a negative weight, hence $W(z_1) < 0$. So, it is not possible to have $x_1, x_2 \in [C]$. Indeed, if $W(x) + i = 0$ then $W(x_1) < 0$ and x_1 does not satisfy C. Otherwise, one has $W(x_2) = W(x) + i > 0$ and x_2 does not satisfy C (note that $z_2 \in \Sigma_0^*$). So, μ is injective on $L(A') \cap [C]$.

Now, we prove that $L(A) = L(A') \cap [C]$.

$(L(A) \subseteq L(A') \cap [C])$ Let $w \in L(A)$. If w is accepted without incrementing the counter then, on the input $\tilde{w}$ obtained from w by replacing each symbol σ with σ_0, the automaton A' enters a final state (see Transition 1 of Table 1-M), hence $\tilde{w} \in L(A')$. Moreover, one has $\tilde{w} \in [C_1]$ and so $\tilde{w} \in [C]$. Otherwise, A increases the counter at least once and then decreases it before accepting w, and we write $w = x\sigma y$, where σ is the rightmost symbol that is counted negatively. Consider the sequence of transitions $(\dot{q}, x\sigma y\$, 0) \overset{|x|}{\Rightarrow} (p, \sigma y\$, r)$ and note that no negative cycle is traversed when reading x (otherwise the counter drops to zero and can not be decreased on reading σ). One can find a word $x' \in \Gamma^*$ such that $\mu(x') = x$ and, for any σ and i, the symbol σ_i' does not occur in x' (x' is obtained by replacing σ by σ_i if A adds i to the counter on reading σ in x). Once x' has been read, A' enters either the state $p_1(j)$ or $p_2(j)$, where $j = r \bmod \pi$ and r is equal to the sum of the weights of the symbols in x', $r = W(x')$. Now, consider the transition $s = (p, \sigma y\$, r) \Rightarrow (q, y\$, 0)$ of A. If s contains a negative cycle, then the corresponding transition in A' necessarily occurs on σ'' and A'

enters the state $q_3(0)$ (see Transitions 8 and 11 of Table 1-M). If in A one has $(q, y\$, 0) \overset{|y|}{\Rightarrow} (v, \$, 0) \overset{*}{\to} (q_F, \$, 0)$ then, on the input $\tilde{y}$ obtained by replacing each σ in y with σ_0, A' will enter the final state $v_3(0)$ (starting from $q_3(0)$). Therefore, the word $w' = x'\sigma''\tilde{y} \in \Gamma^*$, with $\mu(w') = w$, is accepted by $L(A')$ and satisfies C_3, $\sum_{\sigma''} |w'|_{\sigma''} = 1 \wedge \sum_{\sigma'_i} |w'|_{\sigma'_i} = 0 \wedge \sum_{\sigma_i} i|w'|_{\sigma_i} = W(x') = r > 0$. Otherwise, s does not contain a negative cycle and so when A' is in $p_1(j)$ (or in $p_2(j)$) and reads σ'_{-r} it enters the state $q_3(0)$ (see Transitions 7 and 10 of Table 1-M). Lastly, let $\tilde{y}$ be the word obtained from y by replacing each symbol σ with σ_0. Then, $w' = x'\sigma'_{-r}\tilde{y} \in \Gamma^*$ is accepted by $L(A')$ and satisfies C_2, since $\sum_{\sigma'_i} |w'|_{\sigma'_i} = 1 \wedge \sum_{\sigma''} |w'|_{\sigma''} = 0$ and $\sum_{\sigma_i, \sigma'_i} (i|w'|_{\sigma_i} + i|w'|_{\sigma'_i}) = W(x') + W(\sigma'_{-r}) + W(\tilde{y}) = r - r + 0 = 0$.

$(L(A') \cap [C] \subseteq L(A))$ Let $w \in L(A') \cap [C]$. If $w \in \Sigma_0^*$ then, by Definition 7, in A one has $(\dot{q}, \mu(w)\$, 0) \overset{|w|}{\Rightarrow} (p, \$, 0) \overset{*}{\to} (\ddot{q}, \$, 0)$, that is, $\mu(w) \in L(A)$. Otherwise, w can be uniquely written as $w = x\tau y$, where $y \in \Sigma_0^*$ and τ is either σ'_{-r} (for a suitable $r > 0$) or σ''. By Definition 7, it follows that the state reached by A' on reading x is either $p_1(j)$ or $p_2(j)$, with $j = r \mod \pi$, where $r = W(x)$ and p is the state of A such that $(q_0, \mu(x\tau y)\$, 0) \overset{|x|}{\Rightarrow} (p, \mu(\tau y)\$, r)$. By Transitions 8 and 11 of Table 1-M, if $\tau = \sigma''$ then A has a negative cycle that resets the counter and such that $(p, \sigma\mu(y)\$, r) \Rightarrow (u, \mu(y)\$, 0)$. This means that, on reading $x\sigma''$, A' enters the state $u_3(0)$, and then $(u_3(0), y) \overset{|y|}{\Rightarrow} (q_3(0), \epsilon)$ for a suitable $q_3(0) \in F'$. So, by Definition 7, there exists a sequence of stable transitions such that $(u, \mu(y)\$, 0) \overset{|y|}{\Rightarrow} (q, \$, 0) \overset{*}{\to} (\ddot{q}, \$, 0)$, that is, $\mu(x\tau y) = \mu(w) \in L(A)$. Lastly, if $\tau = \sigma'_{-r}$ one has $W(x) = r$, $W(y) = 0$ and $W(\sigma'_{-r}) = -r$ (w satisfies C_2). This implies that in A one has $(\dot{q}, \mu(x)\sigma\mu(y)\$, 0) \overset{|x|}{\Rightarrow} (p, \sigma\mu(y)\$, r) \Rightarrow (u, \mu(y)\$, 0)$. Since in A' one has $(u_3(0), y) \overset{|y|}{\Rightarrow} (q_3(0), \epsilon)$, it follows that in A there exists a sequence of stable transitions $(u, \mu(y)\$, 0) \overset{|y|}{\Rightarrow} (q, \$, 0) \overset{*}{\to} (\ddot{q}, \$, 0)$, hence $\mu(w) \in L(A)$.   □

Example 3. The language L of Example 2 is in RCM. Indeed, one has $L = \langle R, C, \mu \rangle$ where R is the language recognized by the s-automaton of Fig. 1, μ is the morphism defined by $\mu(a_0) = \mu(a_1) = a$ and $\mu(b_{-1}) = \mu(b_0) = \mu(b_1) = b$, and C is given by $|w|_{b'_{-1}} = 1 \wedge |w|_{a_1} - |w|_{b_{-1}} - |w|_{b'_{-1}} = 0$.

A language in $\mathcal{L}_{\mathsf{DFCM}(1,0,1)}$ is unambiguos context-free [14] and then its generating function is algebraic, hence holonomic (any algebraic function is also holonomic). This result can also be obtained as an immediate consequence of Theorem 1 and [11, Theorem 3], which states that the generating function of a language in RCM is holonomic. A more significant result can be obtained by considering a property [13] regarding the left or the right quotient of languages in $\mathcal{L}_{\mathsf{DFCM}(1,0,1)}$ with languages from many families. In particular, by considering the class $\mathcal{L}_{\mathsf{NPCM}}$ of the languages recognized by nondeterministic pushdown automata augmented by a fixed number of reversal bounded counters, one has:

Corollary 1. *Let $L \in \mathcal{L}_{\mathsf{DFCM}(1,0,1)}$ and $L_1, L_2 \in \mathcal{L}_{\mathsf{NPCM}}$. Then, both $(L_1^{-1}L)L_2^{-1}$ and $L_1^{-1}(LL_2^{-1})$ are in RCM.*

Proof. By [13, Theorem 3], both $(L_1^{-1}L)L_2^{-1}$ and $L_1^{-1}(LL_2^{-1})$ belong to DFCM and are a finite union of languages in $\mathcal{L}_{\text{DFCM}(1,0,1)}$. As RCM is closed under union [11, Theorem 4], the result follows from Theorem 1.   □

Since RCM is closed under union and intersection [11, Theorems 4 and 5], from Theorem 1 we also obtain the following corollary.

Corollary 2. *Let $\mathcal{L}_{DFCM(1,0,1)}^{fin}$ be the class containing all the languages L such that $L = L_1 op_1 L_2 \cdots L_{k-1} op_{k-1} L_k$, where $k \in \mathbb{N}$, $L_1, \ldots, L_k \in \mathcal{L}_{\text{DFCM}(1,0,1)}$ and $op_1, \ldots, op_{k-1} \in \{\cap, \cup\}$. Then, one has $\mathcal{L}_{DFCM(1,0,1)}^{fin} \subsetneq \text{RCM}$.*

5   Conclusions

We have shown that $\mathcal{L}_{\text{DFCM}(1,0,1)} \subsetneq \text{RCM}$. This result may be considered as the first step in the investigation of the relationship between RCM and other well-known classes of languages defined by means of reversal bounded counter machines or Parikh automata. In particular, the ideas behind s-automata and m-automata seem to be generalizable to counter machines in $\text{DFCM}(k, 0, 1)$, for any fixed $k > 1$. This would prove the conjecture $\mathcal{L}_{\text{DFCM}} \subsetneq \text{RCM}$ stated in [11]. We stress that proving this conjecture would lead to an important result concerning the holonomicity of the generating functions of languages in $\mathcal{L}_{\text{DFCM}}$. As far as we know, there is not a general result regarding the generating functions of languages recognized by suitable classes of reversal bounded counter machines (apart the case $k = 1$). This makes the previous conjecture of particular interest.

References

1. Chomsky, N.: Schützenberger, M.P.: The algebraic theory of context-free languages. In: Computer Programming and Formal Systems, pp. 118–161 (1963)
2. Flajolet, P.: Ambiguity and transcendence. In: Brauer, W. (ed.) ICALP 1985. LNCS, vol. 194, pp. 179–188. Springer, Heidelberg (1985). doi:10.1007/BFb0015743
3. Flajolet, P.: Analytic models and ambiguity of context-free languages. Theor. Comput. Sci. **49**, 283–309 (1987)
4. Stanley, R.: Differentiably finite power series. Eur. J. Combin. **1**(2), 175–188 (1980)
5. Zeilberger, D.: A holonomic systems approach to special functions identities. J. Comput. Appl. Math. **32**(3), 321–368 (1990)
6. Bertoni, A., Massazza, P., Sabadini, N.: Holonomic generating functions and context free languages. Int. J. Found. Comput. Sci. **3**(2), 181–191 (1992)
7. Massazza, P.: Holonomic functions and their relation to linearly constrained languages. RAIRO-Theor. Inf. Appl. **27**(2), 149–161 (1993)
8. Klaedtke, F., Rueß, H.: Parikh automata and monadic second-order logics with linear cardinality constraints. Technical report, Dep. of Computer Science, Univ. of Freiburg (2002)
9. Klaedtke, F., Rueß, H.: Monadic second-order logics with cardinalities. In: Baeten, J.C.M., Lenstra, J.K., Parrow, J., Woeginger, G.J. (eds.) ICALP 2003. LNCS, vol. 2719, pp. 681–696. Springer, Heidelberg (2003). doi:10.1007/3-540-45061-0_54

10. Cadilhac, M., Finkel, A., McKenzie, P.: Affine parikh automata. RAIRO-Theor. Inf. Appl. **46**(4), 511–545 (2012)
11. Castiglione, G., Massazza, P.: On a class of languages with holonomic generating functions. Theor. Comput. Sci. **658**, 74–84 (2017)
12. Ibarra, O.: Reversal-bounded multicounter machines and their decision problems. J. ACM **25**(1), 116–133 (1978)
13. Eremondi, J., Ibarra, O.H., McQuillan, I.: Deletion operations on deterministic families of automata. In: Jain, R., Jain, S., Stephan, F. (eds.) TAMC 2015. LNCS, vol. 9076, pp. 388–399. Springer, Cham (2015). doi:10.1007/978-3-319-17142-5_33
14. Valiant, L., Paterson, M.: Deterministic one-counter automata. J. Comput. Syst. Sci. **10**(3), 340–350 (1975)

Synchronization Problems in Automata Without Non-trivial Cycles

Andrew Ryzhikov[1,2(✉)]

[1] Laboratoire G-SCOP, Université Grenoble Alpes, 38031 Grenoble, France
ryzhikov.andrew@gmail.com
[2] United Institute of Informatics Problems of NASB, 220012 Minsk, Belarus

Abstract. We study the computational complexity of various problems related to synchronization of weakly acyclic automata, a subclass of widely studied aperiodic automata. We provide upper and lower bounds on the length of a shortest word synchronizing a weakly acyclic automaton or, more generally, a subset of its states, and show that the problem of approximating this length is hard. We also show inapproximability of the problem of computing the rank of a subset of states in a binary weakly acyclic automaton and prove that several problems related to recognizing a synchronizing subset of states in such automata are NP-complete.

Keywords: Synchronizing automata · Computational complexity · Weakly acyclic automata · Subset rank

1 Introduction

The concept of synchronization is widely studied in automata theory and has a lot of different applications in such areas as manufacturing, coding theory, biocomputing, semigroup theory and many others [25]. Let $A = (Q, \Sigma, \delta)$ be a deterministic finite automaton (which we simply call an *automaton* in this paper), where Q is a set of states, Σ is a finite alphabet and $\delta : Q \times \Sigma \rightarrow Q$ is a transition function. Note that our definition of an automaton does not include initial and accepting states. An automaton is called *synchronizing* if there exists a word that maps all its states to a fixed state. Such word is called a *synchronizing word*. A state $q \in Q$ is called a *sink state* if all letters from Σ map q to itself.

In this paper synchronization of weakly acyclic automata is studied. A *simple cycle* in an automaton $A = (Q, \Sigma, \delta)$ is a sequence $q_1, \ldots, q_k$ of its states such that all the states in the sequence are different and there exist letters $x_1, \ldots, x_k \in \Sigma$ such that $\delta(q_i, x_i) = q_{i+1}$ for $1 \leq i \leq k-1$ and $\delta(q_k, x_k) = q_1$. A simple cycle is a *self-loop* if it consists of only one state. An automaton is called *weakly acyclic* if all its simple cycles are self-loops. In other words, an automaton is weakly acyclic if and only if there exists an ordering $q_1, q_2, \ldots, q_n$ of its states such that if $\delta(q_i, x) = q_j$ for some letter $x \in \Sigma$, then $i \leq j$ (such ordering is called a *topological sort* [6]). Using topological sort, this class can be recognized in polynomial time. Weakly acyclic automata are called acyclic in [10] and partially

© Springer International Publishing AG 2017
A. Carayol and C. Nicaud (Eds.): CIAA 2017, LNCS 10329, pp. 188–200, 2017.
DOI: 10.1007/978-3-319-60134-2_16

ordered in [4], where in particular the class of languages recognized by such automata is characterized.

Weakly acyclic automata arise naturally in synchronizing automata theory. Section 3 of this paper shows several examples of existing proofs where weakly acyclic automata appear implicitly in complexity reductions. Surprisingly, most of the computational problems that are hard for general automata remain very hard in this class despite of its very simple structure. Thus, investigation of weakly acyclic automata provides good lower bound on the complexity of many problems for general automata. An automaton is called *aperiodic* if for any word $w \in \Sigma^*$ and any state $q \in Q$ there exists k such that $\delta(q, w^k) = \delta(q, w^{k+1})$, where w^k is a word obtained by k concatenations of w [23]. Obviously, weakly acyclic automata form a proper subclass of aperiodic automata, thus all hardness results hold for the class of aperiodic automata.

One of the most important questions in synchronizing automata theory is the famous Černý conjecture stating that any n-state synchronizing automaton has a synchronizing word of length at most $(n-1)^2$. The conjecture is proved for various special cases, including orientable, Eulerian, aperiodic and other automata (see [25] for references), but is still open in general. For more than 30 years, the best upper bound was $\frac{n^3-n}{6}$, obtained in [15]. Recently, a small improvement on this bound has been reported in [22]: the new bound is still cubic in n but improves the coefficient $\frac{1}{6}$ at n^3 by $\frac{4}{46875}$.

The concept of synchronization is often used as an abstraction of returning control over an automaton when there is no a priori information about its current state, but the structure of the automaton is known. If the automaton is synchronizing, we can apply a synchronizing word to it, and thus it will transit to a known state. If we want to perform the same operation when the current state is known to belong to some subset of states of the automaton, we come to the definition of a synchronizing set. A set $S \subseteq Q$ of states of an automaton A is called *synchronizing* if there exists a word $w \in \Sigma^*$ and a state $q \in Q$ such that the word w maps each state $s \in S$ to the state q. The word w is said to *synchronize* the set S. It follows from the definition that an automaton is synchronizing if and only if the set Q of all its states is synchronizing. Consider the problem SYNC SET of deciding whether a given set S of states of an automaton A is synchronizing.

SYNC SET

Input: An automaton A and a subset S of its states;

Output: Yes if S is a synchronizing set, No otherwise.

The SYNC SET problem is PSPACE-complete [20], even for binary strongly connected automata [26] (an automaton is called *binary* if its alphabet has size two, and *strongly connected* if any state can be mapped to any other state by some word). In [14] it is shown that the SYNC SET problem is solvable in polynomial time for orientable automata if the cyclic order respected by the automaton is provided in the input. The problem of deciding whether the whole set of states of an automaton is synchronizing is also solvable in polynomial time [25]. In [19] the complexity of finding a synchronizing set of maximum size in an automaton is investigated.

While there is a simple cubic bound on the length of a synchronizing word for the whole automaton, there exist examples of automata where the length of a shortest word synchronizing a subset of states is exponential in the number of states [26]. On the other hand, a trivial upper bound $2^n - n - 1$ on the length of a shortest word synchronizing a subset of states in a n-state automaton is known [26]. In [5] Cardoso considers the length of a shortest word synchronizing a subset of states in a synchronizing automaton.

We assume that the reader is familiar with the notions of an NP-complete problem (refer to the book by Sipser [21]), an approximation algorithm and a gap-preserving reduction (for reference, see the book by Vazirani [24]).

Given an automaton A, the *rank* of a word w with respect to A is the number $|\{\delta(s, w) \mid s \in Q\}|$, i.e., the size of the image of Q under the mapping defined in A by w. More generally, the rank of a word w with respect to a subset S of states of A is the number $|\{\delta(s, w) \mid s \in S\}|$. The *rank* of an automaton (resp. of a subset of states) is the minimum among the ranks of all words $w \in \Sigma^*$ with respect to the automaton (resp. to the subset of states).

In this paper we provide various results concerning computational complexity and approximability of the problems related to the subset synchronization in weakly acyclic automata. In Sect. 2 we prove some lower and upper bounds on the length of a shortest word synchronizing a weakly acyclic automaton or, more generally, a subset of its states. In Sect. 3 we investigate the computational complexity of finding such words. In Sect. 4 we give strong inapproximability results for computing the rank of a subset of states in binary weakly acyclic automata. In Sect. 5 we show that several other problems related to recognizing a synchronizing set in a weakly acyclic automaton are hard.

2   Bounds on the Length of Shortest Synchronizing Words

Each synchronizing weakly acyclic automaton is a 0-automaton (i.e., an automaton with exactly one sink state), which gives an upper bound $\frac{n(n-1)}{2}$ on the length of a shortest synchronizing word [18]. The same bound can be deduced from the fact that each weakly acyclic automaton is aperiodic [23]. However, for weakly acyclic automata a more accurate result can be obtained, showing that weakly acyclic automata of rank r behave in a way similar to monotonic automata of rank r (see [1]).

Theorem 1. *Let $A = (Q, \Sigma, \delta)$ be a n-state weakly acyclic automaton, such that there exists a word of rank r with respect to A. Then there exists a word of length at most $n - r$ and rank at most r with respect to A.*

Proof. Observe that the rank of a weakly acyclic automaton equals to the number of sink states in it. The conditions of the theorem imply that A has at most r sink states.

Consider a topological sort $q_1, \ldots, q_n$ of the set Q. Consider sets $S_1, \ldots, S_t$ constructed in the following way. Let $x_i, 1 \leq i \leq t$, be a letter mapping the state in S_{i-1} with the smallest index in the topological sort which is not a sink state to some other state, where $S_i = \{\delta(q, x_i) \mid q \in S_{i-1}\}, 1 \leq i \leq t$, and $S_0 = Q$. Since A has at most r sink states, the word $w = x_1 \ldots x_t$ exists for any $t \leq n - r$ and has rank at most r with respect to A.   □

The following simple example shows that the bound is tight. Consider an automaton $A = (Q, \Sigma, \delta)$ with states $q_1, \ldots, q_n$. Let each letter except some letter x map each state to itself. For the letter x define the transition function $\delta(q_i, x) = q_{i+1}$ for $1 \leq i \leq n - r$ and $\delta(q_i, x) = q_i$ for $n - r + 1 \leq i \leq n$. Obviously, A has rank r and shortest words of rank r with respect to A have length $n - r$.

Theorem 2. *Let S be a synchronizing set of states of size k in a weakly acyclic n-state automaton $A = (Q, \Sigma, \delta)$. Then the length of a shortest word synchronizing S is at most $\frac{k(2n-k-1)}{2}$.*

Proof. Consider a topological sort $q_1, \ldots, q_n$ of the set Q. Let q_s be a state such that all states in S can be mapped to it by some word $w = x_1 \ldots x_t$. We can assume that the images of all words $x_1 \ldots x_j, j \leq t$, are pairwise distinct, otherwise some letter in this word can be removed. Then a letter x_j maps at least one state of the set $\{\delta(q, x_1 \ldots x_{j-1}) \mid q \in S\}$ to some other state. Thus the maximum total number of letters in w sending all states in S to q_s is at most $(n - k) + (n - k + 1) + \ldots + (n - 1) = \frac{k(2n-k-1)}{2}$, since application of each letter of w increases the sum of the indices of reached states by at least one.   □

Consider a binary automaton $A = (Q, \{0, 1\}, \delta)$ with n states $q_1, \ldots, q_{k-1}$, $s_1, \ldots, s_\ell, t$, where $\ell = n - k$. Define $\delta(q_i, 0) = q_i, \delta(q_i, 1) = q_{i+1}$ for $1 \leq i \leq k - 2$, $\delta(q_{k-1}, 1) = s_1$. Define also $\delta(s_i, 0) = s_{i+1}$ for $1 \leq i \leq \ell - 1$, $\delta(s_i, 1) = t$ for $1 \leq i \leq \ell - 1$. Define both transitions for s_ℓ and t as self-loops. Set $S = \{q_1, \ldots, q_{k-1}, s_\ell\}$. The shortest word synchronizing S is $(10^{l-1})^{k-1}$ of length $(k - 1)(n - k)$. The automaton in this example is binary weakly acyclic, and even has rank 2. As was noted by an anonymous reviewer, for alphabet of size $n - 2$, a better lower bound of $\frac{(k-1)(2n-k-2)}{2}$ can be shown.

3   Complexity of Finding Shortest Synchronizing Words

Now we proceed to the computational complexity of some problems, related to finding a shortest synchronizing word for an automaton. Consider first the following problem.

SHORTEST SYNC WORD
Input: A synchronizing automaton A;
Output: The length of a shortest synchronizing word for A.

First, we note that the automaton showing inapproximability of SHORTEST SYNC WORD in the construction of Berlinkov [2] is weakly acyclic.

Proposition 1. *For any* $\gamma > 0$, *the* SHORTEST SYNC WORD *problem for n-state weakly acyclic automata with alphabet of size at most* $n^{1+\gamma}$ *cannot be approximated in polynomial time within a factor of $d \log n$ for any $d < c_{sc}$ unless $P = NP$, where c_{sc} is some constant.*

In Berlinkov's reduction to the binary case, the automaton is no longer weakly acyclic. However, the binary automaton showing NP-hardness of SHORTEST SYNC WORD in Eppstein's construction [7] is weakly acyclic.

Proposition 2. SHORTEST SYNC WORD *is NP-hard for binary weakly acyclic automata.*

Consider now the following more general problem.

SHORTEST SET SYNC WORD
Input: An automaton A and a synchronizing subset S of its states;
Output: The length of a shortest word synchronizing S.

It follows from Theorem 2 that the decision version of this problem (asking whether there exists a word of length at most k synchronizing S) is in NP for weakly acyclic automata, so it is reasonable to investigate its approximability.

Theorem 3. *The* SHORTEST SET SYNC WORD *problem for n-state binary weakly acyclic automata cannot be approximated in polynomial time within a factor of $O(n^{\frac{1}{4}-\epsilon})$ for any $\epsilon > 0$ unless $P = NP$.*

Proof. To prove this theorem, we construct a gap-preserving reduction from the SHORTEST SYNC WORD problem in p-state binary automata, which cannot be approximated in polynomial time within a factor of $O(p^{1-\epsilon})$ for any $\epsilon > 0$ unless $P = NP$ [8]. Let a binary automaton $A = (Q, \{0,1\}, \delta)$ be the input of SHORTEST SYNC WORD. Let $Q = \{q_1, \ldots, q_p\}$. Construct a binary automaton $A' = (Q', \{0,1\}, \delta')$ with the set of states $Q' = \{q_i^{(j)} \mid 1 \leq i \leq p, 1 \leq j \leq p^3 + 1\}$. Define $\delta'(q_i^{(j)}, x) = q_k^{(j+1)}$ for $1 \leq i \leq p$, $1 \leq j \leq p^3$, $x \in \{0,1\}$, where k is such that $q_k = \delta(q_i, x)$. Define $\delta'(q_i^{(p^3+1)}, x) = q_i^{(p^3+1)}$ for $1 \leq i \leq p$ and $x \in \{0,1\}$. Take $S' = \{q_i^{(1)} \mid 1 \leq i \leq p\}$.

Observe that any word synchronizing S' in A' is a synchronizing word for A because of the definition of δ'. In the other direction, as a shortest synchronizing word for a p-state automaton has length at most p^3 [15], a shortest synchronizing word for A also synchronizes S' in A'. Thus, the length of a shortest synchronizing word for A equals to the length of a shortest word synchronizing S' in A', and we get a gap-preserving reduction with gap $O(p^{1-\epsilon}) = O(n^{\frac{1}{4}-\epsilon})$, as A' has $O(p^4)$ states. Finally, it is easy to see that A' is binary weakly acyclic. $\square$

As was kindly reported by an anonymous reviewer, by reducing from the automata in the construction of Gawrychowski and Straszak [8], the inapproximability factor in the theorem can be improved to $O(n^{\frac{1}{3}-\epsilon})$, because the automata in their construction satisfy the Černý conjecture.

4 Computing the Rank of a Subset of States

Assume that we know that the current state of the automaton A belongs to a subset S of its states. Even if it is not possible to synchronize S, it can be reasonable to minimize the size of the set of possible states of A, reducing the uncertainty of the current state as much as possible. One way to do it is to map S to a set S' of smaller size by applying some word to A. Recall that the size of the smallest such set S' is called the rank of S. Consider the following problem of finding the rank of a subset of states in a given automaton.

> SET RANK
> *Input*: An automaton A and a set S of its states;
> *Output*: The rank of S in A.

The rank of an automaton, that is, the rank of the set of its states, can be computed in polynomial time [16]. However, since the automaton in the proof of PSPACE-completeness of SYNC SET in [17] has rank 2 (and thus each subset of states in this automaton has rank either 1 or 2), it follows immediately that there is no polynomial c-approximation algorithm for the SET RANK problem for any $c < 2$ unless P = PSPACE. It is possible to get much stronger bounds, as it is shown by the results of this section.

We shall need the CHROMATIC NUMBER problem. A *proper colouring* of a graph $G = (V, E)$ is a colouring of the set V in such a way that no two adjacent vertices have the same colour. The chromatic number of G, denoted $\chi(G)$, is the minimum number of colours in a proper colouring of G. A set of vertices in a graph is called *independent* if no two vertices in this set are adjacent. A proper colouring of a graph can be also considered as a partition of the set of its vertices into independent sets.

> CHROMATIC NUMBER
> *Input*: A graph G;
> *Output*: The chromatic number of G.

This problem cannot be approximated within a factor of $O(p^{1-\epsilon})$ for any $\epsilon > 0$ unless P = NP, where p is the number of vertices in the graph [27].

Theorem 4. *The SET RANK problem for n-state weakly acyclic automata with alphabet of size $O(\sqrt{n})$ cannot be approximated within a factor of $O(n^{\frac{1}{2}-\epsilon})$ for any $\epsilon > 0$ unless $P = NP$.*

Proof. We shall prove this theorem by constructing a gap-preserving reduction from the CHROMATIC NUMBER problem. Given a graph $G = (V, E)$, $V = \{v_1, v_2, \ldots, v_p\}$, we construct an automaton $A = (Q, \Sigma, \delta)$ as follows. The alphabet Σ consists of letters $\tilde{v}_1, \ldots, \tilde{v}_p$ corresponding to the vertices of G, together with a *switching* letter ν. We use p identical *synchronizing* gadgets $T^{(k)}, 1 \leq k \leq p$, such that each gadget synchronizes a subset of states corresponding to an independent set in G. Gadget $T^{(k)}$ consists of a set $\{s_i^{(k)}, t_i^{(k)} \mid 1 \leq i \leq p\} \cup \{f^{(k)}\}$ of states.

The transition function δ is defined as following. For each gadget $T^{(k)}$, for each $1 \le i \le p$, the state $s_i^{(k)}$ is mapped to $f^{(k)}$ by the letter $\tilde{v}_i$. For each $v_i v_j \in E$ the state $s_i^{(k)}$ is mapped to $t_i^{(k)}$ by the letter $\tilde{v}_j$, and the state $s_j^{(k)}$ is mapped to $t_j^{(k)}$ by the letter $\tilde{v}_i$. All yet undefined transitions corresponding to letters $\tilde{v}_1, \ldots, \tilde{v}_p$ map a state to itself.

It remains to define the transitions corresponding to ν. For each $1 \le k \le p-1$, ν maps $t_i^{(k)}$ and $s_i^{(k)}$ to $s_i^{(k+1)}$, and $f^{(k)}$ to itself. Finally, ν acts on all states in $T^{(p)}$ as a self-loop.

Define $S = \{s_i^{(1)} \mid 1 \le i \le p\}$. We shall prove that the rank of S is equal to the chromatic number of G. Consider a proper colouring of G with the minimum number of colours and let $I_1 \cup \ldots \cup I_{\chi(G)}$ be the partition of G into independent sets defined by this colouring. For each I_j, consider a word w_j obtained by concatenating the letters corresponding to the vertices in I_j in some order. Consider now the word $w_1 \nu w_2 \nu \ldots \nu w_{\chi(G)}$. This word maps the set S to the set $\{f^{(i)} \mid 1 \le i \le \chi(G)\}$, which proves that the rank of S is at most $\chi(G)$.

In the other direction, note that after each reading of ν all states except $f^{(k)}, 1 \le k \le p - 1$, are mapped to the next synchronizing gadget (except the last gadget $T^{(p)}$ which is mapped to itself). By definition of δ, only a subset of states corresponding to an independent set of vertices can be mapped to some particular $f^{(k)}$, and the image of S after reading any word is a subset of the states in some gadget together with some of the states $f^{(k)}, 1 \le k \le p$. Hence, the rank of S is at least $\chi(G)$.

Thus we have a gap-preserving reduction from the CHROMATIC NUMBER problem to the SET RANK problem with gap $\Theta(p^{1-\varepsilon})$ for any $\varepsilon > 0$. It is easy to see that $n = \Theta(p^2)$, A is weakly acyclic and its alphabet has size $O(\sqrt{n})$, which finishes the proof of the theorem. $\square$

Using the classical technique of reducing the alphabet size (see [26]), $O(n^{\frac{1}{3}-\epsilon})$ inapproximability can be proved for binary automata. To prove the same bound for binary weakly acyclic automata, we have to refine the technique of the proof of the previous theorem.

Theorem 5. *The* SET RANK *problem for n-state binary weakly acyclic automata cannot be approximated within a factor of $O(n^{\frac{1}{3}-\epsilon})$ for any $\epsilon > 0$ unless $P = NP$.*

Proof. To prove this theorem we construct a gap-preserving reduction from the CHROMATIC NUMBER problem, extending the proof of the previous theorem.

Given a graph $G = (V, E), V = \{v_1, v_2, \ldots, v_p\}$, we construct an automaton $A = (Q, \{0, 1\}, \delta)$. In our reduction we use two kinds of gadgets: p *synchronizing gadgets* $T^{(k)}$, $1 \le k \le p$, and p *waiting gadgets* $R^{(k)}$, $1 \le k \le p$. Gadget $T^{(k)}$ consists of a set $\{v_{i,j}^{(k)} \mid 1 \le i, j \le p\}$ of states, together with a state $f^{(k)}$, and $R^{(k)}$, $1 \le k \le p$, consists of the set $\{u_{i,j}^{(k)} \mid 1 \le i, j \le p\}$.

For each i, j, k, $1 \leq i, j, k \leq p$, the transition function δ is defined as:

$$\delta(v_{i,j}^{(k)}, 0) = \begin{cases} u_{i,j}^{(k)} & \text{if } i = j, \\ v_{i+1,j}^{(k)} & \text{otherwise} \end{cases}$$

$$\delta(v_{i,j}^{(k)}, 1) = \begin{cases} u_{i,j}^{(k)} & \text{if there is an edge } v_i v_j \in E, \\ v_{i+1,j}^{(k)} & \text{otherwise} \end{cases}$$

Here all $v_{p+1,j}^{(k)}, 1 \leq j \leq p$, coincide with $f^{(k)}$. We set $\delta(u_{i,j}^{(k)}, x) = u_{i+1,j}^{(k)}$ for $x \in \{0, 1\}$, $1 \leq i, k \leq p - 1$, $1 \leq j \leq p$, and $\delta(u_{p,j}^{(k)}, x) = v_{1,j}^{(k+1)}$ for $1 \leq j \leq p$, $1 \leq k \leq p - 1$, $x \in \{0, 1\}$. The states $u_{i,j}^{(p)}$ are sink states: both letters 0 and 1 act on them as self-loops. Finally, we set $S = \{v_{1,j}^{(1)} \mid 1 \leq j \leq p\}$.

The idea of the presented construction is similar to the construction in the proof of Theorem 4. A synchronizing gadget $T^{(k)}$ synchronizes a set $S^{(k)} \subseteq S$ of states corresponding to some independent set in G. All the states corresponding to the vertices adjacent to vertices corresponding to $S^{(k)}$ are mapped to the corresponding waiting gadget $R^{(k)}$, and get to the next synchronizing gadget $T^{(k+1)}$ only after the states of $S^{(k)}$ are synchronized (and thus mapped to $f^{(k)}$). Hence, the minimum size of a partition of V into independent sets equals to the rank of S. We omit the details because of the space limitations. The number of states in A is $O(p^3)$. Thus, we get $O(n^{\frac{1}{3} - c})$ inapproximability. □

Mycielski [13] provides an example of a series of graphs which do not have three pairwise adjacent vertices, but have arbitrary large chromatic number. The reduction in Theorem 5 together with this example can be used to prove the following result showing that there is almost no connection between subset rank and pairwise synchronization of elements in this subset in binary weakly acyclic automata.

Corollary 1. *There exists a pair of a binary weakly acyclic automaton A and a subset S of its states such that for any three states in S at least two of them form a synchronizing subset, but the rank of S is arbitrary large.*

5 Subset Synchronization

In this section, we obtain complexity results for several problems related to subset synchronization in weakly acyclic automata. We adapt Eppstein's construction from [7], which is a powerful and flexible tool for such proofs. We shall need the following NP-complete SAT problem [21].

SAT
Input: A set X of n boolean variables and a set C of m clauses;
Output: Yes if there exists an assignment of values to the variables in X such that all clauses in C are satisfied, No otherwise.

Theorem 6. *The* SYNC SET *problem in binary weakly acyclic automata is NP-complete.*

Proof. Because of the polynomial upper bound on the length of a shortest word synchronizing a subset of states proved in Theorem 2, we can use such word as a certificate. Thus, the problem is in NP.

We reduce the SAT problem. Given X and C, we construct an automaton $A = (Q, \{0, 1\}, \delta)$. For each clause c_j, we construct $n+1$ states $y_i^{(j)}, 1 \leq i \leq n+1$, in Q. We introduce also a state $f \in Q$. The transitions from $y_i^{(j)}$ correspond to the occurrence of x_i in c_j in the following way: for $1 \leq i \leq n$, $1 \leq j \leq m$, $\delta(y_i^{(j)}, a) = f$ if the assignment $x_i = a$, $a \in \{0, 1\}$, satisfies c_j, and $\delta(y_i^{(j)}, a) = y_{i+1}^{(j)}$ otherwise. The transition function δ also maps $y_{n+1}^{(j)}$ to itself for all $1 \leq j \leq m$ and both letters 0 and 1.

Let $S = \{y_1^{(j)} \mid 1 \leq j \leq m\}$. The word $w = a_1 a_2 \ldots a_n$ synchronizes S if a_i is the value of x_i in an assignment satisfying C, and vice versa. Thus, the set is synchronizing if and only if all clauses in C can be satisfied by some assignment of binary values to the variables in X. □

The proof of Theorem 6 can be used to prove the hardness of a special case of the following problem, which is PSPACE-complete in general [11].

> FINITE AUTOMATA INTERSECTION
> *Input*: Automata $A_1, \ldots, A_k$ (with initial and accepting states);
> *Output*: Yes if there is a word which is accepted by all automata, No otherwise.

Theorem 7. FINITE AUTOMATA INTERSECTION *is NP-complete when all automata in the input are binary weakly acyclic.*

Proof. Observe first that if a word which is accepted by all automata exists then a shortest such word w has length at most linear in the total number of states in all automata. Indeed, for each automaton consider a topological sort of the set of its states. Each letter of w maps at least one state in some automaton to some other state, which has larger index in the topological sort of the set of states of this automaton. Thus, the considered problem is in NP.

For the hardness proof, we use the same construction as in Theorem 6. Provided X and C, define A in the same way as in Theorem 6. Define $A_j = (Q_j, \{0, 1\}, \delta_j)$ as following. Take $Q_j = \{y_i^{(j)}, 1 \leq i \leq n+1\} \cup \{f\}$ and δ_j to be the restriction of δ to the set Q_j. Set $y_1^{(j)}$ to be the input state and f to be the only accepting state of A_j. Then there exists a word accepted by automata $A_1, \ldots, A_m$ if and only if all clauses in C are satisfiable by some assignment. □

To obtain the next results, we shall need a modified construction of the automaton from the proof of Theorem 6, as well as some new definitions. A *partial automaton* is a triple (Q, Σ, δ), where Q and Σ are the same as in the definition of a finite deterministic automaton, and δ is a partial transition function (i.e., the transition function which may be undefined for some argument values). Given an instance of the SAT problem, construct a partial automaton $A_{base} = (Q, \{0,1\}, \delta)$ as following. We introduce a state $f \in Q$. For each clause c_j, we construct $n + 1$ states $y_i^{(j)}, 1 \leq i \leq n + 1$, in Q. For each c_j, construct states $z_i^{(j)}$ for $h_i + 1 \leq i \leq n + 1$, where h_i is the smallest index of a variable occurring in c_j. The transitions from $y_i^{(j)}$ correspond to the occurrence of x_i in c_j in the following way: for $1 \leq i \leq n$, $\delta(y_i^{(j)}, a) = z_{i+1}^{(j)}$ if the assignment $x_i = a$, $a \in \{0,1\}$, satisfies c_j, and $\delta(y_i^{(j)}, a) = y_{i+1}^{(j)}$ otherwise. For $x \in \{0,1\}$, we set $\delta(z_i^{(j)}, a) = z_{i+1}^{(j)}$ for $h_i + 1 \leq i \leq n$, $1 \leq j \leq m$, $a \in \{0,1\}$. The transition function δ also maps $z_{n+1}^{(j)}, 1 \leq j \leq m$, and f to f for both letters 0 and 1.

A word w is said to *carefully synchronize* a partial automaton A if it maps all its states to the same state q, and each mapping corresponding to a prefix of w is defined for each state. The automaton A is then called *carefully synchronizing*. We use A_{base} to prove the hardness of the following problem.

‖ CAREFUL SYNCHRONIZATION
‖ *Input*: A partial automaton A;
‖ *Output*: Yes if A is carefully synchronizing, No otherwise.

For binary automata, CAREFUL SYNCHRONIZATION is PSPACE-complete [12]. We call a partial automaton *aperiodic* if for any word $w \in \Sigma^*$ and any state $q \in Q$ there exists k such that either $\delta(q, w^k)$ is undefined, or $\delta(q, w^k) = \delta(q, w^{k+1})$.

Theorem 8. CAREFUL SYNCHRONIZATION *is NP-hard for aperiodic partial automata over a three-letter alphabet.*

Proof. We reduce the SAT problem. Given X and C, we first construct A_{base}. Then we add an additional letter r to the alphabet of A_{base} and introduce m new states $s^{(m)}$. For $1 \leq i \leq n, 1 \leq j \leq m$, we define $\delta(s^{(j)}, r) = y_1^{(j)}$, $\delta(y_i^{(j)}, r) = y_1^{(j)}$, $\delta(z_i^{(j)}, r) = y_1^{(j)}$, $\delta(f, r) = f$. All other transitions are left undefined. Let us call the constructed automaton A.

The automaton A is carefully synchronizing if and only if all clauses in C can be satisfied by some assignment of binary values to the variables in X. Moreover, the word $w = rw_1w_2\ldots w_n0$, is carefully synchronizing if w_i is the value of x_i in such an assignment.

Indeed, note that the first letter of w is necessarily r, as it is the only letter defined for all the states. Moreover, each word starting with r maps Q to a subset of $\{y_i^{(j)}, z_i^{(j)} \mid 1 \leq j \leq m + 1\} \cup \{f\}$. The only way for a word to map all states to f is to map them first to the set $\{z_{n+1}^{(j)} \mid 1 \leq j \leq m\}$, because there are no transitions defined from any $y_{n+1}^{(j)}$, except the transitions defined by r. But this exactly means that there exists an assignment satisfying C.

The constructed automaton is aperiodic, because each cycle which is not a self-loop contains exactly one letter r.   □

By using the trick from [9] of adding one new letter mapping the state f to all states and undefined for all other states, and considering the transition matrices of the obtained non-deterministic automaton, the complexity of the following problem can be obtained from Theorem 8.

> POSITIVE MATRIX
> *Input*: A set $M_1, \ldots, M_k$ of $n \times n$ binary matrices;
> *Output*: Yes if there exists a sequence $M_{i_1} \times \ldots \times M_{i_k}$ of multiplications (possibly with repetitions) providing a matrix with all elements equal to 1, No otherwise.

Corollary 2. POSITIVE MATRIX *is NP-hard for two upper-triangular and two lower-triangular matrices.*

Finally, we show the hardness of the following problem (PSPACE-complete in general [3]).

> SUBSET REACHABILITY
> *Input*: An automaton $A = (Q, \Sigma, \delta)$ and a subset S of its states;
> *Output*: Yes if there exists a word w such that $\{\delta(q, w) \mid q \in Q\} = S$, No otherwise.

Theorem 9. SUBSET REACHABILITY *is NP-complete for weakly acyclic automata.*

Proof. Consider a topological sort of Q. Let w be a shortest word mapping Q to some reachable set of states. Then each letter of w maps at least one state to a state with a larger index in the topological sort. Thus w has length $O(|Q|^2)$, since the maximum total number of such mappings is $(|Q|-1) + (|Q|-2) + \ldots + 1 + 0$. Thus, the considered problem is in NP.

For the NP-hardness proof, we again reduce the SAT problem. Given an instance of SAT, construct A_{base} first. Next, add a transition $\delta(y_{n+1}^{(j)}, a) = f$ for $1 \leq j \leq m$, $a \in \{0, 1\}$, resulting in a deterministic automaton A.

Similar to the proof of Theorem 8, C is satisfiable if and only if the set $\{z_j^{(n+1)} \mid 1 \leq j \leq m\} \cup \{f\}$ is reachable in A.   □

Acknowledgments. We would like to thank Vladimir Gusev and Ilia Fridman for very useful discussions, and Mikhail V. Volkov and anonymous reviewers for their great contribution to the improvement of the paper.

References

1. Ananichev, D., Volkov, M.: Synchronizing monotonic automata. Theor. Comput. Sci. **327**(3), 225–239 (2004)
2. Berlinkov, M.V.: On two algorithmic problems about synchronizing automata. In: Shur, A.M., Volkov, M.V. (eds.) DLT 2014. LNCS, vol. 8633, pp. 61–67. Springer, Cham (2014). doi:10.1007/978-3-319-09698-8_6
3. Bondar, E.A., Volkov, M.V.: Completely reachable automata. In: Câmpeanu, C., Manea, F., Shallit, J. (eds.) DCFS 2016. LNCS, vol. 9777, pp. 1–17. Springer, Cham (2016). doi:10.1007/978-3-319-41114-9_1

4. Brzozowski, J., Fich, F.E.: Languages of R-trivial monoids. J. Comput. Syst. Sci. **20**(1), 32–49 (1980)
5. Cardoso, A.: The Černý Conjecture and Other Synchronization Problems. Ph.D. thesis. University of Porto, Portugal (2014)
6. Cormen, T.H., Leiserson, C.E., Rivest, R.L., Stein, C.: Introduction to Algorithms, 3rd edn. MIT Press (2009)
7. Eppstein, D.: Reset sequences for monotonic automata. SIAM J. Comput. **19**(3), 500–510 (1990)
8. Gawrychowski, P., Straszak, D.: Strong inapproximability of the shortest reset word. In: Italiano, G.F., Pighizzini, G., Sannella, D.T. (eds.) MFCS 2015. LNCS, vol. 9234, pp. 243–255. Springer, Heidelberg (2015). doi:10.1007/978-3-662-48057-1_19
9. Gerencsér, B., Gusev, V.V., Jungers, R.M.: Primitive sets of nonnegative matrices and synchronizing automata. CoRR abs/1602.07556 (2016)
10. Jirásková, G., Masopust, T.: On the state and computational complexity of the reverse of acyclic minimal dfas. In: Moreira, N., Reis, R. (eds.) CIAA 2012. LNCS, vol. 7381, pp. 229–239. Springer, Heidelberg (2012). doi:10.1007/978-3-642-31606-7_20
11. Kozen, D.: Lower bounds for natural proof systems. In: Proceedings of the 18th Annual Symposium on Foundations of Computer Science, pp. 254–266 (1977)
12. Martyugin, P.V.: Complexity of problems concerning carefully synchronizing words for PFA and directing words for NFA. In: Ablayev, F., Mayr, E.W. (eds.) CSR 2010. LNCS, vol. 6072, pp. 288–302. Springer, Heidelberg (2010). doi:10.1007/978-3-642-13182-0_27
13. Mycielski, J.: Sur le coloriage des graphs. Colloquium Mathematicae **3**(2), 161–162 (1955)
14. Natarajan, B.K.: An algorithmic approach to the automated design of parts orienters. In: Proceedings of the 27th Annual Symposium on Foundations of Computer Science, pp. 132–142 (1986)
15. Pin, J.É.: On two combinatorial problems arising from automata theory. Ann. Discrete Math. **17**, 535–548 (1983)
16. Rystsov, I.K.: Rank of a finite automaton. Cybern. Syst. Anal. **28**(3), 323–328 (1992)
17. Rystsov, I.K.: Polynomial complete problems in automata theory. Inform. Process. Lett. **16**(3), 147–151 (1983)
18. Rystsov, I.K.: Reset words for commutative and solvable automata. Theor. Comput. Sci. **172**(1), 273–279 (1997)
19. Ryzhikov, A.: Approximating the maximum number of synchronizing states in automata. CoRR abs/1608.00889 (2016)
20. Sandberg, S.: Homing and synchronizing sequences. In: Broy, M., Jonsson, B., Katoen, J.-P., Leucker, M., Pretschner, A. (eds.) Model-Based Testing of Reactive Systems. LNCS, vol. 3472, pp. 5–33. Springer, Heidelberg (2005). doi:10.1007/11498490_2
21. Sipser, M.: Introduction to the Theory of Computation. Cengage Learning, 3rd edn. (2012)
22. Szykuła, M.: Improving the upper bound the length of the shortest reset words. CoRR abs/1702.05455 (2017)
23. Trahtman, A.N.: The Cerný conjecture for aperiodic automata. Discrete Math. Theor. Comput. Sci. **9**(2), 3–10 (2007)
24. Vazirani, V.V.: Approximation Algorithms. Springer, Heidelberg (2001)

25. Volkov, M.V.: Synchronizing automata and the Černý conjecture. In: Martín-Vide, C., Otto, F., Fernau, H. (eds.) LATA 2008. LNCS, vol. 5196, pp. 11–27. Springer, Heidelberg (2008). doi:10.1007/978-3-540-88282-4_4
26. Vorel, V.: Subset synchronization and careful synchronization of binary finite automata. Int. J. Found. Comput. Sci. **27**(5), 557–578 (2016)
27. Zuckerman, D.: Linear degree extractors and the inapproximability of max clique and chromatic number. Theory Comput. **3**(6), 103–128 (2007)

Syntactic Complexity of Bifix-Free Languages

Marek Szykuła[1]([✉]) and John Wittnebel[2]

[1] Institute of Computer Science, University of Wrocław,
Joliot-Curie 15, 50-383 Wrocław, Poland
msz@cs.uni.wroc.pl
[2] David R. Cheriton School of Computer Science,
University of Waterloo, Waterloo, ON N2L 3G1, Canada
jkwittnebel@hotmail.com

Abstract. We study the properties of syntactic monoids of bifix-free regular languages. In particular, we solve an open problem concerning syntactic complexity: We prove that the cardinality of the syntactic semigroup of a bifix-free language with state complexity n is at most $(n-1)^{n-3} + (n-2)^{n-3} + (n-3)2^{n-3}$ for $n \geqslant 6$. The main proof uses a large construction with the method of injective function. Since this bound is known to be reachable, and the values for $n \leqslant 5$ are known, this completely settles the problem. We also prove that $(n-2)^{n-3} + (n-3)2^{n-3} - 1$ is the minimal size of the alphabet required to meet the bound for $n \geqslant 6$. Finally, we show that the largest transition semigroups of minimal DFAs which recognize bifix-free languages are unique up to renaming the states.

1 Introduction

The *syntactic complexity* [11] $\sigma(L)$ of a regular language L is defined as the size of its syntactic semigroup [17]. It is known that this semigroup is isomorphic to the transition semigroup of the quotient automaton $\mathcal{D}$ and of a minimal deterministic finite automaton accepting the language. The number n of states of $\mathcal{D}$ is the *state complexity* of the language [19], and it is the same as the *quotient complexity* [2] (number of left quotients) of the language. The *syntactic complexity of a class* of regular languages is the maximal syntactic complexity of languages in that class expressed as a function of the quotient complexity n.

Syntactic complexity is related to the Myhill equivalence relation [16], and it counts the number of classes of non-empty words in a regular language which act distinctly. It provides a natural bound on the time and space complexity of algorithms working on the transition semigroup. For example, a simple algorithm checking whether a language is *star-free* just enumerates all transformations and verifies whether none of them contains a non-trivial cycle [15].

Syntactic complexity does not refine state complexity, but used as an additional measure it can distinguish particular subclasses of regular languages from the class of all regular languages, whereas state complexity alone cannot.

M. Szykuła—Supported in part by the National Science Centre, Poland under project number 2014/15/B/ST6/00615.

A. Carayol and C. Nicaud (Eds.): CIAA 2017, LNCS 10329, pp. 201–212, 2017.
DOI: 10.1007/978-3-319-60134-2_17

For example, the state complexity of basic operations in the class of star-free languages is the same as in the class of all regular languages (except the reversal, where the tight upper bound is $2^{n-1} - 1$ see [8]).

Finally, the largest transition semigroups play an important role in the study of *most complex* languages [3] in a given subclass. These are languages that meet all the upper bounds on the state complexities of Boolean operations, product, star, and reversal, and also have maximal syntactic semigroups and most complex atoms [10]. In particular, the results from this paper enabled the study of most complex bifix-free languages [12].

A language is *prefix-free* if no word in the language is a proper prefix of another word in the language. Similarly, a language is *suffix-free* if there is no word that is a proper suffix of another word in the language. A language is *bifix-free* if it is both prefix-free and suffix-free. Prefix-, suffix-, and bifix-free languages are important classes of codes, which have numerous applications in such fields as cryptography and data compression. Codes have been studied extensively; see [1] for example.

Syntactic complexity has been studied for a number of subclasses of regular languages (e.g., [4–6,8,13,14]). For bifix-free languages, the lower bound $(n-1)^{n-3} + (n-2)^{n-3} + (n-3)2^{n-3}$ for the syntactic complexity for $n \geqslant 6$ was established in [6]. The values for $n \leqslant 5$ were also determined.

The problem of establishing tight upper bound on syntactic complexity can be quite challenging, depending on the particular subclass. For example, it is easy for prefix-free languages and right ideals, while much more difficult for suffix-free languages and left ideals. The case of bifix-free languages studied in this paper requires an even more involved proof, as the structure of maximal transition semigroup is more complicated.

Our main contributions are as follows:

1. We prove that $(n-1)^{n-3} + (n-2)^{n-3} + (n-3)2^{n-3}$ is also an upper bound for syntactic complexity for $n \geqslant 8$. To do this, we apply the general method of injective function (cf. [7,9]). The construction here is much more involved than in the previous cases, and uses a number of tricks for ensuring injectivity.
2. We prove that the transition semigroup meeting this bound is unique for every $n \geqslant 8$.
3. We refine the witness DFA meeting the bound by reducing the size of the alphabet to $(n-2)^{n-3} + (n-3)2^{n-3} - 1$, and we show that it cannot be any smaller.
4. Using a dedicated algorithm, we verify by computation that two semigroups $\mathbf{W}_{\text{bf}}^{\leqslant 5}$ and $\mathbf{W}_{\text{bf}}^{\geqslant 6}$ (defined below) are the unique largest transition semigroups of a minimal DFA of a bifix-free language, respectively for $n = 5$ and $n = 6, 7$ (whereas they coincide for $n = 3, 4$).

In summary, for every n we have determined the syntactic complexity, the unique largest semigroups, and the minimal sizes of the alphabets required; this completely solves the problem for bifix-free languages.

The full version of this paper is available at [18].

2   Preliminaries

Let Σ be a non-empty finite alphabet, and let $L \subseteq \Sigma^*$ be a language. If $w \in \Sigma^*$ is a word, $L.w$ denotes the *left quotient* or simply quotient of L by w, which is defined by $L.w = \{u \mid wu \in L\}$. The number of quotients of L is its *quotient complexity* [2] $\kappa(L)$. From the Myhill-Nerode Theorem, a language is regular if and only if the set of all quotients of the language is finite. We denote the set of quotients of regular L by $K = \{K_0, \ldots, K_{n-1}\}$, where $K_0 = L = L.\varepsilon$ by convention.

A *deterministic finite automaton (DFA)* is a tuple $\mathcal{D} = (Q, \Sigma, \delta, q_0, F)$, where Q is a finite non-empty set of *states*, Σ is a finite non-empty *alphabet*, $\delta \colon Q \times \Sigma \to Q$ is the *transition function*, $q_0 \in Q$ is the *initial* state, and $F \subseteq Q$ is the set of *final* states. We extend δ to a function $\delta \colon Q \times \Sigma^* \to Q$ as usual.

The *quotient* DFA of a regular language L with n quotients is defined by $\mathcal{D} = (K, \Sigma, \delta_\mathcal{D}, K_0, F_\mathcal{D})$, where $\delta_\mathcal{D}(K_i, w) = K_j$ if and only if $K_i.w = K_j$, and $F_\mathcal{D} = \{K_i \mid \varepsilon \in K_i\}$. Without loss of generality, we assume that $Q = \{0, \ldots, n-1\}$. Then $\mathcal{D} = (Q, \Sigma, \delta, 0, F)$, where $\delta(i, w) = j$ if $\delta_\mathcal{D}(K_i, w) = K_j$, and F is the set of subscripts of quotients in $F_\mathcal{D}$. A state $q \in Q$ is *empty* if its quotient K_q is empty. The quotient DFA of L is isomorphic to each complete minimal DFA of L. The number of states in the quotient DFA of L (the quotient complexity of L) is therefore equal to the state complexity of L.

In any DFA $\mathcal{D}$, each letter $a \in \Sigma$ induces a transformation on the set Q of n states. We let $\mathcal{T}_n$ denote the set of all n^n transformations of Q; then $\mathcal{T}_n$ is a monoid under composition. The *image* of $q \in Q$ under transformation t is denoted by qt, and the *image* of a subset $S \subseteq Q$ is $St = \{qt \mid q \in S\}$. If $s, t \in \mathcal{T}_n$ are transformations, their composition is denoted by st and defined by $q(st) = (qs)t$. The identity transformation is denoted by $\mathbf{1}$, and we have $q\mathbf{1} = q$ for all $q \in Q$. By $(S \to q)$, where $S \subseteq Q$ and $q \in Q$, we denote a *semiconstant* transformation that maps all the states from S to q and behaves as the identity function for the states in $Q \setminus S$. A *constant* transformation is the semiconstant transformation $(Q \to q)$, where $q \in Q$. A *unitary* transformation is $(\{p\} \to q)$, for some distinct $p, q \in Q$; this is denoted by $(p \to q)$ for simplicity.

The *transition semigroup* of $\mathcal{D}$ is the semigroup of all transformations generated by the transformations induced by Σ. Since the transition semigroup of a minimal DFA of a language L is isomorphic to the syntactic semigroup of L [17], the syntactic complexity of L is equal to the cardinality of the transition semigroup of $\mathcal{D}$.

The *underlying digraph* of a transformation $t \in \mathcal{T}_n$ is the digraph (Q, E), where $E = \{(q, qt) \mid q \in Q\}$. We identify a transformation with its underlying digraph and use usual graph terminology for transformations: The *in-degree* of a state $q \in Q$ is the cardinality $|\{p \in Q \mid pt = q\}|$. A *cycle* in t is a cycle in its underlying digraph of length at least 2. A *fixed point* in t is a self-loop in its underlying digraph. The *orbit* of a state $q \in Q$ in t is a connected component containing q in its underlying digraph, that is, the set $\{p \in Q \mid pt^i = qt^j \text{ for some } i, j \geqslant 0\}$. Note that every orbit contains either exactly one cycle or one fixed point. The *distance* in t from a state $p \in Q$ to a state $q \in Q$ is the length of the path in the underlying digraph of t from p to q, that is, $\min\{i \in \mathbb{N} \mid pt^i = q\}$, and is undefined if no such path exists. If a state q does not lie in a cycle, then the *tree of q* is the underlying digraph of t restricted to the states p such that there is a path from p to q.

2.1 Bifix-Free Languages and Semigroups

Let $\mathcal{D}_n = (Q, \Sigma, \delta, 0, F)$, where $Q = \{0, \ldots, n-1\}$, be a minimal DFA accepting a bifix-free language L, and let $T(\mathcal{D}_n)$ be its transition semigroup. We also define $Q_M = \{1, \ldots, n-3\}$ (the set of the "middle" non-special states).

The following properties of bifix-free languages, slightly adapted to our terminology, are well known [6]:

Lemma 1. *A minimal DFA* $\mathcal{D}_n = (Q, \Sigma, \delta, 0, F)$ *of a bifix-free languages* L *satisfies the following properties:*

1. *There is an empty state, which is* $n-1$ *by convention.*
2. *There exists exactly one final quotient, which is* $\{\varepsilon\}$, *and whose state is* $n-2$ *by convention, so* $F = \{n-2\}$.
3. *For* $u, v \in \Sigma^+$, *if* $L.v \neq \emptyset$, *then* $L.v \neq L.uv$.
4. *In the underlying digraph of every transformation of* $T(\mathcal{D}_n)$, *there is a path starting at 0 and ending at $n-1$.*

The items (1) and (2) are sufficient and necessary for prefix-free languages, while (3) and (4) follow from the properties of suffix-free languages. Following [9], we say that an (unordered) pair $\{p, q\}$ of distinct states in Q_M is *colliding* (or p *collides* with q) in $T(\mathcal{D}_n)$ if there is a transformation $t \in T(\mathcal{D}_n)$ such that $0t = p$ and $rt = q$ for some $r \in Q_M$. A pair of states is *focused* by a transformation $u \in \mathcal{T}(n)$ if u maps both states of the pair to a single state $r \in Q_M \cup \{n-2\}$. We then say that $\{p, q\}$ is *focused to the state* r. By Lemma 1(3), it follows that if $\{p, q\}$ is colliding in $T(\mathcal{D}_n)$, then there is no transformation $u \in T(\mathcal{D}_n)$ that focuses $\{p, q\}$. Hence, in the case of bifix-free languages, colliding states can be mapped to a single state only if the state is $n-1$. In contrast with suffix-free languages, we do not consider the pairs from $Q_M \times \{n-2\}$ being colliding, as they cannot be focused.

For $n \geqslant 2$ we define the set of transformations

$$\mathbf{B}_{\mathrm{bf}}(n) = \{t \in \mathcal{T}_n \mid 0 \notin Qt, \ (n-1)t = n-1, \ (n-2)t = n-1, \text{ and for all } j \geqslant 1,$$
$$0t^j = n-1 \text{ or } 0t^j \neq qt^j \ \forall q, \ 0 < q < n-1\}.$$

In [6] it was shown that the transition semigroup $T(\mathcal{D}_n)$ of a minimal DFA of a bifix-free language must be contained in $\mathbf{B}_{\mathrm{bf}}(n)$. It contains all transformations t which fix $n-1$, map $n-2$ to $n-1$, and do not focus any pair which is colliding from t.

Since $\mathbf{B}_{\mathrm{bf}}(n)$ is not a semigroup, no transition semigroup of a minimal DFA of a bifix-free language can contain all transformations from $\mathbf{B}_{\mathrm{bf}}(n)$. Therefore, its cardinality is not a tight upper bound on the syntactic complexity of bifix-free languages. A lower bound on the syntactic complexity was established in [6].

We study the following two semigroups that play an important role for bifix-free languages.

Semigroup $\mathbf{W}_{bf}^{\geq 6}(n)$. For $n \geqslant 3$ we define the semigroup:

$$\mathbf{W}_{bf}^{\geq 6}(n) = \{t \in \mathbf{B}_{bf}(n) \mid 0t \in \{n-2, n-1\}, \text{ or}$$
$$0t \in Q_M \text{ and } qt \in \{n-2, n-1\} \text{ for all } q \in Q_M\}.$$

The following remark summarizes the transformations of $\mathbf{W}_{bf}^{\geq 6}(n)$ (illustrated in Fig. 1):

Remark 2. $\mathbf{W}_{bf}^{\geq 6}(n)$ contains all transformations that:

1. map $\{0, n-2, n-1\}$ to $n-1$, and Q_M into $Q \setminus \{0\}$, or
2. map 0 to $n-2$, $\{n-2, n-1\}$ to $n-1$, and Q_M into $Q \setminus \{0, n-2\}$, or
3. map 0 to a state $q \in Q_M$, and Q_M into $\{n-2, n-1\}$.   ∎

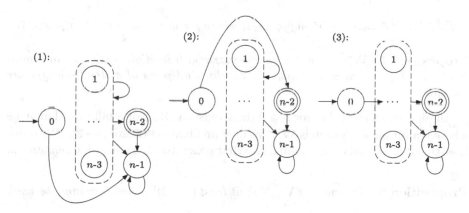

Fig. 1. The three types of transformations in $\mathbf{W}_{bf}^{\geq 6}(n)$ from Remark 2.

The cardinality of $\mathbf{W}_{bf}^{\geq 6}(n)$ is $(n-1)^{n-3} + (n-2)^{n-3} + (n-3)2^{n-3}$.

Proposition 3. $\mathbf{W}_{bf}^{\geq 6}(n)$ *is the unique maximal transition semigroup of a minimal DFA $\mathcal{D}_n$ of a bifix-free language in which there are no colliding pairs of states.*

In [6] it was shown that for $n \geqslant 5$, there exists a witness DFA of a bifix-free language whose transition semigroup is $\mathbf{W}_{bf}^{\geq 6}(n)$ over an alphabet of size $(n-2)^{n-3} + (n-3)2^{n-3} + 2$ (and 18 if $n = 5$). Now we slightly refine the witness from [6, Proposition 31] by reducing the size of the alphabet to $(n-2)^{n-3} + (n-3)2^{n-3} - 1$, and then we show that it cannot be any smaller.

Definition 4 (Bifix-free witness). *For $n \geqslant 4$, let $\mathcal{W}(n) = (Q, \Sigma, \delta, 0, \{n-2\})$, where $Q = \{0, \ldots, n-1\}$ and Σ contains the following letters:*

1. b_i, for $1 \leqslant i \leqslant n - 3$, inducing the transformations $(0 \to n - 1)(i \to n - 2)$ $(n - 2 \to n - 1)$,
2. c_i, for every transformation of type (2) from Remark 2 that is different from $(0 \to n - 2)(Q_M \to n - 1)(n - 2 \to n - 1)$,
3. d_i, for every transformation of type (3) from Remark 2 that is different from $(0 \to q)(Q_M \to n - 1)(n - 2 \to n - 1)$ for some state $q \in Q_M$.

Altogether, we have $|\Sigma| = (n - 3) + ((n - 2)^{n-3} - 1) + (n - 3)(2^{n-3} - 1) = (n - 2)^{n-3} + (n-3)2^{n-3} - 1$. For $n = 4$ three letters suffice, since the transformation of b_1 is induced by $c_i d_i$, where $c_i \colon (0 \to 2)(2 \to 3)$ and $d_i \colon (0 \to 1)(1 \to 2)(2 \to 3)$.

Proposition 5. The transition semigroup of $\mathcal{W}(n)$ is $\mathbf{W}_{\mathrm{bf}}^{\geqslant 6}(n)$.

Proposition 6. For $n \geqslant 5$, at least $(n - 2)^{n-3} + (n - 3)2^{n-3} - 1$ generators are necessary to generate $\mathbf{W}_{\mathrm{bf}}^{\geqslant 6}(n)$.

Semigroup $\mathbf{W}_{\mathrm{bf}}^{\leqslant 5}(n)$. For $n \geqslant 3$ we define the semigroup

$$\mathbf{W}_{\mathrm{bf}}^{\leqslant 5}(n) = \{t \in \mathbf{B}_{\mathrm{bf}}(n) \mid \text{for all } p, q \in Q_M \text{ where } p \neq q, pt = qt = n - 1 \text{ or } pt \neq qt\}.$$

Proposition 7. $\mathbf{W}_{\mathrm{bf}}^{\leqslant 5}(n)$ is the unique maximal transition semigroup of a minimal DFA $\mathcal{D}_n$ of a bifix-free language in which all pairs of states from Q_M are colliding.

In [6] it was shown that for $n \geqslant 2$ there exists a DFA for a bifix-free language whose transition semigroup is $\mathbf{W}_{\mathrm{bf}}^{\leqslant 5}(n)$ over an alphabet of size $(n-2)!$. We prove that this is an alphabet of minimal size that generates this transition semigroup.

Proposition 8. To generate $\mathbf{W}_{\mathrm{bf}}^{\leqslant 5}(n)$ at least $(n - 2)!$ generators must be used.

3   Upper Bound on Syntactic Complexity

Our main result shows that the lower bound $(n-1)^{n-3} + (n-2)^{n-3} + (n-3)2^{n-3}$ on the syntactic complexity of bifix-free languages is also an upper bound for $n \geqslant 8$.

We consider a minimal DFA $\mathcal{D}_n = (Q, \Sigma, \delta, 0, \{n - 2\})$, where $Q = \{0, \ldots, n - 1\}$ and whose empty state is $n - 1$, of an arbitrary bifix-free language. Let $T(\mathcal{D}_n)$ be the transition semigroup of $\mathcal{D}_n$. We will show that $T(\mathcal{D}_n)$ is not larger than $\mathbf{W}_{\mathrm{bf}}^{\geqslant 6}(n)$.

Note that the semigroups $T(\mathcal{D}_n)$ and $\mathbf{W}_{\mathrm{bf}}^{\geqslant 6}(n)$ share the set Q, and in both of them 0, $n - 2$, and $n - 1$ play the role of the initial, final, and empty state, respectively. When we say that a pair of states from Q is colliding we always mean that it is colliding in $T(\mathcal{D}_n)$.

First, we state the following lemma, which generalizes some arguments that we use frequently in the proof of the main theorem.

Lemma 9. *Let* $t, \hat{t} \in T(\mathcal{D}_n)$ *and* $s \in \mathbf{W}_{\mathrm{bf}}^{\geqslant 6}(n)$ *be transformations. Suppose that:*

1. *All states from* Q_M *whose mapping is different in* t *and* s *belong to* C, *where* C *is either an orbit in* s *or is the tree of a state in* s.
2. *All states from* Q_M *whose mapping is different in* $\hat{t}$ *and* s *belong to* $\hat{C}$, *where* $\hat{C}$ *is either an orbit in* s *or is the tree of a state in* s.
3. *The transformation* $s^i t^j$, *for some* $i, j \geqslant 0$, *focuses a colliding pair whose states are in* C.

Then either $C \subseteq \hat{C}$ *or* $\hat{C} \subseteq C$. *In particular, if* C *and* $\hat{C}$ *are both orbits or both trees rooted in a state mapped by* s *to* $n - 1$, *then* $C = \hat{C}$.

The following is our main theorem:

Theorem 10. *For* $n \geqslant 8$, *the syntactic complexity of the class of bifix-free languages with* n *quotients is* $(n - 1)^{n-3} + (n - 2)^{n-3} + (n - 3)2^{n-3}$.

Proof (Idea). We construct an injective mapping $\varphi \colon T(\mathcal{D}_n) \to \mathbf{W}_{\mathrm{bf}}^{\geqslant 6}(n)$. Since φ will be injective, this will prove that $|T(\mathcal{D}_n)| \leqslant |\mathbf{W}_{\mathrm{bf}}^{\geqslant 6}(n)| = (n - 1)^{n-3} + (n - 2)^{n-3} + (n - 3)2^{n-3}$.

The mapping φ is defined by 23 (sub)cases covering all possibilities for a transformation $t \in T(\mathcal{D}_n)$. Let t denote a transformation of $T(\mathcal{D}_n)$, and s denote the assigned transformation $\varphi(t)$.

The whole proof is split into three Supercases, depending on t. Supercase 2 and Supercase 3 are split into a number of cases, and the cases are split into subcases. To show injectivity, in every (sub)case we prove *external injectivity*, which is that there is no other transformation $\hat{t}$ that fits to one of the previous (sub)cases and results in the same s, and we prove *internal injectivity*, which is that no other transformation $\hat{t}$ that fits to the same (sub)case results in the same s. We use there various kinds of arguments of analysis orbits, cycles, longest paths, and focused states. Often, we use Lemma 9 to argue that if another $\hat{t}$ yields the same s (so φ is not injective) and s is obtained by a local modification of t or $\hat{t}$, then the difference between t and $\hat{t}$ is also only local – restricted to the same orbit or tree. All states and variables related to $\hat{t}$ are always marked by a hat.

Supercase 1: $t \in \mathbf{W}_{\mathrm{bf}}^{\geqslant 6}(n)$.
We take $s = t$. The internal and external injectivity are obvious. ◁
For all the remaining cases let $p = 0t$. Note that all t with $p \in \{n - 2, n - 1\}$ fit in Supercase 1. Let $k \geqslant 0$ be a maximal integer such that $pt^k \notin \{n - 2, n - 1\}$. Then pt^{k+1} is either $n - 1$ or $n - 2$, and we have two supercases covering these situations.

Supercase 2: $t \notin \mathbf{W}_{\mathrm{bf}}^{\geqslant 6}(n)$ and $pt^{k+1} = n - 1$.
Here we have the chain

$$0 \xrightarrow{t} p \xrightarrow{t} pt \xrightarrow{t} \cdots \xrightarrow{t} pt^k \xrightarrow{t} n - 1.$$

Within this supercase, we always assign transformations s focusing a colliding pair, and this will make them different from the transformations of Supercase 1.

Also, we use only transformations s of type 1 from Remark 2, that is, we will always have $0s = n - 1$.

As an example, we show the full proof of the first case:

Case 2.1: t has a cycle.

Let r be the minimal state among the states that appear in cycles of t, that is,

$$r = \min\{q \in Q \mid q \text{ is in a cycle of } t\}.$$

Let s be the transformation illustrated in Fig. 2 and defined by:

$$0s = n - 1, \; ps = r,$$
$$(pt^i)s = pt^{i-1} \text{ for } 1 \leqslant i \leqslant k,$$
$$qs = qt \text{ for the other states } q \in Q.$$

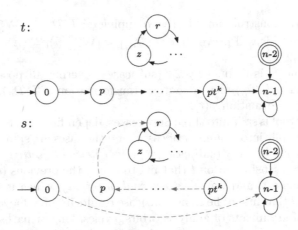

Fig. 2. Case 2.1.

Let z be the state from the cycle of t such that $zt = r$. We observe the following properties:

(a) Pair $\{p, z\}$ is a colliding pair focused by s to state r in the cycle, which is the smallest state of all states in cycles. This is the only colliding pair which is focused to a state in a cycle.

Proof: Note that p collides with any state in a cycle of t, in particular, with z. The property follows because s differs from t only in the mapping of states pt^i ($0 \leqslant i \leqslant k$) and 0, and the only state mapped to a cycle is p.   ◁

(b) All states from Q_M whose mapping is different in t and s belong to the same orbit in s of a cycle. Hence, all colliding pairs that are focused by s consist only of states from this orbit.

(c) s has a cycle.

(d) For each i with $1 \leqslant i < k$, there is precisely one state q colliding with pt^{i-1} and mapped by s to pt^i, and that state is $q = pt^{i+1}$.

Proof: Clearly $q = pt^{i+1}$ satisfies this condition. Suppose that $q \neq pt^{i+1}$. Since pt^{i+1} is the only state mapped to pt^i by s and not by t, it follows that $qt = qs = pt^i$. So q and pt^{i-1} are focused to pt^i by t; since they collide, this is a contradiction.   ◁

External injectivity: By (a), $\{p, z\}$ is a colliding pair focused by s, therefore t and s cannot be both present in T_n and so s was not used in Supercase 1.   ◁

Internal injectivity: Let $\hat{t}$ be any transformation that fits in this case and results in the same s; we will show that $\hat{t} = t$. From (a), there is the unique colliding pair $\{p, z\}$ focused to a state in a cycle, hence $\{\hat{p}, \hat{z}\} = \{p, z\}$. Moreover, p and $\hat{p}$ are not in this cycle, so $\hat{p} = p$ and $\hat{z} = z$, which means that $0t = 0\hat{t} = p$. Since there is no state $q \neq 0$ such that $qt = p$, the only state mapped to p by s is pt, hence $p\hat{t} = pt$. From (d) for $i = 1, \ldots, k-1$, state pt^{i+1} is uniquely determined, hence $p\hat{t}^{i+1} = pt^{i+1}$. Finally, for $i = k$ there is no state colliding with pt^{k-1} and mapped to pt^k, hence $p\hat{t}^{k+1} = pt^{k+1} = n - 1$. Since the other transitions in s are defined exactly as in t and $\hat{t}$, we have $\hat{t} = t$.   ◁

Then we have four other cases, which together cover all possibilities for t.

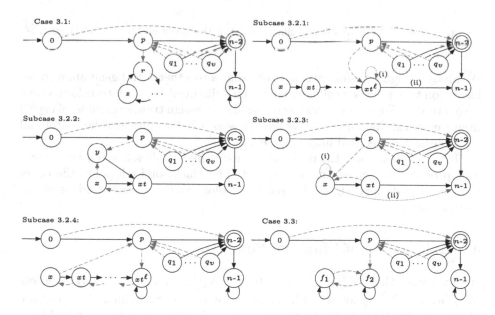

Fig. 3. Map of the (sub)cases of Supercase 3 in the proof of Theorem 10 (part 1).

Supercase 3: $t \notin \mathbf{W}_{\mathrm{bf}}^{\geqslant 6}(n)$ and $pt^{k+1} = n - 2$.
Here we have the chain

$$0 \xrightarrow{t} p \xrightarrow{t} pt \xrightarrow{t} \cdots \xrightarrow{t} pt^k \xrightarrow{t} n - 2 \xrightarrow{t} n - 1.$$

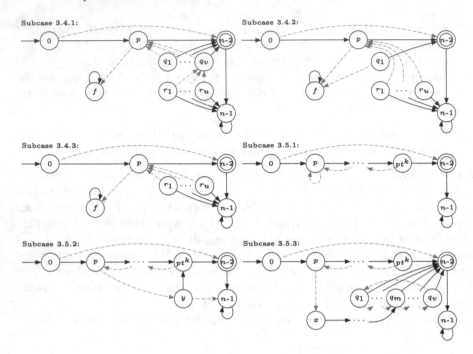

Fig. 4. Map of the (sub)cases of Supercase 3 in the proof of Theorem 10 (part 2).

We always assign transformations s such that s together with t generate a transformation that focuses a colliding pair, which distinguishes such transformations s from those of Supercase 1. Moreover, we always assign transformations of type 2 from Remark 2, that is, we always have $0s = n - 2$. This distinguishes s from all the transformations used in Supercase 2.

To show briefly how the construction looks like, in Figs. 3 and 4 we present a map of the (sub)cases for Supercase 3. The black solid edges are the edges of t, and the dashed edges (also red in a color printout) are the edges of the corresponding s.   ◁

4   Uniqueness of Maximal Semigroups

Here we show that $\mathbf{W}_{\mathrm{bf}}^{\geq 6}(n)$ for $n \geq 6$ and $\mathbf{W}_{\mathrm{bf}}^{\leq 5}(n)$ for $n \in \{3, 4, 5\}$ (whereas $\mathbf{W}_{\mathrm{bf}}^{\geq 6}(n) = \mathbf{W}_{\mathrm{bf}}^{\leq 5}(n)$ for $n \in \{3, 4\}$) have not only the maximal sizes, but are also the unique largest semigroups up to renaming the states in a minimal DFA $\mathcal{D}_n = (Q, \Sigma, \delta, 0, \{n - 2\})$ of a bifix-free language.

Theorem 11. *If $n \geq 8$, and the transition semigroup $T(\mathcal{D}_n)$ of a minimal DFA $\mathcal{D}_n$ of a bifix-free language has at least one colliding pair, then*

$$|T(\mathcal{D}_n)| < |\mathbf{W}_{\mathrm{bf}}^{\geq 6}(n)| = (n - 1)^{n-3} + (n - 2)^{n-3} + (n - 3)2^{n-3}.$$

Proof (Idea). This is done by finding one more s (under the assumption that there exists a colliding pair) that was not assigned by φ in the proof of Theorem 10. Thus, since φ is injective and $\varphi(T(\mathcal{D}_n)) \subseteq \mathbf{W}_{\mathrm{bf}}^{\geq 6}(n)$, $s \in \mathbf{W}_{\mathrm{bf}}^{\geq 6}(n)$ but $s \notin \varphi(T(\mathcal{D}_n))$, it follows that $\varphi(T(\mathcal{D}_n)) \subsetneq \mathbf{W}_{\mathrm{bf}}^{\geq 6}(n)$, so $|T(\mathcal{D}_n)| < |\mathbf{W}_{\mathrm{bf}}^{\geq 6}(n)|$.   □

Corollary 12. *For $n \geqslant 8$, the transition semigroup $\mathbf{W}_{\mathrm{bf}}^{\geq 6}(n)$ is the unique largest transition semigroup of a minimal DFA of a bifix-free language.*

Proof. From Theorem 11, a transition semigroup that has a colliding pair cannot be largest. From Proposition 3, $\mathbf{W}_{\mathrm{bf}}^{\geq 6}(n)$ is the unique maximal transition semigroup that does not have colliding pairs of states.   □

The following theorem solves the remaining cases of small semigroups:

Theorem 13. *For $n \in \{6, 7\}$, the largest transition semigroup of minimal DFAs of bifix-free languages is $\mathbf{W}_{\mathrm{bf}}^{\geq 6}(n)$ and it is unique. For $n = 5$, the largest transition semigroup of minimal DFAs of bifix-free languages is $\mathbf{W}_{\mathrm{bf}}^{\leq 5}(n)$ and it is unique. For $n \in \{3, 4\}$, $\mathbf{W}_{\mathrm{bf}}^{\geq 6}(n) = \mathbf{W}_{\mathrm{bf}}^{\leq 5}(n)$ is the unique largest transition semigroup of minimal DFAs of bifix-free languages.*

Proof (Idea). We have verified this with the help of computation, basing on the idea of conflicting pairs of transformations from [6, Theorem 20]. We have developed an algorithm which verified for a given $n \leqslant 7$ that no transformation from $\mathbf{B}_{\mathrm{bf}}(n)$ can belong to a transition semigroup of a minimal DFA $\mathcal{D}$ of a bifix-free language of size at least $\max\{\mathbf{W}_{\mathrm{bf}}^{\leq 5}(n), \mathbf{W}_{\mathrm{bf}}^{\geq 6}(n)\}$ that is different from $\mathbf{W}_{\mathrm{bf}}^{\geq 6}(n)$ and $\mathbf{W}_{\mathrm{bf}}^{\leq 5}(n)$.   □

Since the largest transition semigroups are unique, from Propositions 6 and 8 we infer the sizes of the alphabets required in order to meet the bound for the syntactic complexity.

Corollary 14. *To meet the bound for the syntactic complexity of bifix-free languages, $(n-2)^{n-3} + (n-3)2^{n-3} - 1$ letters are required and sufficient for $n \geqslant 6$, and $(n-2)!$ letters are required and sufficient for $n \in \{3, 4, 5\}$.*

5   Conclusions

We have solved the problem of syntactic complexity of bifix-free languages and identified the largest semigroups for every number of states n. In the main theorem, we used the method of injective function (cf. [7,9]) with new techniques and tricks for ensuring injectivity (in particular, Lemma 9 and the constructions in Supercase 3). This stands as a universal method for solving similar problems concerning maximality of semigroups. Our proof required an extensive analysis of 23 (sub)cases and much more complicated injectivity arguments than those for suffix-free (12 cases), left ideals (5 subcases) and two-sided ideals (8 subcases). The difficulty of applying the method grows quickly when characterization of the class of languages gets more involved.

It may be surprising that we need a witness with $(n-2)^{n-3} + (n-3)2^{n-3} - 1$ (for $n \geqslant 6$) letters to meet the bound for syntactic complexity of bifix-free languages, whereas in the case of prefix- and suffix-free languages only $n+1$ and five letters suffice, respectively (see [6,9]).

Finally, our results enabled establishing existence of most complex bifix-free languages ([12]).

References

1. Berstel, J., Perrin, D., Reutenauer, C.: Codes and Automata. Cambridge University Press, Cambridge (2009)
2. Brzozowski, J.A.: Quotient complexity of regular languages. J. Autom. Lang. Comb. **15**(1/2), 71–89 (2010)
3. Brzozowski, J.A.: In search of the most complex regular languages. Int. J. Found. Comput. Sci. **24**(6), 691–708 (2013)
4. Brzozowski, J.A., Li, B.: Syntactic complexity of R- and J-trivial languages. Int. J. Found. Comput. Sci. **16**(3), 547–563 (2005)
5. Brzozowski, J.A., Li, B., Liu, D.: Syntactic complexities of six classes of star-free languages. J. Autom. Lang. Comb. **17**, 83–105 (2012)
6. Brzozowski, J.A., Li, B., Ye, Y.: Syntactic complexity of prefix-suffix-, bifix-, and factor-free regular languages. Theoret. Comput. Sci. **449**, 37–53 (2012)
7. Brzozowski, J., Szykuła, M.: Upper bounds on syntactic complexity of left and two-sided ideals. In: Shur, A.M., Volkov, M.V. (eds.) DLT 2014. LNCS, vol. 8633, pp. 13–24. Springer, Cham (2014). doi:10.1007/978-3-319-09698-8_2
8. Brzozowski, J.A., Szykuła, M.: Large aperiodic semigroups. Int. J. Found. Comput. Sci. **26**(07), 913–931 (2015)
9. Brzozowski, J., Szykuła, M.: Upper bound on syntactic complexity of suffix-free languages. In: Shallit, J., Okhotin, A. (eds.) DCFS 2015. LNCS, vol. 9118, pp. 33–45. Springer, Cham (2015). doi:10.1007/978-3-319-19225-3_3
10. Brzozowski, J.A., Tamm, H.: Theory of átomata. Theoret. Comput. Sci. **539**, 13–27 (2014)
11. Brzozowski, J., Ye, Y.: Syntactic complexity of ideal and closed languages. In: Mauri, G., Leporati, A. (eds.) DLT 2011. LNCS, vol. 6795, pp. 117–128. Springer, Heidelberg (2011). doi:10.1007/978-3-642-22321-1_11
12. Ferens, R., Szykuła, M.: Complexity of bifix-free languages. In: Carayol, A., Nicaud, C. (eds.) CIAA 2017. LNCS, vol. 10329, pp. 76–88. Springer, Cham (2017)
13. Holzer, M., König, B.: On deterministic finite automata and syntactic monoid size. Theoret. Comput. Sci. **327**, 319–347 (2004)
14. Iván, S., Nagy-György, J.: On nonpermutational transformation semigroups with an application to syntactic complexity (2014). http://arxiv.org/abs/1402.7289
15. McNaughton, R., Papert, S.A.: Counter-free automata (M.I.T. Research Monograph No. 65). The MIT Press (1971)
16. Myhill, J.: Finite automata and representation of events. Wright Air Development Center Technical report, pp. 57–624 (1957)
17. Pin, J.E.: Syntactic semigroups. In: Rozenberg, G., Salomaa, A. (eds.) Handbook of Formal Languages, Volume 1 Word, Language, Grammar, pp. 679–746. Springer, Heidelberg (1997)
18. Szykuła, M., Wittnebel, J.: Syntactic complexity of bifix-free languages (2017). http://arxiv.org/abs/1604.06936
19. Yu, S.: State complexity of regular languages. J. Autom. Lang. Comb. **6**, 221–234 (2001)

Author Index

Printed in the United States
By Bookmasters